J. Stitt Wilson

Socialist, Christian, Mayor of Berkeley

Stephen E. Barton

ISBN 978-1-878050-01-4

Published by
Berkeley Historical Society
P.O. Box 1190
Berkeley, CA 94701
510-848-0181
www.berkeleyhistoricalsociety.org

For Barbara
And in memory of our son, Andre

CONTENTS

ILLUSTRATIONS

ACKNOWLEDGMENTS

Any human activity, no matter how apparently individual, builds on the work of many others and is made possible by the larger society and culture of which it is a part. This biography of J. Stitt Wilson began as a pastime while I worked for the City of Berkeley as its housing director. During that time, Phyllis Gale and Steven Finacom of the Berkeley Historical Society asked that I prepare talks on Wilson's work with the women's suffrage movement and on his life more generally. Douglas Firth Anderson's two splendid articles on Wilson's social Christianity provided models and inspired me to try to fill in the gaps in the story. He read an early draft of my book and provided helpful comments as well. Suggestions from Sherry Jeanne Katz led me to archives where I found Wilson's few remaining personal letters. Alan Lessoff, then editor of the *Journal of the Gilded Age and Progressive Era*, and Alexandra Wagner Lough, editor of a special issue of the *American Journal of Economics and Sociology* on Progressive Era mayors, encouraged my work and published articles that included some of the material in this book.

Rebecca Darby, head librarian for the Newspaper and Microfilm Collection at the University of California, Berkeley, made an essential contribution to my research. I needed access to material in microfilm collections around the U.S. but as an independent scholar I was not entitled to interlibrary loan privileges. Ms. Darby waived the technicalities and obtained the needed materials for me, generously following up on my seemingly endless stream of requests. I am also grateful to the many other libraries that had preserved materials essential to my research and the library staff who helped me find them and e-mailed scans of documents to me, usually at no or modest cost. These include the Balliol College, Bancroft Library, Berkeley Historical Society, Berkeley Public Library, British Library, Duke University, Huntington Library, Newberry Library, Northwestern University, Stanford University, the University of Oregon, the Wisconsin Historical Society and the libraries of the University of California at Berkeley, Davis, Los Angeles, and Santa Barbara.

Vance A. Fisher, a descendant of J. Stitt Wilson's older sister Sara Fisher, generously provided me with "The Autobiography of J. Stitt Wilson," which describes his youth in Canada. It was copied by Vance E. Fisher, son of Sara Fisher, from her original typewritten copy. Steve Pichel, great-grandson of Wilson, and grandson of his daughter, Violette, generously provided me with copies of an additional chapter of Wilson's autobiography, "The Zetland Schoolmaster Falls in Love," and Wilson's brief chronology of his life, "My Crowded Years" (1942), which was intended as a preface to now-lost letters and scrapbooks of material from his public life. Carol Guy provided copies of Wilson's letters regarding the death of his son, William Gladstone Wilson.

Unlike J. Stitt Wilson, I am a secular person and had a secular upbringing. I share some of his democratic socialist political views and some of his analysis of capitalism. I do not, however, share his religious beliefs. My primary focus is on setting his beliefs and actions within the broader context of the issues involved in building a movement for social and economic democracy. Nonetheless, Wilson's Christian beliefs were central to his life, so I have tried to explain them clearly and follow their evolution in some detail. I thank Douglas Firth Anderson and the authors of numerous works on the history of socially oriented Christianity for helping me to better understand Wilson's religious tradition. Any errors are, of course, my own and not attributable to those who have tried to assist me in understanding Wilson's life and thought.

This biography was made possible by technological advances that put vast quantities of 19th- and early 20th-century books, magazines, newspapers, and pamphlets on the web in searchable form. Only a few years ago a historian could have spent a lifetime visiting libraries around the U.S., U.K., and Canada searching through old newspapers and magazines to find a fraction of what can now be turned up from the comfort of one's home. The Library of Congress "Chronicling America" project, the California Digital Newspaper Collection, the HathiTrust Digital Library, the Marxists Internet Archive, the International Association for the Preservation of Spiritualist and Occult Periodicals, and the School of Cooperative Individualism, which has an archive of Georgist and single-tax journals, make their material freely available. Many other newspapers are available for a fee through various competing genealogical websites, and participants on these websites have been very generous in sharing information and documents. The public interest in genealogy supports searchable access to a great deal of important material, but it is characteristic of the declining support for public institutions over the past generation that these materials are provided for profit rather than made freely available through public libraries.

I am grateful to the Publications Committee of the Berkeley Historical Society: co-chairs John Aronovici and Ann Harlow, Jeanine Castello-Lin, Ed Herny, Linda Rosen, John Underhill, and Charles Wollenberg. Ann Harlow was especially helpful in guiding the production process, referring me to Rose Marie Cleese for editing, Susan Gerber for formatting, and Carl Wikander for indexing. She also designed the cover and proofread the final formatted book. Charles Wollenberg reviewed the manuscript in both an early version and its final form and provided a statement for the back cover.

Many people have assisted me in this work over the years. If I have omitted some people it is a failure of record-keeping rather than a lack of appreciation.

Artist unknown, portrait of J. Stitt Wilson, used as frontispiece
for his *How I Became a Socialist and Other Papers*

Chapter 1

"Socialism Is Applied Christianity"

Rev. J. Stitt Wilson . . . has been a staunch and fearless advocate of the principles of Socialism and has done his full share to augment the power and influence of the movement. Comrade Wilson speaks from the heart and his message is always eloquent and effective.

—Eugene Victor Debs[1]

Jackson Stitt Wilson (1868–1942) was mayor of Berkeley for only two eventful years—from July 1, 1911, to June 30, 1913, but he was active in California politics from the time he arrived in the state in 1901 until he died in 1942. During Wilson's life, we see the movement for democratic socialism intertwined with union organizing, women's suffrage, the single-tax and urban reforms such as public ownership of utilities, and with Christianity and various forms of spiritual seeking. Wilson experienced occasional political triumphs but also many political disappointments to which he responded with resilience and new initiatives. Despite his political setbacks and personal tragedies, he remained optimistic about humanity.

One can consider Stitt Wilson's life on several levels. There are the many interesting and largely unknown stories, some of which reflect the tensions between "Berkeley Bohemia" and the respectable Republican college town that preceded the Civil Rights and Free Speech movements of the 1960s. There is the way his life illustrates the creativity and experimentation characteristic of the movements for social justice so well-represented in Berkeley and in California as a whole. Then there is the way his life story fills out some rarely studied aspects of the history of socialism in the United States.

Wilson stated that "socialism is applied Christianity," a way to organize the economy so that it would support rather than undermine Jesus's message to "love thy neighbor as thyself." It followed from this that democracy and cooperation should pervade all aspects of society, including the economy. Modern civilization makes workers immensely productive, and society, as a society, creates tremendous value above and beyond the value that any individual creates on their own. A democratic society should produce and distribute this socially created wealth in a way that enables all people to own sufficient personal property and have access to the collective goods they need to realize their God-given human potential. Capitalism, in contrast, Wilson considered a social sin because it allowed the "one percent" to take most of the socially created value for private profit. This made even those who led apparently blameless private lives complicit in a system in which competition reduced millions to poverty and destroyed their human dignity. Starting out as an ordained Methodist minister in Chicago, he resigned his ministry in 1897 in protest over the church's complacency in the face of economic injustice. Wilson believed there could be no individual salvation without participating in social salvation—the effort to bring society closer to the Kingdom of God "on earth as it is in heaven."

Stitt Wilson was a practical politician and political strategist as well as a religious idealist. He first came to national prominence in 1910, when he ran a creditable campaign for governor of California as a socialist by forming an alliance with organized labor. The next year he was elected mayor of Berkeley, then the state's fifth-largest city. Wilson understood that democratizing the economy could be done only through democratic means. He supported workers' efforts to organize unions and campaigned for women to have the right to vote. He believed that just as the public school system and the postal service had broad popular support, so public ownership of utilities and transportation systems, land value taxation, and worker and consumer cooperatives would expand democratic control over the economy and further demonstrate the practicality of socialism.

Over the course of his life, Wilson won a great many people to the socialist cause. He was a noted public speaker in an era before radio and television, when public speaking was a major form of communication and entertainment. He routinely drew audiences of hundreds and often thousands. He was just under six feet tall, extremely handsome as a young man, and distinguished in his later years. He gave "forceful and eloquent" speeches, delivered with great sincerity and enthusiasm. Despite the difficulties of frequent campaigns and travel, for the most part he loved his work. During his term as mayor of Berkeley, a speaker introducing him commented that "the Mayor would not enjoy his usual health unless he had a chance to make at least one speech a day."[2] His skill as a performer was passed on to his children. Both of his daughters became successful actresses, and one went on to be a movie star in the silent film era. His only son to survive into adulthood had leading roles in college theatricals and regularly filled in for his father as a public speaker before his death in pilot training during World War I.

It is hard to trace the effect of public speaking, but a rare example of his influence shows up in a story that was often told by the noted American author and socialist, Kurt Vonnegut. The novelist's friend, Powers Hapgood, was a union organizer in the 1920s, served on the national executive committee of the Socialist Party from 1932 to 1940, and was a regional officer in the Congress of Industrial Organizations (CIO) in Indiana when Vonnegut met him in 1945. Hapgood told Vonnegut how he had once been called as a witness in a case about violence on a picket line. When the judge asked him why a Harvard graduate from a good family was spending his time on picket lines. Hapgood replied, "Why, the Sermon on the Mount, Sir!" Vonnegut then commented that this summed up his own beliefs as well.[3] And how did Powers Hapgood come to connect the labor movement with the Sermon on the Mount? In the summer of 1919, he went to a YMCA conference for college students where he was deeply moved by a speech by Wilson and decided to dedicate his life to working for the oppressed.[4]

The public Wilson is well documented, but we have only glimpses of his private life. He published some of his speeches in pamphlet form (his one published book, *How I Became a Socialist and Other Papers*, is a collection of nine of his pamphlets), and accounts of many other speeches, campaigns, and his work as mayor of Berkeley can be found in newspapers and now-obscure journals. There are stretches of his public life where it is possible to trace his activities day by day. At the end of his life he described his youth and young adulthood in an unfinished autobiography, filling in the period for which there is no other record. After that, his interpersonal relations and actions when out of the public eye often remain obscure, only occasionally illuminated by a few surviving personal letters, statements made in times of personal tragedy, and infrequent personal references in his speeches. Even in his book, he warns the reader, "You will need to read between the lines . . . I wish to be perfectly frank and yet I cannot tell all. The soul shudders to expose itself."[5]

Wilson dedicated his life to the ethics of Jesus, striving for a society that would value people in all aspects of their lives, rather than treating them as children of God in church on Sunday and as commodities during the working week. He dreamed of a society in which there was no poverty and the people would socially own and democratically control all major economic institutions just as they do public school systems or cooperative grocery stores. He believed in equal rights for women and that women, much more than men, carried an ethic of care that was essential for a more cooperative society. He believed in democracy and freedom as necessary means as well as ultimate goals. He made some serious mistakes along the way, as with his advocacy of the prohibition of alcoholic beverages, but he took an open, pragmatic approach to building a movement for social justice and democracy. He knew that he and his comrades were "groping in the dark" as they searched for a path forward and he hoped "our concern will be, as we grope in our ignorance, to receive whatever light is available."[6]

Significance of Wilson in the history of the socialist movement in America

After a lifetime of campaigning for socialism, what Wilson had to show for it depends on your perspective. The first step for any movement is that it must attract a critical mass of people sufficient to exercise some degree of political power and this the socialist movement was able to accomplish. The second step is that it must act effectively to make the changes that are possible with what political power it has. Wilson contributed both to attracting public support for socialism and to strategic use of that support.

Historians of the Socialist Party during the Debs period often overemphasize the role of Marxism and downplay the role of Christian and moral appeals and the economic analysis that grew from ethical premises. Eugene Victor Debs was the nation's best-known socialist and a socialist candidate for president in 1900, 1904, 1908, 1912, and 1920. In his speeches and writings he appealed to the ideal of citizenship, to manhood, to Christ on the Cross, to Karl Marx, and to the Declaration of Independence.[7] Much of Debs's and the Socialist Party's economic analysis blended easily with the moral and religious claims from which it was largely derived—the workers are entitled to the product of their labor, the land belongs to all God's children, the wealth of the nation is a product of society, and no individual has a right to take a disproportionate share of it. These were basic elements of the Cooperative Commonwealth, another name for socialism that was widely used because it emphasized the importance of cooperation and the common ownership of wealth. Marxism had a more difficult relationship with moral appeals.

Marxism was influential because its portrayal of class conflict and the increasing domination of the economy by large corporations was a living reality. Anyone involved in the union movement had practical experience with capitalist hostility to workers' efforts to organize and obtain a decent standard of living and with the role of the state in protecting capitalism. For some, Marxism served as an alternative religion. The Marxist belief in the

Eugene V. Debs, circa 1908 (from the frontispiece
of *Debs: His Life, Writings and Speeches*).

inevitability of a final crisis of capitalism leading to a proletarian revolution was as much an apocalyptic vision of judgment and redemption as anything found in the Bible, and it could provide similar comfort. But Marxism was purportedly a rigorous system based on a scientific, materialist analysis of society in which moral judgement had no place.

For most socialists, the moral basis of the movement was extremely important, even if they agreed with other aspects of Marxism. Few could understand Marx's labor theory of value, but it was usually taken as a moral truth rather than an economic theory. Marx's hostility to religion as "the opiate of the masses" created continual tension between his true believers and religious socialists. But for socialist Christians, Marx's views on religion were an overreaction to the conservatism of the established churches and separable from his social analysis of class conflict.

Religious socialists drew on their belief in the benevolent intentions of a God who made the earth for everyone and on the ethic of love expounded by Jesus, the carpenter. Even Socialist Party members who were "anticlerical and religiously unorthodox" often derived their ethics from the pervasive Christian culture around them.[8] Historians have demonstrated the importance of socially oriented Christianity in the Socialist Party organizations in Oklahoma, which had the largest party membership proportional to population of any state in the union, as well as in nearby areas of Texas, Kansas, and Louisiana.[9] Jim Bissett criticizes those who treat the Christian contribution to the movement in Oklahoma as rural backwardness in comparison with Marxism. He argues that "Marxist ideas . . . energized the democratic, communitarian strains in evangelical Protestantism, religion simultaneously deepened and made (Marxism) relevant."[10] This synergy was not limited to the fundamentalist tenant farmers of the Southwest. Mari Jo Buhle describes the socialist women of the small towns of the Midwest, the Plains, and California as "visionary, moralistic and militantly Protestant . . . class-conscious revolutionaries."[11]

Wilson was one of those who enabled the Socialist Party to combine secular and religious appeals. The socialist movement embodied his religion and he explained why in clear and forceful language. Wilson's economic analysis borrowed from the "moral economy" arguments of Henry George and Samuel "Golden Rule" Jones, as well as from Karl Marx. He described an economy increasingly dominated by monopolies, in which "the laborer is being deprived of the just product of his toil." He supported this statement not with the labor theory of value, but by contrasting the power of those who owned the means of production over those who had only their own labor and competed with each other for employment. Wilson considered industry to be the collective, cumulative product of civilization and that, therefore, the decision as to how to distribute its products rightly belonged to the public, not to private individuals or corporations. From this perspective, everyone but major capitalists was exploited, in that they were denied their democratic and economic rights as collective inheritors and creators of civilization.[12]

This perspective enabled Wilson, who identified himself as an "evolutionary" and "constructive" socialist, to make a broad appeal to the public as workers, whether in factories, offices, shops, or in the home. In contrast, the "revolutionary" socialists believed that only the industrial proletariat could lead the way, whether through elections, a general strike, or an armed insurrection, and that the workers would be motivated by their material economic interests rather than by morality. Looking for ways to strengthen moral commitment, Wilson drew on the thinking of feminist reformers such as Elizabeth Cady Stanton, Frances Willard, and Jane Addams, who argued for women's equality on the grounds that women held an ethic of care that was essential for creation of a society based on cooperation rather than conflict.

Socialism in the United States is usually portrayed as a failure because there is no major Socialist or Labor Party here. While systems that provide proportional representation for multiple parties make it easy for a new party to enter the political system, America's winner-take-all elections result in a two-party system. The British, Australian, and New Zealand Labour Parties cleared a similar hurdle, but Daniel Bell argued that American socialists were too sectarian and unwilling to form a broad-based Labor Party that would include socialists but not be limited to them.[13] Seymour Martin Lipset and Gary Marks agreed with Bell and suggested that socialists could also have contested primaries within the major parties, as Bernie Sanders and others inspired by his example, such as Alexandria Ocasio-Cortez, have recently done.[14]

During Wilson's lifetime, the socialist movement twice attracted the critical mass of people necessary to have significant political influence, first for the period from about 1908 to 1919 and again during the Great Depression from 1930 to 1940. In the first period, the movement was largely encompassed by the Socialist Party of America, which began in 1901 with 10,000 dues-paying members and grew to a peak of 118,000 in 1912 (proportionately equivalent to about 425,000 people in 2020 when adjusted for today's much larger population), before splintering into fragments in 1919. Eugene V. Debs received more than 900,000 votes for president in 1912, about six percent of the vote, but his similar total in 1920 represented only three percent of an expanded electorate that now included women. Nowhere did the Socialist Party break through to major party status, but there were serious efforts to do so in several states, including California.

Wilson returned to Berkeley in 1909, after two years of lecturing in Great Britain for the Labour Party. From 1910 to 1915 he worked, with some initial success, to position the Socialist Party as the party of the labor movement in California. In his campaign for governor of California in 1910, Wilson received strong labor support and his 12% of the vote was the Socialist Party's best showing ever in a statewide campaign. His election as mayor of Berkeley the following year gave him a platform from which to support socialism and key statewide reforms such as women's suffrage, which was passed by the voters of California later in 1911.

Mayor Wilson proved to be an effective and astute politician. He worked for municipal ownership of water and electric power supply, public parks, street improvements, sewers, shelter for the homeless, and public works jobs for the unemployed. He led a successful campaign to prevent the recall of his allies on the city council and school board. His specifically socialist accomplishments, however, were limited, in large part because Berkeley was in the early stages of development, with unpaved streets, poor water and sewer service, and low taxes, so he had to focus on building the capacity of the city government to provide basic services.

Ultimately, the defeat of the union movement in Los Angeles in the years before World War I precluded a strong statewide labor organization that might have carried the Socialist Party into serious contention. Instead, labor settled for modest reforms under the progressive Republican governor, Hiram Johnson. There were serious moral costs to the Socialist Party's effort to make an alliance with California unions. Wilson believed that people of all races, nations, and religions were equally connected to God. The Socialist Party proclaimed the solidarity of all workers regardless of race, nationality, or religion. Despite this, to gain union support the Socialist Party in California agreed to oppose further immigration from Asia. Asians made up less than four percent of the California population at the time, and most socialists who supported the agreement argued that it was a temporary policy that would become unnecessary after the party won enough votes for socialism to triumph. Several years later, Wilson also used racial appeals as part of his efforts to persuade the public to support peace and oppose militarism, arguing that war would weaken the white race and its leadership position in the world. Soon afterward, however, he replaced this international racial competition framework with an anti-imperialist framework. It is clear, however, that while he regarded women's equality as essential, he regarded racial equality as a secondary issue.

During the Great Depression, the socialist movement lacked a dominant organization. In addition to the Socialist Party and the Communist Party, there were several Trotskyist organizations; left-wing state parties such as the Minnesota Farmer-Labor Party; left-wing state organizations such as EPIC (End Poverty in California) that operated within the Democratic Party; and many independent socialists active in organizing unions, farm organizations, cooperatives, consumer groups, and so on. Socialist Party presidential candidate Norman Thomas received 885,000 votes in 1932, only two percent of the total vote. Upton Sinclair, the famous author and long-time Socialist Party member who formed EPIC, received 880,000 votes running for governor of California as a Democrat in 1934, 39% of the total vote. Wilson joined EPIC after helping lead the Socialist Party in California for the previous three years, as did many other socialists. EPIC avoided using the word socialism. Instead, it called for "production for use" rather than for profit.

EPIC and other regional left-wing campaigns, combined with major strikes such as the San Francisco waterfront strikes and general strike of 1934, had a strong effect on the Roosevelt administration. In 1935 and 1936, the "Second New Deal" passed and implemented many of the immediate reforms that had long been part of the Socialist Party platform, including workers' right to organize, Social Security, unemployment insurance, and a major expansion in government-funded employment for the unemployed. This succeeded in assimilating much of the left into the Democratic Party. EPIC and most of the third-party organizations dissolved. People guided by their socialist beliefs had found strategies and tactics that had real, practical effects on the policies of the New Deal. That did not result in the creation of a large Socialist or Labor Party, but Wilson and tens of thousands of other socialists appreciated the importance of their gains, even as they recognized that much more progress was needed.

Wilson's life alternated between periods of evangelism, when he focused on making the Christian case for socialism, and periods of practical politics, when he focused on building organizations and winning elections on the state and local level. Chapters 2–6 describe the influences that led him first to the ministry and then to socialism. They explain the nature of his Christian and socialist beliefs, how he worked to spread them, his role in building up the Socialist Party in its early years, and the exhaustion of both his personal energies and the evangelical "crusade" model he drew on. Chapters 7–10 describe how his time in England and Wales inspired his belief in the potential of a socialist party backed by organized labor and his attempt to apply that model to California. As mayor of Berkeley he worked to lay the groundwork for socialism by demonstrating the benefits of an active local government that would serve the public interest rather than the real estate industry and private utility companies. Chapters 11, 12, and the first part of 13 describe his return to the crusade model, his disillusionment with the Socialist Party, and his effort to promote socialism under the names of "industrial democracy" and "Christian Democracy." Chapter 12 also describes his campaign for mayor as an independent in 1917 and the "citizen secret service" organization that red-baited him and likely cost him the election. Chapter 13 describes his return to the Socialist Party during the Great Depression, his breakaway to join with Upton Sinclair in the End Poverty in California campaign of 1934, and his subsequent support for Franklin D. Roosevelt and the New Deal.

A revival of democratic socialism?

Wilson did not live to see the end of World War II. After the war, the United States entered an era of unprecedented economic growth and broad prosperity, driven by the New Deal's social compromise in which government agencies regulated large corporations, supported workers' rights to form

unions, and provided a basic social safety net. Socialism became identified in the public mind with the grim, authoritarian communism of the
Soviet Union and few people openly identified themselves as socialists. Martin Luther King, Jr., for example, adopted a democratic socialist perspective based on Christian ethics as early as 1950 while he attended seminary,
but kept the term out of his writings and speeches.[15] Although not directly
influenced by Wilson, King drew on the same current of social Christian
thought that Wilson had adopted and helped to sustain. In the 1950s and
1960s, the nation entered a long-delayed fight for democratic inclusion of
its non-white citizens, women, and sexual minorities—forms of liberation
long neglected by the socialist movement.

In the late 1970s, feeling threatened by broadening democracy and
increasing discontent with "the system," the capitalist class reasserted its
political and economic power, drawing particularly on white resentment of
black demands for equality. Average wages stagnated, and the incomes and
wealth of the top one percent increased dramatically. It is now common-
place to describe America as having entered a new Gilded Age. Worse still,
as climate change threatens the future of world civilization, large corporations and the wealthy engage in denial and delay in order to maintain their
wealth and power. That once-obsolete word, "plutocracy," or rule by the
wealthy, is again relevant to discussions of American government. Critiques
of the American economic system developed more than a century ago still
have surprising resonance today.

The collapse of Soviet communism and, ironically, decades of right-
wing attacks on the legacy of the New Deal as "socialist" helped lead to a
revival of public support for socialism. Bernie Sanders's campaigns in the
Democratic Party presidential primaries further popularized socialism but
left its meaning open to many possible interpretations. Over the course of
its history, perhaps the most consistent meaning of socialism is the ideal of
a democratic and ethical economy and society. Wilson and many others in
the early socialist movement recognized the role of society as a whole in
creating value and claimed the moral right of society to direct the creation
and distribution of that value through the democratic process. There is no
blueprint that can define in advance how such a society would be organized
and what steps must be taken to get there. Americans working for social
justice in this New Gilded Age, with democracy and civilization itself at
risk, may find Stitt Wilson's lifelong effort both inspiring and sobering as a
picture of the difficulty of the task, the need for creativity, experimentation,
and sustained effort over many years, and the value spiritual beliefs can have
in sustaining that commitment.

CHAPTER 2

THE EDUCATION OF A MINISTER

Jackson Stitt Wilson came of age at a time when large corporations were beginning to dominate American economic life and a rapidly growing urban population was overtaking the rural majority. The Jeffersonian vision of a democratic society sustained by the rural virtues of independent farmers and artisans in small communities was never an accurate picture of reality in a nation that incorporated plantation slavery in its beginnings, but it was a fair description of the part of rural Canada where Wilson grew up. When he moved to the Chicago area as a young married man, he was exposed to extremes of wealth and poverty. He saw the great depression of 1893–1897 reduce millions of working people to destitution despite the nation's great wealth and industry. This demonstrated to Wilson, as to many others, that America needed to find a new basis to sustain democracy and community, and he searched for an effective way to apply his Christian beliefs in an urban and industrial society.

Early life[1]

Wilson was born on March 19, 1868, in the little town of Auburn in Huron County, Ontario, Canada, a rural area along the Maitland River not far from Lake Huron. Auburn had two general stores, two blacksmith shops, a wagon shop, a cabinet shop, a harness shop, a tailor shop, his father's shoe-maker's shop, his uncle's tannery, two taverns, three churches (Presbyterian, Anglican, and Methodist), and a public school. His parents had a one-acre lot located on the gravel main road that ran through town, with the shoe repair shop set by the road and the house with a flower garden behind it. He recalled his father working long hours in the window of the shop, making or repairing shoes with his journeyman helper, and remembered his father's willingness to extend credit to neighbors when farm prices were low.

Jackson was the third of thirteen Wilson children born between 1866 and 1887 to William James Wilson (1841–1897) and Sarah Ann Stitt Wilson (1842–1909); ten of the children lived into adulthood. His parents were born in Ireland, the descendants of Protestants who moved from Scotland to Northern Ireland in the 1600s and 1700s, and were brought to Canada as small children in the 1830s and 1840s. Jackson's brother, Benjamin Franklin Wilson, born sixth in 1874, would become his lifelong ally, coworker, and neighbor. During his childhood, Wilson was called Jackie or Jackson by his family and friends. In adulthood, he is always referred to in writing as J. Stitt Wilson or J. S. Wilson and his friends likely called him Stitt or Wilson.

Jackson spent his childhood within a twelve-mile radius of home, the distance that he or his parents could travel on foot or in a horse-drawn wagon and return home on the same day. Less than three miles away was the farm owned by his maternal grandmother, Ann Stitt. The family visited frequently to help out his widowed grandmother; Jackson's grandfather, Jackson Stitt, after whom Wilson was named, had died several years before he was born. Jackson's paternal grandparents, Jonathan and Ann Wilson, lived twelve miles west of Auburn in the county seat of Goderich, located at the mouth of the Maitland River overlooking Lake Huron. The area included a great many Wilsons and Stitts since his parents were both one of thirteen children.

Wilson recalled near-universal literacy in the area and a strong belief in the value of education, the result being that he and several of his schoolmates went on to become teachers and ministers. Looking back, Wilson felt that the nature of the community gave him an early education in democracy and cooperation.

> The great majority of [the farmers of Huron County] owned or were in fair prospect of owning each his own hundred acres. There was no laboring class as such either. Most of the work on these farms was done by the farmer and his sons, or with the cooperation of neighbors. There were few, if any, absentee landlords and no super-rich anywhere holding anyone in dependence.[2]
>
> They helped one another in the larger undertakings, such as barn-raising or a heavy crop that required immediate attention, or in getting out the winter's wood . . . As among the men, so among the women, with their quilting bees or fruit preserving . . .[3]

The river was a major factor in the community economy. A dam near its mouth provided power for the mills that ground wheat into flour and sawed logs into lumber. It provided boating and fishing and there was ice skating every year when it froze over. Wilson recalled the "spring break-up of the ice" as a great annual community event.

> The dam below held the solid ice-field intact until the spring thaw and spring rains swelled the river far above. Then it began to crack and break. The villagers and even men and women from the countryside would get out of bed in the dead of night, if need be, to see and hear the ice begin to move . . . This was a real moving picture before the days of the movies, quite a thriller to a growing country boy, especially if the boy had to leap out of bed and watch the scene under the bright moonlight or at grey dawn.[4]

His parents were devout members of the Methodist Church and their home "was often turned into a place of worship and prayer."[5] His father, William, was "a class-leader—that is, a layman in the church who had a group which he met with every week, and with whom he counseled concerning their spiritual progress."[6] Jackson described him as "a man of great spiritual power . . . one of those men in early Methodism who were said to be 'powerful in prayer'." Even so, his father had a sense of humor and was fond of a comment made by his brother Abram, about loud praying, "What's the use of shouting as if the Lord was in California?"[7] Jackson described his mother as "undemonstrative" but with "great kindness of heart" and recalled her sending him "out one night through the winter storm to take a pail of soup to a family where there was sickness."[8] Wilson's parents taught him to read the Bible early on and he recalled having a "spiritual illumination" at around the age of 13, "the memory of which still brings me to silence and tears."[9]

Alcoholism was a serious problem in the Auburn area and it affected several family members. Jackson recalled, for example, that his great-uncle Abram would go on drunken sprees, spending all his money, pawning anything of value to get more liquor and reducing his wife and daughter to tears; he eventually converted to Methodism and gave up liquor entirely. Jackson neither drank nor smoked. He recalled that one hot summer, as a boy, he had turned on the tap of a keg of home-brewed ale his grandfather kept in his cellar and drank directly from the keg. When he emerged from hiding "staggering drunk," his grandfather "laughed till the tears ran down his cheeks" and Jackson apparently never touched alcohol again.[10]

At the age of six he had an accident that blinded him permanently in his left eye. His family was bringing in the hay at Grandmother Stitt's farm that summer and as he was bouncing on the growing haystack he was struck in the eye by a loose pitchfork. When the family brought in a doctor some days later, it was too late to save his sight in that eye. Wilson never mentioned this disability to people outside the family, and it left no mark that is visible in his many photographs, but he notes in his reminiscences that he "probably never lived a day without some pain." As a university student years later, he studied with his left eye covered to avoid the distraction of the glimmer of light that remained in that eye.[11]

Wilson described himself as "a hearty, healthy, robust lad, insanely fond of boyish sport and often the victim or aggressor in the rows that were not infrequent in our school days."[12] As was customary in the community, Wilson left home at the age of 13 to live with a family in Goderich and learn a trade. He started with printing, then worked as a telegraph operator and a clerk in a grocery store, then at a law office, and in a dry goods store supervised by his older brother, Will. At the age of 18 he decided to become a teacher. He moved back in with his parents, who were now farming, attended Goderich High School, and after a few months' study was able to pass his entry level teachers' certification. In the fall of 1886, he spent three months teaching at the Goderich Model School, a training school for teachers. In January of 1887, he took a position as the schoolteacher in nearby Morris Township and began preaching in the nearby Methodist Church. In January of 1888 he was hired as the "master" of a one-room school in Zetland with between forty and fifty students. He boarded with a farm family whose home was just across the road from the schoolhouse and soon his 14-year-old brother, Ben, came to live with him and attend the school.

In Zetland, Wilson changed his teaching method to rely less on punishments and more on building community ties and positive reinforcement.

> I was strapped by every teacher I ever had as a boy. In my first school, as a schoolmaster, I had a fine big strap that was used occasionally and apparently with success. I relented in my second school and made a public demonstration of the elimination of the strap, which, however it pleased the pupils, was not considered a wise procedure either by the parents or by the school board or other teachers.[13]

Scarcely older than his oldest students, Wilson joined their noon games and arranged for football matches with neighboring schools, becoming very popular because "I was a very devil on the soccer field."[14] He used his popularity to maintain order and encourage learning.

> I would quietly praise any good work and take extra pains
> to help a dull boy or girl. I made it my business to visit the
> homes of the biggest and most threatening fellows, making
> my visit most casual and not about "anything." To stand in
> the barnyard and just chat with big Henry who was cleaning out a cow-stable was a poor prelude to any sort of a row
> next day at school.[15]

His success as a teacher gained him respect in the surrounding community, including the larger nearby town of Wingham, where he was invited to join a mock parliament that included editors, teachers, and an actual member of parliament; there he could practice public speaking and debate.[16] Among his acquaintances in Wingham was the Agnew family, which included two daughters, Anna and Emma Jane. The Agnews were a devout Methodist family, and three of Emma's brothers would later go on to careers in the Salvation Army. In late January of 1888, Anna invited him to join a group of their friends on a sleigh ride. He recalled:

> A group of young people would hire big sleighs and fine
> teams of horses, with their sparkling harness and jingling
> sleigh-bells, and away they would go out into the country
> to some appointed farmhouse . . . No ride is quite so fine
> as a sleigh ride through the country, up hill and down glen,
> the full moon glorifying the entire landscape, the keen frost
> and the fresh winter air making the blood tingle, and all
> the while the right boy or girl, or at least some boy or girl,
> bundled in beside you and all packed in like sardines in a
> box and all brimming full of the glee and hilarity and exuberance of youth.[17]

As it happened, Wilson was bundled in next to Emma, who formed an immediate attachment to the young schoolmaster. Wilson joined other sleighing parties, often preceded or followed by parlor games such as charades or drop the handkerchief, and soon developed a similar attachment to Emma. Many years later, he described his feelings towards Emma as "indescribable reverence, something akin of worship of the character, the personality of this lovely girl."[18] Further, he said, "In the presence of this lovely being, though a mere girl, I felt a sense of unworthiness that fifty years has not changed."[19]

During the succeeding months, Wilson would walk to the Agnew home several times a week after school ended at 4 p.m. and would also stop by on the weekend. On these visits he was often accompanied by his brother, Ben, who would play on the lawn with Emma's 9-year-old sister, Leila, while their older siblings talked. Once Anna persuaded Emma to wear an engagement ring when Wilson visited them, as if she had become engaged to someone else. Wilson collapsed in shock and even after learning it was a practical joke it took him several days to recover. Emma's relatives suggested that she should not remain committed to a young man who showed such weakness, but she remained devoted to him.[20]

Early in 1888, Wilson's parents and several younger siblings moved across Lake Huron to a farm in Grant Township in Michigan. In 1889, Wilson moved in with them, attended the local Normal School for three months in the summer of 1889, and obtained an American teaching certificate. That fall he moved to nearby White Rock to take a position as schoolteacher. Used to the deeply religious Auburn area, he recalled that he was so disturbed by "the almost universal disregard for the Sabbath . . . irreligiousness . . . and Godlessness" he found on his first Sunday in his new home that he "sat down on the edge of the sidewalk and just wept."[21] He was sustained, however, by close family ties. His 16-year-old sister, Ida May, moved in with him and attended Normal School. Wilson tutored her and helped her become a teacher at a nearby school. His brother, Ben, also moved in with him and attended the school where he taught.

Wilson made frequent visits back to Wingham to continue courting Emma Jane, his "first and only sweetheart," and they exchanged hundreds of letters while they were apart. They married at noon on December 26, 1889, at the Minnie Street Methodist Church in Wingham. He would prove to be a devoted husband and father and, often separated from Emma by his frequent travels, continued to send frequent loving letters throughout their marriage. He regarded their marriage as a partnership in all things, describing her as "my superior in perception, in reason and in wisdom . . . I never published an article or pamphlet without reading it over to her."[22]

After they wed, Wilson returned to teaching at White Rock and began preaching at local Methodist churches. In the summer of 1890, he filled in as pastor of the Methodist Episcopal Church in Grindstone City and decided to attend a seminary to study for ordination in the ministry. His uncle, Dr. James Steele Stitt, urged him to "come here to the great metropolis, Chicago, where you can watch the tides of history as you study." As a further incentive, Dr. Stitt sent him a check for $50 (equivalent to around $1,400 in 2020).[23]

A minister's education

In September of 1890 Wilson rented a house for himself and his wife in Evanston, Illinois, a university town and well-to-do suburb of Chicago, where he enrolled at the Garrett Biblical Institute, located on the campus of the Methodist-affiliated Northwestern University.[24] Methodism was the largest Protestant denomination in America in 1890, accounting for 22% of all church membership. Between them, Methodists, Baptists, Lutherans, and Presbyterians made up 54% of all church members, Catholics totaled 30% and were concentrated in large cities, and other Protestant denominations accounted for most of the remainder.[25] Garrett Biblical Institute and Northwestern University in Evanston were the leading Methodist educational institutions serving the Midwest and central Canada. Also headquartered in Evanston was the world's largest women's organization, the Woman's Christian Temperance Union (WCTU), led since 1879 by Frances Willard, possibly the world's most famous Methodist at the time.

Once Stitt and Emma were established in Evanston, the Wilsons encouraged other members of the family to join them and attend school there. (In addition to the educational opportunities, the setting was lovely, with the campus located right on the shore of Lake Michigan.) They were soon joined by his sister, Sarah Ann, who enrolled in the Northwestern Academy, a preparatory school for attending Northwestern University that was located on the University campus. The Wilsons' first child, Gladys Viola, was born on March 5, 1891. During this time, they sublet a room to two divinity students, one of whom was Albert L. Fisher, who successfully courted Sarah Ann although he was five years her junior. They married on September 7, 1892, then moved into their own house in Evanston, a few blocks away from Stitt and Emma. Sarah Ann left school for motherhood and Albert graduated and became a minister in the Methodist Episcopal Church. They and their children became lifelong friends of Stitt and Emma.

Soon the Wilson family was joined by a second child, William Gladstone Wilson, born on April 27, 1893. Naming his first son after the Liberal Party prime minister of the United Kingdom reflects both Wilson's attachment to Great Britain and his mainstream political views at the time. Gladstone supported free trade, small government with low taxes, civil service reform, expanded public education, and home rule for Ireland. Perhaps most focused on public education, Wilson was taken aback when his grandfather, Jonathan Wilson, told him, "Jackson . . . , I wouldn't call a dog Gladstone," objecting to the idea of home rule for Ireland because the Protestant minority would be subject to the Catholic majority.[26]

Also arriving at the Wilsons' home in 1893 and staying for some months were two of Emma's brothers, Fletcher and Stanton, and her sister Leila, all of whom enrolled in the Academy. The following year they were joined by their widowed mother, Eliza, and two more of Emma's brothers, Ernest and Gilbert. All five Agnews subsequently rented a house together. Subletting rooms helped pay the rent, but Stitt still needed an income to support his family while attending school. He took positions as pastor at a series of churches on the outskirts of the Chicago area, first in Lee, a rural town 80 miles away, and then at locales closer to home as they became available.[27] Chicago was surrounded by a dense network of rail lines, so he likely traveled out on Friday or Saturday, stayed with a local family, and returned on Monday.

After two years of study on the Bible, theology, church history, and pastoral psychology among other courses, Wilson completed his studies at Garrett. Explaining that he was "passionately fond of study and books," he decided that he would continue his studies and get a college degree at Northwestern University.[28] To meet the entry requirements, he attended the Northwestern Academy for a year, studying Greek, Latin, history, English, mathematics, physics, and astronomy, and was accepted to the B.A. program in English at Northwestern.[29] In the fall of 1893, Wilson enrolled at Northwestern University and on October 6th he was ordained a deacon of the Methodist Church. Soon afterward he became pastor at the Erie Street Methodist Episcopal (M.E.) Church in a working-class area of Chicago, only ten miles from Evanston, with an annual salary of $800 (about $23,000 in 2020).[30]

Up to this point, Wilson had lived entirely in small towns and in Evanston, which he described as "the richest suburb of Chicago, where wealth and luxury were displayed on every hand."[31] Chicago was a dramatically different place. A major rail, mercantile, and manufacturing center, the city saw its population double every 10 years from 1850 to 1890 and was still growing rapidly, reaching 1.6 million in 1900. Wealthy industrialists and financiers lived in mansions designed by fashionable architects with all the modern conveniences, while over a quarter of a million residents working in the garment industry, slaughterhouses, packinghouses, and other industries lived in squalid, makeshift residences and tenements without running water or indoor plumbing, a setting that would soon be made famous in Upton Sinclair's best-selling book, *The Jungle*. Wilson recounted his new surroundings:

Northwestern University, circa 1907 (Library of Congress).

> The church which I served was well-located . . . On one
> side not far away were the beautiful boulevards along which
> the motor cars and glittering equipage of the rich rolled
> past spacious lawns and magnificent and palatial residences.
> The north and west was densely populated with artisans
> and labourers and eastward, towards the throbbing center
> of the metropolis, along the river . . . slumdom. Thus, the
> scene of my labours in the city was to me an education in
> economics.[32]

Also in the fall of 1893, the Columbian Exposition was attracting visitors to Chicago from around the United States and the world for its displays of modern science, technology, and culture. This 400th-anniversary celebration of the arrival of Columbus in the Americas (one year removed) was set in large neoclassical buildings designed by major architects, built specially for the fair, and illuminated by electricity. Earlier that year, America had begun to sink into what would soon become the worst depression in U.S. history, not to be surpassed until the Great Depression of the 1930s. By 1894, unemployment nationally was close to 20 percent.[33] In Chicago the extra employment provided by the fair, including construction, fair operations, and tourism, kept the city from the worst effects of the depression until the fair came to an end in October; nonetheless, by August thousands of unemployed were demonstrating outside the exposition grounds calling for food and jobs.[34]

Wilson was shocked by what he saw as he began his pastoral duties in Chicago and as the months went on his dismay only deepened. He later recounted what he saw and how he felt during this time in several pamphlets and articles:

> I have buried children who did not have enough rags to cover them in their coffins. I have slept with men to keep them from committing suicide. I have seen the great armies of the unemployed live worse than animals, hungry in the streets.[35]
>
> I remember Nellie, who worked in the soap factory of the great benevolent soap makers, known over the world, millionaires. Nellie fainted at one of my meetings one Sunday night. She actually disturbed God's service with her secular cries, "the soap is heavy—is heavy—too heavy." She died—a suicide—at nineteen.[36]

Initially he tried to help individuals in need, encouraging them to follow the path of individual righteousness and morality and providing them with his personal assistance.

> I saw my brothers hunt for a job, offer themselves for sale to master after master, in vain, day after day. I helped them hunt. I went with Tom or Mack to "use my influence" and found fifty others looking for the same job.[37]

His fellow churchmen seemed oblivious to the injustice around them.

> I sat down one day to a chicken banquet in a west side church parlor with a group of preachers who were praying for a revival, while a detachment of the army of the unemployed marched through the alley and ate the refuse from our table out of the garbage box . . .[38]

He studied history, sociology, and political economy, searching for explanations and solutions, finding little of use in his classes at Northwestern.

> In political economy my professors were "sound," the textbooks used were properly stale with orthodoxy . . . my head professor in sociology . . . had a contempt for the working classes and a fawning devotion to the privileged and powerful.[39]

He visited Christian missions doing outreach to the poor but found no recognition of systemic injustice or even recognition of the harm done by the transit monopolies, usually obtained by bribing local officials.

> Missions for Jesus' sake were carried on with great success . . . I heard it boasted that souls of working-class men and women, under deep religious conviction, had made restitution of the fares they had avoided to pay to tram companies and railways. But I never heard of any accusation of the tramway bandits that had plundered tens of thousands of profits annually out of the pockets of the working class—to say nothing of any restitution of their ill-gotten gains.[40]

He visited Hull House, founded just a few years earlier in 1889, and was deeply impressed by the work of Jane Addams and the other Hull House residents.[41] They did outreach to the surrounding low-income neighborhood, supported organizing to obtain better services from the City of Chicago, backed union organizing, sponsored evening education classes for adults, and hosted presentations and debates over social reform. Although they did not offer an answer to the problems of poverty and exploitation, they engaged in a multitude of efforts to ameliorate slum conditions and to empower the residents of the surrounding community.

The labor movement and the churches

Wilson had been pastor at Erie Street for less than a year when the Pullman strike erupted in June and July of 1894. The Pullman Company, founded and owned by George Pullman, constructed and refurbished Pullman Palace Cars, which provided overnight sleeping accommodations for railroad passengers. Pullman had moved his facilities to the outskirts of Chicago, where he incorporated the town of Pullman and built homes and churches for the workers. He gave preference in employment to workers who were willing to live in Pullman rather than in neighboring towns and charged rents that made his ownership of the town quite profitable. He maintained a network of informants throughout the town, who kept the management apprised of dissent and union organizing efforts, and he also used the powers of the company to ensure that supporters ran the town government. Pullman claimed that he was creating a model community that would end labor problems at a profit. When the depression hit, Pullman reduced the workers' wages and hours of work, but did not reduce rents. Nor did he lower quarterly dividends to stockholders or lower the salaries of management and supervisors. Many workers had little left after paying the rent, but they were afraid to move to cheaper quarters for fear of being laid off if they ceased to reside in Pullman.

Some of the Pullman workers reached out to the American Railway Union (ARU), founded only the previous year. The ARU was led by Eugene Victor Debs, previously a popular official of the Brotherhood of Locomotive Firemen and editor of its magazine. Debs had concluded that the many separate railroad worker brotherhoods, which represented only about one-quarter of all railroad workers, had insufficient power to stand up to the railroad companies. What was needed was an "industrial" union, one representing all workers in the railroad industry. At the beginning of May 1894, the new union won a strike against wage reductions on the Great Northern Railroad and, in an era in which union victories were few and far between, railroad workers around the country joined the ARU. By the time of the union's first annual convention in June, it had 150,000 members, more than all the other railroad brotherhoods combined.

Assisted by an ARU organizer, the Pullman workers presented a list of grievances to the company, which promptly fired the workers who presented it. The workers went on strike and came to the ARU convention asking for support. The delegates were deeply moved by their plight and, over objections from Debs, who warned that a larger strike could endanger the union, voted to refuse to operate any trains with Pullman cars unless Pullman would accept arbitration of the workers' grievances. The railroad companies wanted a confrontation with the ARU and refused to remove the Pullman cars, forcing a strike that shut down the railroads in the West and Midwest where the ARU membership was concentrated.

The State of Illinois and the City of Chicago used their law enforcement powers to maintain order but refused to use them to break the strike. The federal government, under President Grover Cleveland, arranged to attach mail cars to all trains with Pullman cars, then obtained an injunction against the strike on the grounds that it interfered with the U.S. mail. Cleveland sent in the army to prevent picketers from blocking trains, arrested the union leadership, and quickly broke the strike and the union. The close collaboration between railroad corporations and the federal government, overriding state and local authorities, provided a dramatic illustration of capitalist control of the government, but it would take some time for Wilson to fully assimilate the experience as, indeed, it did for Eugene Debs himself.

In the wake of the Pullman strike, Wilson wrote in his diary of the need for a "religious culmination of the labor movement to rescue from the infidels the body of Christ's thought" and searched for guidance. He did not find it in the church. From the Civil War to the early 1900s, American Protestant denominations were deeply conservative in economics and politics. Virtually all church leaders and ministers of that era believed that poverty was largely the result of individual sin and dissipation. The role of the church was to show people the path to a righteous life and to assist widows and orphans. This perspective was reinforced by the belief that God had ordained the laws of nature and that the market economy based on private ownership of capital followed natural law. Theologically liberal ministers and university faculty might accept the Darwinian idea of evolution, but then extended it to society in the form of "social Darwinism," another way of describing economic competition and "survival of the fittest" as part of God's natural order.[42]

Ministers' solutions to social problems ranged from urging thrift and Christian living on the part of the workers to appeals to the wealthy to act with charity or even to treat the workers as brothers. Church publications argued that collective action through unions interfered with the freedom of the individual worker. Faced with labor unrest, protests, strikes, and efforts to prevent strikebreakers from taking the jobs of striking workers, the churches sometimes responded with ferocious hostility. The editors of the journal of the Congregational Church, for example, called for the use of Gatling guns to mow down the "mob" and restore order after violence broke out during the railroad strike of 1877 and again in 1886 after an unknown individual threw a bomb at police moving in to break up a rally in support of the eight-hour day in Chicago's Haymarket Square.[43] The vast majority of churchmen in virtually all denominations were opposed to the Pullman strike and supported Pullman as a Christian gentleman. Some went so far as to call for the strikers to be shot down in the streets.

With no support from the churches, labor and other social reform movements developed an alternative social Christian tradition that supported collective action. Proponents of this tradition understood that while some capitalists and monopolists might respond to moral appeals, most of those who profited from human suffering would not. It was necessary for people to use the power of organization to gain recognition of their human dignity. They rooted their appeal in God's love for all humanity, exemplified above all by Jesus the carpenter and his message of love and sacrifice in service to others. Added to this were appeals to the example of the prophets. Moses as a labor leader was a frequent theme, with the exodus from Egypt treated as a form of strike. The more radical proponents argued that through organizing and the democratic process, an economy based on competition could be replaced by an economy of cooperation, bringing about God's Kingdom "on earth as it is in heaven."[44] These were major themes of groups such as the Knights of Labor, the Farmers Alliance, the People's Party, the Woman's Christian Temperance Union under Frances Willard, and the American Railway Union of Eugene Debs. Social Christianity, which supported movements for social change, was developed and spread not by ministers and religious evangelists but by organizers and activists.

Social Christianity and church Christianity competed for support among the workers of Chicago.[45] In the wake of the Great Depression of 1893–1897 and the Pullman strike, some clergy became concerned that workers were avoiding the church and began searching for a middle path. Rev. William H. Carwardine, pastor of the First Methodist Episcopal Church in Pullman, was the best known of the sympathetic ministers. He gave a strong sermon on the text, "the laborer is worthy of his hire," in which he stated that the strikers' grievances were real, even though he opposed the strike itself and argued in favor of arbitration of the issues, something the workers had asked for before they went on strike.[46] As the depression continued, an increasing number of clergy came to recognize that the workers had legitimate grievances and that it could be appropriate to support organization of trade unions. They opposed measures such as strikes and boycotts that involved direct conflict, but many of them supported such significant social reforms as women's suffrage and the eight-hour day. This perspective came to be called the Social Gospel.[47]

Carwardine and some other proponents of the Social Gospel went so far as to call themselves Christian socialists. At that time, the term socialism meant opposition to economic "individualism" and could refer to a wide range of institutional arrangements that might foster social responsibility, ranging from government ownership to worker and consumer cooperatives to simple profit-sharing that would otherwise leave the capitalist system intact. The Christian socialists hoped the spread of a social understanding of Christianity would, through a gradual, voluntary, and peaceful evolution, convert the competitive economy to an economy based on cooperation. In the years after the Pullman strike, the views of some Social Gospel proponents crossed over into overt support for the labor movement and political action.

Major influences: Henry George, Frances Willard, and George Herron

The very limited support for labor organizing in the early Social Gospel did not meet Wilson's need to find a way to overcome the severe injustices he witnessed. Instead, he began to find answers in the social Christian organizing tradition. Three people in particular had a lifelong influence on Wilson.

These were Henry George, founder and leader of the single tax movement; Frances Willard, president of the Woman's Christian Temperance Union; and Rev. George Herron, who was the first Midwestern minister to cross over and adopt that alternative tradition.

Henry George combined a religious appeal that God made the earth for all of humanity with an astute economic analysis of how land value was created by the larger society but then taken for private profit by private landowners. George argued that the study of political economy had an inherently moral aspect. God had created the earth for man, and therefore all people were entitled to their fair share of the land and its fruits. God was beneficent and had provided a sufficiency for all people, so that poverty could be ended and was not a simple fact of nature. This argument appealed to the Christian beliefs of the vast majority of those who heard him speak or read his books.[48]

Rather than abolish private ownership of the land, George proposed to tax the land value and use this revenue to replace all other taxes, hence the Single Tax. He argued that land value taxation was both the fairest and most economically efficient tax system. It was fair because land values were created by society as a whole rather than by the enterprise of the landowner. It was economically efficient because it taxed the "unearned increment" in land value that was siphoned off by land owners and other "monopolists" and allowed government to pay for its operations without taxing work, consumption, or productive investment.[49] (Like Adam Smith, Henry George used the term "monopoly" to describe any beneficiary of imperfect competition.) This tax would end the practice of holding land for speculation, strengthen the bargaining power of labor by making more land available for workers to start small farms and small businesses, and fund bountiful public services.

George was also the first major American reformer to see the immense value of cities and proposed strengthening them, rather than calling for a return to the supposedly greater virtues of rural and small-town life. He had spent the years from 1857 to 1879 in San Francisco observing the explosive growth of that metropolis in its early years and he understood the productive role of urban density, how it increased urban land values, and how landlords siphoned off this increased value through rent. As he stated in 1879:

> Production is here carried on upon a great scale, with the
> best machinery and the most favorable facilities, the division
> of labor becomes extremely minute, wonderfully multiplying
> efficiency; exchanges are of such volume and rapidity that

they are made with the minimum of friction and loss. . . . Here intellectual activity is gathered into a focus, and here springs that stimulus which is born of the collision of mind with mind . . . All these advantages attach to the land; it is on this land and no other that they can be utilized, for here is the center of population—the focus of exchanges, the marketplace and workshop of the highest forms of industry. . . . And rent, which measures the difference between this added productiveness and that of the least productive land in use, has increased accordingly.[50]

In contrast with the socialists, George valued the market as a means of facilitating production of complex goods. Having once sailed before the mast, he argued that while a sailing ship needed a captain to direct its operations, production of all the materials and equipment needed for construction of that ship was too complex for one enterprise and required a market from which the many needed products could be drawn together.[51] Inherent in his view of the market as a form of social cooperation, as well as of competition, was that market exchange took place among equals, without any subordination of one person to another. George recognized that there were natural monopolies and argued that these should be publicly owned to reduce the corrupting effect of private monopolies on a democratic society. He suggested that public ownership should be extended from the post office to the telegraph system and from ownership of the roads to ownership of the railroads. The socialists argued that this limited view of natural monopolies was obsolete and that capitalism had a natural tendency to create monopolies and cartels that would dominate markets, bankrupt small businesses, and eliminate competition. Socialists were generally enthusiastic about the part of George's analysis showing that socially created land value was taken for private profit by landlords, and they supported land value taxation. They disagreed with his view that the single tax was the only necessary reform.

Like most American social reformers of his time, George held a deep belief in democracy and democratic government as the vehicle for social change. He believed that all that was standing in the way of the single tax was a small group of monopolists who held large tracts of land for speculation and used political privileges to gain control of land, railroads and municipal transportation, and utility systems. Once the mass of the people came to understand this, they would elect representatives who would pass laws that would sweep away the class privileges of the land monopolists and allow progress to end poverty. Ironically, given his opposition to socialism, George was probably the single greatest recruiter for socialism. Once people understood the concept of socially created value, they rarely stopped with land.

Perhaps equally famous and influential was Frances Willard, a resident of Evanston, who was president of the Woman's Christian Temperance Union from 1879 until her death in 1898. Wilson referred to her often as a major influence on his life, although it's not known that he ever met her personally. At about the time Wilson arrived in Evanston in 1890, Willard had been spending a great deal of time in England, on public speaking tours around the U.S., and in various health spas due to her deteriorating health.

Most of the prohibition movement regarded alcoholism as one of the many moral failings responsible for poverty. As Willard gained experience with the problems of cities such as Chicago, she concluded that poverty was a major cause of alcoholism and looked for ways to end poverty. In the late 1880s, influenced especially by Edward Bellamy's book, *Looking Backward*, she declared herself a Christian socialist, arguing that civilization itself should be "the common property of all the people." Her biographer, Ruth Bordin, points out that Willard was part of a milieu that believed women had a "talent for mutual aid and sisterly sharing of responsibility and rewards" and was attracted to the idea that "the whole society adopt what women viewed as their special affinity for cooperation."[52]

Willard was also a strong proponent of voting rights for women. She argued that women needed to be involved in politics for "Home Protection,"

Frances Willard speaking from a church pulpit in England
in 1894 (courtesy Northwestern University Library).

by which she at first simply meant protection of the home from the effects of alcoholism on the man of the house by prohibition of the sale of alcoholic beverages. Over time, her concept of the home broadened to encompass the surrounding neighborhood, and city and home protection broadened to include a demand for women's right to vote in order to ensure proper "municipal housekeeping."[53] As Willard put it in a letter to Susan B. Anthony, "Men have made a dead failure of municipal government, just about as they would of housekeeping, and government is only housekeeping on the broadest scale."[54] Willard worked to ally the WCTU with the Knights of Labor and then with the People's Party, trying to create a broad political coalition for social and economic change.

In the coming years, Wilson often worked closely with the WCTU, sharing Willard's support for labor, women's right to vote, prohibition, and socialism, and he was influenced by other feminist thinkers as well. Many socialists, including many socialist women, argued that since women could achieve equality only under socialism, the struggle for socialism should take priority over the struggle for women's rights. Some feminists had developed an alternative theory that it was womanly virtue that would provide the necessary basis for the moral reconstruction of society.[55]

Elizabeth Cady Stanton, a women's suffrage leader who espoused socialism toward the end of her life, developed a synthesis of these two views. She argued that replacing competition with cooperation was essential to enable women to develop their human potential, but at the same time women's nature provided the essential basis for a cooperative society. Said Stanton, "Before we can realize the dream of socialism, we must establish the equilibrium of the masculine and feminine elements in humanity."[56] This view made a lasting impression on Wilson. As he turned toward socialism in the coming years, he came to believe that women's role as mothers imbued them with the ethic of care necessary for the Cooperative Commonwealth and that women's equality was therefore essential to the socialist project.

Social Christianity received no visible clerical support in the Midwest until the mid-1890s, when Congregationalist minister George Herron, a professor at Iowa College (now Grinnell College), an institution affiliated with the Congregationalist church, published a series of sermons in which he moved from appeals to individual morality as the solution for social problems to appeals for collective action to change society. He first came to public attention with his widely reprinted sermon, "The Message of Jesus to Men of Wealth." In it he made an unusually forceful condemnation of the existing economic system as a social Cain, in which murderous self-interest resulted in "torn, bleeding, mangled, sorrowing, famishing multitudes." As usual, however, the solution was individual action. He stated, "Self-sacrifice is the law which God asserts in Christ over against the law of self-interest which Satan asserts in Cain." Society could be redeemed if only men of wealth would follow the cross and sacrifice themselves to God's will. He continued, "God is calling today for able men who are willing to be financially crucified in order to establish the World's market on a Golden Rule basis."[57] This appeal so moved Mrs. Caroline Rand, a wealthy widow in his congregation, that she endowed a professorial chair in "Applied Christianity" for him at Iowa College.

After Herron began teaching at the college, his message became much more radical. In September of 1893, he and its president, George Gates, created the "Kingdom Movement," declaring that there is social as well as individual sin and calling for social as well as individual redemption.[58] In his new book, *The New Redemption: A Call to the Church to Reconstruct Society According to the Gospel of Christ*, Herron argued that "capital is a social creation, and its administration a social responsibility . . . An industrial democracy would be the social actualization of Christianity. It is the logic of the Sermon on the Mount, which consists of the natural laws by which industrial justice and social peace can be obtained."

Now the action required was not simply individual sacrifice but social change to restructure property rights and administer the production and distribution of goods to provide "every man full opportunity to develop all his powers." The vehicle for action would be the church, reborn with the true message of Jesus, since "the call of the cross alone has power to summon the moral heroism of the world to action."[59] A few months later Herron's message radicalized again. Through "the social movement," the people were manifesting the message of Jesus and when they established a Christian State based on that message, they would also redeem the Church.[60]

Wilson described how, in late 1894, he was introduced to Herron's work by a classmate who "called me a heretic and said that I was worse than this man Herron . . . My curiosity was aroused, and I concluded to find out what the stranger's teachings were."[61] Wilson finally met Herron at the end of August 1895 while the professor was delivering a series of lecture-sermons in Chicago. Sitting down with him privately, Wilson recalled that "I poured out my own heart to him, telling him of my own soul's awakening." In Herron, "a poetic-souled mystic," Wilson found inspiration and a mentor.[62]

Bringing the labor movement to church

As Wilson searched for ways to help change society, he found a kindred spirit at Northwestern in acting assistant professor of physics Hiram B. Loomis. Loomis and Wilson joined the Single Tax Club of Chicago in the summer of 1895 and Wilson spoke on September 6th on "The Gospel of Social Reform."[63] The two also joined a Chicago-based effort by a small group of American Railway Union members to form a new broadly based union of all workers.

In April of 1895, the union's vice president, George W. Howard, the organizer originally assigned to the Pullman workers, resigned from the now-shattered ARU to establish the American Industrial Union. Howard urged that "all trades should combine in self-defense" in a union representing "all classes of workmen whether unskilled, mechanical or professional." He called for an eight-hour day, arbitration, and appeals to public opinion rather than strikes and added a mélange of self-help ideas, including refusal of overtime to spread the work, employment bureaus to help workers relocate to areas where work was available, and purchase of agricultural land where unemployed workers could make a subsistence living in "colonies" until other employment could be found. The union drew about 100 workers to its initial meetings including Wilson and Loomis.[64] In May, the U.S. Supreme Court upheld the federal government's power to issue injunctions against the ARU for supporting the Pullman strike, and Debs, Howard, and the rest of the ARU leadership went to jail for violating the anti-strike injunction. While Howard languished in jail, the union's Local 1 in Chicago debated whether to endorse a resolution denouncing the Supreme Court for its decision. When the decision was put off for a week, both the Local 1 president and vice president resigned in protest and were replaced by Hiram B. Loomis as president and by Wilson as vice president.[65] Howard returned from jail in August, but the organization folded soon after.

That summer Wilson finally became an American citizen and on June 12th, he and his wife added a third child, Violette Rose Wilson, to the family. They also welcomed to the household his brother Ben, who had been living with their parents in Michigan and preaching in local Methodist churches. Now 21 years old, Ben enrolled in the Northwestern Academy and his older brother helped him secure a position as pastor of the Methodist Episcopal Church in Spring Valley, a mining town 116 miles west of Evanston. Miners in Spring Valley had a history of conflicts with the mine owners going back to when the town was built in the mid-1880s.[66] Ben arrived in Spring Valley nine months after the defeat of a miner's strike that had taken place at the same time as the Pullman strike.[67] Ben's response to conditions in the mining town was very similar to his brother's response to conditions in Chicago. He related:

> The awful need of the miners impressed me profoundly and
> led me to investigate the cause of their condition. Their dire

poverty was appalling. During the first days spent in visiting, my heart almost bled within me. At first my response was one of charity and I frequently gave away all the money I had to buy bread for the needy, yet as the days passed into weeks and the weeks lengthened into months, I came to the irresistible conclusion that individual charity, good as it was in its place, was sadly inadequate to meet the needs of the poor.[68]

On Sunday, September 29th, Stitt Wilson was ordained as an elder in the Methodist Episcopal Church, completing the full ordination process, and his annual salary was raised to $1,200. He obtained the permission of his church trustees to hold a conference on "the labor question" at the Erie Street M.E. Church, to be followed by weekly evening meetings, and he issued an open invitation to the workingmen of Chicago to a first meeting on Friday, December 6th, at 8 p.m. "I hope to bring together on common ground all classes, trade-unionists, socialists, single-taxers, laborers. We want even the plutocrat to come in and give his side of the question if he will," said Wilson.[69] The conference was attended by about 300 people, mainly manual laborers. Opening exercises included the singing of "The Jubilee of Labor" to the tune of "Marching Through Georgia," asserting that "music is the enemy of tyranny and wrong," that "God is with the workingman," and that "ballot, voice and pen" will bring freedom to labor.

Rev. Wilson delivered the main address, demonstrating both his moral fervor and his uncertainty about how to proceed.

It would be moral suicide for me not to give vent to my feelings on the labor question. . . . I believe that the cause of labor today is as the cry that went up to Moses to deliver the children of Israel from the land of bondage . . . I have little faith in professional agitators or organizations, but I do admire Eugene V. Debs for his manly fight for the rights of labor. . . . It is not a question of higher wages only, it is not simply providing for the poor people, but it is a fight for freedom . . . We won't have any political meeting or any organized society, but we will hold a meeting of brother love and do all in our power to aid in cutting the chains which now bind the wage slave.[70]

Wilson's Friday evening lecture series at the Erie Street M.E. Church included Henry Demarest Lloyd, author of the recently published book

Wealth Against Commonwealth, and Eugene Debs, who spoke at the church early in January.[71] Debs had only just gotten out of jail after serving six months for violating the court injunction against the Pullman strike. At that point Debs was committed to working for a "cooperative commonwealth" but hoped the People's Party could lead the way.[72] Another Friday evening speaker was Dr. George Herron. In his talk on "Economics and Religion," Herron argued that "the hope of social democracy is itself the religious aspiration and effort of the common life" and criticized the church, saying that it "must repent of its manifest subjection to money and free its institutions from servile dependence thereupon."[73]

Wilson was the first minister in Chicago to try to bring social movement Christianity into a mainstream church. His activities and the speakers he brought in offended some of the better-off members of the Erie Street M.E. Church. Some members responded by reducing contributions to the church. Pastor Wilson's salary was set at $1,200, but he received only $925.[74] They also appealed to his superiors to rein Wilson in. He lamented:

> When it was reported to the higher church authorities . . .
> that I was preaching one sermon on the Labour Question
> each month, and holding a mass-meeting of working men
> to discuss the problems of Labour on Friday nights in the
> church, my bishop (presiding elder) wrote me a letter of
> severe chastisement. He wanted to know if I was going to
> be a loyal Methodist and was amazed at my youthful stupid-
> ity in thinking that I could learn anything about the Labour
> Problem by gathering a mass of work people into my church
> to "talk" about it. He warned me that to do this in order to
> get light on the Social Problem was like "hunting rabbits
> with a brass band." One of the higher officials, who had
> known me in some of my spiritual hungers and searchings,
> expressed the fear that my soul was lost . . .[75]

Rather than quiet down, Wilson moved beyond his expressions of general ethical concern with the labor problem and a lack of faith in "agitators or organizations." He denounced the current economic system and gave open support to unions, strikes, and boycotts. In mid-March of 1896, thousands of garment workers in Chicago went out on strike over the manufacturers' refusal to bargain with their unions. On Sunday, March 29th, a mass meeting in support of the strike and in opposition to the sweatshop featured such notables as labor and civil liberties lawyer Clarence Darrow, author Henry Demarest Lloyd, United Garment Workers of America president Charles Reichers, and several members of the clergy, including the Reverend J. Stitt Wilson.

Wilson insisted that it was immoral to treat "labor" as if it were separable from the human beings who labored. This separation he denounced as wage slavery.

> When we ride across our wide prairies, we must get our palace cars from the slave pens of Pullman City. When we wear fine clothing, we are conscious of the fact it is the product of the dungeons of the sweatshop district. What if the clothing in this room could tell its history? What a story of tears, misery, starvation, low wages, long hours and abject slavery we would hear. We, the public, have a right to know where and at what dreadful cost of human life and comfort our garments are made. A hundred years hence such evils will be referred to as hideous; let us begin to call them hideous today.[76]

Wilson suggested that arbitration of grievances, a key demand of the workers and widely supported in Social Gospel circles, would not be enough to eliminate sweatshops. He called on the garment workers to broaden the strike and for supporters to boycott non-union goods until the union won recognition. He proposed, "As to the ethics of the question, let me urge more practice of ethics and less preaching of it."[77] Two weeks later, on April 10th, Eugene Debs came to Chicago and joined Wilson in speaking at an evening meeting of strike supporters at the Erie Street Church, after which the two men spoke to a union meeting of "cutters and trimmers." In spite of Debs's and Wilson's efforts, a few days later the strike collapsed.[78]

By the end of May, the trustees at the Erie Street Church apparently reached the end of their tolerance for their pastor's radical views on workers and poverty and for bringing attention to the church by inviting noted radicals such as Debs, Herron, and Lloyd. In early June, Lizzie Holmes, a "special correspondent" with connections to radical and social reform circles in Chicago reported that "Rev. Stitt Wilson of this city, who but last week lost his pulpit for his noble winter's work, said: 'From the beginning of my ministry I assisted in and promoted the work of charity, until I saw that it could not cure poverty. The labor question lies at the bottom of that, and cold victuals and bundles of old clothes will never solve the labor problem.'"[79] Despite opposition from the trustees, Wilson had strong support from many church members who did not want to see him go. Evidently something was worked out between Wilson and the trustees, and he was reinstated to serve as the pastor of the Erie Street Church for one more year.

With a family to support, and a year to go in his studies at Northwestern, it appears that Wilson agreed to tone down his activism and he disappeared from the city newspapers for the 1896–97 school year.[80] Instead, he redirected his energies and honed his speaking skills by joining the Northwestern University debate team and winning a prize for "extemporaneous speaking."[81] (His debate team included Harry F. Ward, who became a leading Social Gospel minister and wrote the "Social Creed of the Churches" ten years later.) Although Wilson was not visibly active in politics that year, it is likely that he, like Debs, placed his hopes in the growing People's Party, which joined with the Democratic Party to endorse Senator William Jennings Bryan for president. With Bryan's defeat, Debs gave up the hope of major immediate economic reforms and declared, "The issue is Socialism versus Capitalism. I am for Socialism because I am for humanity."[82]

Wilson graduated from Northwestern with a B.A. in English in June of 1897. He then resigned his position as pastor, gave up his ordination in the ministry, and left the Methodist Church. He ensured his family's economic security over the next academic year by arranging an appointment as a part-time instructor in English at Northwestern, where his duties would include teaching oratory and coaching the debate club. He also enrolled as a graduate student in the College of Liberal Arts at Northwestern, which he could do tuition-free since he was now on the university teaching staff. Wilson's resignation shook the Erie Street M.E. Church. Membership declined from 123 in 1897 to 60 in 1898. (Membership meant people who made a formal commitment to the church; attendance at sermons and other events was typically much larger.) His successor as pastor was offered a reduced salary, suffered large deficiencies in his pay, and moved on after unsuccessful efforts to rebuild the church membership.[83]

The details of Wilson's conflict with the church are not known, nor are the reasons for his resignation not only as pastor but from ordination and the church itself.[84] His resignation would seem to be an expression of both his anger over the church's compromises with economic sin and of his desire to distance himself from a painful part of his own life. In light of Wilson's previous statement that "it would be moral suicide not to give vent to my feelings on the Labor Question," perhaps this pain came in part from his compromise with the church authorities, keeping quiet to support his family while finishing his B.A.

CHAPTER 3

THE SOCIAL CRUSADE

On August 29, 1897, Wilson gave the keynote address at the annual conference of Chicago's Cooperative College of Citizenship. His address, "The Ethical Aspect of the Labor Problem," gained wide notice. Benjamin O. Flower called it a "remarkable sermon that should be placed in the hands of every minister and church member in America" and published it in the November 1897 issue of his magazine, *The New Time: A Magazine of Social Progress*. He also reprinted it as a pamphlet.

Wilson began his speech by presenting a two-part question: "What is the labor problem and under the light of what ethical system do we consider that problem?" The first third of the talk defined the labor problem, arguing that the competitive system not only created wealth for a few and deprivation for many but also destroyed the moral character of both rich and poor while portraying this tragedy as the God-given "natural order."

Wilson proposed to compare the then-current "industrial relations" with the ethical standard set by the teachings of Jesus. He showed that the capitalist market economy contradicts Jesus's teachings of the Golden Rule, brotherhood, love, service, and sacrifice for others. Saying that "if Jesus was right, our industrial situation is wrong," Wilson then turned towards what is to be done:

> Charity cannot do it. Individualistic piety cannot do it. Justice, social justice . . . our associated loves and sacrifices alone can do it . . . to put into social and industrial practice the teachings of Jesus must ultimately result in . . . Co-operative Industry—the only solution of the labor problem.[1]

The call for cooperative industry left open the form that cooperation would take. His audience included proponents of building an alternative economy and of political action, gradualists and revolutionaries, populists and Marxists. Colonizers wanted to establish new towns and associated agricultural areas that would operate on a cooperative basis and use their growing socialist population to gain control of a state government. Party-builders wanted to establish a socialist or labor party that would gain control of the national government and use it to nationalize industry. Political reformers wanted the initiative and referendum to establish "direct democracy" so the people could vote for social change themselves. Some wanted to organize the working class for the inevitable class struggle and others believed in appealing to the common interests of all people regardless of class. There was a good deal of overlap among the different groups. George Herron, for example, supported both colonization and the Socialist Labor Party, despite the fact that leaders of each group fervently denounced the other.[2]

Wilson did not pretend to know the ultimate solution. At this point, he simply wanted to increase the number of people who would reject capitalism and join the effort to create a better society. He had models in the histories of Methodism and the abolition of slavery. John Wesley, the founder of Methodism, had sent Francis Asbury from England to America a few years before the American Revolution, when Methodism was a minor sect with at most a few thousand adherents. Asbury traveled throughout the colonies recruiting young, single ministers who would accept a subsistence stipend to travel a circuit of hamlets and towns preaching and recruiting people into Bible study groups. The itinerant ministers worked in conditions of great hardship and personal sacrifice, traveling by horseback in all kinds of weather, and regularly being sent into new territories. By the time of Asbury's death in 1816, Methodism was a major denomination in the U.S.[3] Advocates of the abolition of slavery had also traveled around the U.S. for decades, often facing violent hostility, presenting a biblically based message of brotherhood that eventually helped bring about a Southern reaction to preserve slavery that precipitated the Civil War and brought about emancipation.

Inspired by Herron's call to follow Jesus and sacrifice oneself for humanity, Wilson hoped to start a Christian revival movement for the end of "wage slavery" through industrial cooperation. Unlike the early Methodist circuit riders, however, he had a wife and three children to support. But Emma, who had come to share his socialist views, urged him to follow his heart. He considered waiting until Herron returned from a year-long tour of Europe, but he felt called to action.[4] A few weeks prior to his keynote address at the Cooperative College of Citizenship conference, on the evening of Wednesday, August 11th, as people were returning home from work, he picked out a busy Chicago street corner, put up a "white banner with the word, 'Humanity,' across the top in gold and the uplifted cross in crimson below surrounded by the words, 'Social Crusade,' and addressed the passersby."[5] Despite his support for a militant labor movement, Wilson was initially ambivalent about even the democratic use of the powers of government to support social change. He urged that cooperation come about voluntarily, rather than being "forced from men by political tyrants, even at the hands of a majority."[6] Like many less radical Christian socialists he started with the hope that the spirit of God would sweep through humanity and make cooperation its joyful expression.

Wilson established his base of operations at the Northwestern University Settlement House, modeled on Hull House and located in a poor neighborhood. The Settlement House accepted Wilson as a "resident."[7] Residents were not paid—they paid the Settlement for their room and board, but the cost was modest and it gave Wilson a place to stay overnight in Chicago and receive mail for business purposes while still maintaining his family in a rented house in Evanston. Emma recalled years later that at the start he had to pawn his library to fund his socialist preaching, "but together we fought the battle."[8] Wilson had at least some support from former members of the Erie St. M.E. Church, one of whom, Donald Noble, served as treasurer of the Social Crusade.

Wilson described the early days of his Social Crusade as a period of intense loneliness, assuaged by reading "the life of Jesus, of his struggle and sorrow and grief" and Professor Herron's book, *The Call of the Cross*. "All alone in the silent woods on the shores of Lake Michigan . . . I read and re-read this 'Song of the Cross' as a liturgy to the music of the waves as they lapped upon the beach . . ."[9] Herron returned to the U.S. that fall to take up his teaching duties at Iowa College and Wilson was again able to seek his counsel and moral support.

That winter Wilson toured nearby towns, taking advantage of the dense rail network in the Chicago area, as well as ship service to coastal communities along Lake Michigan. This allowed him to visit for a day or two and return to Chicago to teach or attend class, speaking to "churches, labor unions, cooperative societies and clubs for economic study," wherever he could find an audience.[10] The February 28, 1898, edition of the *Daily Chronicle* of Marshall, Michigan (a small town roughly halfway between Chicago and Detroit) was typical of the usually friendly local reporting:

> Rev. J. Stitt Wilson spoke in this city four times Sunday. He
> occupied the pulpit of the Christian church in the morning,

lectured at the opera house in the afternoon, made an address to men on the labor question at the Christian church and took part in the union meeting at the Baptist church in the evening. A fair-sized audience was present at the opera house in the afternoon to hear his address on Christ's solution of the labor problem. He took for his subject the Sermon on the Mount and drew from it a lesson which, if it could be spread broadcast throughout the land, could not help but benefit the cause of labor. Mr. Wilson is working in the interest of the Social Crusade. He is a forcible, enthusiastic speaker and is doing a work which must eventually result in much good.

In April, Wilson reported that more than 20,000 people heard him speak over about a six-month period, that he and his local supporters had distributed thousands of tracts (probably "The Ethical Aspect of the Labor Problem"), and inspired people to hold "meetings for prayer and the study of social problems."[11] These local meetings he called Social Crusade Circles, democratically organized groups that discussed the issues of the day, studied recommended readings, and helped spread the good word. He also recommended books by his two main mentors: *Social Problems* by Henry George and *The Christian State* by George Herron.[12]

Wilson returned to Marshall in May, speaking to "large audiences" in three different venues on Sunday, May 1st, and giving a new talk on "The Sublime Task of the Twentieth Century." The reporter for the town's other newspaper, the *Marshall News*, predicted that "he will be given a warm reception whenever he chooses to visit Marshall again."[13] Not all the reviews were good. After Wilson spoke in Greencastle, Indiana, home of DePauw University, the editor of the student newspaper (Charles Beard, who later went on to fame as a progressive historian) criticized Wilson, saying that his "communistic visions are only the nightmares of disturbed dreamers" and that it was wrong to agitate the masses with "a vision of an unattainable state of society."[14]

Searching for a path to socialism:
cooperation and colonization

Around this time Wilson met William Ross Wallace. Wallace was four years older than Wilson and, like Wilson, a Canadian of Scotch-Irish descent who had moved to the U.S. as a young man and had become a naturalized citizen.[15] A man with strong organizational skills, Wallace had started a grocery and general store with the intention of turning it into a cooperative with profit-sharing for employees and consumers. He had plans for cooperative manufacturing ventures as well. Wilson was deeply impressed by a man whose commitment to cooperation was so strong that he would invest his time and money to build up a business that he planned to give away. For his part, Wallace needed to attract employees motivated to work in a cooperative and customers motivated to patronize it. The two agreed to make the cooperative a part of the Social Crusade. In May of 1898, Wilson announced that the Social Crusade was entering the "industrial" aspect of its work and now included a grocery, market, and dairy. He encouraged people to patronize the store and use it to sell and distribute goods in the Chicago area.[16]

A few months later, Wilson learned that Wallace was not what he had appeared to be but rather was a missionary of the Koreshan Unity. Members of this communal organization believed that Koresh (Dr. Cyrus R. Teed) was the new messiah and successor to Jesus. A physician and alchemist, Teed had given himself a severe electrical shock in an experiment in 1869 and returned to consciousness believing that God had designated him as the messiah. He taught that the world was on the inside of the earth rather than the outside, with the sun in the center of the hollow sphere. He practiced mental healing and taught that the races and sexes were equal and that celibacy brought people closer to God. The combination of belief in celibacy and women's equality made the organization a refuge for abused women. The majority of the members were women and they filled most of the leadership positions in the organization. People who joined the group gave it all their worldly possessions. Koresh proclaimed that the ideal society would be a "theocratic socialism" under his leadership and proposed to implement his theocratic socialism through groups of secretly committed followers, like Wallace, who would permeate the political and economic system.[17]

At the beginning of September, while Wilson was speaking in Benton Harbor, Michigan, Wallace convened a meeting of people associated with the store to discuss its future. Wallace proposed that the cooperative become a branch of the Bureau of Equitable Commerce of the Koreshan Unity. Wallace's plan was opposed by several people who wanted a democratic organization, among them a skilled craftsman with many years in the cooperative movement. With his reputation as the founder of the coop and the backing of fellow Koreshans who packed the meeting, Wallace carried the support of the majority of those attending. The editor of the Koreshan magazine, *The Flaming Sword*, ridiculed the craftsman for his ungrammatical English, dismissed democracy as "delusional" since there is always a "central power . . . hidden from the masses," and praised Wallace's "scientific" approach.[18] (The unscientific craftsman probably believed that humanity lived on the outside rather than the inside of the earth.) Wallace had used the cooperative store (and Wilson) as a front to bring in people he could then try to recruit for the Koreshan Unity.[19] In January of 1899, *The Flaming Sword* proudly announced that the cooperative had expanded to include a grocery and produce store, bakery, restaurant, meat market, sausage factory, broom factory, and shoe manufactory.[20] None of the enterprises survived for long. By 1903, Wallace and the Chicago Koreshans had all moved to Estero, Florida, which they incorporated as a town and where Wallace ended up serving on the City Council.[21]

In August of that year, after a full year of the Social Crusade, Wilson was at last joined by another Crusader, Rev. Thaddeus S. Fritz, an ordained Methodist minister from the Kansas City area who was two years older than Wilson. He had moved to Chicago a few months earlier and was now teaching elocution and oratory at the Mrs. John Vance Cheney School of Music and Oratory. He became active in the Cooperative College of Citizenship, where he spoke on "The Relation of the Church to Social Reform" and most likely met Wilson through this organization.[22] Inspired by the idea of the Social Crusade, Fritz joined Wilson as a resident of the Northwestern University Settlement. (Also new at the settlement that fall was Harry Ward, Wilson's former classmate, who had just taken over as head resident after having earned his master's degree at Harvard.)[23]

Wilson and Fritz went on a speaking tour that August. With two leading speakers and the network of supporters that Wilson had built up over the previous year, they could make an impressive showing when they came into a town, and they built on successful campaigns with multiple visits. A good example is their work in Benton Harbor and St. Joseph, Michigan, small manufacturing and shipping towns about 60 miles from Chicago on the east shore of Lake Michigan. They visited the towns three times in the span of seven days, speaking mornings, afternoons, and evenings in places such as the Methodist Church, on the streets, and in front of the Hotel Benton, owned by the mayor of Benton Harbor, Edward Brant, a supporter of the Crusade.[24] Some meetings drew hundreds but others were less successful. Benton Harbor's *Evening News* reported with chagrin that two meetings on serious issues held the evening of Thursday, September 1st, including "the street meeting where Rev. J. Stitt Wilson preached the doctrines of Christ as applied against the trusts that are sucking the life-blood of the people," had each had an attendance of only 20 people, while boxing and a melon-eating contest at the bicycle track had drawn 400.[25]

The grand final meeting of the Social Crusade in Benton Harbor was advertised for the evening of Friday, September 2nd, at the bicycle track. The mayor would preside at the meeting and an orchestra would provide music. The Rev. Thaddeus S. Fritz, "a master of the art of elocution," would give a rendition of the chariot race from the novel, *Ben Hur*, and Wilson would give "his popular lyceum lecture on the sublime task of the Twentieth Century," a lecture previously delivered "at Battle Creek to 2,500 people at the Tabernacle." Alas, the electric arc lights burned out and the Crusaders had to speak on a nearby street corner instead. Although the orchestra was unable to play, Fritz led the audience in song and did his dramatic recitation of the chariot race from *Ben Hur*, after which Wilson gave a shortened version of his speech.[26] They regarded their campaign in the two cities as a success, having organized a Social Crusade Circle in each city.[27] On their return to Chicago, they learned about the loss of the coop to the Koreshans and took a few days' break before resuming their whirlwind speaking routine.

One August evening, in between visits to Benton Harbour, Wilson spoke to a crowd of about 500 people on State Street in Chicago, backed by the Social Crusade banner "floating resplendent beneath the electric light." A passing patrol wagon stopped to indicate that the crowd was blocking the walkway and he moved his portable speaking stand into the street and continued speaking. (In Chicago at that time it was customary for open air speakers, such as the Salvation Army, to use business streets in the evening to address passersby after the businesses closed.) Wilson later recounted that after he bid the crowd goodnight, a never-identified "well-dressed businessman" approached and told him, "I will publish a paper for you for three months if you will be the editor. We want your message in print and we want to keep in touch with your work. Will you do it?" Once he determined that the offer was serious, Wilson was happy to accept, and the September 1898 premiere issue of *The Social Crusader* appeared two weeks later.[28]

The lead article in the first issue presented the objectives of the Crusade: first, to present "a beautiful and inspiring message of social brotherhood, . . . arouse the social conscience of the people . . . (and) herald the social ideal of Jesus, the kingdom of heaven upon the earth;" second, to carry out "an active and unceasing campaign of social education" by establishing thousands of study circles that provide "centers of social Light and Truth;" and third, to support a "colony movement" to establish settlements in Western states "where men would be guaranteed the full product of their toil . . . and creating the material basis for . . . social emancipation." Dues were established at a 10-cent initiation fee and 25 cents every three months to support "the propaganda and colony work of the Crusade."

The *Social Crusader* was established as a monthly, usually sixteen pages long, with one or two long articles, news of the Social Crusade, suggested readings, and exhortations for readers to subscribe and donate funds. After the initial three months, subscriptions and contributions were apparently sufficient to keep the news magazine going for the next two years. Later on, after visits by Wilson to Battle Creek, Michigan, the *Social Crusader* also ran a regular monthly advertisement for Granola, invented by Dr. Kellogg at the Battle Creek Sanitarium.[29]

Wilson and Fritz announced their support for colonization just as the colonization movement was falling apart. After Eugene Debs's January 1897 announcement of his conversion to socialism, he had begun to work with a group called the Brotherhood of the Cooperative Commonwealth, which planned to establish cooperative settlements in Western states with small populations, growing the "colonies" until they had a voting majority in the state. In June, the American Railway Union had held a convention in which it dissolved the union and reorganized as the Social Democracy of America. The convention became a struggle between proponents of colonization and proponents of organizing as a political party to contest elections, ending in an agreement to do both. The colonists searched for sites to buy, made plans that required millions of dollars they didn't have and couldn't raise, and came into the June 1898 convention in Chicago proposing to buy and develop a gold mine in order to raise the necessary funds. As the colonists held a majority of the delegates, the political action group walked out and formed a new Social Democratic Party, led most notably by Eugene Debs and Victor Berger of Milwaukee. The Social Democracy of America managed to establish two small colonies in the state of Washington with a total of just over 100 members before falling apart.

The Social Crusade endorsement of colonization did not last long. Two months later, the November issue of the *Social Crusader* responded to inquiries by saying that "our work at present is purely educational and evangelistic. We have no colony or other institution under way. When future developments of our work fruit in a colony plan or cooperative school we shall fully inform our readers." The eclectic nature of Wilson's political views at this point in his life were displayed at one of his speeches in Benton Harbor when he responded to a question from the crowd on what he thought of Michigan governor, Hazen Pingree. Pingree was a progressive Democrat who, as mayor of Detroit, had fought for reduced streetcar fares and public ownership of the streetcar lines. Wilson won applause from the crowd when he predicted that Pingree would become president of the United States.[30] By January of 1899, the *Social Crusader* would refocus on political action.

Searching for a path to socialism: political action

Writing and editing a monthly publication pushed Wilson to air his developing views on Christianity and society. Wilson had enrolled in Northwestern University's M.A. program to study sociology and economics. Years later he recalled, "My professors, knowing my socialistic tendencies, required extensive reading and study of conservative and individualistic authorities," particularly of Herbert Spencer.[31] Spencer had coined the phrase "survival of the fittest" and applied evolutionary theory to society, arguing both that people were mutually dependent on each other as part of a social organism and that untrammeled capitalist competition would improve the human race by weeding out the unfit. He was opposed to most government activity except protection of private property, arguing that humane relations among people must be voluntary and based on Christian morality. Wilson's reading program resulted in a long essay in the *Social Crusader*, which laid out themes that would be important to him for decades to come.

Wilson's essay, "Analysis of Social Conditions," started with a familiar broad-brush economic analysis. He posited that since the competitive economic system has winners and losers, a small number of winners gradually monopolize the land, machinery, and money, dominating those who have only their labor. "Pay must constantly decrease when multitudes of toiling men, their wives and their children are all pleading for a chance to work the lands and the machines of those who have them." Then he drew on recent sociological work by two writers who were influenced by Spencer to argue that their analysis logically pointed towards socialism.

In *Principles of Sociology* (1896), Prof. Franklin Giddings optimistically claimed that "antagonism is self-limiting . . . the exceptionally strong (will be defeated) by the combined resistance of individuals of average power." Wilson recalled that he had recently heard "a cigar-maker curse in fiery hate the Jew who is gradually controlling that branch of labor," and argued for the necessity of "reconciliation and class-conscious combination among the great laboring and working classes" to provide that combined resistance.[32]

Modifying his previous denunciations of competition, Wilson now suggested that "strife" could be "creative as well as destructive," thinking of college sports, chess, and his own participation on the debate team. But, quoting from Benjamin Kidd's *Social Evolution* (1894), he points out that this requires that "we have obtained for all members of the community the necessary opportunity for the full exercise of their faculties . . . equal social opportunity." Wilson argued that equal opportunity requires socially guaranteed employment, which could only be provided by socialism. Only then would "a new form of competition" on "a higher plane" benefit society. Wilson was uncertain what such an economy would eventually look like, but he was clear that the socialist full-employment economy he envisioned would still have room for private enterprise.

> As private schools still exist and compete with the public school, and yet have no power to debar a single child from the privilege of an education, so we may let the private individual run his factory or shop if he so chooses . . . but he shall be powerless to keep an army of willing workers from a chance to live, and thus to profit enormously both from those who toil and those who toil not.

Kidd believed that Christianity was the underlying moral force behind the progressive evolution of society; that it was due to Christianity that human equality was recognized, slavery was abolished, and political democracy was won. Wilson agreed and argued that Christianity would provide the moral force leading to socialism as the next step in social evolution.

The next major article to appear in the *Social Crusader* was by Algie Martin Simons. Simons had graduated from the University of Wisconsin and moved to Chicago, where he worked for the Bureau of Charities while living at Hull House and the University of Chicago Settlement House. Searching for the causes of poverty, he had studied Marx and joined the tiny Socialist Labor Party (SLP), then the only Marxist political party in America. The group was made up largely of German socialists who emigrated to the U.S. when Germany banned the Social Democratic Party in the 1880s and was run by Daniel De Leon.[33] Simons's article, "Socialism: A Philosophy of Social Development," was a concise ten-page Marxist analysis of the process of social evolution through class conflict, describing the working class as the class that would finally end the tyranny of one class over another. His definition of the working class was a broad one that included educated people whose work included "organization and direction." The socialist parties were the vehicles for this social revolution and were growing rapidly in Europe, where they had received almost five million votes in 1898. He concluded that the class interests of American workers were best represented by the Socialist Labor Party.[34]

Wilson was evidently persuaded by the strategy of educating the public about socialism, electing a socialist government, and viewing socialism as an international movement. It is not clear that he believed that the Socialist Labor Party was the right vehicle, especially given his ties to Eugene Debs and the Social Democratic Party, but he added works by Marx, Engels, and DeLeon to the books and pamphlets available from the *Social Crusade*.[35]

Wilson followed up the next month with the article, "An Appeal to the Working Classes," which presented the idea of class conflict in less ideological language. He argued the need for a revolution (preferably peaceful) in the organization of the economy and characterized the economy as the "national house-keeping" of the American family, language borrowed from Frances Willard. He reviewed the dramatic inequality that resulted from "private property without limit" in the land and means of production, "which eventually results in the abolition of private property for the great masses of the people," and called for "the collective or social or common ownership by the people of the means of production and distribution." He called on working people to use their free speech and right to vote to bring about that change by voting for a Labor Party with an explicitly socialist program and pointed out that socialism is an international movement and that "the oppressed laborer of Japan and the Philippines has common cause with the wage-slave of America."[36]

Christian socialism in Great Britain

In 1899, Wilson gained both reinforcements and a significant new perspective on the socialist movement. The January 1899 edition of the *Social Crusader* announced that "members and friends" of the Social Crusade were about to send him to England for two or three months, where he would study the cooperative movement, municipal reform, socialist organizations, settlement houses, and the work of socially conscious churches. The *Social Crusader* had brought Wilson's work to the attention of other Christian socialist organizations and among them was the Brotherhood Church in London, founded by Rev. Bruce Wallace. Wallace invited Wilson to visit and arranged for him to stay at Mansfield House, a social settlement. The trip meant giving up the Social Crusade presence at the Northwestern University Settlement, and its business address was moved to the Wilsons' home in Evanston. Rev. Fritz would continue the work of the *Social Crusade* while Wilson was away.

Wilson would be joined on his tour by two highly regarded Methodist Episcopal ministers who planned to join the Social Crusade. In January he had toured several towns in Indiana, revisiting Greencastle, where he had long conversations with Rev. William H. Wise and invited him to join the trip to England. Wise took a three-month leave from his pastorate to join Wilson on the trip. Wise, two years younger than Wilson, had graduated from DePauw University in 1891 and done graduate studies in philosophy and ethics. He went into the ministry, serving as pastor of a Methodist church in Lafayette, Indiana. After reading Herron's *The Larger Christ*, he took a leave of absence and spent the 1894–95 school year studying with Herron at Iowa College.[37] In June of 1895, he married a DePauw classmate and in 1897 he was ordained and appointed pastor of the 400-member College Avenue Church in Greencastle. Wise was deeply impressed by Wilson and the way he was acting on Herron's message. Wise thought that the social movement "but awaits a really moral and truly spiritual dynamic to make it irresistible . . . and incarnate itself in just and righteous social institutions. . . . Any movement that hopes to be redemptive must be both spiritual and economic. It must be Christian. It must be Socialist. The feeling deepens in me that such a movement is close at hand, is already here."[38]

In Frankfort, Indiana, Wilson met with Rev. James H. Hollingsworth, who reciprocated by visiting Wilson in Chicago. Hollingsworth was so impressed by Wilson's activities that on his return to Frankfort he informed the church that he would resign his pastorate to unite with the Social Crusade movement, although he would maintain his membership in the Northwest Methodist Episcopal Conference. He decided to join Wilson and Wise on their trip to England. Hollingsworth was 49 years old, married with children, and for 22 years a highly respected Indiana minister. In 1897 he had transferred from Greencastle to Frankfort, where the church had a membership of over 1,000. His salary of $1,800 a year (about $56,000 in 2020 dollars) was more than twice the average U.S. household income of the time and sixth-highest among the 107 pastors of the Northwest Indiana Conference. He explained that he saw a civilization "based on selfishness and greed" and that the Church "is painfully indifferent at an hour when it should be ablaze with holy passion for the social emancipation of the people." The Social Crusade, he continued, expresses Christ's message to the world.[39]

The three men booked tickets from Boston to Liverpool on the S.S. *Canada*, departing on Thursday, February 16th. Wilson's train was snowed in by a blizzard near Baltimore and just made it to Boston before the ship sailed. During the voyage, Wilson spoke at the religious services held for first-class passengers on Sunday morning. That afternoon Wilson and Hollingsworth spoke in the common area reserved for second-class passengers. In the evening all three spoke at a meeting for passengers in "steerage." They held a follow-up meeting the following Thursday that attracted about 60 passengers from all over Europe, the U.S., and Canada as well as some members of the crew.[40]

After a smooth voyage, the ship arrived in Liverpool on the morning of Saturday, February 25th. They covered the 200 miles to London by train, going "50 miles per hour through the most beautiful countryside, plotted like a garden and already bearing indications of the approaching springtime." They were met at the station by Rev. Wallace and Edward Stavenon, "an old Chicago friend," Wilson recalled, "who a few years ago used to attend the labor meetings which we held in the Erie St. Methodist Church." The welcoming committee took them to dinner at the restaurant run by the Cooperative Brotherhood Trust and then on through the slums of London to Mansfield House, where they would stay for most of their trip. The next day, although "still feeling the motion of the vessel," Wilson gave an address at the Brotherhood Church on how his personal experiences had led him to socialism.[41]

Wasting no time, the trio filled the next weeks, meeting with leaders in the many overlapping social movement organizations located in London: Marxist, Fabian, and Christian socialists; trade unions; cooperatives; and settlement houses. They attended services at major churches including Westminster Abbey, St. Paul's Cathedral, and City Road Chapel, where John Wesley had preached. They attended a conference where they heard talks by the leaders of English Methodism. They visited Salvation Army shelters and workshops and Ruskin College in Oxford, a workers' education project that is still flourishing today. (It had just been established by two Americans, Walter Vrooman and Charles Beard, who had criticized Wilson in the DePauw student newspaper the previous year.) They also took in some of the major sights, visiting a session of Parliament, the Tower of London, and the British Museum, among others. Years later Wilson recalled that on the second Sunday after they had arrived, "I went as far as the famous London buses would take me and there I got on a bicycle and spent the day in the lands and by-paths and . . . villages of rural England."[42]

The socialist movement that Wilson encountered in England had several currents. The Social Democratic Federation (SDF) was a Marxist political party similar to the Socialist Labor Party in America. The Americans attended two SDF conferences that had brought major European socialist leaders to England. The Fabian Society focused on producing socialist educational materials and critical studies of industrial society from a non-Marxist, gradualist perspective. The leading Christian socialist organization was the Christian Social Brotherhood, "a society composed of ministers and workers in social reconstruction," whose activities were primarily educational, but who also worked in settlement houses and cooperatives. The *Social Crusader* printed a speech by its leader, Rev. John Clifford, on "The

Effect of Socialism on Personal Character," arguing that "commercial-ism" destroyed physical and mental character through unemployment and deprivation, while socialism would provide the basis for people to engage in meaningful work and develop their human capacities. Wilson reported that England had thousands of cooperative societies with a total of more than 1.5 million members and strong ties to Christian socialism.[43]

London's Christian socialists welcomed the Social Crusaders and their message. Wilson spoke at the Christian Social Brotherhood's monthly meeting on "Spiritual Dynamics in Social Reconstruction."[44] The Brotherhood Church set aside an entire week for them. Wilson, Wise, and Hollingsworth conducted afternoon and evening meetings on Sunday, March 19th, followed by meetings every evening during the week and concluding on Sunday, March 26th, with five meetings in all at the Brotherhood Church, Mansfield House, and Westminster Chapel. Following these meetings, they went out on Barking Road, the street passing Mansfield House, and held forth to the passing crowd. They had brought copies of "Christ's Solution of the Labor Problem," which quickly sold out, and it was then reprinted and distributed by the Brotherhood Church.[45]

Wilson and his two traveling companions were most impressed with the Independent Labor Party (ILP), which was explicitly socialist and more influenced by Christian socialism than by Marxism. It gave priority to working with unions and supporting immediate reforms as well as looking to an ultimate revolution in the structure of the economy. The ILP had won control of several town councils including the Borough of West Ham in the part of East London where Mansfield House was located. Percy Alden, warden of Mansfield House, was a representative on the West Ham Council and supported the ILP although he was not a member. Wilson attended a meeting of the West Ham Council with him and was deeply impressed to see a government body run by "representatives of the working classes" who had created public parks, libraries, and baths and were considering taking ownership of the street railways. During his visit, the council voted to construct a hospital using its own public works department and to require that businesses contracting with the council pay union wages. Wilson was inspired by seeing the Independent Labor Party control a municipal government and it had a lasting effect on his views about the path to social justice.

At the beginning of April, the Crusaders traveled to Northern England, and attended the ILP annual conference in Leeds. Wilson, after being invited to say a few words, commented that he "saw in this body a prophesy of the parliament of the twentieth century . . . where the elected representatives of the working classes would discuss and carry into effect the program of Socialism." He urged them to "work together with hope and courage for the success of the common cause throughout the world" as part of "the great international brotherhood of labor."[46]

The Americans then visited nearby Bradford, England's ninth-largest city with a population of 280,000 people, a woolen manufacturing center where the ILP was founded in 1892.[47] There they spoke at the Bradford Labour Church, part of a network of more than 50 churches dedicated to the idea that the Kingdom of God would be established on earth through the labour movement.[48] They met local leaders of the ILP at the home of Arthur Priestman, an ILP member of the Bradford Council, a socialist, and a Quaker whose family owned a factory employing 800 people. Among them, city councilmember Fred Jowett, who had started work in the mills at age eight, had helped organize a textile union and led a major strike. He was a founding member of the Labour Church and the Independent Labor Party, and had served on the city council since 1892, shortly after the right to vote was extended to most male heads of households in 1889.[49] (Women and the lowest-income one-third of men were excluded from the vote until 1918.)

As the Social Crusaders' speaking reputation grew, they received invitations to speak from throughout England and planned to move on to the town of Tunbridge Wells, but on Monday, April 10th, Wilson received a telegram informing him of a severe illness in his family. They immediately abandoned their plans and made arrangements to return home. Since the fastest available ship did not leave for another three or four days, they took advantage of the delay, going on a bicycle trip into the nearby Lake District. They arrived back in New York City aboard the S.S. *Umbria* on April 22nd and took the train back to Chicago where Wilson rejoined his family. There is no indication which member of the family was ill or the nature of the illness, but evidently the person recovered over the next few weeks because Wilson was soon back working on the Social Crusade. With Wilson back, Rev. Thaddeus Fritz set out for Los Angeles, where he was well-received by the active Christian socialist movement in that city. Fritz initially introduced himself as part of the Social Crusade, but he soon set up his own organization called the Forward Movement.

Wilson, Hollingsworth, and Wise

At the beginning of May 1899, Rev. James Hollingsworth moved his family from Frankfort to Evanston, renting a house next door to the Wilsons. Wilson and Hollingsworth spent three weeks getting into the flow by speaking every noon at Willard Hall in downtown Chicago and every evening in Fountain Square in downtown Evanston. Then they were back on the road, revisiting towns with Social Crusade Circles and trying to start new ones.

In September, Rev. William Wise and his family moved in with the Hollingsworth family in Evanston. Wise issued a statement calling for people "to repent not only of personal sin, but of the selfishness upon which the present competitive system is based."[50]

The visit to England and the news that Hollingsworth and Wise had resigned their pastorates to join the Social Crusade gave it a new aura of legitimacy. Previously, Wilson's Crusade work had primarily been in street meetings and at a small number of Methodist churches. Now Wilson, Hollingsworth, and Wise were receiving requests to appear in Methodist, Presbyterian, Congregational, and Baptist churches all over the Midwest. A visit from three respected ministers who had given up their churches "to go out, as did the apostles of old, preaching and teaching for the kingdom's sake" helped legitimize the concerns of local reform-oriented pastors, especially those with working-class congregations, and appealed to Christians becoming disaffected by church support for the status quo.[51] Hollingsworth was initially criticized by some ministers when he joined the Social Crusade, but after a few months, the local press reported that "the church and his brethren recognize his sincerity and admire his bravery. The conviction has also been growing that the work he is in is very important and that his real usefulness will not be diminished but enhanced."[52]

The Social Crusade had particular success in Eugene Debs's hometown of Terre Haute, Indiana. A group of ministers, including Rev. Worth Tippy of the Centenary Methodist Episcopal Church, along with the heads of the YMCA and the Terre Haute Central Labor Council arranged for Wilson, Hollingsworth, and Wise to come hold a series of meetings. After an opening address on the evening of Thursday, June 8th, the three held quiet meetings for prayer and individual counseling on Friday and Saturday mornings. Wilson and Hollingsworth gave speeches on Friday afternoon and Friday evening; Wise spoke on "Industrial Freedom." On Saturday evening Wilson spoke at the Central Labor Council on "The Cry of Labor, the Demand of Christ." On Sunday, the Crusaders split up, with Hollingsworth speaking at the Centenary and Trinity Churches and Wilson speaking at the Presbyterian Church, the YMCA, and a "union" meeting of members of several churches in the evening. The meetings drew so much interest that the visit was extended another three days, through the evening of Wednesday, June 14th. A Social Crusade Circle was formed, and 110 subscriptions were taken for the *Social Crusader*.

The Central Labor Council invited Wilson to return to Terre Haute in September as the principal speaker at its Labor Day celebration, although not all were welcoming. The trustees of the Centenary Church were so angry about the presentation in their church that they barred the Crusaders from returning there unless they promised not to teach socialism "either directly or indirectly."[53] Rev. Tippy moved on to other churches, remained committed to the Social Gospel, and eventually served as the executive secretary of the Commission on the Church and Social Service of the Federal Council of Churches of Christ in America.

The work in Terre Haute brought a rare new recruit, although she only stayed with the Crusade for about eight months. Martha Biegler was a graduate of Indiana State University in Terre Haute, where she worked as a teacher and became a member of the Terre Haute Social Crusade Circle. In the summer of 1899 she studied at Indiana State University in Bloomington and arranged for Wilson to come speak to a union meeting of Protestant churches there, drawing an audience of 500 people.[54] Biegler then joined the Social Crusade and began holding socialist meetings in the coal mining camps in the region around Terre Haute.[55] The Social Crusade reading list added *Woman and the Social Problem* (1899) by May Wood Simons (married to Algie Simons) and *Women and Economics* (1898) by Charlotte Perkins Stetson (later Gilman), likely reflecting the combined influence of Biegler and of socially conscious leaders in the WCTU.[56]

Biegler left the Crusade in May 1900 and moved to Indianapolis. She attended the convention there in 1901 that founded the Socialist Party of America, and she was the party candidate for Indiana Superintendent of Public Instruction in November 1902, losing but receiving 6,900 votes (1.2 percent). She left Indiana to work on the *Chicago Socialist* newspaper and became well known in radical circles in Chicago as "Red Martha," speaking in Washington Square Park and participating in debates at the bohemian Dill Pickle Club. She fell on hard times due to alcoholism but recovered and spent the years before her death in 1937 running a boarding house for the impoverished and homeless.[57]

Toward the beginning of July, Chicago Chief of Police Joseph Kipley ordered police to disperse "unlawful assemblies." Wilson met with Chief Kipley, who told Wilson he would "be arrested the next time he preached in the street." When Wilson asked him whether he would also "arrest the Salvation Army people," the chief was evasive. Wilson was scheduled to speak to the Chicago Single Tax Club on "The Social Crusade" on July 21st and, since the Single-Taxers had recently begun open-air speaking in the parks and streets of Chicago, they were also a potential target. Wilson used the club meeting to protest the threat to free speech. He was joined at the meeting by George Herron, who argued that the order was a response to criticism of the city administration and of the war against Philippine independence, not real concern with potential violence. (Jane Addams was also present but did not speak.) Wilson announced that he would defy the order, saying "I intend to preach in the street until I am arrested and then I will fight it out in the courts." Wilson held two open-air meetings in August, one in front of a church where he was scheduled to speak inside an hour later and another outside a church that sponsored the meeting. These venues seemed carefully chosen to make the best possible case against any police interference but apparently there was none. Single Tax Club members continued speaking in the streets and parks and were assured that they would be left alone and that the order would be limited to "disorderly gatherings which are without laudable purpose and obstruct traffic."[58]

Individual and social salvation

The Social Crusaders attempted to appeal to members of all classes of society on the basis of a shared religious faith. They were particularly proud of the way their Crusade meetings drew in large numbers of working men, while typical church attendance was disproportionately made up of women. Wilson described the subscribers to their magazine as including the laborer, college professor, music teacher, architect, capitalist, broker, farmer, lawyer, and mechanic; the settings in which it was received included the tenement attic, the suburban parlor, the machine shop, and the kitchen.[59] The greater level of detail given to middle-class occupations suggests that the magazine's message was particularly attractive to professionals and skilled workers who were active in established churches. Wilson also indicated that their readers were Catholics, Protestants, and Jews, but it is unlikely that Catholics and Jews made up any significant proportion of the readership. The appeal to the essential message of Jesus avoided specific issues that divided Christian denominations but was unmistakably part of the dominant Protestant culture.

With their many speaking engagements in Protestant churches, the Social Crusade leaders grappled with how to respond to a Protestant tradition focused on individual redemption as the essential basis for improving the larger society. Conservatives argued that socialism, with its focus on material conditions and economic institutions, was essentially hostile to religion. Hollingsworth responded with "Christianity and the Competitive System: a Word to the Church" (also published as a pamphlet and reprinted in the *Frankfort Standard*, his former hometown newspaper). He described himself as "a staunch advocate of individual regeneration" but argued that the system "unregenerates faster than we can regenerate . . . Let us cease expecting men to walk with God when we keep them chained to mammon." Rejecting arguments that conversion of capitalists to Christian brotherhood would solve social problems, he pointed out that business owners who attempted to live by the principles of the Sermon on the Mount would be driven into bankruptcy by their competition. The only solution, then, was "a co-operative commonwealth in harmony with the principles declared by Christ."[60]

Wilson followed with "Individual and Social Salvation," explaining how the two were inextricably linked. (Eight years later this essay was reprinted in *The Christian Socialist* and described by its editor as "one of the best ever printed" in his journal.) In his piece, Wilson described several great movements for individual salvation, starting with the early Christians, who had no chance of overthrowing the tyranny of the Roman Empire but who could achieve inner spiritual freedom, and continuing with Wesley and the early Methodists. He then argued that membership in society, even by a saved individual, makes that individual complicit in the social sins of that society. "Paul the apostle was a partaker in Roman Tyranny as a Roman citizen . . . No saint before the [American Civil] War could escape the social guilt of chattel slavery." Similarly, the capitalist economic system is "anti-Christian" and sinful.

Wilson then briefly described several great movements for social salvation, beginning with Moses, "the greatest labor leader in all history," and continuing with "the establishment of government of the people, by the people, for the people." Eventually freedom must come to the wage slave through "the international socialist labor movement of the present day, which is as distinctly Christian in its content as the abolition movement of a half century ago." In order to advance this movement for social salvation, however, we must also remember "the grandeur of great moral movements in which men were dealt with as individuals . . ." He called for a "revival" that would bring out the "inner spiritual liberty and a quality of divine life" in the individual."[61]

Wilson elaborated on his view of the importance of the individual in the social movement two months later in the article, "The Ideal Reformer." Here he argued that "every reformer who seeks to get the whole society to renew itself ought to reform himself."

> Shall the partisan demagogue, intolerant almost to hatred of every man's view but his own, reform society, bringing the longed-for state where each man may seek out the fullness and freedom and sacredness of his own life? No!
>
> If a man would be a savior of his fellows, he must be saved himself . . . The social salvation of the people will never be permanent except as wrought out and accompanied by the highest type of individual life and character . . . that and that alone will constitute you an Ideal Reformer.

At this point, having made a closely reasoned argument and searching for a means to achieve the necessary individual salvation, Wilson segued into an exposition of "New Thought," although it was not labeled as such.[62]

New Thought was a spiritual belief system that focused on enabling the mind to commune with and apply the infinite power and presence of God or the divine in daily life. As with Christian Science, it held that the physical world was a creation of and controlled by the spiritual realm. Adopting a Universalist perspective, New Thought held that it had discovered the essential truth underlying all religions and all sacred texts. A person who learned to bring their mind "in tune with the infinite" could ensure themselves health and prosperity. Proponents argued that just as physical science had developed techniques to power modern civilization, so the science of the mind would generate techniques to enable people to reach and draw on the universal power of the divine.[63] Wilson enthusiastically embraced this view. He suggested that just as there are physical laws, there is a "law and method of the soul's liberation" if only people "seek it, find it and obey it."[64]

Adherents to New Thought used techniques such as silent meditation, visualization, and affirmations to attune themselves to the divine power and direct it toward helping them reach their desired goals. (The San Francisco New Thought journal was called *Now: A Journal of Affirmation*.) New Thought teachers would do guided meditations to help people learn these techniques, some of which are still in common use today, especially in sports psychology, but without the spiritual framework of divine immanence.[65] New Thought could be understood in an entirely individualistic manner, making everyone responsible for their own health and success in life based on their own thoughts and providing one more way to blame the poor for their condition because they had failed to think correctly. But many proponents argued that love of and service to one's fellow humans, the path that Jesus had proclaimed to reach the Kingdom of God, was an essential part of attuning oneself to the divine and thus essential to achieving individual and social health. This view easily incorporated the Christian socialist idea that a society based on service to one's fellows was the path that Jesus had proclaimed to reach the Kingdom of God. Many leading New Thought writers advocated for or were sympathetic to socialism.[66]

Perception of the immanence of God enabled Wilson to have an ecstatic identification with humanity and the physical environment.[67]

> Sometimes I catch joyous glimpses of what it is to be at home in this lovely world; as the lily, as the bird in the air, as the wavelet in the stream, . . . a man in Nature's glorious movement. Not a stranger, nor a pilgrim, not bound

for some other world, but here and now . . . The listening
soul is touched with the breath of the Infinite and lives—the
inspired life—which alone is free.

And to live the "inspired life" meant that "my comrades are all peoples,
all colors, all creeds—all." William Wise made a similar New Thought-
influenced leap into ecstatic religious hope.[68]

It is unclear what influenced Wilson and Wise to take up New Thought
at this time, but Chicago was a center of New Thought teaching and Wilson's milieu was full of people who were proponents of or influenced by it.
One of its founding theorists, Emma Curtis Hopkins, taught there.[69] Rev.
Fritz had become a proponent before he left the area. George Herron was
influenced by it and was a friend of Ralph Waldo Trine, who was both a
socialist and author of the New Thought bestseller, *In Tune with the Infinite*
(1897).[70] Rev. Wallace D. Wattles, pastor of the M.E. Church in North Judson, Indiana, regularly invited the Crusaders to speak at his church. Wattles
had come to socialism after hearing Herron speak in 1896 and contributed
a New Thought article to the *Social Crusader*, calling for people to awake to
"the Gospel of the Divine Immanence."[71]

Samuel "Golden Rule" Jones

In the fall of 1899, Samuel M. Jones, mayor of Toledo, Ohio, sent a letter
requesting that Wilson and Hollingsworth join in his campaign for governor
of Ohio.[72] The man commonly known as "Golden Rule" Jones was at that
point America's most prominent Christian socialist. An inventor and manufacturer with no previous involvement in politics, he had been selected as
the Republican candidate for mayor in 1897 only because opposing factions
in the party had deadlocked. The Republican leaders who asked him to
run knew nothing about his political beliefs, other than that he was popular
with labor because he paid high wages. Jones manufactured oil extraction
equipment and was protected from competition by his patents. This enabled
him to charge prices high enough to pay his workers well and still make
substantial profits.

Jones had worked his way up from poverty in the oil fields of Pennsylvania and was initially a conventional conservative. As he began setting up
his factory in Toledo, the Depression of 1893 arrived and convinced him
that poverty was not simply a matter of individual morality but rather was
caused by society. Reacting against the long lists of rules he saw posted in
other factories he visited, in his business he posted the following sign: "The
Rule That Governs This Factory: Therefore, Whatsoever Ye Would That

Samuel Jones (from frontispiece of Jones's book, *The New Right: A Plea for Fair Play through a More Just Social Order*).

Men Should Do Unto You, Do Ye Even So Unto Them." Influenced by George Herron's writings, he came to regard the Golden Rule as the appropriate guidance not only for business but for government and the entire society.[73]

In his book, *The New Right: A Plea for Fair Play Through a More Just Social Order* (1899), Jones argued that society must provide everyone "the right to work" at wages that could support a family, the eight-hour day, and the right to organize unions; that cities should take public ownership of public utilities; and that society should be organized on a cooperative basis of partnership.[74] Jones was influenced by Henry George, but argued that the concept of socially created value extended much farther.

> That which is created by society should belong to society; but land is not the only property which is in its very nature social and not individual. . . . Is not machinery a

social product, the result of centuries of experiment and invention? In short, is not our whole civilization essentially a social product? Back of every inventor stand a thousand others who made his invention possible. Back of every enterprising capitalist stands the entire nation, without which not one of his schemes could succeed. . . . No man can point to his pile of gold and say, "Alone I earned it." What is called Socialism is not a visionary plan for remodeling society; it is a present fact, which is not yet recognized in the distribution of wealth.[75]

Once elected mayor of Toledo, Jones horrified the Republican establishment by calling for public ownership of the streetcar system and the utilities that provided water, gas, and electricity. He instituted the eight-hour day for municipal workers and public kindergartens and expanded public parks, playgrounds, swimming pools, and other amenities. He fought corruption in criminal justice and tried to reorient it from punishment to reforming the drunks, prostitutes, and petty criminals who churned through the system. He also brought George Herron to Toledo to give talks at Golden Rule Hall, which Jones had built on Golden Rule Park, next to his factory. In 1899, now understanding the type of man they had run for mayor, the Republican leadership repudiated him. The nominating convention split, however, and only by a narrow margin selected the party leaders' candidate. Jones ran as an independent and on April 3rd he was reelected with 69% of the vote over the Republican and Democratic candidates.[76]

Jones decided that political parties were themselves part of the problem because they divided people and that society needed to be redeemed through nonpartisan elected officials who maintained the essential unity of humanity. In all of his subsequent campaigns, he would run as an independent and he refused to create any kind of permanent organization. Jones also saw that political campaigns were a way to reach and educate the public on the changes needed in American politics and society. Having won such a remarkable victory in Toledo, he decided to take his message of nonpartisan democracy to the voters of Ohio through a campaign for governor.

Jones needed allies. He and his supporters had enthusiasm, but they lacked experienced public speakers who shared and could articulate Jones's message. The various socialist parties vehemently opposed nonpartisanship and refused to support candidates who did not run as party members, so he could get no help there.[77] Jones asked George Herron for his support in the campaign, and Herron gladly agreed. Wilson visited Herron at Iowa College and arranged to spend ten days at Iowa College in late October, taking over Herron's teaching and lecture duties while Herron joined the Jones campaign. Then, in the final week of the campaign, all three Social Crusaders joined the Jones campaign, with Jones paying their expenses and providing some family support. Wise and Hollingsworth spoke ahead of Mayor Jones in Cincinnati, while Wilson campaigned in the streets of Toledo. Wilson spoke ahead of the mayor in Cleveland, Lorain, and Toledo, while Wise and Hollingsworth campaigned in Sandusky, Perrysburg, North Baltimore, and other small and mid-size towns. On Election Day, Jones received 107,000 votes, only 12% of the total, coming in third after the victorious Republican and the Democrat. Jones and his supporters declared that getting over 100,000 votes was "a mass movement for social righteousness" and a great "moral victory."[78]

Jones and Wilson quickly became friends. Jones was very ambivalent about his personal wealth, which he believed was a social product of which he received a disproportionate share under the existing economic structure. He admired Wilson, who dedicated himself to his socialist Christian beliefs and lived modestly at best, and stated that:

> There are a lot of us who do a great deal of talking of the right kind, but our message lacks the force that Wilson's carries for the very good reason that we do not "live the life." Wilson does and comes as near being true to the Higher Self as any soul I know on the planet.[79]

Wilson's work with Jones and his strengthened ties with Herron now gave him entry into broader social reform circles and in December of 1899 he was an invited speaker at the national conference of the Social Reform Union held in Chicago. The Social Reform Union was a nonpartisan organization whose aim was to bring together a broad coalition of reformers around five principles: direct legislation and proportional representation; public ownership of public utilities; taxation of land values, franchises, inheritances, and incomes; money to be issued only by the government and in sufficient quantity to prevent deflation; and opposition to militarism.[80] The president of the Social Reform Union was the Rev. William Dwight Porter Bliss, author of an *Encyclopedia of Social Reform* (1897), and the union's long list of vice presidents had three governors, including Hazen Pingree of Michigan; several mayors, including Samuel Jones; and leading editors and writers, including Henry Demarest Lloyd, George Herron, Benjamin O. Flower, Lawrence Gronland, and Florence Kelly; and several ministers.[81] The organization was initially headquartered in the Los Angeles area, where it received financial support from Dr. John Randolph Haynes and Mrs. Caroline Severance, both of whom had affinities with Christian socialism and the Fabian socialist strategy of gradualism. The organization lasted only two more years, but Wilson's involvement gave him contacts that would prove invaluable.

A return to England

Shortly after the first of the year, Wilson made a return trip to England. He held a final conference with Herron the night before he left and placed the management of the Social Crusade in the hands of Hollingsworth and Wise for the next three months.[82] On this trip he was accompanied by his wife, Emma, and his four-year-old daughter Violette, leaving his older daughter Gladys, age eight, and son William, age six, with family in Evanston where they were attending school. Leaving New York City on January 4, 1900, aboard the *Kaiser Wilhelm Der Gross*, then one of the world's largest and fastest passenger ships, they arrived at Southampton on Wednesday, January 10th, after a pleasant voyage across the Atlantic with unusually good weather. Taking the train to London, they were met at Waterloo Station by Rev. Bruce Wallace, spent a few days in London sightseeing and visiting friends from the previous visit, and went to Wallace's Brotherhood Church, where Wilson gave a Sunday sermon.[83]

At the time of their visit, Great Britain was three months into the Boer War, which ultimately resulted in the incorporation of the Orange Free State and the Transvaal Republic, two Dutch settler-states, into the British-controlled Union of South Africa. Wilson was surprised to find that his support for peace was "received in marked coldness or with open disapprobation."[84] The Wilsons took a four-hour train ride to Bradford, again staying with Arthur Priestman, the Quaker cloth manufacturer and his wife. Both were members of the Independent Labor Party and elected officials, he on the city council and she on the Board of Guardians that administered poor relief. Here Wilson resumed his daily round of public speaking, mostly at churches—Anglican, Methodist, Friends, Congregationalist, and the nondenominational Labour Church, as well as at the trades council and other interested groups. He also spent several days speaking in the nearby town of Rawdon, sponsored by socially-minded Friends.[85]

Wilson was impressed by the peace meetings and anti-war sentiment he found in Bradford, contrasting it with London, which he described as "war mad." Wilson found the Society of Friends to be particularly interested in his message that peace required abolition of capitalism and spoke to several

Quaker meetings and organizations. In a letter to readers of the *Social Crusader*, Wilson engaged in an extended reflection on the similarity of aspects of the theology of the Society of Friends with his own.

> If there is any spiritual truth which is to be prominent in the theology of the twentieth century it is the re-statement of Christ's idea of inspiration, viz., that every human being is the abode of the indwelling God . . .

He considered the Friends' belief in the "inward light" within all people to be the equivalent to his own belief in the divine immanence. He approved of their rejection of war and urged them to also reject the economic warfare of competitive and ruthless capitalism.[86]

The Brownroyd Congregational Church, located in a working-class district of Bradford, was temporarily without a pastor, so the governing committee made the church available to Wilson as his headquarters and provided the organizational assistance needed to arrange talks at the church and around Bradford. In between speaking engagements, he and Mrs. Wilson visited the sick and needy around the church. Wilson's talks on "Practical Christianity" at the church were so successful that they were moved into Bradford's large Central Hall and concluded with afternoon and evening talks on Sunday, March 11th, at St. George's Hall, the largest in Bradford, before audiences of between 4,000 and 5,000 people. The Wilsons then took a few days off and then moved on to a week of Wilson speaking in Tunbridge Wells, a town south of London known for its health resorts built around mineral springs.[87]

The Wilsons returned to London on Tuesday, March 27th, for a farewell gathering at the Brotherhood Church, and the next day the Wilsons embarked for America on the German steamer *Lahn*, with Wilson's record of smooth transatlantic voyages about to be broken. The weather on the return trip was terrible and the ship "was tossed like a tub on the angry Atlantic." Wilson was seasick for three days but after he recovered, he "had the sailors tie me in a chair and lash me on deck and there, hour after hour, I let the wild sea do its worst while I watched . . . in a strange exultation . . . the sublime spectacle."[88]

On his return to Evanston, Wilson learned that Hollingsworth and Wise had done successful campaigning in Chicago, where a Social Crusade Circle met weekly, and in numerous small towns. The Social Crusade had more speaking invitations than it had speakers, but it also had a new recruit. Wise and Hollingsworth had held a week of meetings in Crete, Illinois, where Wilson's brother, Ben, was the new pastor. Ben decided to leave the pastorate and join his brother in the Social Crusade.[89] After his experiences as pastor in the mining town of Spring Valley and the steelmaking town of Joliet, he could no longer settle for pastoral duties and occasional visits from his brother and the other members of the Social Crusade.

The now *four* Crusaders traveled and spoke at a hectic pace, taking advantage of the long summer days, but there was occasional relaxation. On Saturday, August 11th, the third anniversary of the beginning of the Social Crusade, they held a picnic with their families in Evanston, on the shore of Lake Michigan. They were joined by members and families of the Social Crusade Circle of the West Side of Chicago, and lunch and dinner were accompanied by boating, baseball, ring toss, and other games. Immediately after, Wilson headed off to Humboldt, Iowa, where he gave a week of lectures to the annual assembly and training school of the Iowa chapter of the International Order of Good Templars, a temperance organization. In his final lecture, to an audience estimated by the press to be 1,000 people, he predicted that a 19th century dedicated to business would give way to a 20th century dedicated to brotherhood.[90]

Chapter 4

The Herron Fiasco

The Social Crusaders spoke to thousands of people each week, but their audience was not responding with the fervent Christian socialist awakening they themselves had experienced. Wilson had hoped to recruit dozens, even hundreds, of Social Crusaders. He had drawn in five, and only three remained: Hollingsworth, Wise, and his own younger brother, Ben. Back in July of 1899, Wilson had reported that "about twelve or fifteen young men whose hearts are aflame with the New Gospel of Brotherhood are coming . . . to spend the week with us. Meetings will be held every day of that week at noon in Willard Hall. In the afternoons we will hold conferences and in the evening street meetings."[1] But the training program did not bring in any new Crusaders. The February 1900 issue of the *Social Crusader* announced that in April "the brothers of the Social Crusade will open a two- or three-week school of Applied Christianity" at Hull House in Chicago and invited laymen and clergy to participate.[2] But with no subsequent reports, it is evident that the school was canceled.

At the end of the summer, James Hollingsworth's health gave out and he was forced to quit the Social Crusade. He had begun his career as a circuit-riding pastor in his 20s and had overestimated his ability to return to a traveling life at the age of 50. He returned to the North-West Indiana Conference of the Methodist Episcopal Church and took a small, vacant pastorate near South Bend to rest and to recover his health. At first, he hoped to eventually rejoin the Social Crusade. Early the next year he gave a series of socialist talks in nearby Friends churches and spoke at a Labor Day celebration in Elkhart, Indiana, but he then came down with a serious illness.[3] A year later, in September 1902, Hollingsworth resigned from the Methodist ministry due to ill health and moved to Terre Haute, where he had relatives.[4] Several years later he recovered enough to found a People's Church in Terre Haute. Its members met at the Nickelodeon on Sunday mornings to hear him preach the gospel of socialism.[5] He became a lifelong friend of Eugene and Theodore Debs and published a pamphlet countering personal attacks on Debs by providing testimonials of the high regard in which he was held in Terre Haute, even by those who disagreed with his politics.[6] After Hollingsworth's death in 1943, at the age of 93, Theodore Debs wrote that he "was one of the most Christ-like men we ever knew; sweet, gentle, kind and loving, coupled with a high degree of moral courage."[7]

Even if Wilson and Wise could recruit more Social Crusaders, they were too short on money to sustain them. Passing the hat often brought in less than the cost of the handbills and newspaper advertisements publicizing their work. The lead article in the August 1900 *Social Crusader* was an almost desperate appeal for funds.

> We have all sacrificed heavily to carry on this work. We are facing the rough edge. And this we joyously choose to do. And the gladness of our sacrifice and labor often hides from the eyes of our sympathizers the real needs of our work. The brothers who have joined me in the work have sacrificed everything for the cause. . . . this special letter . . . is an appeal to your heart from our hearts, frankly asking you to stand by us nobly in our labor of love. . . . send at once a contribution, however small . . .

In the first flush of enthusiasm after hearing Wilson and Wise speak, many people subscribed to the *Social Crusader* and joined Social Crusade Circles but they did not stay. People could join a Social Crusade Circle, study social problems, and support the speakers the next time they came back to town, but Wilson and his associates could not explain how this would lead to the Cooperative Commonwealth.

New direction, new energy

The state of the socialist movement at that time was confusing to say the least. In the summer of 1900 there were three competing socialist political parties: the De Leon faction of the Socialist Labor Party, the Hillquit faction of the Socialist Labor Party, and the Social Democratic Party of Eugene Debs and Victor Berger. In addition, there were smaller local organizations and nonpartisan socialists like Mayor Jones. There were few ideological differences between the Debs and Hillquit groups, and they agreed to support a unified national campaign ticket of Eugene Debs for president and Job Harriman for vice president. Harriman was a prominent member of the Socialist Labor Party in Los Angeles. A lawyer and former minister, he had been the SLP candidate for governor of California in 1898.[8]

Wilson announced his intention to vote for Debs and Harriman.[9] His friend Samuel Jones endorsed William Jennings Bryan on the grounds that the anti-imperialist Bryan was pledged to withdraw American troops from the Philippines and give its people the right of self-government instead of simply changing their status from a colony of Spain to a colony of the U.S. Wilson argued that even if Bryan were elected, fear of his policies by the "leading financiers, bankers and businessmen" would precipitate another economic crisis and, blaming Bryan and the Democrats, the people would go back to the Republicans. The only way out was to elect socialists who, unlike Bryan, would be ready to change fundamental economic institutions to end the crisis and guarantee full employment.[10] Despite their difference over the election, Wilson and Jones remained good friends.

During October, Wilson and the others campaigned for Debs, working closely with the Social Democratic Party in Chicago, Milwaukee, and other nearby cities.[11] In Kalamazoo, Michigan, Wilson spoke on "The Ethics of Socialism and the Issues of the Current Campaign" at the corner of Main and Rose streets, drawing a large crowd and receiving "generous applause."[12] Mary Collson, the probation officer for Chicago's Juvenile Court, later recalled that she became an enthusiastic socialist after hearing Wilson speak at Hull House, where she was a resident.[13] On November 6th, Debs and Harriman received only 88,000 votes, but this was more than double what the Socialist Labor Party had received in 1896 and the prospect of a larger, unified organization gave the socialists reason to hope for future growth.

Under fire from the Iowa College trustees for his increasing radicalism, George Herron had resigned from his position at Iowa College at the end of 1899 and went traveling in Egypt, the Holy Land (Palestine), and Europe, accompanied by his sponsor, the elderly Mrs. Rand, and her daughter, Miss Carrie Rand. In late September of 1900, Herron cut short his extended travels and returned to the U.S. to campaign for Debs and Harriman. During his trip, Herron had been thinking about next steps. He was increasingly estranged from the church, especially after his resignation from Iowa College, and he now wanted to establish a new spiritual and religious movement based on the teachings of Jesus outside of the churches. On his return, he wrote to the Wilson brothers and Wise and asked them to join him in a new "social apostolate," which they agreed to do after the election.

Herron gave an overview of his thinking in his keynote address to the September 29th meeting of the Social Democratic Party marking the beginning of the Debs-Harriman campaign in Chicago. He described the developing American socialist movement as the synthesis of three movements: the European socialist labor movement, with its analysis of class conflict and its call for the oppressed laboring class to win its liberty; the democratic individualism on which America was founded; and a new religious movement that imbues daily life with spiritual value. Together they call for a social and economic reformation to provide liberty for all through democratic cooperation. The socialist society must be "thoroughly democratic and spiritual" so that its government becomes an expression of the people. Otherwise, unchecked monopolistic capitalism is likely to evolve into a "Bismarckian" imperialist socialism, in which the people become the property of the state.

Herron argued that only if the socialist movement itself becomes an alternative religious movement as well as a movement for economic reorganization could it inspire the people to a great spiritual awakening and to "become noble and courageous enough to adopt the cooperative commonwealth as a working ideal . . . in the spirit of goodwill toward all men . . . In its essence, socialism is a religion; it stands for the harmonious relating of the whole life of man; it stands for a vast and collective fulfilling of the law of love."[14]

Wilson was enthusiastic about this approach and wrote two articles based on Herron's ideas.[15] In these articles Wilson argued that modern technology, the "railroad, steamship, telegraph and telephone," were transforming all of humanity into one worldwide community "irrespective of color, creed and custom" and that production and distribution of goods were now social rather than individual. But the new technology had been implemented through older forms of private property and individualistic morality that were not adapted to the larger interdependence of the modern world. As a result, the economy based on small farms and small businesses he had grown up with had become an economy of "capitalistic . . . industrial monsters" and turned the older individual morality into immoral complicity with injustice. "Sin is social as well as individual and evil is the pain of life un-adapted to the environment and in violation of the common good." At the same time, it is not enough to simply place all moral responsibility upon "the social systems." Wilson argued that an "awakened conscience" is needed, grounded in the recognition that "all human life . . . is sacred and divine."

Wilson, like Herron, was arguing against the view, prevalent in the socialist movement, that the economy was fundamental, and all other aspects of society and culture were mere epiphenomena. Many Marx socialists believed that the transition to socialism would be the inevitable result of the underlying economic processes of capitalism. Herron and Wilson agreed with much of the Marxist analysis of capitalism, but they believed people would have to change not only their economic institutions but their moral beliefs and spiritual understandings. Despite their criticisms of existing religions, the proposed new spiritual understanding was largely a socialist version of Protestant Christianity combined with New Thought.

With the election over, Herron decided to go ahead with his idea of a Social Apostolate. Wilson and Wise had for several years regarded Herron as their mentor and they and Wilson's brother, Ben, happily joined him, providing him with an instant organization. As Wilson put it, "Our natural leader had appeared and had called us to his side."[16] Even before the details were worked out, they began to work towards bringing together the Social Democrats and the Hillquit group from the Socialist Labor Party. Herron, the Wilsons, and Wise were not directly affiliated with either group and had good relations with both, so they were able to help mediate. On November 18th, Chicago's joint campaign committee held a day-long rally for unity whose featured speakers included Herron, who gave the main speech; Wise; and Wilson, who chaired the Resolutions Committee. Wilson spent the rest of the month traveling to Kentucky and Ohio to speak to local socialist groups urging formation of a unified Socialist Party.[17]

Herron brought substantial resources to the Social Apostolate, as his work was funded by Mrs. Rand and a group of wealthy sympathizers. He hired Franklin H. Wentworth, a 35-year-old businessman who had recently converted to socialism, to serve as business manager and editor of the new, expanded *Social Crusader*. Miss Carrie Rand served as treasurer. It appears that the Wilsons and Wise were also provided with modest salaries. Herron announced his new venture two days after Christmas and it received national publicity.[18] Article headings typically referred to a "new system of religion," "new gospel," "new religion," and "new belief." The first public event introducing the Social Apostolate took place on Sunday, January 6, 1901, at the Central Music Hall in Chicago, the city's largest indoor venue, with a packed house of over 1,000 people. The meeting opened with the Wilsons, Wise, and Wentworth on stage flanking Herron. Wilson began with a prayer for divine guidance, Wentworth did the introductions, and Herron gave his opening speech, "The Need of a New Religious Synthesis."[19]

After its initial use of the term "Social Apostolate," the group reverted to calling itself a "Social Crusade." The Social Crusaders were in great demand, and with five speakers the group was able to conduct a quite demanding schedule of meetings. When one of the group was forced to miss a meeting, another could usually fill in for him. Herron's effort to reclaim the message of Jesus from the Christianity of the "official church" and his description of Protestantism as "a performance, not a faith" naturally drew a reserved and even hostile response from many churches. They spoke mostly at house meetings, rented halls, and alternative churches such as the "Church of the Soul," but continued to work with sympathetic clergy in mainstream Protestant churches.[20] A group of Chicago socialists rented a former church and on the evening of February 24th Herron gave the opening address at the new "Socialist Temple." The Crusaders became regular Sunday speakers there. Wilson told the Michigan Congress of Religions held in Benton Harbor that "other centuries have discovered new continents, but the mission of the 20th century is to discover new continents in the soul of man and his relations to God."[21]

Secretary Wentworth reported that news of the formation of the Social Apostolate had resulted in a deluge of letters and so many offers from ministers to join their fellowship that they could expand their numbers tenfold if only they had the resources to support them all. However, despite the large numbers attending Herron's lectures, "Chicago contributions have so far paid only the bare expenses of the lecture course. The half-dozen earnest people who have undertaken to feed and clothe us in our beginnings, and the little band of self-sacrificing comrades who are paying our office rent, cannot do more than they are now doing."[22] Wentworth called for supporters in the ministry to follow the example of Rev. Carl D. Thompson, who had regularly invited Wilson to speak at his church. On January 1st, Thompson resigned from the pastorate of the Prospect Street Congregational Church of Elgin, Illinois, and, with the assistance of the socialists in his congregation, had leased the Elgin Opera House for Sunday evenings and established a new People's Church, also described as a "Church of the Social Conscience."[23] Herron hoped to bring the small number of existing politically radical churches into his organization, inspire the creation of new ones, and create a socialist church federation, similar to the British Labour Churches.

With the stability that Herron's funding provided, Wilson renewed his enrollment in the M.A. Program at Northwestern University. (He had allowed it to lapse when he first traveled to England.) He arranged to study with two supporters of the Social Gospel, Professor William Caldwell, who served on the governing council of the Northwestern University Settlement when Wilson was a resident, and Professor George A. Coe. Wilson's thesis was to be on the "Social Value of Religious Work of a Section of the City of Chicago," a sociological study in which he would attempt to interview a minister, priest, or rabbi from every church and temple in the two-square-mile "West Town" area of Chicago.[24] Wilson, and his brother, Ben, were also able to take time off to go to Denver to attend the funeral of their older brother William, who died in mid-February at the age of only 35, and to spend time with surviving family members. William was married with children and had also taken responsibility for support of his and his brothers' mother and several younger siblings after the death of their father in 1897. Wilson believed that William had worked himself to death and that capitalism at least shared in the blame.[25]

The end of the social crusade in the Midwest

March began well for Wilson. He visited Sandusky, Ohio, for a week of presentations and then moved on to Knox, Indiana, where he spoke at two churches, at a teacher's institute, and to high school students. The local *Starke County Democrat* said, "No thinking person can afford to miss these lectures . . . Mr. Wilson is an intensely earnest and eloquent man, whom it is a pleasure to hear."[26] The paper's competitor, the *Starke County Republican*, published a lengthy excerpt from Wilson's concluding lecture in Knox on "Socialism: The Logic of Christianity."[27] A high point was Wilson's visit to Toledo, speaking at Golden Rule Hall, and staying with Samuel Jones. Wilson later wrote to him, saying, "I shall not soon forget the last morning I was under your roof, when you danced into my room in your shirt singing a "Song of the Free Soul" which you had written that morning."[28]

Herron missed several lectures, ostensibly due to an illness, and Wilson filled in for him in South Bend and Battle Creek on March 19th and 20th. What was actually going on was that Herron was dealing with the crisis he had precipitated in his marriage. On March 21st, his wife, Mary, filed for divorce on the grounds of desertion and cruelty. George Herron did not contest the suit and the divorce was granted the same day. This was the culmination of several years of ever-closer relations between Herron and Miss Carrie Rand. Soon after her mother, Mrs. Caroline Rand, created the professorship for Herron at Iowa College, the Rands purchased a house near the campus and Herron had spent a great deal of time visiting them. Mrs. Rand made a number of generous contributions to the school, and it appointed Carrie Rand its dean of women. Mrs. Rand financed Herron's trips to Europe, and Mrs. Rand and her daughter had accompanied him on his most recent trip, while his wife and four children remained home in Grinnell. Upon his return in September of 1900, Herron asked his wife for a divorce and she eventually decided that she had no alternative but to comply. She received custody of the four children and $60,000 (about $1.8 million in 2020 dollars), which was provided by Mrs. Rand.

As soon as the divorce was granted, Herron left for New York City, where he announced that he would marry Carrie. The Christian socialist Rev. William T. Brown conducted the ceremony on May 25th with a number of notables in attendance including the famous poet Edwin Markham and Ralph Waldo Trine, author of *In Tune with the Infinite*. There was a strong backlash from many former allies in social Christianity. Rev. Josiah Strong, a nationally known reform-oriented Social Gospel minister, had been a friend and supporter of Herron for years. He now denounced him and refused to appear with him at a meeting in New York City. Another minister scheduled to share the platform with Herron and Strong also refused to appear, saying "I cannot hear what Herron says, because the sobs of his deserted babies thunder in my ears."[29] In Knox, Indiana, the local newspaper that had given Wilson such favorable mention two weeks earlier commented on Herron, stating that "a man who abandons his wife and children for some other woman would scarcely be chosen by ordinary decent people as a teacher of right living and he exhibits monumental egotism and impudence if he poses in that character."[30] The First Congregational Church of Grinnell, where Herron was a member, convened a council of representatives of Congregational churches to consider charges against him for actions unbecoming a minister. Herron wrote a letter defending his conduct but agreed that it was contrary to received doctrine and resigned from the ministry and the church.

Herron's actions destroyed the Social Crusade in its Midwestern heartland and put an end to his vision of leading a nationwide religious socialist movement that would retrieve Jesus from official Christianity. Many socialists had more modern ideas about marriage, love, and individual freedom, but Herron's main contribution to the socialist movement was his ability to reach out to Protestant Christians, winning support for socialism on the basis of Jesus's teachings on the poor and love of one's neighbor. Many Christians sympathetic to his politics now found his actions unacceptable and his religious claims a sham. He had also blindsided the Wilsons and Wise, who likely held then-conventional views on the sanctity of marriage and divorce as a last resort. They soon learned that Herron had asked his wife for a divorce immediately after his return from Europe, well before they joined his Social Apostolate. Yet Herron had given them no advance warning that accepting his leadership would require accepting a different view of marriage and a willingness to engage in conflict with the churches over the issue. Herron had simply taken their support for granted.

For Wilson, this was a personal and organizational disaster. The scandal destroyed what he had built up over four years of intense effort, and

Herron's failure to fully inform Wilson and Wise before they joined him changed Wilson's view of the man he had regarded as a mentor. The Social Crusade ground to a halt. Wentworth accompanied Herron to New York to manage his schedule and assist him at meetings, leaving Ben Wilson to manage the organization from Chicago. The Wilsons and Wise completed their scheduled meetings, including those held in churches, drawing on their own personal credibility in an environment that was becoming much less welcoming. They held few meetings in May, and these were largely within the socialist movement. In previous years, the summer had been a time of intense effort by the Social Crusade, with late evenings and warm weather making it easy to speak on the streets after the working day. Instead, Ben went camping in the woods of Wisconsin with a group of friends and the Wise family vacationed with friends in a suburb of Chicago.[31]

A new start in the West

Wilson responded by preparing to take the Social Crusade to the West coast. He knew leading Christian socialists in the Los Angeles area and had received invitations from socialists in Oregon. He and Emma arranged what was initially described as a three-month trip west for the summer. In preparation, Wilson quickly wrapped up his M.A. thesis. As D. Scott Cormode describes it, "Running out of time in completing his Master's degree at Northwestern University, he did what generations of students have done before and since; he turned in what he had. What he left for historians was his map, his notes from the interviews he could get, and a set of statistics he accumulated along the way."[32] If Wilson had intended to return to the Chicago area, where he could continue his interviews, there would have been no need to rush his thesis to completion. His thesis advisor signed off on it two months after he left, but his M.A. was not actually awarded until June of 1902, as it awaited payment of final fees.[33]

In preparation for his trip west, Wilson obtained glowing letters of recommendation from Mayor Samuel M. Jones, Eugene V. Debs, Algie M. Simons (now editor of the *International Socialist Review*), and Rev. Edward A. Steiner (pastor of the First Congregational Church of Sandusky, Ohio).[34] Notably absent from this list was George D. Herron. Just before he left on his trip, Wilson congratulated Jones on his reelection as mayor of Toledo in a letter that gives evidence of his emotional state.

> When I read the clipping as I walked down the street I was quite filled with emotion and my tears blinded me so that I could not finish reading. But I do not say it was over what

people would call your "victory." . . . "Our Kingdom is not
of this world." What I felt was an onrushing of prayer that
divine inspiration would be upon you that you might wor-
thily fulfill your priesthood . . . I would like to have spent a
day with you before I left for the West for the inspiration you
are always to me. You warm and enrich my soul with your
strength and simplicity and naturalness. As I leave for an
absence of three months, I am sure your benediction follows
me as my simple prayer remains for you.[35]

On Saturday, April 20th, a month after Herron's divorce, Wilson got
on the train and headed west, with many lecture stops, ranging from a day
to a week, along the way. His audiences were diverse. In Omaha he was
sponsored by the Central Labor Union, the Humanitarian Association, the
Women's Club, the Social Literature Club, and the Social Democratic Party.
He delivered a series of lectures on "Evils of the Competitive System" at
the First Congregational Church, then at Woodman Hall, and the last in a
large tent on a vacant lot downtown.[36] In Denver, Colorado, he was joined
by Emma, who had left the children in care of the Agnew family.[37] They
visited with his mother, brothers, sisters, and their families, and on Sunday,
May 12th, he spoke twice at the Church of Humanity and the next day
at the Church of Divine Science, a New Thought church. Notably absent
from news reports of his talks was any mention of affiliation with Herron.
Instead he was described as "the Chicago clergyman who left his pulpit to
advocate the principles of socialism," "recently from Europe where he has
studied social questions," and "connected with the Northwestern University
Settlement and Hull House in Chicago."[38]

The Wilsons traveled on to Cheyenne, Wyoming, where they spent several days, with Wilson speaking on Sunday May 19th, at the First Congregational Church. Its pastor that year was Rev. George A. Gates, who had
just the previous year stepped down as president of Iowa College and the
following year would become the president of Pomona College in California. The following week, the Wilsons traveled to Livingston, Montana,
where Wilson spoke to a full house at Union Hall and was invited to speak
the following Sunday at the Congregational Church. In between these and
other local speaking engagements, the Wilsons were taken riding and hiking
in the Yellowstone Valley, guided by local socialists including Frank Mabie,
a local architect best known for Socialist Hall in Butte, Montana.

While he and Emma were there, Wilson wrote to Mayor Jones requesting a loan of $250 (six months' pay for an average worker in 1901 and
around $7,600 in 2020 buying power), expressing the hope that this request

would not mar their friendship. Jones replied with a check and assurances of his continuing friendship.[39] On Monday, May 27th, they traveled on to Helena, Montana, where Wilson had three days of meetings in "church, hall, club, parlor." Wilson wrote a letter of thanks to Jones and described the political situation.

> This is a wonderful and beautiful commonwealth speaking conventionally. But the whole life of the state is almost completely dominated and controlled by the huge copper interests of these mountain cities. No one seems to dare to *claim their own souls*. Men live in social, political, religious and economic fear.[40]

Having spent extra time enjoying the scenic wonders of Montana, the Wilsons moved on to two weeks of hectic travel in order to make all of Wilson's promised appearances in Washington and Oregon and get to San Francisco in time to open a series of scheduled talks at the Academy of Sciences. On May 30th, they visited Spokane, followed by Puyallup, Olympia, Portland, Oregon City, Salem, Albany, and Medford. Arriving on short notice, local socialists were not always fully prepared to receive them. In Salem, "on account of the room engaged being occupied by the rummage sale, the lecture this afternoon was cancelled" although Wilson was able to deliver his evening talk.[41] He put the free afternoon to good use, finishing an article for the *International Socialist Review* in which he strongly criticized mainstream churches, saying "the basis of fellowship in the Christian societies was changed from character and conduct to belief (in) metaphysical dogmas. . . . It is doubtful that Jesus himself could have passed a creditable examination for license to preach on these paganized creeds . . ."[42]

The Wilsons reached San Francisco just in time for him to open a previously scheduled series of talks at the Academy of Sciences, beginning with "The Ethical Aspect of the Labor Problem" on the evening of Saturday, June 15, 1901.[43] Wilson arrived in the midst of a growing class conflict. The recently formed San Francisco Employers Association was determined to break the growing power of San Francisco's unions. The Wholesale Butchers' Association had announced a boycott of unionized meat retailers, forcing them to repudiate agreements with the Butchers' Union and a butchers' strike was quickly defeated in May. The Association then refused to supply meat to union restaurants, and in return the Central Labor Council announced a boycott of non-union restaurants. Meanwhile 4,000 metal workers went on strike for a nine-hour day against their employers, who maintained unity by refusing metal supplies to any company that settled with the union. The conflict would intensify over the coming months and in November the voters would elect a Union Labor Party mayor and board of supervisors, which consolidated union strength in San Francisco but would create interesting dilemmas for the soon-to-be-formed Socialist Party.[44]

Thaddeus Fritz and the Forward Movement cult

Thaddeus Fritz had moved from Los Angeles to Oakland, and Wilson had told friends in the Midwest that letters could be sent in care of Fritz for him to pick up when he reached the Bay Area.[45] Wilson had been enthusiastic about Fritz's work in Los Angeles. "His work is our work and ours is his and we are ONE in this common cause of human redemption."[46] He did not realize that the Forward Movement had collapsed into a small cult, and once he picked up his mail and became familiar with the situation, it appears that Wilson broke off all contact with him.

In Los Angeles, "Professor Fritz," as he called himself, set to work teaching New Thought and forming a Christian socialist organization. In Fritz's version of New Thought, just as people could now tune in to Marconi's new wireless telegraphy, people could learn to attune their "thought vibrations" to a higher mental level. Instead of using prayer to petition a "reluctant God," people should "trust the power of the living Christ within," "hold the thought," and "vibrate our spirit."[47] Soon after he arrived, Fritz made a New Thought presentation to a conference of the teachers of the Los Angeles School District, gaining numerous contacts.[48]

In June and July of 1899, he presented a series of lectures that combined Christian Socialism and New Thought. Lecture topics ranged from "Social Problems of America" to "Mental Concentration, Health Exercises and Psychic Culture."[49] He called for an independent, nonpartisan organization to unify reformers, a "forward movement." In October, Fritz introduced his new Forward Movement, dedicated to Christian Socialism and New Thought, to an audience of several hundred people at Blanchard Hall. His presentation drew heavily on the work of Herron and Wilson, but he disagreed with their turn towards a socialist party and away from colonization and nonpartisanship.

The mission of the Forward Movement would be twofold. First, it would work for "social awakening," seeking a gradual shift toward an economic system based on cooperation and Christian ethics, starting with public ownership of utilities and use of the initiative and referendum to place "power in the hands of the people." Second, the movement would provide working examples of "the Christ life of service working through the power of commonwealth instead of private wealth." A sympathetic businessman offered him use of an unused farm on the outskirts of Los Angeles, where he established a "Health Farm" with cottages and tents, treating people with fresh air, rest, exercise, baths, healthy food, and New Thought mental exercises.[50] He hoped to found a "colony" that would show the way to "an Industrial Republic."[51]

Fritz's Forward Movement was taken quite seriously in labor and reform circles in Los Angeles. He was invited to the Economic Club, whose leading light was Henry Gaylord Wilshire, a millionaire socialist. He was a featured speaker at a labor protest after a tunnel cave-in killed several workers, with the reporter commenting that "he succeeded in arousing more enthusiasm among those present than did any of the (other) speakers." He obtained funding and organized an event bringing 400 newspaper boys together with volunteer teachers who would assist them in getting at least some education.[52] He started a newsletter for Forward Movement members that he was soon able to convert to a weekly magazine.

Late in 1900, the apparently promising Forward Movement fell apart after a lawsuit revealed that Fritz was running a cult. At the beginning of August 1899, he had led a group of thirty people, mostly women and many of them public school teachers, on a three-week retreat at a camp in the San Gabriel Mountains east of Los Angeles where they would "commune with each other, with nature and with God." Five women in the group agreed to become his disciples and vowed on a silver half dollar placed on a Bible to commit themselves, their time, and their money to the Forward Movement. They moved into a communal home on South Flower Street in Los Angeles.[53] Mrs. Gertrude M. Caldwell, one of his disciples, filed suit for the recovery of money she had given Fritz. She testified that while living in the communal house in Los Angeles she was not allowed to speak to her mother without being accompanied by one or two of the other women in the group. After Caldwell learned that her mother had fallen on hard times, she asked Fritz for the return of some of the $350 he had gained from sale of her interest in a mining claim (equivalent to about $10,700 in 2020). He refused and when she announced her decision to leave to help her mother, she was sent away that evening, penniless. The lawsuit also brought to light that Fritz and his disciples were working with Margaret Brannon Sheehan, a spiritualist medium, who had gone on the mountain retreat with Fritz and Caldwell. They recorded in "sacred records" her visions in which "the Spoken Word of God through the Lord Jesus Christ" was revealed.[54] Support for the Forward Movement collapsed.

Fritz, Sheehan, her husband, and some of the disciples moved to Oakland in early 1901, then into a communal house in San Francisco's Richmond District.[55] The group continued on in obscurity, showing up briefly in the press after the San Francisco Earthquake and Fire of 1906, when they set up a tent and held a sewing school for children living in a refugee camp.[56] Fritz and Sheehan made a fundraising visit to Los Angeles, where they gave a highly exaggerated description of their work and lectured on "The Decline and Rise of San Francisco" and "Intelligent Parenthood the Most Vital Need of the American Nation Today."[57] "Professor" Fritz continued to teach his version of New Thought and went on lecture tours in the West and Midwest, addressing spiritualist groups with an offer that "spirit messages" would be heard.[58]

In May of 1909, Fritz and his group made another effort at colonization. They purchased a ten-year lease with an option to buy "Lawndale Ranch," 1,280 acres of eucalyptus forest near the City of Santa Rosa, north of San Francisco, and sold shares. The plan was to log and sell the eucalyptus ten years later, when it reached maturity, and use the proceeds to buy the property and build a utopian community. In 1911 several investors filed suit, saying that the Forward Movement had taken thousands of dollars from them and had told them it was a safe investment because the value of the property was over $20,000, whereas the company owned only the ten-year option to buy the property, valued at $1,000.[59] After several years of lawsuits, the Forward Movement Syndicate filed for bankruptcy.[60] Thaddeus Fritz and Margaret and Edward Sheehan moved back to Southern California and apparently remained together for the rest of their lives, all three showing up as a household in the 1920 census and Fritz and the widowed Margaret Sheehan in the 1930 census.

A new home in California

After a week in San Francisco, Wilson and his wife moved on to Los Angeles, a stronghold of Christian Socialism. Unlike San Francisco, Los Angeles and the surrounding cities were predominantly Protestant and many residents came from small and mid-size towns in the Midwest—the kinds of places where the Social Crusade had been most successful. In mid-1900, a group of wealthy Social Reform Union members formed the Economic Club, a monthly dinner and discussion group. Later in the year, many of the same people were part of a group of about twenty clergy and thirty laypeople who formed a League of Christian Socialists. The League members decided to form a socialist church in Los Angeles, initially called the

Christian Socialist Union and later the Church of the Commonwealth. As pastor they brought in Rev. R. M. Webster, the minister of Palo Alto's Unitarian Church and a frequent socialist lecturer.[61]

Notable members of the Economic Club and the League of Christian Socialists who would play important roles in Wilson's future included Henry Gaylord Wilshire, a wealthy real estate investor after whom Wilshire Boulevard is named. A militant socialist, he had recently begun publication of a weekly magazine called *Challenge*, soon to become *Wilshire's Monthly Magazine*. John Randolph Haynes was a physician and successful real estate investor who became the first president of the League of Christian Socialists. Mrs. Caroline Seymour Severance was a wealthy widow known as the "Mother of Clubs" for her role in founding the first Women's Club in 1868 in Boston. C.C. Reynolds was a well-to-do undertaker and Friends minister who was elected to the Pasadena city council as a nonpartisan in April 1901. Mary Garbutt was president of the Southern California Woman's Christian Temperance Union. James T. Van Rensselaer was an experienced journalist.

These people were far from being of one mind on the issues or on the relationship between Christianity and socialism. Some were proponents of nonpartisanship along the lines of "Golden Rule" Jones and others were members of the Social Democratic Party. Webster and many others believed Christianity would play a major role in gaining support for socialism, while Gaylord Wilshire and others believed that Christianity was a matter of personal belief with no particular effect on the larger society.[62] Despite these differences, these were people with the motivation and the means to provide Wilson with significant support. Shortly before his arrival, Wilshire's *Challenge* printed an article by Wilson on "The Present Moral Conflict" and ran notices of Wilson's availability to speak in return for payment of expenses for himself and his wife.[63] The Economic Club sent out postcards on behalf of the "Socialists of Los Angeles" proclaiming "Stitt Wilson Week" and announcing his upcoming series of three talks followed by a dinner at the Economic Club.[64]

Wilson's eloquence and his comfort with the local reform culture made him an immediate success and soon gained him the support and friendship of local Christian socialists. Wilshire gave an enthusiastic review of his initial talks ("few, if any, have ever listened to a speaker of greater intellectual clearness and power"), printed his schedule and letters of recommendation, and provided *Challenge* as a mailing address for people to reach him.[65] James T. Van Rensselaer made speaking arrangements in Los Angeles and throughout Southern California for him.[66] Severance, Reynolds, and

Haynes assisted with his travel expenses.[67] The elderly Mrs. Severance soon became a close friend, to whom Wilson could write of both his hopes and his difficulties. His surviving letters to her preserve a side of Wilson's life that would otherwise be rarely visible.

Upon his arrival in Los Angeles, Wilson plunged into lecturing at his usual intense pace. He spoke almost daily for two weeks in Los Angeles on topics including "The Competitive System Impeached," "The Great Social Sin," "The Class Struggle: The Drama of History," and "Program of Freedom for Labor." He was the featured speaker at the July 4th social-ist picnic at Long Beach, attended by socialists from throughout the Los Angeles area. Then he moved on to surrounding communities, speaking in Pasadena on "Socialism and Christianity" on Saturday evening, July 6th, and at the Grand Army of the Republic Hall on Sunday, followed by three days in Redlands speaking at the Christian Church.[68] He had to cancel four speeches planned for three days in Riverside due to "throat trouble brought on by overwork," but then he gave speeches for four days in nearby San Bernardino.[69]

On July 15th, he was back in Los Angeles, where he addressed a gath-ering of Protestant ministers of various denominations at the First Con-gregational Church and told them that justice, mercy, and brotherly love were essential religious principles and that all were violated by the existing, un-Christian economic system.[70] On July 18th, he was the featured speaker for Christian Socialist Day at the annual Long Beach Chautauqua. This fol-lowed Anti-Saloon Day and preceded Science Day. After an opening invo-cation by Rev. R. M. Webster, minister of the Christian Socialist Union, Wilson gave morning, afternoon, and evening addresses on the topic of the day. (The news reports gave far more attention to Miss Dromgoole's lecture on "Folk Lore of the South" in which she expounded on "the quaint, beau-tiful legends and lore of the humble folk.")[71] Payment for his work at the Chautauqua and donations from the audience after his speeches enabled him to repay Mayor Jones for the loan of $250.[72]

Wilson took the train to San Diego where he spoke twice on a Sunday and for the next three evenings. Local newspapers gave his visit to San Diego extensive coverage, describing packed halls and providing summa-ries of his talks.[73] One of them provides a rare description of Wilson as a speaker.

> Mr. Wilson is more than an interesting speaker. He is a man
> with a message, and he speaks with all the earnestness of a
> prophet, although he is by no means devoid of a sense of

humor. Moreover, he has no unpleasant mannerisms. He reiterates a great deal, but his evident object is to compel attention and agreement with certain truths, more or less self-evident. He is aggressive, but never abusive, and constantly calls attention to the fact that he does not attack men but systems. Throughout his discourse the audience accorded him the utmost attention . . .[74]

The article also printed an excerpt from his speech, which provides an example of his earnest humor.

Everything in this world by which we live is open to the limitless private ownership of . . . him who has the business ability to get and keep it. . . . Fifty people in New York own and control the real estate on which 3,000,000 people exist. . . . Suppose a fiat should go forth that all the material resources of this world were open to the limitless private ownership of any individual or group of individuals who could write the best poetry. You would say: "This is manifestly unjust, and I protest. I cannot write poetry and it is not right to give away what rightly belongs in part to me on any such basis!" But when the offer comes to him who has the greatest financial ability you say "Oh, I'm for that all right" and you strip for the race. My friend, you can write poetry better than you can finance and you will find it out some day.[75]

He returned to Los Angeles to give a lecture arguing that spiritual and economic needs could not be treated as separate issues and, a constant theme, pointing to the treatment of children as a moral touchstone.

Let us build a church for 70,000,000 people, all that are in the United States, and gather into all mankind, without regard to creed or condition, race or color, and with the sole view of enabling them to live the best, sweetest and most useful lives possible. . . . The wonderful forces of intellect inherent in every human mind should be set free and allowed to ripen to their fullest extent. The laborer's child possesses these as well as the heir to wealth, but poverty and constant drudgery stunts their growth. This is the greatest crime of all.[76]

As Wilson was speaking in Los Angeles, the socialist Unity Convention of July 29–August 1 had begun in Indianapolis, bringing together delegates from the Social Democratic Party led by Eugene Debs and Victor Berger, the Hillquit group from the Socialist Labor Party, and several state and local organizations. George Herron chaired the initial meeting, as he was regarded as a neutral party. The 128 delegates, including current and former Social Crusaders William Wise, Martha Biegler, and James Hollingsworth, formed the new Socialist Party of America.

Herron came out to Chicago from New York for a last conference with Wentworth, Wise, and Ben Wilson on July 26th before the convention. They apparently agreed on an amicable separation. After the convention, Herron and his assistant, Franklin Wentworth, went back to New York and formed a new Fellowship of the Socialist Spirit.[77] Herron's group planned to continue "as in the social crusade," publishing *Socialist Spirit* magazine and providing speakers whenever they were requested. Ben Wilson and William Wise announced that they would join Wilson on the Pacific Coast and continue the Social Crusade for a year, then return to Chicago. The *Indianapolis News* commented that "the separation of Dr. Herron from the crusade will greatly relieve the friends of Mr. Wise and Mr. Wilson."[78] Neither group made any public criticism of the other.

In September of 1901, Herron, his wife, and his mother-in-law left for another year in Europe. Historians writing about Herron have emphasized his desire to escape the hostile and sensationalist news stories about him, but the fact that his own disciples, his chosen Apostles, refused to accept his actions must have hurt deeply. His parting comment was "A Menacing Friendship," published in *Wilshire's Magazine*, which ensured it would be read by Wilson and his new friends and supporters in California. Herron charged that Christianity and Christian Socialism were a threat to the socialist movement. "The spirit of Jesus cannot escape until Christianity is destroyed . . . Christianity stands for all that is worst in capitalism; for all that is weak and mean in the human spirit . . . Materialistic Socialism is in a far better way to give Jesus a hearing in the world . . ."[79] Wilson did not respond to this and never again mentioned Herron in any of his published articles or speeches.

Herron returned to the U.S. at the end of 1902 and disbanded the Fellowship of the Socialist Spirit the next year. He did public speaking, provided financial assistance to

Socialist Party membership button, circa 1900 (from the author's collection)

young writers, including Upton Sinclair early in his career, and founded the Rand School of Social Science in New York City with the inheritance from his mother-in-law. For all his talk about sacrifice for humanity in emulation of Jesus on the cross, he was unwilling to live with constant vilification by the American press. In 1907, he and his wife left the U.S. for good and settled down on an estate in Florence, Italy, with their two children.[80] With the onset of World War I, Herron served as an informal advisor on European affairs to President Woodrow Wilson and urged support for Wilson's ideas of a just peace and a League of Nations. After the Versailles peace settlement of June 1919, he warned that the unjust treaty forced on Germany would set the stage for future wars. He died in 1925.[81]

CHAPTER 5

THE SOCIAL CRUSADE IN THE WEST

> The Social Crusader, the Reverend Stitt Wilson, has not a
> very large band but it is a faithful one. It will never desert
> him, as he is it.
> —*Daily People* (Socialist Labor Party), August 9, 1901

Wilson's tour of the western states showed that a well-delivered Christian socialist message had an enthusiastic audience there. Regrouping after the Herron debacle, Stitt and Ben Wilson arranged to restart the Social Crusade in Denver, where they could stay with family.[1] With his brother Ben taking on most of the administrative work, Wilson plunged into his usual heavy speaking schedule, starting with talks on Sunday, August 11th, at the Church of Divine Science (New Thought) and the Bethany Baptist Church. During the week he spoke every evening at Denver's Unity Church (Unitarian), followed by morning and evening speeches at the Church of Humanity on Sunday, the 19th, and again nightly at the Unity Church the following week.[2] (Wilson later recalled that his mother attended many of these talks.) By the end of the first month after the Wilsons had arrived, the new Denver Social Crusade Circle had 150 members, but it would turn out to be the last Social Crusade Circle.[3]

Rev. Charles H. Vail, a Universalist minister and author of *Principles of Scientific Socialism* (1899), arrived in Denver and joined Wilson for several evenings at the Unity Church. As the new national organizer for the Socialist Party of America, he had as his mission to help state parties organize local chapters.[4] Since the Socialist Party now offered an effective national organization, capable of organizing and supporting local party branches, there was no need for a separate Denver Social Crusade group, and it dissolved into the Denver local of the Socialist Party. The Social Crusade soon described itself as "a group of speakers assisting the socialist movement in the Western States."[5] Rev. Carl Thompson arranged a leave of absence from his People's Church in Elgin, Illinois, to join the Wilsons in their work for the next few months. Stopping at towns along the way to lecture on socialism, Thompson arrived in Denver at the beginning of October. He spent a few days with the Wilsons and then took over speaking duties in Colorado while Stitt and Ben went off to lecture in Sacramento, Oakland, Alameda, and San Francisco.[6]

In San Francisco, Wilson participated in a debate on socialism and then gave a series of speeches supporting the Socialist Party candidates in the upcoming municipal election.[7] The newly formed Union Labor Party, which elected Eugene Schmitz, president of the Musicians Union, as the city's new mayor, cut deeply into Socialist Party support. The 912 votes for the Socialist Party's candidate for mayor were far less than Wilson's audience in the city's Metropolitan Temple, where he gave a series of well-attended talks.[8] The "revolutionary" wing of the party was particularly strong in San Francisco where more-moderate socialists had been drawn into the Union Labor Party; the group protested that his lectures "contain too much Christianity and too little class consciousness."[9]

In November, Wilson returned to the Los Angeles area, accompanied by Ben and Rev. Thompson. They received extensive press coverage, particularly from the pro-labor *Los Angeles Herald*, which was then engaged in fierce competition with the ultraconservative and anti-labor *Los Angeles Times*. The *Herald* published long stories on each of their first four days in Los Angeles; these articles included photographs of the Social Crusaders and substantial excerpts from their speeches.[10] The fourth Social Crusader, William Wise, joined them three weeks later, coming out from Chicago.[11]

The Social Crusaders split up to cover as many different neighborhood halls, churches, YMCAs, women's clubs, and other venues as possible. After three weeks in Los Angeles, the Social Crusaders toured throughout Southern California, from Pasadena to Riverside to San Diego. Wilson was the star attraction, with audiences that typically ran to several hundred and reached over a thousand a few times. According to a news report, "though cosmopolitan to a degree, the audiences of Rev. Mr. Wilson are made up largely from the working classes . . ."[12] The collections taken up from their large audiences and help with expenses from a number of well-to-do Christian socialists brought in enough money to sustain several more months of touring.[13]

Wilson's morning talks usually addressed how people could live an "inspired life," and his evening talks focused on socialism as the solution for the social and economic problems of society. His morning "Inspired Life" talks were rooted in New Thought, although not identified as such.

He argued that God was present in everyone and that people should work to create a "relationship of the soul to the Infinite" so they could recognize their own divine nature. All the great artists, poets, musicians, philosophers, inventors, discoverers, and prophets had established this relationship and the greatest example of inspired living was that of Jesus. Wilson urged his audiences to follow the example of the Redeemer, who said, "I am come that they may have life and may have it more abundantly." Such a life was accessible to "open-souled people" in any walk of life who contribute to human happiness rather than using others for "power and gain." Wilson concluded by arguing that a scientific understanding of society would demonstrate that only socialism could provide the basis for an inspired life for all people, and that this would be the topic of his evening speech.[14]

His evening speeches followed standard socialist lines. He described the current conditions of suffering, explaining their roots in capitalism and the competitive system. He expounded on the need for economic freedom through cooperation and referenced the postal system and public education as examples of what the people can achieve through government. He reminded the audiences of past struggles for religious and political freedom and concluded with a call for expansion of the labor movement and for the working class to use its power at the ballot box to bring about a peaceful social revolution.

When speaking in a church or to a conference of ministers, he would emphasize his argument that socialism was a practical program for implementing the message of Jesus in economic life—that people cannot claim to follow Jesus if they proclaim brotherhood on Sunday and accept that the working class is subject to exploitation and autocracy on the other six days of the week. When speaking on behalf of the Socialist Party, he would point out that socialism was the scientific answer to the social problems of industrial society and that it should be supported by all—people of any or no religious faith.

The Social Crusaders had similar views on socialism but different styles of presentation. The editor of the *Los Angeles Socialist* preferred William Wise, because "his manner of presenting the subject of Socialism is a trifle more scientific and less florid than Comrade Wilson's."[15] But after praising a "fine address" by Wise, he noted that "it seems many members and others want oratory more than scientific Socialism, judging by the number of vacant chairs in the rear of the hall."[16]

They also differed in their interest in New Thought. Wise shared Stitt Wilson's enthusiasm and gave New Thought talks on "the Inspired Life."[17] Ben Wilson's viewpoint was similar to that of the Quakers, saying that "God has planted a spark of individual divinity in every human breast."[18] He urged people to work on developing a "stainless character" as part of the work of social change and praised the YMCA for supporting physical, mental, and spiritual development.[19] Like the others, Thompson argued that "Socialism (is) the only possible program for realizing the ideals of Jesus. To us it is the logic of Christianity." In a pamphlet, he briefly mentioned "a new movement, vaguely called the 'New Thought Movement,' which seems to be a very sincere effort to vitalize religious truth . . ."[20]

The Social Crusaders followed a grueling touring schedule (not unlike those of musicians today) and spent a great deal of time on trains. The trip from Oakland to Los Angeles on the Southern Pacific Railroad, for example, was twelve to fifteen hours long, depending on the route and the time of day. But one can work while riding a train, and during these train trips, Wilson produced his first substantial pamphlet, *The Impending Social Revolution: or The Trust Problem Solved.*[21] This was a straightforward, thirty-six-page overview of the political, economic, and ethical arguments for socialism and for joining the Socialist Party that Wilson typically covered in his sequence of lectures, but entirely omitted any reference to Christianity, Jesus, or other spiritual arguments that non-religious party members might object to.

In California, for the first time, Wilson began to speak on women's issues.[22] The Socialist Party was, at the time, the only political party that

The Impending Social Revolution!

IS THE TITLE OF

MR. WILSON'S LAST PAMPHLET.
Startling, Clear, Convincing.

☞ DON'T FAIL TO GET IT.
Price 10 Cents.

For Sale at This Meeting,

Or Address, **SOCIAL CRUSADE,**
531 Byrne Building,
Los Angeles, Cal.

STITT WILSON.

Flyer promoting one of Wilson's pamphlets (from the author's collection).

allowed women to be members and officers. Women were only a small percentage of the Socialist Party's national membership, but they played a substantial role in the Socialist Party of California. They had organized a statewide Woman's Socialist Union of California with many local branches and provided much of the leadership in the California chapters of the Woman's Christian Temperance Union and in the "social" wing of the New Thought movement.[23] The leaders of both the Northern and Southern California chapters of the WCTU were prominent members of the Socialist Party and became friends of the Wilsons.[24]

The Social Crusaders brought in hundreds of new members for the Socialist Party. Historian Grace Stimson has called Wilson "the outstanding organizer for the Socialist Party of California."[25] The Los Angeles local credited him with doubling their membership.[26] The relationship was not entirely harmonious. The Los Angeles local held regular Sunday evening meetings, but it was forced to cancel them when Wilson was speaking because he drew away so much of the party membership. At regular party meetings, the leadership tried to help members develop their speaking skills by encouraging questions and statements from the audience. Wilson declined to set aside time for that, although he would take written questions from the audience and speak informally with members after his talks. After much discussion, they compromised by having the L.A. local sponsor some of Wilson's talks.[27]

The party constitution adopted by a statewide convention in the first week of January 1902 included a provision that "No independent Socialist propaganda, periodical or school of Socialism shall receive official endorsement by the party."[28] Despite this, Wilson and his associates continued to work both under official party auspices and independently. When the Los Angeles Council of Labor held a parade and mass rally on January 25th to demonstrate public support for unions and for boycotts of nonunion businesses, Wilson was the featured speaker and the only Socialist Party representative chosen to address the crowd.[29]

By the end of 1901, the Social Crusade seemed firmly established in California and Colorado, so Thompson returned home to Elgin, Illinois, and gave notice that he would resign his People's Church pastorate. He quickly completed his University of Chicago M.A. thesis on "The Need of Cooperation of the Rochdale Type in and About Chicago" and settled in Denver at the beginning of April 1902.[30] Wise returned home to Chicago and he and his wife also arranged to move to Denver, where he took on the role of secretary for the Social Crusade, planning the speaking tours of his fellows and himself.[31] The Wilsons' children remained in Evanston with the Agnew family while Stitt and Emma searched for a place to settle down.

In January 1902, the Social Crusaders were joined by Rev. Robert M. Webster, minister for the Los Angeles Christian Socialist Union, who gave speeches occasionally on behalf of the Social Crusade in the Los Angeles area, and Socialist Union member James T. Van Rensselaer. Van Rensselaer was the author of *The Church and Scientific Socialism*, in which he urged "Scientific Socialists . . . never to forget that the Church as a moral agent immeasurably surpasses all other institutions in its power of aiding and abetting your advance."[32] An experienced journalist, he had just become the editor of the *Los Angeles Socialist*, the weekly voice of the Socialist Party of America in the Los Angeles area, and added the editing and publishing of the revived *Social Crusader* to his responsibilities.[33]

The *Social Crusader* lasted only six or seven months. Wilson later explained that "the obligation we feel to stimulate to the utmost degree the state and county socialist papers now springing into existence wherever we

From left to right: Ben Wilson, William Wise, Robert Webster, J. Stitt Wilson, Carl Thompson, and James Van Rensselaer (from *The Comrade*, November 1902, page 43; courtesy of the Huntington Library).

go has led us to discontinue the publication."[34] Just as there was no need to create "Social Crusade Circles" now that there were Socialist Party locals to join, there was no longer a need for a Social Crusade publication to give people a sense of being part of a larger movement.

Making a home in Berkeley

At the beginning of March 1902, Stitt and Emma Wilson decided to establish their home in Berkeley, which was then a small town of just over 13,000 people, divided between the largely middle-class neighborhoods near the University of California at the base of the hills and the working-class neighborhoods two miles to the west, near the waterfront. He recalled years later, "We went to Berkeley, where we had decided to make our home, without ever having seen the city. It was the seat of the State University—that was enough."[35]

> We arrived at night. The next day was perfectly glorious. The real estate men . . . showed us the town . . . Toward evening we . . . started out on foot. The atmosphere on the hillside was divine. Every light all about the bay sparkled like a gem. The moon shone down on the fair waters before us. I can remember how we spoke to each other almost in subdued tones as the silent glory of that wonderful night fell upon us. And that night I walked to the owner of the lot we stood on and bought it.[36]

They stayed temporarily at the Albany, a middle-class residential hotel in downtown Oakland, and a few days later rented a house from Laura Hall at 1745 Highland Place at the top of Ridge Road near the lot they had just purchased. Emma's younger sister, Leila Agnew, brought the three Wilson children from Evanston, moving in with the family. When they traveled west with their aunt, Gladys was 11, Gladstone 8, and Violette 6.[37] Two years later, in 1904, Wilson sold the lot and instead purchased the house they were renting from Ms. Hall and lived there for the rest of his life. Architectural historians refer to this house as the Laura G. Hall House, after its first owner, but Wilson always referred to it as "Highland Home."

Built in 1896, Highland Home was a large house, two stories high on the uphill side and three stories on the downhill side. It featured a flowing, open-plan interior with exposed post-and-beam construction surrounded by redwood-paneled walls, while the exteriors were done in brown shingles that blended into the hillside landscape and featured large windows that looked out over the Bay to San Francisco and the Golden Gate.[38] The lower level featured a "den" with wide windows offering an expansive view. The ground floor included the entryway, living room, dining room, kitchen, and small work room. Sliding wall panels between the living room and dining room could be opened so that the two rooms worked as one space with the bay view as a backdrop. Wilson's older daughter, Gladys Viola, would later stage plays here, since the combined rooms could accommodate an audience of up to 50 people. The top floor had six small bedrooms.[39]

The house was one of a cluster of five homes, all designed by Bernard Maybeck, that played a major role in establishing the Berkeley brown-shingle house as a major Bay Area style.[40] (The first was Maybeck's own home, built in 1892, followed by the home built in 1895 for Charles Keeler, author of *The Simple Home* (1904).)

For Wilson, living the traveling life much of the year, Highland Home was a source of deep satisfaction.

> Any kind of day in Berkeley seems sweeter than the best anywhere else. Let the winds blow or the storm fret or the rains fall or the fogs come sweeping up like bridal wreaths— it is perfect. The bay of San Francisco, never hidden from our window . . . I have watched its moods as if it were a child at play or an old sage in his meditation. And the dear, dear hills right out of my back door . . . the city should own them as a natural park . . .[41]

Wilson may not have realized it at the time but moving to Berkeley ensured that he would spend a great deal of time traveling to Southern California. In 1906, 51% of church members in Los Angeles were Protestant, while in San Francisco only 15% were Protestant and in Oakland 35%.[42] The Catholic Church was uniformly hostile to socialism, while Protestantism in California had opened up to the Social Gospel and, to some extent, to Christian Socialism. And, indeed, no sooner had Wilson rented Highland Home and settled his family there than he was on the road again, heading to speaking engagements around Southern California.[43]

While he was there, his friend Samuel Jones, mayor of Toledo, arrived in Los Angeles for a visit and Caroline Severance gave a reception in his honor. Speaking on Jones's life and work was Nelson O. Nelson, himself a successful industrialist from just outside St. Louis, who shared the profits of his business with his workers and planned to eventually turn it into a cooperative employee-owned enterprise.[44] Alfred Dolge, who was rebuilding his fortune in Los Angeles, described how he had built a successful business offering profit-sharing and old-age pensions in Dolgeville, N.Y. before being driven into bankruptcy in the depression. Wilson spoke on how the work of Jones, Nelson, and Dolge demonstrated the practicality of socialism.[45]

While in Los Angeles, Jones suffered an attack of pleurisy and stayed with Nelson for three weeks until he recovered enough to return to Toledo.[46] Wilson visited him during his recovery and became friends with Nelson, who often came to Southern California to visit a cooperative colony he had founded for people suffering from tuberculosis.[47] It was the last time Wilson and Jones would see each other. Reelected mayor again in 1903, Jones died in office in 1904.

Wilson next embarked on a tour that took him to Denver, Albuquerque, Omaha, Ogden, Oklahoma City, and back to Denver, stopping at many smaller cities in between. In Albuquerque, New Mexico, he spoke to the local branch of the Socialist Party and to railway and foundry workers on behalf of the Socialist slate in the municipal elections, denouncing control of the economy by the 2% who were experts at financial manipulation. He also discoursed on the nature of education at the university and spoke on Christian socialism at the Congregational church.[48] In Colorado, he gave a speech to several thousand people at the Denver Coliseum, after being introduced by Edward Boyce, president of the Western Federation of Miners, a militant industrial union that had adopted socialism as its ultimate economic objective.[49] After a month of touring, Wilson finally returned to Berkeley for two weeks to spend time with his family and attend the wedding of his brother and sister-in-law.[50] On May 7, 1902, Ben and Leila Agnew were married and moved into the Wilsons' bottom-floor den.[51] Their honeymoon was short. Two weeks later Ben joined his older brother and Thompson, campaigning in Oregon for the Socialist Party candidate for governor.[52]

The two families lived together in Highland Home for the next five years. This was undoubtedly a great help for the two sisters, since their husbands were engaged in almost constant travel throughout the West, the Southwest, and the Mountain states, and both had children on the way, Emma's fourth and Leila's first. In the first four months after moving to Berkeley, Wilson spent less than six weeks at home.

In September of 1902, Wilson set out on the road again, lecturing on socialism in Southern California, Washington, Montana, and British Columbia, and then in October moved on to Wyoming and Colorado supporting the Socialist Party ticket in the November elections. Ben, who had started his career as a minister in a mining town, was a favorite speaker among union miners. He did not avoid giving his views on temperance as well as on socialism. He praised the work of the Woman's Christian

Temperance Union, but took a good-humored approach, suggesting that under socialism "the world would be such a grand sweet song that a man would not want to get drunk for fear he would miss half the show."[53] In the November 1902 election, he was the sacrificial Socialist Party candidate for Alameda County administrator, but actually spent his time touring mining towns, mostly in Montana and Idaho.[54] The Socialists did not get any of their candidates elected, nor did they really expect to. The elections were an opportunity to introduce their new party and educate the voters about socialism.

The Socialist Party had especially high hopes in Colorado. The miners were in an ongoing struggle for an eight-hour day law and the Western Federation of Miners had officially endorsed the Socialist Party. Eugene Debs spent the entire month of August touring the state and all of the Social Crusaders came at various times to speak at election rallies and help organize locals in areas where the party did not yet have an organization. Edward Boyce, the union president, chose Wilson to accompany him on the speaking platform, and Wilson's subsequent speaking tour was mostly organized out of local union offices.[55] A talk he gave in Denver to an audience estimated at 2,000 people was described by a hostile reporter:

> Mr. Wilson spoke for two hours. He is a man . . . of striking appearance. His make-up is rather Byronic, clean shaven, long locks parted on the side and the Byron collar and flowing tie. He was formerly a minister and his platform style is that of the evangelist. He is forceful and has the power to stir men. He gave vent to a number of blasphemies that had a bad effect on many auditors.[56]

The party's growing importance became manifest when Colorado Lieutenant Governor David Coates, who had been elected on a Populist-Democratic fusion ticket, joined the Socialist Party, although he declined to run for reelection. This broader interest in the Socialist Party drew an outraged response from the "revolutionary" wing of the party in Colorado, which denounced Coates as a "grafter" and "corruptionist," the Social Crusaders as "sentimentalists," and the Denver local, many of whom had been recruited after hearing the Social Crusaders, as "cockroaches." In their view, middle-class people such as ministers and lawyers who joined the party were opportunists who planned to use the party's inevitable rise to power to get themselves jobs and elected to offices. The leading historical account of the Socialist Party during this period takes the revolutionists' charges against the Social Crusade at face value, claiming that their tours of Colorado were sponsored by "right wing" socialists when in fact they were sponsored by the militant Western Federation of Miners. Several subsequent writers simply repeat this version of the story.[57] The last word should go to Eugene Debs, who expressed his gratitude to Wilson and Wise for their support in the difficult days after his release from prison and said that while the critics "talk about 'revolutionary Socialism' and 'opportunism'; these and a few other stock phrases complete their vocabulary . . . Such men may organize a sect, but never a party."[58]

The Social Crusade comes to an end

Changes in the leadership of the California Socialist Party now affected the Social Crusade. Wilson's experience in Great Britain had left him with a strong belief in the strategy of close collaboration between the union movement and a labor party. Many California Socialists, including Wilson, had been impressed by the success of the Union Labor Party in the San Francisco elections in 1901, after the Democrats and Republicans had both supported use of the police against a major strike by teamsters and waterfront workers. Socialists found its leadership and program unacceptable, and for good reason. The leadership was a group that had been defeated in the Republican Party primary election and took over the effort to organize a Union Labor Party in order to get a second chance at controlling city government. The platform they wrote called for police neutrality during strikes, public ownership of utilities, and exclusion of immigrants from Asia and said nothing about restructuring the economy. Once in control of the city, they proved to be thoroughly corrupt.[59]

Union leaders in Los Angeles were much closer to the Socialist Party and hoped that in Los Angeles they could create a genuine Labor Party with a socialist program. The California Socialist Party convention in September adopted a platform stating that it did not oppose formation of "bona fide working class parties," and the Los Angeles Union Labor Party convention adopted a socialist program that called for "abolition of the wage system." The Los Angeles local of the Socialist Party then endorsed the Union Labor Party candidates for local office. This de facto fusion of the Socialist Party in Los Angeles with another party drew furious opposition from other locals around the state. The revolutionary wing was, of course, opposed. In addition, many "evolutionary" socialists had previously supported the People's Party and were traumatized when the effect of the 1896 endorsement of Democrat William Jennings Bryan for president was to destroy the People's Party as an effective political force. The result was that most members of the Socialist Party were inflexible on the issue of "fusion," regardless of the local circumstances. Indeed, the Los Angeles effort was highly unusual within the national organization.

The Union Labor Party effort there failed, and its candidate for mayor, George McGahan, president of the Retail Clerks Union, received only 16% of the vote. Socialist Party sentiment in California swung decisively against further such efforts. Job Harriman, vice-presidential candidate with Eugene Debs in 1900 and a pro-fusion leader in the Socialist Party, moved to Colorado for several years. The revolutionary wing won control of the state executive committee and they stopped employing Wilson as a lecturer.[60]

Wilson's speechmaking on behalf of socialism slowed drastically and he now spent more time at home. This was no doubt welcomed by his family. Emma was in her eighth month of pregnancy and Leila her seventh when Wilson and his brother, Ben, returned home from campaigning. Jackson Stitt Wilson, Junior, was born at Highland Home on December 4, 1902. Leila gave birth to her first child, Royce Agnew Wilson, at Highland Home on January 17, 1903.

The 1902 election campaigns were the last hurrah for the Social Crusade. In February, the brothers of the Social Crusade dissolved their organization and went their separate ways.[61] Although hostility from the revolutionary wing of the party was certainly difficult to deal with, the main problem for the Social Crusade was raising enough money to support its speakers.[62] The Social Crusade arrived just after the Socialist Party was formed and successfully brought in members to newly organized locals in the Western states, but once the party became more organized, the Social Crusade was less important.

The Socialist Party organized its own speakers bureau and began to send lecturers all over the United States. Among them was Ben, who for the next five years traveled throughout the Pacific Coast, Mountain and Southwestern states, from California to Washington, from Montana to Texas, and all the states in between. He was especially popular in mining areas and in summer socialist encampments in hard-pressed farming communities.[63] He and his family continued to live in Berkeley, sharing Highland Home with his brother and sister-in-law and their children, and the two families remained connected for the rest of their lives.

Carl Thompson became the Socialist Party state organizer for Minnesota in 1904, then for both Minnesota and Wisconsin in 1905.[64] He moved to Milwaukee and was elected to a two-year term in the Wisconsin legislature in 1906. After the election of socialist Emile Seidel as mayor of Milwaukee in April 1910, Thompson was appointed city clerk, serving until 1912 when Seidel was defeated for reelection. In 1911 he was chosen to form a new Socialist Party Information Bureau, where he tracked and publicized the accomplishments of elected socialists. He broke with the party to support American entry into World War I on the side of the Allies. After the war, he founded and led the Public Ownership League, which lobbied for and did studies in support of public ownership of utilities. He authored numerous books and pamphlets on public ownership of utilities, railroads and mines.

William Wise continued to speak on behalf of the Socialist Party in Denver and elsewhere for at least another year. Sometime between 1904 and 1910, he and his wife moved to Los Angeles. He reported his occupation as real estate agent in the 1910 and 1920 Censuses and then as manager for a mining company in the 1930 and 1940 Censuses.

Wilson's Social Crusade had helped articulate a Christian theology compatible with socialism and opened the way for a growing cadre of Protestant ministers for whom Christian Socialism meant active support for the Socialist Party of America based on Christian ethics, not a vague hope that brotherly love might transform capitalism. After the *Social Crusader* and the *Socialist Spirit* were closed down, a new journal started up. *The Christian Socialist*, with its subtitle, "The Golden Rule Against the Rule of Gold," grew rapidly and subscribers started calling for a new organization of socialist Christians, pointing to the model of the Social Crusade. In 1906, the Christian Socialist Fellowship was formed and declared its loyalty to the Socialist Party.[65] The 1907 conference issue of *The Christian Socialist* featured Wilson's article, "Individual and Social Salvation," which the editor declared one of the best articles he had ever published.[66] By 1910, hundreds of ministers joined the Christian Socialist Fellowship. With the end of the Social Crusade, however, Wilson moved on and it would be several years before he reconnected with the movement he had done so much to support. He had larger aspirations than simply joining the Socialist Party's speakers bureau.

CHAPTER 6

SOCIALISM AND NEW THOUGHT

Stitt Wilson needed to support his family and pay the rent, and occasional speaking to unions, churches, or socialist locals was not enough to do that. He joined in creating a "Labor Lyceum" in San Francisco, a pro-labor educational forum, but it did not last long.[1] While he was home in August of 1902, he experimented with teaching New Thought. At the beginning of the month, he gave a free Sunday lecture on "The Social and Religious Revolution" at Golden Gate Hall in San Francisco to bring in potential students. The following week he began a course on "The Inspired Life," for which he charged a fee, meeting two or three evenings a week in the Academy of Sciences Building at 819 Market Street.[2]

After the 1902 election campaigning was over, Wilson went back to teaching New Thought and kept it up for the next four years, teaching month-long courses in San Francisco, Denver, and Los Angeles, and shorter versions in smaller cities like San Diego and Riverside.[3] The venture was successful enough that he could hire a secretary to take dictation of letters, arrange travel, and rent rooms for his classes and lectures, likely working out of a spare room at Wilson's house.[4]

Commuting to San Francisco was not difficult. The Key Route streetcar and ferry system offered a thirty-six-minute service between downtown Berkeley and San Francisco.[5] From Highland Home he could walk downhill along the north side of the university to downtown, take a streetcar down University Avenue to the waterfront ferry terminal, board the ferry to San Francisco, and then walk or take streetcars to reach the halls he rented for his talks and classes (the Academy of Sciences Building, for example, was ten blocks from the Ferry Building). He could then reverse the process to return home, perhaps taking a horse-drawn cab up the hill.

Wilson's New Thought teaching normally involved one or more public lectures on "The Life Message," given free with a collection at the end. This was followed by a class that met two or three times a week for several weeks, which students paid for. The overview began with the idea of the "Inspired Life," as described earlier, which urged people to take inspiration from the life of Jesus, realize the divine within themselves, and use that creative power to work for freedom both for themselves and all of humanity. This was followed by a description of three "hypnotisms," false understandings that block the inspired life. First, "there is no matter. There is only Being and Consciousness." Second, heredity does not control your life. People are neither conceived in sin, nor are they limited because they evolved from lower forms of life. They have a "divine inheritance." Third, Jesus came "to deliver men from the false notion that they were separate from God." As Wilson put it, "You don't have to ring up central and say, 'Give me God.' You are on an automatic board and can get direct communication."[6]

After the public lectures recruited enough paying students, he gave a course, meeting two or three times a week for four or five weeks. The course lessons provided "detailed, personal instruction . . . in the deep truths of the free and divine life, including the art of healing."[7] There is apparently no surviving copy of his class pamphlet, *Life Lesson—The Mission of Jesus to Our Time*, but there is an excerpt from a class, giving what appears to be a guided visualization followed by an affirmation, intended to help students attune themselves to the presence of God.[8] A few sentences from each gives a sense of the style and content.

Visualization:

> Old Sol pours down his glory upon me from the half-afternoon sky . . . The light shines on me. The heat warms me . . . It seems as if the whole of his power were concentrated on me. . . . All for me! True. But I look about me and the trees are stretching out their branches and gathering in the golden harvest of his rays. The little lake in the park shimmers like a mirror of the gods as it receives the light upon its placid bosom. The birds are holding high carnival and it seems as though they too were claiming that old Sol is lighting up the world for them alone. . . . And away yonder in the ocean of blue I see a fleecy cloud hanging like a tiny feather, and I can almost feel it claiming the day as its own. But nay! The democracy of creation joins in an anthem of delight to the Light. . . . Light is Truth. Truth is God.[9]

Affirmation:

> O Truth, thou . . . art my Divinity and thou art my Comrade. Let us throw our arms over each other's shoulders and saunter along—forever. Let me be a little child learning the Truth, for Truth is Mother as well as Comrade. When tired let me cast myself on her bosom as a babe in its mother's arms. . . . I feel thou gather me up into thine everlasting arms and hold me to thy heart of Infinite Love. O Truth thou art my Mother dear.[10]

Having established himself as a New Thought teacher, Wilson reached out to the broader New Thought community with his socialist message. During the election campaign, Wilson and Wise spent the last week of October 1902 speaking in Colorado Springs. The morning after their arrival, they walked to the nearby suburb of Roswell to visit Edgar Wallace Conable, editor and publisher of a successful monthly magazine, *The Path-Finder*, which propounded New Thought, vegetarianism, raw food, and fasting. Wilson pressed Conable on whether he would publish arguments for advances in social institutions as well as in individual consciousness. Two days later, Conable walked into town and offered to take over the mailing list for the *Social Crusader*, fulfill all of its subscriptions with issues of *The Path-Finder*, and publish monthly articles by Wilson on "Socialism and Life." Wilson and Wise immediately accepted the offer.[11]

Wilson believed that New Thought and socialism in combination could bring "a great spiritual and social awakening."[12] He used his platform in *The Path-Finder* to urge the importance of social as well as individual change and denounced the "refined selfishness" of those who considered poor people responsible for their own poverty. Poor children, who suffered stunted growth from hunger and workplace injuries as child laborers, could hardly be held responsible for failing to learn correct thinking.[13] Many adherents to New Thought did support socialism, but other than general references to "the law of love" they rarely tried to explain why. Rev. Wallace D. Wattles had several times brought the Social Crusade to his church in Indiana. A few years later he wrote the New Thought classic, *The Science of Getting Rich*, in between running as a Socialist Party candidate for Congress in 1908 and for district attorney in 1910, with no explanation of how socialism and getting rich using New Thought fit together.[14]

Wilson tried to build a coherent argument for socialism within a New Thought framework. He noted the inherent contradiction in individualistic versions of New Thought. "Making each individual a separate entity . . .

is an impossibility to Idealism, a philosophy based on the Unity and intercommunion of the All."[15] Wilson agreed that the individual must engage in "facing his own problems" through the "true science of living," but collective action is also necessary. Even if, as many proponents of New Thought believed, an individual master of the powers of thought could drink contaminated water and yet suffer no harm, unless all those who live in the neighborhood can do the same, many will suffer and die. Fortunately, "there is Sanitary Science as well as Mental Science" and modern sewer and water systems should also be considered a "Great Thought of Mind."[16] The economic system that exploited children and failed to provide clean water was itself poisonous and needed to be changed according to true social science.

With his usual good humor, Wilson argued that socialism did not conflict with other beliefs that might be held by *Path-Finder* readers.

> You are a vegetarian . . . I may be deeply sympathetic with that position. You believe in re-incarnation. All right. Come back as often as you like. I shall be glad to see you if I am here too. You believe in "holding the thought" of opulence . . . Go ahead . . . (I) offer to introduce you to a Great Idea . . . This Great Idea [Socialism] will not quarrel with all the others inside [your mind] even though some of the people who hold it are intolerant dogmatists.[17]

Wilson made no claim to having all the answers and urged people to investigate conditions in their own communities. "Life has no final solution, either for the individual or for society . . . Forward, ye Children of the Light!"[18]

Some of Wilson's friends were distressed with his outlandish ideas of a "science" of human engagement with divinity.[19] Van Rensselaer, who had served as editor of the *Social Crusader* in its waning days and was now working for *Wilshire's Magazine*, ridiculed Wilson's teachings in a public lecture. Taking up the idea that the universe is made up of and can be controlled by thought, Van Rensselaer continued, "If you stand in front of one of Mr. Huntington's street cars, I will guarantee that you will be run over or a policeman will arrest you."[20] Wilson maintained his characteristic dedication to his own beliefs. "All the Life and Light and inward power that now possesses me I have found in refusing any voice but God's and going on. First, rejecting the church, and on to Socialism. Then refusing to let the Socialists hinder me in my Life Message to the Individual . . ."[21]

Illness, tragedy, burnout

In late May, Wilson went to Denver to speak on socialism to the annual convention of the American Labor Union, the association of unions created by the Western Federation of Miners, and he remained in Denver for the next five weeks teaching New Thought. While he was in Denver, his wife, Emma, became ill back in Berkeley with fever and chills and was unable to get out of bed. A physician stopped by daily but was unable to diagnose the problem or find a cure. Wilson finished his classes and returned to Berkeley at the end of June. After being bedridden for three months and trying many remedies, Emma sent a lock of her hair to a psychic healer, Dr. Nellie Beighle, who responded that she could provide a cure. As Emma described it:

> I was taken out of bed, wrapped in blankets and conveyed by means of cabs, railways and ferries to Dr. Beighle's office in San Francisco. I was placed in one of her treating cots and received from her her usual method of treatment, which consists solely and entirely of the wonderful power which emanates from her hand . . . after her wonderful treatment, I was able to return home by streetcar, was not confined to my bed any more but was able to travel daily from Berkeley to San Francisco to receive her treatment; in six weeks my health was completely restored so that I was able to take long walks, attend to my household duties and in fact do anything I wished.[22]

Emma provided this testimonial two years later, when Ms. Beighle was charged with practicing medicine without a license. Beighle argued that she never claimed to practice medicine, she only claimed to heal people, and the jury quickly acquitted her.[23]

Wilson stayed close to home for the rest of the year, teaching in San Francisco, Oakland, and San Jose, with only a one-week trip to San Diego in September after Emma was on the road to recovery. In November, the household was struck by diphtheria, for which there was not yet either a vaccine or an effective treatment. Ben cancelled the rest of his lecture tour of Washington and rushed home to Berkeley to help care for the two families.[24] Ben's wife, Leila, had lost a baby in childbirth in February, leaving them with their two-year-old son, Royce. Stitt and Emma and their three older children survived (as did Ben, Leila, and Royce), but their youngest, Jackson Stitt Wilson, Junior, died on December 10th, shortly after his first birthday.

Over the course of the next two years, the couple showed increasing signs of mental and physical fatigue and sought comfort in Spiritualism, beginning a lengthy, yet quiet, involvement in the belief. They were impressed by the work of the Society for Psychical Research in England, which drew the support of a number of leading scientists and, while it debunked a number of fraudulent mediums, also argued for the reality of the psychic accomplishments of others.[25] Wilson later wrote:

> I believe—we of this household believe in Immortality. Ever since we lost our little boy nine years ago, we have followed every hint that would open up the invisible. . . . the research . . . together with some very singular and remarkable personal experiences have brought our minds to the conviction that personality not only persists after what we call death, but that all life is one vast association and our loved ones may and do under the necessary conditions communicate with us. Beside the grave of sorrow stands the Angel of the Resurrection.[26]

Like proponents of New Thought, many Spiritualists were sympathetic to socialism and Wilson began to speak to Spiritualist groups. In March of 1904, Wilson spoke at the San Francisco home of Dr. Cora Morse, an osteopath who edited a monthly journal of spiritualism and social reform called *The Coming Light*.[27] Later that month, Wilson was the keynote speaker at the annual meeting of the California State Spiritualists' Association, giving a well-received talk on the socialist movement.[28]

In a letter to Caroline Severance, Wilson expressed his mental fatigue and an uncharacteristic lack of certainty about what to do next. "Nelson writes me to give up the platform and go wandering or at some other physical labor. I think I should if it were not for the supposed inner voice that ever urges & compels me thus. Perhaps I misinterpret the voices within. The Little Woman has an undying faith in me—and practically says daily to me, 'See what one man may do'."[29]

Wilson joined Berkeley's Ruskin Club, a literary, philosophical, and social reform discussion group oriented toward the arts and crafts movement. It met in the First Unitarian Church, a recently built brown-shingled building (now a National Historic Landmark) next to the University campus. At the club's meeting in February 1904, Wilson arranged to hold a public debate with the evening's guest speaker, Rev. Dr. E.E. Baker, a leading Presbyterian minister in Oakland who had preached against socialism in his church.[30] The debate drew more than 2,000 people to the Alhambra Theater in San

Francisco.[31] Perhaps encouraged by his continued ability to draw a crowd, Wilson became more active in the Socialist Party.

He was still a popular figure among rank-and-file socialists, who often did not see the clear distinctions drawn by their more ideological comrades.[32] He ran for and was elected to be one of the two delegates representing the Oakland area at the Socialist Party national convention in Chicago at the beginning of May. Before leaving for the convention, Wilson gave a talk to the Oakland local on "Dogmatism and Life in the Socialist Movement," which presumably laid out some of his concerns with the state of the Socialist Party.[33] In a classic example of Socialist Party sectarianism, upon his arrival in Chicago he found his right to serve as a delegate challenged by another delegate. He was charged with disloyalty for sending a telegram the previous year congratulating his friend Samuel Jones on his reelection as mayor of Toledo as an independent, defeating Republican, Democratic, and Socialist Party opponents. (The telegram read, "Mayor Jones, Hilarious congratulations. Nelson & Wilson.)[34] Wilson responded that Nelson O. Nelson had sent the telegram in good faith after a conversation with Wilson, but he had not authorized it and would have asked that his name not be included if he had known Nelson's intentions. With no further evidence before them, the credentials committee unanimously approved Wilson as a delegate.[35] He continued to have concerns about dogmatism.

On his return from the convention, Wilson found Emma "wearied and spent." He cancelled a planned trip to Los Angeles, writing to Caroline Severance:

> I have been away from home too much in recent years and especially since my dear wee boy left his mamma. Mrs. Wilson says Go!—with the light in her eyes that . . . always inspires me, but I can see that the constant burden of the home falling on her alone is proving too much for her. . . . You know how dear, how unspeakably precious she is to me. This I say not merely as a Lover but whatever I am to the world seems impossible without her.[36]

In August of 1904, with the new school year about to begin, a new state law took effect requiring all children attending public schools to be vaccinated against smallpox. The law drew strong opposition from many parents, including Wilson and, for the first time, he became involved in a local political activity, helping organize a Berkeley organization opposing compulsory vaccination.[37] An Oakland group soon formed and together they founded a statewide organization to lobby for the bill's repeal.

Today we know that anti-vaccinationists are profoundly wrong and, indeed, endanger the health of others when they reduce the percentage of people vaccinated below the level needed to provide group immunity. At the time, however, the quality of vaccines was often poor and there had been several episodes in which a number of children had died due to contaminated vaccines.[38] In response, Congress passed the Biologics Control Act of 1902 and began annual inspections of vaccine producers, but quality control was not as strong as it would later become.

Wilson regarded compulsory vaccination as both a violation of individual freedom and an effort to avoid dealing with the social causes of disease. Poverty, he pointed out, resulted in people not seeking treatment until too late because they lacked the money to pay for care. Harsh working conditions and poor food weakened workers and their families and lowered their resistance to disease. Society was not yet providing clean water, sewer systems, and decent quality housing for all. He correctly cited statistical studies showing that the highest rates of disease were in major cities and that the major reductions in disease up until then were the result of improved sanitation rather than vaccination.[39] He joined in lobbying the state legislature, which passed a bill repealing compulsory vaccination in January 1905. Governor George Pardee, a physician, vetoed the bill.[40] Later in the year, Wilson spoke on behalf of an unsuccessful effort to establish a private school that would not require students to be vaccinated.[41]

Wilson arranged a series of lectures at Bay Area churches on "The Message of Socialism to the Church," concluding the series at a regional conference of Congregationalist ministers.[42] His theme was that a cooperative economy based on universal brotherhood would embody Christian ethics and end the injustices of a system that pitted people against each other in a remorseless struggle for economic supremacy. He published the talk as a pamphlet and a few years later reported that he had printed and sold more than 25,000 copies.[43] Shortly afterward he joined the editorial board of *The Christian Socialist*, the new journal that was founded after the *Social Crusader* ceased publication.

Wilson persevered in his work for the Socialist Party, serving as a delegate to the state and county conventions to select candidates for the upcoming elections. As the November 8, 1904, Election Day neared, he toured Southern California, speaking in cities large and small, including Los Angeles, San Diego, Riverside, Corona, Hemet, and Santa Ana.[44] Wilson was energized by the election campaign. "Everywhere the interest is great. I do not have to beat about the bush to try to interest my audiences & then to replant the socialist seed. They are already interested. . . . I am feeling well. My voice is as mellow as that of a canary tho I am speaking two hours every night."[45] He cancelled his appearance at the Convention of the New Thought Federation in St. Louis in late October, where he was scheduled to talk about socialism and New Thought, in order to continue campaigning.[46] The Socialist Party was happy with the result. In 1904, Eugene Debs received nearly 9% of the presidential vote in California, the highest percentage of any state and more than three times the vote he received there in 1900.

Once the election was over, Wilson stayed in Los Angeles and taught New Thought classes from late November through mid-January. He brought the family down during the winter break from school, so the Wilsons were able to visit with friends in Southern California.[47] Edgar Conable had recently moved to Los Angeles and he treated Wilson, his wife, and his brother, Ben, who was on his way home after his own election work, to dinner and a musical evening.[48] They also had a literary evening at the home of Caroline Severance, attended by Jack London and other writers and friends such as Mary Garbutt of the WCTU.[49] Their daughter, Gladys Viola, then 13, took the occasion of a rainy day to begin writing a play and recruited her younger brother and sister to help act it out.[50] Wilson's classes in Los Angeles were highly successful so, after returning to Berkeley for several weeks, he was back in Los Angeles in late February for another six-week engagement, reporting that 600 people signed up for the class in "metaphysics and the science of healing."[51] The large number of paying students enabled Wilson to support his family and take considerable time off to campaign for socialism.

In May, Gladys Viola completed the play she had started in Los Angeles and staged the work and acted the lead role before an audience of fifty neighbors and friends of the family in the large dining/living room area of her parents' home. Her cast, none of whom was older than her, included her brother and sister, schoolmates, and neighbors, with her brother, Gladstone, also serving as the electrician handling the lighting. *Dorothea* was a melodrama set in colonial Virginia and in high-society and poverty-stricken neighborhoods of London. Dorothea marries for wealth rather than love, becoming Lady Dunstanwold, but finds her life empty, repents, and searches for her true love, Richard Melnotte, finding him on his death bed in a tenement in East London.

The several-months-long upswing in Wilson's socialist and New Thought activities was followed by an equally rapid decline as he again struggled with fatigue and burnout. The Socialist Party, which supposedly embodied the ideal of universal brotherhood, was characterized by constant, often vicious infighting. "The continuous attacks upon me personally have practically silenced me in the party—not only in its counsels but in its propaganda."

Wilson worried that even if the party could win elections, "the caliber of the men and the spirit of them in the party seems scarcely adequate."[52]

Far more stressful than his conflicts with other socialists was his grief over the loss of his son, anxiety over his wife's often-precarious health and, quite likely, difficulties reconciling this with the supposed extraordinary powers of New Thought. And perhaps he was simply exhausted by the years of constant travel. By the summer of 1905, friends in the New Thought movement reported that he was going off the deep end. According to one prominent New Thought exponent:

> (Wilson) has been drinking at the metaphysical stream until he has become "woozy" about the "nothingness" of things . . . He has become so filled with the "I am God" idea that he talks quite earnestly of his creations, the Rocky Mountains and other big things. But . . . bye-and-bye he will throw off this mass of metaphysical wordy "nothingness" which afflicts all of us who have tried to solve the Riddle of the Universe with our finite minds and he will . . . laugh at his present attempts to express the unexpressible.[53]

Wilson's friend Edgar Conable, now based in Los Angeles, wrote:

> The last seen of J. Stitt before leaving for the North, he was pacing up and down the mountain slopes saying to himself, "I made all these mountains—the rocks and the trees and the birds and the flowers: are they not beautiful and wonderful! And still they are nothing." . . . a summer's work in his garden will straighten him out all right.[54]

On August 25, 1905, the editor of the *Hemet News* announced that the "noted lecturer" J. Stitt Wilson had purchased a five-acre ranch with a small orchard in that small Southern California community and planned to move there with his family at the beginning of October.[55] Located 35 miles southeast of Riverside, Hemet had a temperate climate and was home to less than a thousand people. Wilson paid $2,000 for the ranch (around $60,000 in 2020 dollars). He told his friends that he had been thinking about such a move for the past two years and he had been looking at places where he had lectured as potential places to move to.

> This quiet release from the public eye, I am somewhat securing by an early retreat to a ranch that I have bought in

> Hemet . . . in the beautiful San Jacinto Valley . . . I don't seem anxious to "save" anybody or anything. I have no ambitions. . . . I shall rear my little one for a period at least in the Joys of country life. Don't think I am going to live the "simple life." I have no moral or spiritual purpose in going. I am going there to make a living, to be released for periods at least from all public activity, to think without having a "meeting" or a "purpose" ahead of me; to relax . . . as a member of human society who seems unable to "fit" anywhere . . . Mrs. Wilson is with me entirely in my new venture. I shall be home. I shall have rest after the long hard years.[56]

On September 12, 1905, Emma Wilson gave birth to a son, Arnold Melnotte, named after the male lead in his big sister, Gladys Viola's, play, *Dorothea*. Wilson was extremely happy that the birth had been an easy one but remained concerned, since "of course she is never strong."[57] Emma's mother, the widowed Eliza Agnew, had joined them at Highland Home to assist with the last months of Emma's pregnancy, and Wilson took her and Gladstone, now age 12, to Hemet a mere week after Arnold Melnotte had been born. Once they were settled, he returned to Berkeley and in mid-October took Gladys Viola, now age 14, to Hemet; Emma, Violette, and the baby followed by the end of the month. Ben, Leila, and their son, Royce, remained in the downstairs unit of Highland Home, and the rest of the house was put up for rent.

> *Berkeley Daily Gazette*, October 12, 1905: "For Rent—Beautiful home on the Berkeley hills; head of Ridge road; one block from University grounds; unsurpassed marine and mountain view; artistic redwood finish; only recommended parties. Address J. Stitt Wilson, Berkeley, Cal."

At the beginning of November, Wilson, Emma, and their four children were ensconced in a "splendid six room house" with piped water on a ranch with apricot and peach trees, alfalfa, two cows, twenty hives of bees, and an unknown number of Brown Leghorn chickens.[58] They were decidedly in farm country.

> *Hemet News*, December 1, 1905: "Strayed—on to my premises, Nov. 29, a yearling Jersey steer. Owner may have by

claiming and paying expense. J. Stitt Wilson, Corn
and Florida"

At the end of January 1906, Highland Home had still ɪ
Wilson and Emma went back to Berkeley to visit with E.........
Salvation Army Adjutant Fletcher Agnew, who was in the Bay Area for a
week accompanying his commander. The Wilsons used their time at Highland Home to reconsider. Wilson wrote to Caroline Severance saying that
"instead of my ranch experience silencing my soul concerning the world
affairs, I have lived all these great questions over again & my soul is hot
within me. And I am more than ever convinced that I should make my
contribution to the social reconstruction . . ."[59]

Hemet News, February 2, 1906:
"Prof. J. Stitt Wilson to Leave Hemet"[60]

By mid-February, Wilson was back to lecturing on socialism and teaching
his New Thought classes in San Francisco. In mid-March, the whole Wilson
family moved back to Berkeley and Mrs. Agnew went off to Kansas City
to visit with one of her sons.[61] The move to Hemet had lasted only four
months, but its costs lingered on. The ranch was not sold until December
1906.[62]

> *Hemet News*, March 16, 1906: "For Sale: J. Stitt Wilson offers
> for sale at the ranch, corner Yale St. and Florida avenue,
> at a bargain if taken at once, the following, two good cows,
> $55; 20 hives of bees, the lot $40; one new barrel churn
> cost $6.50 for $4; one new cook stove complete, cost $30,
> for $20."[63]

While back in Hemet selling off the contents of the ranch, Stitt Wilson
made a side trip to Los Angeles to join a protest sponsored by a coalition of unions and socialists. In February 1906, Charles Moyer, president
of the Western Federation of Miners; "Big Bill" Haywood, its secretary;
and George Pettibone, a former member, were falsely charged with the
murder of a former governor of Idaho. They were arrested by Colorado
police and put on a train to Idaho in the early morning hours to face trial
without being allowed to contact their lawyers or appeal the extradition
to the courts. Ultimately, they would be acquitted, but unionists justifiably
regarded this as a kidnapping by the mine owners (who paid the costs of the

osecution) and an effort to break the union. Wilson took the train from Hemet to the Los Angeles protest, held on the evening of March 13th, and was asked to be the final speaker. The *Daily People*, which usually mentioned Wilson only to ridicule and attack him, reported, "J. Stitt Wilson's impassioned measures aroused the audience to such a pitch of excitement that they began throwing their dollars on the platform in response to his appeal for money to fight the United Mine Owners Association."[64]

Wilson returned to Berkeley and resumed his regular lectures in San Francisco, but on April 18, 1906, they were brought to an abrupt halt by the San Francisco earthquake. The earthquake started fires that burned for the next four days, leveling much of the city's downtown. Berkeley was flooded with thousands of San Franciscans fleeing the fire. Within a few days, the number of refugees equaled the previous population of Berkeley, with most of them living in tents.[65] Wilson's activities during the first few days after the earthquake are unknown, but by the end of April and into early May he was in Southern California traveling from city to city speaking to raise money for earthquake relief. Wilson took no money for these speeches. The socialist locals covered his expenses and everything that was donated was sent to the Socialist Party of San Francisco for its relief efforts.[66]

In "Capitalism: The Nation's Perpetual Disaster," Wilson contrasted the nation's response to the suffering caused by earthquake and fire with its response to the ongoing suffering caused by our economic system.[67]

> We were appalled by the sudden death by earthquake of 500 to 1,000 people in our sister city. Are we appalled when I tell you that . . . ten times as many men were unnecessarily killed in the steel and coal industries of the Pittsburg district last year, because of sheer neglect to protect the lives of the laborers in the mad gamble for profit?
>
> Again, we were thunderstruck to learn that perhaps 300,000 people were rendered temporarily homeless, hungry and destitute. And our hearts leaped to help. The soul of the nation was touched and the purse responded. But a state of comparable homelessness, hunger and destitution affects immeasurably more of our citizenship perpetually. . . . We call a natural calamity a terrible disaster, but the poverty and want of 10 million people, caused by social injustice, we call even such names as prosperity and national well-being.
>
> When the announcement was sent out the other morning that there was not a hungry man in all San Francisco,

few reflected that that was the first time in the city's history that it could be truthfully said. That the people are now being fed is owing to the application of the co-operative principle instead of the competitive principle. Cooperative industry is the hope of the world. It is the practical Christianity of the Twentieth Century.

Wilson's speech in Pasadena made a deep impression on newlyweds Graham Phelps Stokes and Rose Pastor Stokes. Graham was an Episcopalian millionaire and Rose was a radical Jewish journalist who had interviewed him when he was living in the University Settlement House on the Lower East Side of Manhattan. After hearing Wilson, they talked about what to do next on the long drive back to New York and decided that they would both join the Socialist Party.[68]

Wilson returned to his busy schedule, teaching New Thought on weekday mornings, followed by talks on socialism in the evenings and on Sundays.[69] He made periodic visits to other cities, ranging from San Jose to San Diego, teaching New Thought and lecturing on the moral case for socialism, often in local churches.[70] His new pamphlet, *The Tragic Game of Capitalism*, concluded with "What we seek is: A union of all who suffer on behalf of themselves; and a union of all who love on behalf of all who suffer."[71] Some of his Christian socialist friends offered to contribute money in support of his work, but he refused to accept it. Instead, Constance Severance sent the checks to Emma, who apparently handled the household finances. Emma explained that while her husband felt it necessary to maintain his independence, "considering the sources . . . I feel that I may accept it."[72]

While Wilson was away lecturing that summer, his 13-year old son, Gladstone, saved Highland Home from a fire. Summer is California's dry season, when fire danger is high. Gladstone and a friend were in a field behind the house watching the flight of a small hot air balloon powered by an alcohol lamp when it crashed into the field, setting the dry grass on fire. The friend ran away, but Gladstone took his coat and used it to beat out the fire, which was threatening Highland Home and the other houses nearby. Fire Chief James Kenney praised young Gladstone and promised to ban the use of fire balloons in the city of Berkeley.[73] The news reports made no mention of who had launched the balloon.

During this time, 15-year-old Gladys Viola continued her theatrical efforts. She appeared in a small part in the biblical play *Mizpah* at Ye Liberty Playhouse in Oakland, her first paying role.[74] She wrote another play of her own, *The Light of Mithra*, set in ancient Persia, and staged it at Wilkins

Hall near the University. The cast wore elaborate costumes, with Gladys Viola playing the female lead and the rest of the roles played by siblings, schoolmates, and neighborhood children.[75]

Wilson's estrangement from the current revolutionary leadership of the Socialist Party in California was demonstrated when he responded negatively to an inquiry from the state committee asking people who spoke on the Party's behalf in the 1904 election campaign if they would be available in the 1906 campaign.[76] The party candidate for governor in 1906 was fellow Berkeley resident Austin Lewis, a labor lawyer and revolutionary theorist who argued that only the unskilled workers, the "proletarians," could make a socialist revolution.

After the Wilsons' ranch finally sold in December of 1906, the couple rented out their house and left with their children for England in June of 1907.[77] Wilson had greatly enjoyed his visits to England several years earlier, and he knew that his Christian and ethical case for socialism was popular there. It was an exciting time for British socialists. The breakthrough 1906 elections resulted in 29 Labour representatives in Parliament and the founding of the Labour Party by a coalition of unions and the Independent Labour Party. Wilson had kept up correspondence with friends in England and he and Emma were eager for a return visit.

Ben and Leila moved to Girard, Kansas, with their two children, including their youngest, Paul Benjamin, who was born on September 22, 1906, at Highland Home. Girard was a small town with one main industry, socialist publishing. It was the home of Julius Wayland and his socialist weekly newspaper, *Appeal to Reason*. To handle a regular nationwide circulation of more than a quarter-million copies, the largest of any weekly in the U.S., he had built up a major printing plant and mailing operation. These facilities were also used by other socialist publications, such as *Socialist Woman*. Ben and Leila quickly became popular members of a large socialist community, and Ben continued to lecture on socialism throughout the western and southwestern United States from his home base in Girard.[78]

CHAPTER 7

WITH THE LABOUR PARTY IN GREAT BRITAIN

On their arrival in Great Britain, the Wilsons' first stop was Penmaenmawr, Wales, where Wilson gave a talk at the Summer School of Theology and Applied Religion organized by the Wilsons' old friend Rev. J. Bruce Wallace of the Brotherhood Church.[1] A few days later the Wilsons settled in Idle, a small town on the outskirts of Bradford, in West Yorkshire.

Wilson's friend Arthur Priestman, the Quaker socialist, was still on the Bradford Town Council and had become chairman of the Independent Labour Party branch in Bradford when its long-time leader, Fred Jowett, was elected to Parliament the year before.[2] The Independent Labour Party continued to operate as a socialist organization within the Labour Party. With eleven members on the eighty-four-member Bradford Town Council, the party held the balance of power because neither the Liberals nor the Conservatives could form a majority without their support. They had accomplished this partly by increasing the number of ILP council members and partly by drawing votes away from the Liberal Party so that more Conservatives were elected in three-way races—the Liberals no longer held a clear majority on the council.[3] With the Liberal and Conservative parties competing for working-class votes to elect council members, as well as for Labour support on the council, Bradford implemented many programs that the British referred to as "municipal socialism." These included public medical clinics; school meals; sale of pure milk; municipal water, sewer, and streetcar systems; and "fair wage" requirements for city employees and employees of firms contracting with the city. The council had also carried out a small slum clearance program that relocated the residents in new, affordable municipal housing.[4]

Working with Priestman, Jowett, and other local socialists, Wilson

East Bradford Socialist Sunday School
banner (Working Class Movement Library,
U.K., http://www.wcml.org.uk/).

began a socialist mission, in which he and other volunteers canvassed homes in working-class neighborhoods; held evening meetings in chapels, halls, and schools; and held Sunday meetings in St. George's Hall, which could seat up to 4,000 people. At these Sunday meetings, Wilson was joined by other prominent socialist clergy from various denominations, including Rev. Bruce Wallace. Wilson worked mostly in Bradford and nearby cities such as Leeds and Blackburn, but also traveled to speak in Halifax, Glasgow, and surrounding towns. In Blackburn, he worked with the local Labour M.P. Philip Snowden, later Chancellor of the Exchequer in the first Labour government. Snowden was known for his powerful speeches, described by one biographer as "highly emotional and full of biblical phraseology," making the moral argument for socialism.[5]

Once settled, Wilson began publication of a monthly four-page tabloid version of *The Social Crusader*, featuring a hand holding a bright red Christian cross and selling for a half-penny.[6] This version of the *Social Crusader* featured heated attacks on capitalism as unchristian, cheerleading for socialism, and much less of the intellectual content and reports on Crusade activities that had been featured in the American version.[7] After his initial lecture in Wales, Wilson moved his focus away from the theme of "divine immanence" and focused on the more popular topics of the Hebrew proph-ets and the life of Jesus. He also began to publish his speeches in pamphlet form; most of the chapters in his only book, *How I Became a Socialist*, were initially pamphlets of speeches given in England and Wales.[8]

A socialist skeptic provides us with an unusually detailed description of Wilson's speaking style during a talk in London.

> The star of the evening was the Rev. J. Stitt Wilson, M.A. . . . I think of him as the revivalist of the Socialist gospel . . . and his appeal succeeds where quieter methods would fail . . . a tall, youthful figure, very broad-shouldered and slender-waisted, in a swallow-tail coat, waistcoat cut low, and a big black tie, bow-fashion; . . . a shock of hair . . . nicely parted on one side; voice resonant and appealing, equally effective in loud and soft passages; a dramatic stride about the platform, and emphatic gestures. . . . a great redundancy of words and phrases, six used where one would serve . . . a rough sense of humour . . . the prophet's rightful egotism—"I say," "I tell you," "I am going to threaten." He allows for an unlimited degree of obtuseness on the part of his hearers—"Have you got that?," "I mean to drive it home"—and accordingly his message is delivered with much reiteration, although no one could suppose that it is at any time obscure or difficult. He relies in fact on the great truisms—the dispossession of the worker from the dawn of history; the land as the one thing needful; the principle of production for use.[9]

Another description conveys Wilson's passion and a use of local context that is not preserved in his published speeches.

> Someone before him had spoken of a Bradford woman who had buried her baby in a soapbox because she could not buy a coffin. This Mr. Wilson made the theme of his . . . speech. "I speak for the baby in the box," cried he.[10]

Wilson made a deep impression on a number of Bradford-area social-ists. Rev. David Blythe Foster was inspired to found a Socialist Christian Church in Bradford to replace the Labour Church, which had closed.[11] (Fos-ter was elected to the Leeds City Council two years later and became lord mayor under a labor majority in 1928.) Matthew Armitage was president of the local Gas Workers' Union. His wife, Lillian Armitage, was a teacher in Bradford's Socialist Sunday School and a militant suffragist. They named their first child, born in December 1907, Stitt Wilson Armitage.[12]

In February 1908, after six months in Bradford, the Wilsons moved to Oxford, where Wilson planned to study philosophy and sociology. He was not formally enrolled as a student, but likely attended public lectures, used the libraries, and met with faculty on an occasional basis.[13] He particularly hoped to meet with Edward Caird, former master (president) of Balliol College. Wilson's talks on the divine immanence of God drew directly on Caird's work and Wilson regarded his books on moral philosophy as "a perfect fountain of illumination."[14] Caird died a few months after Wilson's arrival and there is no record of the two of them meeting.

With London and its renowned theater culture just an hour-and-a-half train ride from Oxford, that summer Gladys Viola, now 17, began serious study as an actress, taking on the stage name of Viola Barry.[15] During the rest of her time in England, she studied under two noted Shakespearean actors who were also theater company owners and drama school founders. Viola apparently began studying with Herbert Beerbohm Tree but soon switched over to working with Frank Benson. Benson managed the Stratford-on-Avon Shakespeare Festival, had founded an acting school in 1901, and operated a traveling theatre company that brought Shakespeare to smaller cities. Viola recounted that under Benson she perfected her English accent, studied dance and fencing, then played a number of leading female roles with his theatre company including Juliet (*Romeo and Juliet*), Desdemona (*Othello*), Ophelia (*Hamlet*), and Portia (*The Merchant of Venice*).[16] Gladstone, age 15, and Violette, age 13, attended the Bedales School, a progressive, coeducational boarding school about 50 miles southwest of London that featured arts and drama along with modern languages, science, and sports. Violette later recounted that she was the only female on the school soccer team.[17]

While living at Oxford, Wilson continued his Social Crusade, traveling to industrial areas to give talks on socialism. During the summer of 1908, he spent several weeks in Halifax and then in Cardiff, attracting audiences numbering in the thousands.[18] His speech for the campaign in Halifax in June 1908 was entitled "Moses: The Greatest of Labour Leaders."[19] In it, Wilson asserted that "The Moses of the Working-Class of today is . . . the Socialist Movement." He pointed out that God spoke to Moses about the oppression of the Jews by their "taskmasters," not about individual vices such as "drink and idleness and thriftlessness." God directed Moses to lead the exodus, a form of general strike. Wilson denied charges that socialist materialism neglected the higher life by pointing out that for Moses "a whipped slave is infinitely more valuable than all the obelisks, palaces and pyramids." Moses led an oppressed and suffering people to the material freedom provided by land to work, land that ultimately belonged to God and not to any individual, and by workers' control over the tools needed to work the land. This, he argued, is the essential material basis for everyone to participate in the higher life of the soul.

Wilson's reception among the workers was extraordinary. The *Halifax Labour News* reported on the conclusion of the Social Crusade in Halifax:

> The Social Crusade procession from the Socialist Hall on Sunday Afternoon was, perhaps, the largest that has ever taken place in connection with the Socialist movement. Led by the Clarion cyclists and followed by the Trades Council with their huge banner, the procession spread itself out to the strains of a lively march by the Copley and Skircoat Band. People flocked from all parts of the three Parliamentary Divisions and joined in the procession, which was at least a half-a-mile long. Finally we arrived on the Moor by way of King Cross and Saville Park Road, there to be joined by another huge crowd. Coun. Taylor, J.P. presided over an audience that probably numbered 10,000. He said that they had learned to love Stitt Wilson, and . . . the message Stitt Wilson had come to preach . . .[20]

The same reporter suggested why Wilson's message was so popular among British workers at a time when most of the churches were hostile to socialism.

> He claimed for them the Bible as their property, with its great store of hope and record of the world's struggle for humanity towards a higher life. He linked up their present efforts with those of Moses, of Isaiah, of Amos, of Christ, and of all the great prophets through the ages. . . . He had borne to them the Message from the heart of God to His people.[21]

After concluding his campaign in Cardiff, Wilson spoke at two summer schools of progressive theology, one in Aberystwyth, Wales, and the other in the new Garden City of Letchworth at Wallace's headquarters in the Cloisters, a recently built school for students of psychology, spirituality, and the arts and crafts movement.[22] There he presented three talks that he published as Social Crusade pamphlets. "The Hebrew Prophets and the

Social Revolution" postulated that the prophets had championed the poor at a time when their society had developed a large gap between the rich and the poor, just as the socialist movement does. Having argued that the socialist movement was the modern Moses, he argued in the "Impending Social Revolution" that the socialist movement was the modern Good Samaritan, lifting up all of the oppressed rather than a single individual. And in "The Messiah Cometh Riding on the Ass of Economics," he argued that, like the lowly donkey Jesus rode into Jerusalem, the lowly and apparently materialistic subject of economics was the necessary basis for people to realize their spiritual nature, which could only be realized under socialism.

Wilson had read Henry George's eloquent description in *Progress and Poverty* on how the market could turn myriad individual actions into the cooperation necessary to build something as complex as a sailing ship. In "The Messiah Cometh . . . ," Wilson provided an equally eloquent description of how the market made each individual complicit in the myriad injustices of capitalism.

> No man liveth unto himself. All the world serves all the world. Who picked the tea or gathered the salt or planted the wheat or ground the flour or made the cutlery on your dinner-table? . . . labourers working till their backs gave out; shop-assistants, battling for a decent livelihood; little pale-faced factory girls, spinning and weaving for you; miners, deep in the bowels of the earth, risking life; office girls, clicking typewriters for long hours and low wages, thousands of miles from where you sit—all these and tens of millions more, daily pour out their life-blood in the labour markets of modern industry for YOU. . . . As long as Capitalism remains . . . you are a sinner in its sins . . . I do not say this to accuse you, I say this to point out to you your duty, that you may repent of this social sin. . . .[23]

The November 1908 elections were coming up in America, with Eugene Debs running for president of the United States and Wilson's brother, Ben, running for Congress in Kansas. Wilson sailed out of Liverpool by himself on September 11, 1908, arriving in New York (by way of Quebec) on September 20th, just in time to speak in favor of Debs at a large meeting in Cooper Union under the auspices of the Christian Socialist Fellowship.[24] He also spoke at several churches whose clergy were fellowship members.[25] He spent the next five weeks doing a speaking tour, traveling from New York to California and back, with stops in Chicago, and then two weeks campaigning with his brother in Kansas.[26] In California he spoke in San Diego, Pasadena, Los Angeles, and San Francisco and visited Berkeley to check on Highland Home, which firefighters had narrowly saved from a nearby brush fire during the summer dry season.[27] On his way back to New York, Wilson connected up with Eugene Debs, who was campaigning across the U.S. on a chartered train called the Red Special, and the two spoke to a large crowd in Galesburg, Illinois.[28]

Wilson's tour concluded with a speech at Carnegie Hall in New York City, again sponsored by the Christian Socialist Fellowship.[29] In his remarks, Wilson told the enthusiastic audience:

> What we are to vote for next Tuesday, and continue to vote until we get it, will be, when it comes, a veritable second coming of Jesus Christ. There will be no stained-glass window effects accompanying that coming . . . that event will signalize the opportunity for every man to stand on his feet and free himself of the social and economic shackles that bind him today.[30]

The results were disappointing for the Socialist Party. Eugene Debs received 420,852 votes for president, just under 3% of the total, essentially unchanged from 1904. Ben Wilson received 5,776 votes for Congress, not quite 10% of the total vote.

Wilson returned to England immediately after the election. In December, Ben and his family joined Stitt and Emma in England. (En route, Ben stopped off in Toronto, Ontario, and spent a week lecturing at the Labor Temple there and in several surrounding towns.)[31] Over the next year, the two brothers continued their Social Crusade, speaking mostly in the north of England and Wales. They did take some time to enjoy life and see the sights. A letter from Ben's wife, Leila, published in *The Progressive Woman* (successor to *The Socialist Woman*) described the beauties of Edinburgh, as well as the shame of its slums, recounted a summer visit to the birthplace of poet Robert Burns, and extolled the beauties of the Scottish countryside.[32]

The arms race among the European powers was raising the threat of war, and socialists throughout Europe held demonstrations for peace. In 1909, Wilson spoke at several of these demonstrations, in addition to his usual talks on behalf of the Independent Labour Party.[33] A peace demonstration held in April at Glasgow's City Hall featured socialists from three countries: Ramsey McDonald, M.P., chairman of the Independent Labor Party and a future prime minister of Great Britain; Eduard Bernstein, Social Democratic Party member of the Reichstag (the German parliament) and author of the influential book *Evolutionary Socialism*; and Wilson, representing the Socialist Party of America.[34]

Historians naturally give first importance in the rise of the Labour Party to the unions, but "underpinning much of this political work . . . was the growth of Labour's cultural and social institutions . . . with the rapid emergence of clubs, Labour churches and socialist Sunday schools."[35] Wilson served as a visiting revivalist, bringing in new recruits, generating new enthusiasm among the already converted, and helping maintain a socialist culture among working-class Christians at a time when mainstream churches often removed ministers who were outspoken in support of socialism or militant labour tactics such as strikes. After interviewing people who heard Wilson speak, Rev. Gilbert Binyon commented in 1931 that "for Christianity in the Labour Movement, perhaps the most powerful figure that has ever appeared was the Rev. J. Stitt Wilson."[36]

Wilson and his wife and children left England in November 1909 to return home to Berkeley. Ben and Leila stayed in Great Britain and continued lecturing under the auspices of the Independent Labour Party until August 1910, at which time he and his family returned to Girard, Kansas, so that he could again run as the Socialist Party candidate for Congress. In later years, Stitt Wilson recalled of his time in England that he had been urged to stay and run for Parliament, but returned to Berkeley nonetheless, having great hopes for the Socialist Party in California.

CHAPTER 8

SOCIALIST FOR GOVERNOR

When the Wilsons' ship arrived at the port of St. Johns, Canada, from England, Emma was quite sick and had to be taken directly to the hospital. Wilson had previously been engaged to lecture to labor organizations in Ottawa, so he left Emma at the hospital for several days, bringing 4-year-old Melnotte with him.[1] Gladys Viola, William Gladstone, and Violette were already back in Berkeley, having left England a week earlier, and Emma's mother had moved into Highland Home to help them out.[2] Once Emma was well enough to travel, she and her husband were able to continue their journey home to Berkeley. This was a very different Berkeley from the one they had left. In the aftermath of the San Francisco Earthquake and Fire, so many people moved from San Francisco to the apparent safety of the East Bay that Berkeley's population had grown from 13,000 in 1906 to 40,000 in 1910. It was now the fifth-largest city in California, after San Francisco, Oakland, Los Angeles, and the state capital of Sacramento.

Wilson was inspired after seeing the British Labour Party win significant reforms that improved the lives of working people and provided models for a future socialist society. He returned to a California Socialist Party in which "evolutionary" socialists with close ties to the unions, such as Job Harriman and Fred Wheeler, head of the Los Angeles Central Labor Council, had regained their influence.[3] They looked to the British Labour Party as a model of what they hoped for in the U.S. and admired Wilson's work there. Little talked about was the fact that Labour had achieved its breakthrough by making a tacit coalition with the Liberal Party against the Conservatives. Each party stepped aside in districts where they were unlikely to win but where splitting the vote would ensure a Conservative victory. Such an approach was contrary to America's Socialist Party policy, but unless the Socialist Party obtained a significant vote it would never even become an issue.

The role of socialists in government was the subject of never-ending debate within the Party. As soon as the Socialist Party came together in 1901, infighting began between the "revolutionary" socialists and the "evolutionary" or "constructive" socialists, as each side referred to itself, or between the "impossibilists" and the "opportunists" as each was referred to by the other side.[4] Revolutionaries such as "Big Bill" Haywood of the Western Federation of Miners and the Industrial Workers of the World (IWW); H. C. Tuck, Oakland-based editor of the *Socialist Voice* (later renamed *The World*); and Austin Lewis, the 1906 Socialist candidate for governor, believed that reforms were of little use because only a full transition to socialism could improve the condition of the working class. This economic transformation would come either through election of a socialist national government or through industrial action culminating in a general strike. For the revolutionaries, running for public office at the state and local level was only a means to publicize the virtues of socialism and, if elected, to reduce use of the police to break strikes.

"Constructive" socialists, such as Victor Berger, the Socialist Party leader in Milwaukee; James Maurer in Reading, Pennsylvania; and Harriman, Wilson, and Fred Wheeler in California, argued that the economy could be transformed from capitalism to socialism step by step, through democratic and largely peaceful methods. In their view it was both wrong and politically self-defeating to tell the workers that nothing much could be done short of an immediate and total revolution.[5] Wilson believed that the biggest problem the Socialist Party faced in electoral politics was to be taken seriously as a political party. The "real producers of wealth," the workers of California in industry and agriculture, made up 80% of the voting population. They could win control of the government if they united as a class against the plutocracy.[6] But even workers who agreed that the two capitalist parties had little to offer would still vote for the Democratic or Republican candidate they judged to be slightly better if they believed that candidate had a real chance to win, whereas the Socialist did not.

The class struggle in California

The British had shown that active support from the unions could break the self-perpetuating cycle in which major parties maintained working-class support with promises of minor reforms. But getting union support in America was difficult. The leaders of the American Federation of Labor believed that precisely because government was inevitably controlled by wealthy business owners, workers' power must be built on self-organization of the skilled workers who were hard to replace during strikes. They also believed that union involvement in party politics should be avoided in order to maintain solidarity at the workplace, since workers were divided by party allegiances that often had more to do with cultural and religious differences than with economics.

In 1910, courts throughout the United States routinely issued injunctions against strikes, boycotts, and peaceful picketing. They held that the property rights of business owners included a right to continue their existing relations with other businesses, workers, customers, and the public. Under the law of the time, a business owned its relationships with its workers even if it did not own them as people. Similarly, the business owned its seller-customer relationships. If workers tried to persuade other workers not to work at a business or consumers to stop buying there, they could be ordered to stop interfering with the employer's property rights by court injunction. If they continued, they could be arrested and fined for violating the court's orders, despite any claims they might make to freedom of speech. The AFL leadership hoped to obtain government neutrality in conflicts between labor and capital by supporting candidates who agreed to support union positions regardless of their party affiliation. A substantial minority within the AFL, especially in certain unions and locations such as Milwaukee, San Francisco, and Los Angeles, believed that unions needed to support pro-union political parties such as the Socialist Party and various local Union Labor Parties.[7]

Wilson believed that conditions in California were now such that the Socialist Party could break through and become a major party. In the wake of the San Francisco earthquake of 1906, graft prosecutions had jailed Abraham Ruef, the Republican operator who had gained control of San Francisco's Union Labor Party, and his friend, Mayor Eugene Schmitz. The San Francisco Building Trades Council picked up the pieces of the Union Labor Party, which it had originally opposed, and made it into a party that genuinely represented union labor. Patrick Henry McCarthy, president of the Building Trades Council, was chosen as the candidate for mayor and was elected in November 1909 in a three-way race.

The San Francisco Building Trades Council (SFBTC) had built its myriad specialized craft unions into an effective industry-wide organization of about 15,000 workers. In effect, its members had overcome the split between craft and industrial unionism and built an industrial union out of craft-based organizations. It provided the main support for the California Building Trades Council (CBTC). For Olaf Tveitmoe, who was both secretary-treasurer of the CBTC and recording secretary of the SFBTC, the building trades' highest priority was maintaining and increasing the unity and practical power of building trades workers at the workplace, the essential basis for working-class power. Unlike the American Federation of Labor nationally, however, the building trades' councils had adopted a wide-ranging political reform program similar to the immediate demands of the Socialist Party. Tveitmoe believed that the workers would ultimately back the Socialist Party and was interested in working with constructive socialists who respected the role of the unions.[8]

The San Francisco Labor Council had brought together most of the other unions in San Francisco, with a total membership of about 25,000. Several of its member unions had officers who were active socialists, but due to the importance of the Union Labor Party, they were a small activist group with little influence. The Labor Council lacked the cohesion and power of the SFBTC, but a long-standing rivalry between the two councils had recently been set aside when McCarthy reached out to unify the city's unions behind his candidacy for mayor. Most of the building trades unions were now members of both organizations.[9] Overlapping with both councils was the Iron Trades Council, which brought together unions representing metal workers of all kinds, with the largest group being the Machinists Union.

In Los Angeles, the Central Labor Council was locked in a major struggle with the Merchants and Manufacturers Association (MMA), which was determined to impose the "open shop" and deny unions any right to collective bargaining over wages and working conditions. The open shop campaign was backed by the vehemently right-wing *Los Angeles Times*. Los Angeles business leaders believed that, by refusing to bargain with the unions and setting wages and hours on their own terms, they would gain a competitive advantage over San Francisco. Dominated by larger businesses, the MMA enforced its position against smaller businesses that wanted to bargain with the unions by holding up their supplies and refusing credit. Arthur Harper, the mayor of Los Angeles, and the city council openly backed the MMA and used the police to help break strikes.

The unions' two main weapons were strikes, which were generally defeated, and boycotts against non-union goods that were successful enough to sustain some unions such as the Brewery Workers. Faced with intransigent employers supported by a "nonpartisan" city government, many union leaders in Los Angeles joined the Socialist Party, which they regarded as the necessary political arm of the labor movement. When Mayor Harper resigned rather than face a recall election over credible accusations of corruption, a special election was held in March 1909 to replace him. Fred Wheeler, president of the Los Angeles Central Labor Council as well as of

Carpenters Union Local 158, was the Socialist candidate for mayor and he was only narrowly defeated by George Alexander, who was backed by self-proclaimed reformers from both major parties.[10] The growing conflicts came to a head in 1910.

In 1907, the San Francisco Iron Trades unions had won a gradual reduction in the work week that would lead to implementation of the eight-hour day on June 1, 1910, at the end of a three-year contract. In early 1910, five months before the eight-hour day was to go into effect, the employers' Metal Trades Association threatened to refuse to implement it on the grounds that their competitors in Los Angeles to the south and Portland and Seattle to the north had nine- and ten-hour workdays. The employers agreed to implement the eight-hour day temporarily while engaging in mediation, with the implication that they wanted to see progress toward an eight-hour day elsewhere on the West Coast. The San Francisco Iron Trades unions stepped up their efforts to organize workers in Los Angeles and on June 1, 1910, as the eight-hour day went into effect in San Francisco, 1,500 Los Angeles metal trades workers went on strike for the eight-hour day, the largest strike that had yet taken place in that city.[11] It seemed that workers' right to organize at the workplace would either be extended throughout California or destroyed throughout California. Who, under these circumstances, could deny the reality of class conflict? Who could deny the need for working-class political as well as economic power to meet the capitalists' combined political and economic power?

Wilson spent the first few months of 1910 traveling around California lecturing on socialism, along with taking a trip to Pittsburgh, Pennsylvania, to speak at the annual conference of the Christian Socialist Fellowship. As he traveled, he met with Harriman, Wheeler, and other like-minded socialists, working out plans for a union-oriented campaign in the upcoming California elections. The Los Angeles special election for mayor had shown that if unions united behind a Socialist candidate, large numbers of workers would vote for him. Wilson and the other "constructive socialists" were further encouraged when, on April 5, 1910, Socialist Emile Seidel was elected mayor of Milwaukee in a three-way race, giving the Socialist Party its first victory in a major city.

The constructive socialist leaders decided that Wilson would run for governor, Fred Wheeler for lieutenant governor, and Job Harriman for United States senator on a platform that supported the immediate demands of the unions, democratic reforms, and steps toward social democracy. Labor's immediate demands included an end to court injunctions against workplace actions such as picketing, boycotts, and strikes; government-funded old age pensions; accident insurance; and workplace safety inspections. Democratic reforms included women's suffrage, the abolition of poll taxes, the initiative and referendum, and the right to recall elected officials. Steps toward social democracy included progressive taxation, municipal ownership of utilities, and the ultimate goal of social ownership of the means of production. (Until 1913, United States senators were selected by the state legislature, so the inclusion of Harriman was simply an indication that he would be selected in the unlikely event that the people elected a majority of socialist legislators.) They would not attempt "fusion" with the Union Labor Party (ULP) in San Francisco. That would be contrary to Socialist Party policy because the ULP did not oppose capitalism and so was considered a capitalist party. But they would try to make it as easy as possible for the unions that supported the ULP, which had no candidates for state offices, to support the Socialist Party candidates.

The debate over exclusion of Asian immigrants

In addition to their many social democratic positions, however, California unions were almost unanimous in calling for "Asiatic Exclusion," a ban on further immigration from Asia. Author and historian Alexander Saxton has described the U.S. of that time as a "White Republic," because most white Americans thought of democratic rights as something that applied only to white people.[12] Non-whites were subject to a racial caste system in which they were, at best, tolerated as long as they did not challenge the status quo and, at worst, subject to violent repression. On the West Coast, the group subjected to the most intense discrimination were Asians rather than Blacks as in most of the rest of the U.S. People of Chinese and Japanese origin made up only 3.3% of the California population in 1910, and Blacks were less than 1%. Asians were subjected to deeply held white fears of the "yellow peril," that Asian "hordes" were ever ready to descend on the West Coast to serve as cheap labor for large corporations and destroy white workers' standard of living and the American (i.e., white) way of life. Both the Republican and Democratic parties in California supported Asian exclusion, a popular position that inflicted its harm on people who could not vote.

Under U.S. law, Asian immigrants were barred from becoming naturalized citizens, but their American-born children had birthright citizenship. Congress had already banned further immigration from China in 1882, so in 1910 the focus of exclusion was on California's small population of Japanese immigrants and their children, fewer than 42,000 people or less than 2% of the total state population of 2,378,000. The disproportion between the small size of the group and the enormous hostile attention they received is explained in part by union politics. The bargaining power of California's craft unions was based on organizing skilled workers who were not easy to replace when they went on strike. The unions found that the campaigns for Asian exclusion helped them mobilize unskilled white workers to support pro-union politicians and policies. Opposition to anti-Asian measures primarily came from businesses with interests in trade with Japan, because they opposed measures that would upset the Japanese government.[13]

The San Francisco Building Trades Council provided most of the support for the Asiatic Exclusion League and the secretary of the Building Trades Council, Olaf Tveitmoe, also served as the Exclusion League's president and chief spokesperson.[14] Support for Asian exclusion by Tveitmoe and many others was not based solely on political and economic calculation. The culture of the "White Republic" instilled a deeply held, emotional racism in many white Americans as they grew up. The racial hierarchy was quickly understood and assimilated by European immigrants seeking to demonstrate their own "Americanism."[15] In other parts of the U.S., marginalized ethnic groups worked to position themselves as "not Black." In California, even a group of Mexican revolutionaries based in Los Angeles adopted a program that called for Asian exclusion.[16]

The Socialist Party of America paid relatively little attention to issues of race. Eugene Debs strongly opposed the widespread practice of excluding non-whites from unions and refused to speak to segregated audiences, but like most socialists he believed that racism would vanish once capitalism was replaced by socialism and the issue would resolve itself.[17] Exclusion of immigrants based on race was contrary to the policy of the international socialist movement. In 1907, representatives from socialist parties throughout the world met in Stuttgart, Germany. The Stuttgart Congress opposed the importation of workers under contracts that reduced them to virtual slavery or as strikebreakers and opposed the use of false promises regarding employment and wages to induce immigration. But the congress rejected the exclusion of any group of workers based on race or nationality as "in conflict with the principles of proletarian solidarity."[18] The U.S. representatives to the Stuttgart Congress, led by Morris Hillquit, had argued for a resolution allowing opposition to immigration of workers "incapable of assimilation with the workingmen of the country" to which they immigrated, by which they meant workers from Asia. When this position was rejected, Hillquit loyally opposed further efforts to pass resolutions supporting exclusion based on race or nationality.

For several years after the Stuttgart Congress, exclusion continued to be hotly contested within the Socialist Party of America at both the national and state levels.[19] Only a few party activists professed explicitly biological racism. More typically, racial bias was thinly covered over with the claim that exclusion was appropriate because nearly all Asian immigrants were "contract labor" held in virtual slavery, or that they were "incapable of assimilation" due to their being from "backward" cultures needing generations of uplift (this despite the fact that Japan had defeated Russia in the Russo-Japanese war of 1905). Others argued that while exclusion on the basis of race or nationality was wrong, the party needed to work in harmony with the labor movement and this was a necessary compromise in order to win the power to abolish capitalism. After capitalism was replaced with socialism, the problems of economic deprivation and racism would supposedly disappear, along with any need to limit immigration.[20]

The Socialist Party in California took contradictory and evasive positions regarding Asian workers as they tried to reconcile socialist internationalism with loyalty to organized labor, from whose ranks many of them came. Fred Wheeler persuaded the Los Angeles Labor Council to endorse a strike by Japanese and Mexican farm workers at the same time that he supported a ban on further immigration from Japan.[21] Later on, in 1913, C.W. Kingsley, the first Socialist Party member of the California State Assembly, would oppose bills to create separate schools for Blacks on the grounds that it would be undemocratic and racially discriminatory.[22] At the same time, he supported a bill to prevent Asian immigrants from owning land, saying "I am here to advance the legislation that labor wants."[23] California socialists welcomed Japanese socialists who came to the U.S. to protest repression by the Japanese government and applauded the Chinese Socialist Club when it joined the Labor Parade in San Francisco on May Day.[24] California Socialists elected George Washington Woodbey, a Black minister, to statewide party offices several times.[25] Meanwhile, the Socialist Party's 1906 California State Convention called for "excluding Oriental laborers while the capitalist system lasts" and that remained the party position in California.[26]

Up until 1910, Wilson's pronouncements on race and nationality had always been general statements to the effect that people of every race, religion, and nationality are equally part of the Kingdom of God and that there must be unity and comradeship within the international working class.[27] But like virtually all white Americans of that time, he was immersed in the cultural presumptions of the "white republic" and he was intent on aligning himself with and winning the support of California's labor unions for the Socialist Party.

Wilson was one of five California delegates to the 1910 National Congress of the Socialist Party, held in Chicago from May 15th to May 21st.[28] There he participated in two policy debates, one over immigration and one focusing on women's suffrage. The committee on immigration was chaired by Ernest Untermann, the American translator of Marx's *Das Kapital*, a member of the party's National Executive Committee, a revolutionary, and a proponent of exclusion. His majority report called for an end to immigration from Asian countries, claiming that this was necessary because they were mostly contract laborers and the laws against contract labor were easily evaded. In addition, he argued that since racism could only be eliminated through the elimination of capitalism, it was essential to align with the main form of working-class organization, the trade unions, and gain their support in the class struggle against capitalism even if that meant accepting racial discrimination. He stated, "The Socialist Party, in its present activities, cannot outrun the general development of the working-class but must keep step with it."[29] John Spargo's minority report pointed out that immigrants from various European countries were also used by capitalists to undercut American labor standards, but that in Hawaii, Japanese workers had shown themselves willing and able to organize and strike for better working conditions, demonstrating that it was possible to organize all workers regardless of race or nationality.[30]

After debates that took up an entire day of the conference, Morris Hillquit proposed a substitute motion. It called for preventing immigration of strikebreakers, contract laborers, and mass importation of workers by employers for the purpose of weakening American labor, but the motion opposed exclusion of immigrants based on race or nationality. This, he argued, summarized the intent of the Stuttgart conference. It narrowly passed by a vote of 55 to 50.[31] (The negative votes included some delegates who favored the Spargo report as well as those who supported the Untermann report.)

Wilson spoke in favor of the Untermann report, and when it failed, he moved that a new immigration committee be established to report back to the next party congress in 1912. This was approved by the convention and an election was held to determine its membership. Among those elected to the seven-member committee were Untermann, who received the most votes with 38, and Wilson and Spargo tied for fifth with 28 each. A majority of those elected to the committee had spoken in favor of exclusion, setting up further conflict in 1912.[32] In the aftermath of the national convention, Eugene Debs made an emphatic statement opposing any exclusion based on race as "heartless," "a delusion and a snare," and contrary to "the fundamental principles of the International proletarian movement."[33]

The conference moved on to the report and recommendations from the Women's National Committee regarding women's suffrage. The Women's National Committee recommended that the Socialist Party increase its work for women's suffrage, but that this work should "be carried on under Party supervision and advocated from Party platforms."[34] Theresa Malkiel, coauthor of the report and a leader in New York rent strikes and garment industry organizing, argued that the party should focus on converting people to socialism, which would also ensure their support for women's right to vote and that involvement with bourgeois women, especially those from capitalist families, would harm the Socialist Party message.

Labor organizer Ella Reeve "Mother" Bloor and fiery Kansas orator Kate Richards O'Hare argued that the language of the report would prevent local Socialist Party groups from working as part of broader coalitions and speaking on the same platform as other non-socialist suffrage advocates.[35] Wilson stated his opposition to the committee recommendation in dramatic terms, claiming that it would require him "to have my mouth sewed up" in the name of "party discipline" and that the Socialist Party had to "decide whether it shall be a sect or a political party."[36] May Wood-Simons, coauthor of the report and chair of the committee, responded with a strong critique of mainstream woman suffrage organizations for ignoring class issues, but she then resolved the issue by assuring the delegates that the language did not, in fact, prevent any individual socialists or socialist groups from working in larger coalitions as long as they did so as socialists. The convention then approved the report and recommendations.[37]

The campaign begins

A week after the convention, when Wilson was in Los Angeles, he received a telegram from the state committee informing him that he had easily won the Socialist Party mail ballot election for its nomination for governor.[38] Wilson spoke at the Los Angeles Labor Temple the next day on "Why I Voted for Asiatic Exclusion" to make sure that his audience of union officials and activists knew that on this subject their views were his views. His speech denounced the use of contract labor in Hawaii and urged exclusion to prevent its use in California.[39] Having made his support for the union position very clear, he avoided the topic in his public campaign appearances.

At the end of his speech, a member of the audience offered to loan his automobile for the campaign. Others in the audience demanded that the car be painted red, the color symbolizing the socialist movement, and took up a collection of $106 (about $2,800 in 2020 dollars) to have it repainted. The Berkeley local pledged to raise $100 a month for gas, oil, and maintenance.[40] (Hiram Johnson, who was running an "insurgent" campaign for the Republican nomination for governor in the primary election, was also driven around in a "fire-engine red" automobile, but the color was for purposes of visibility rather than symbolizing his beliefs.)[41]

Although Wilson won the internal Socialist Party mail ballot, the official selection would be in the primary election now mandated by state legislation. It was a foregone conclusion that he would be the Socialist Party candidate, but he began campaigning anyway during the primary election period, working to bring in new members and strengthen the Socialist Party for the general election in November. The Republican Party was engaged in a hotly contested primary election between "old guard" and "reformers" that was getting extensive press coverage. Wilson could not afford to wait until later if he wanted to be taken seriously. The socialist press provided strong support. The Oakland-based *World* was edited by H. C. Tuck, normally a political opponent of Wilson within the party. He agreed to feature Wilson's campaign for the duration of the election and raise its normal weekly printing run to 10,000 copies for broader distribution in Alameda County. The *People's Paper* followed suit in Los Angeles and Southern California.

Wilson's campaign message had three essential points.[42] First, the capitalists were engaged in class war against the workers and the other parties offered no relief. He pointed out that in the previous year five times as many people were killed at work as were killed fighting for the Union at the battle of Gettysburg.[43] Both Republican and Democratic judges issued injunctions to break strikes and boycotts. Elected officials on the Los Angeles city council, from both major parties, responded to strikes by brewery and metal workers by unanimously passing an anti-picketing ordinance, after which police began arresting pickets by the dozen and ultimately by the hundreds. Wilson always included local examples of exploitation and repression in his speeches.

Second, far from abolishing private property, socialists would ensure that private property in the form of homes and the material necessities for a good life were available to the entire working population through social ownership and democratic management of the land and machinery of large-scale industries. The socialists would begin the transition from capitalism to socialism through constructive legislation. They would eliminate the labor injunctions and anti-picketing ordinances that violated workers' rights. They would provide factory safety inspections, accident insurance, free employment agencies, and free legal assistance. Like many socialists, he regarded small farmers as self-employed workers, so he proposed crop insurance, credit at lower interest rates, and land value taxation to break up large landholdings, make more land available for family farms, and reduce taxes on workers.[44] Wilson pledged that passing legislation giving women the right to vote would be a major issue in his campaign.[45]

Third, Wilson argued that he had a real chance to win. He pointed to the Socialist Party's success in Milwaukee and to the strength shown by

Wilson's campaign button
(from the author's collection).

union-backed candidates in San Francisco and Los Angeles. He believed that with hard campaigning the Socialist Party could get 100,000 votes, enough to win in a three-way race. In 1906, Austin Lewis had received 16,036 votes for governor, 5.1% of the total. In 1908, Eugene Debs had received 28,659 votes for president from California, 7.4% of the total. In 1909, the Union Labor Party and Socialist candidates for mayor in San Francisco and Los Angeles had polled a total of 42,000 votes in just the two cities. A vote for the Socialist Party was a practical action, not a wasted vote.

Wilson formally launched his campaign with a speech in Oakland on June 26th and then spent June 28–30 speaking at a socialist encampment in Klamath Falls, Oregon, near the California border, sponsored jointly by the Socialist Parties of California and Oregon.[46] Like the encampments at which Ben Wilson spoke in Texas, the Klamath Falls meeting was patterned after the Chautauquas that provided education and entertainment to the people of rural communities. Several thousand people spent anywhere from a day to a week living in tents, listening to speeches, vaudeville routines, and musical performances.[47] In keeping with the Chautauqua format, Wilson focused on broad themes rather than on his campaign, giving such talks as "The Tragedy of the Ages," "International Socialism," "The Historical Argument for Socialism," "The Socialist Congress in Chicago," and "The Bible Argument for Socialism."[48]

On the road in the "Red Special"

The first week of July he returned to Los Angeles and set out on the road in his "Red Special" automobile. The vehicle allowed him to reach out to small towns that he could not reach by train and also allowed him to stop at each town along his route to give speeches without being constrained by the train schedule. In some towns, his visits were accompanied by a Socialist Party or union band, which helped draw a crowd and provide entertainment between speeches. As Wilson's team gained experience with this mode of campaigning, it developed a routine. Local party members would reserve a hall or a pavilion in a park or pick out a busy street corner, put an announcement in the local newspaper, and give Wilson information on local issues to include in his speech. An advance car with three or four campaign workers would arrive about half an hour before the car with

Wilson, dressed in hats with red hat bands that said, "Red Special," dusters with red straps at the shoulders, and a "Red Special" badge. In the center of town, they would take out two fifes, a bugle, a drum, and a megaphone and march down the street playing. (When school was not in session, the advance party included Wilson's son, Gladstone, then 17.) At each street corner, they would announce that the next governor of California would be speaking at whatever the planned location was and then return to the car and bring out bundles of leaflets with Wilson's "Message to the Working Class" or copies of *The People's Paper* or *The World*. As a crowd gathered, one of the advance men would launch into a warm-up speech. Wilson would arrive in the second car, painted bright red and draped with an American flag. His crew would take over distribution of literature and the advance party would then move on to the next town. Wilson generally talked for about three-quarters of an hour, then asked for contributions to fund his campaign. Wilson reported that in this manner he had spoken in seven towns in one day, going from 10 a.m. to 10 p.m. on a sixty-mile trip from San Bernardino to Los Angeles.[49]

On the Fourth of July, Los Angeles area socialists and their families and friends held their holiday picnic at the beach at Playa Del Rey. After eating, they filled the boardwalk pavilion with anywhere from 2,000 to 3,000 people to hear a program that began with a group of young girls dressed all in white with crimson banners singing "The Red Flag."[50] After hearing from Fred Wheeler, president of the Los Angeles Labor Council and candidate for lieutenant governor, and Stuart Reid, regional organizer for the American Federation of Labor, Wilson received a tumultuous welcome. His speech focused on the role of socialists in supporting the workers in the class struggle. He said:

> The class struggle is not . . . a mere theory of social con-
> flict . . . It is the actual line-up of the workers in their battle,
> right out there in the street and the shop and in the homes
> of the workers, with the capitalist class—a class whose profit-
> hunger drives them on to reduce wages, lengthen hours,
> import strikebreakers and vow destruction to the unions.[51]

There were mishaps large and small along the campaign trail. In Long Beach, Wilson and Gladstone were distributing fliers advertising a speech he was going to give when they were cited by the police for the distribution of handbills without a license and fined $5 (about $135 in 2020 dollars). Wilson tried to talk his way out of the fine, saying "I'm going to be the next governor of California." When this failed to impress the judge, he tried arguing that his son, who was under 18, was the one actually distributing the handbills, but gave up and paid when the judge responded that in that case Gladstone would have to appear in juvenile court.[52]

The cars broke down frequently as early automobile technology and tires met low-quality roads. On several occasions, Wilson had to walk the rest of the way into town, wait for another car (as he did to get to Playa Del Rey) or, when both cars broke down, take the train or cancel planned meetings.[53] This did not prevent him from ridiculing some of the Republican candidates for campaigning on promises to build "good roads":

> Good roads, what do you think of a great big fine-looking man standing on that kind of a platform? Good roads, when the world today is facing some of the gravest and most momentous problems that the human race has ever been called upon to solve. . . . vote for them and . . . within a short time you will be called upon to hit it [the road]![54]

The Los Angeles anti-picketing ordinance and accompanying arrests provided the occasion for the socialists to organize protest meetings that attracted thousands of people in Los Angeles, Oakland, San Francisco, San Diego, and other cities around California. These meetings featured union leaders along with the Socialist Party candidates, Wilson, Wheeler and Harriman, exemplifying the hoped-for socialist-union partnership under circumstances that did not require the unions to formally endorse the Socialist Party candidates. This effort to bring the unions into alliance with the Socialist Party around immediate demands was not acceptable to the party's revolutionary wing. Wilson was severely criticized, particularly by the Oakland local, which now included Austin Lewis. Lewis refused to speak alongside Wilson and sent him letters that Wilson characterized as "nasty and insulting."[55]

Wilson argued that the struggle between the unions and the Merchants and Manufacturers Association in Los Angeles showed that the capitalist class would use its control over government to destroy workers' organizations and their efforts to build economic power at the workplace unless the workers gained at least enough political power to prevent criminalization of class struggle. Immediate reforms were needed to give workers more resources in the struggle to end class society and replace capitalism with the Cooperative Commonwealth. He pointed out that the working class movement could not simply put all ordinary concerns aside until after the revolution, stating:

I want to say for myself that I am not an Opportunist. And I want to say just as emphatically that I am not a Revolutionist, if by "revolutionist" you mean a Socialist who talks phrases and refuses to face the immediate legislative requirements of the working class . . . The question is: What is the working class demanding now? What does organized Labor demand immediately in the form of law, to strengthen them and equip them for the class struggle? WE WILL WORK FOR SUCH LEGISLATION WHETHER DEFEATED OR ELECTED.[56]

The primary election on August 16, 1910, showed the difficulty of the task Wilson had taken on and the importance of his efforts to bring in more members. With participation limited to those already registered with the party at least twenty days before the primary, there were only 4,554 Socialist Party votes for Wilson. Theodore Bell, the only Democratic candidate, received 47,369 votes. Hiram Johnson won a hotly contested Republican primary with 101,666 votes out of a total of 215,605 Republican votes. The candidates were now set for the general election in November.

Wilson's Labor Day speech in Emeryville before an audience of several thousand was a highlight of his campaign and gave him great hope. He began the day in San Francisco, riding in a carriage near the head of a parade of 24,000 members of 107 different unions, complete with floats and bands and some marchers wearing uniforms. Highlights mentioned by the press included the glassblowers' float on which people demonstrated the process of blowing glass, the pile drivers' float with a miniature pile being set in place, and the sheet metal workers' automobile decorated with metal representations of an American bald eagle and a California bear. The plasterers wore blue-and-white uniforms and marched in formation, and the milk delivery drivers carried bottles of milk.

The parade made its way down Market Street from Civic Center to the Ferry Building, and an estimated 10,000 people then took ferries across the Bay to Shellmound Park in Emeryville. There the crowd heard speeches from San Francisco Mayor McCarthy, Democratic candidate Theodore Bell, and Wilson. Hiram Johnson sent word that he was ill. Bell received polite applause for his short speech telling of his working-class upbringing and declaring himself "the friend of organized labor." Wilson received a standing ovation both before and after his speech, in which he declared that his highest ambition "is to do whatever lies in my power to help men in the organized labor movement in the battle they are fighting everywhere to lift labor from (beneath) the feet of organized capital and place it on the throne of the world, where it ought to be."[57] Wilson challenged the opposing candidates to debate with him, but they had no interest in helping Wilson appear to be a serious candidate or to get publicity for his campaign, which received little attention from most major newspapers.

While Wilson was campaigning, his daughter Viola Barry made news of her own. On her return to Berkeley from England, Viola won the leading role in a melodrama staged by the Ye Liberty stock company in Oakland. The play, *Dorothy Vernon of Haddon Hall*, based on a best-selling novel from 1902, was set in England, but Viola was disappointed when the theater manager insisted that she speak with an American rather than an English accent. When that engagement ended in early 1910, she moved to Los Angeles and joined the Burbank stock company.[58] In October, she joined the new Socialist Theater Company. There she played the lead female role of Ona in the stage version of Upton Sinclair's *The Jungle*, which premiered at the Los Angeles Labor Temple auditorium and then went on the road in Southern California.[59] The rising star who declared herself a socialist and women's suffrage supporter proved irresistible to the press.[60]

The home stretch

With its candidates chosen, the Socialist Party of California held its convention in San Jose on September 10th and 11th to establish its political platform. Beginning with a call for socialization of the means of production, it contained a substantial list of reform measures under three categories: political, social, and "advocated by organized labor." Political reforms included a universal right to vote for men and women; initiative, referendum, recall and proportional representation; and home rule for cities, allowing them to own and operate public utilities, manufacture "necessities of life," and sell them at cost. Social reforms included progressive and graduated taxation of unearned incomes and the unearned increase in land values, old age pensions for workers at age 60, free textbooks and school equipment, and an end to land speculation.

"Measures advocated by organized labor" provided affirmative responses to a questionnaire sent to all candidates for state offices by the San Francisco Labor Council. These included support for state employment bureaus controlled by the unions, laws regulating hazardous and unhealthy working conditions, factory inspections by qualified union workers, accident insurance, and laws ending injunctions against peaceful picketing.[61]

The question on exclusion of Asian immigration was listed first on the Labor Council questionnaire, implying that it was considered of the greatest importance to the unions.[62] The Socialist Party statement in response was carefully crafted. It arguably fit within the boundaries of the Hillquit resolution passed by the national convention because it called for Asian exclusion only if "caused or stimulated by the employing classes for the purpose of weakening the organization of American labor," but the intent was clear. It drew substantial opposition at the convention and a proposal to table it was defeated by a single vote.[63] H. C. Tuck, editor of *The World*, wrote a follow-up article criticizing the state convention measure and Tuck also reported that the state secretary of the California Socialist Party had cancelled Debs's planned election tour of the state, fearing that his strong stance against Asian exclusion would offend the unions.[64] This would not have been done without Wilson's knowledge and approval. Tuck's vehement disagreement on Asian exclusion did not, however, prevent him from supporting Wilson's campaign in the pages of *The World*.

Having endorsed the entire platform of the California Building Trades Council and the California Federation of Labor, Wilson met with Olaf Tveitmoe and received the Building Trades Council's support for his campaign, though not its formal endorsement. Quite likely this trade-off had been arranged in advance. Tveitmoe sent W. Flagler, an organizer with the Building Trades Council and business agent for the United Glass Workers, to campaign with Wilson for ten days. Flagler gave opening speeches on Wilson's behalf in which he made it clear that he represented the California Building Trades Council. He criticized Johnson for his ties to the Los Angeles "good government" forces who had passed the anti-picketing law and Bell for criticizing San Francisco's Union Labor Party and making false accusations of embezzlement against Tveitmoe. Flagler said that while he had never voted for a Socialist Party ticket before in his life, Wilson and Wheeler were the only candidates representing the interests of organized labor.

Wilson followed with his own criticisms of Johnson and Bell, who were both running as reformers and promising to kick the Southern Pacific Railroad (the "Octopus" featured in Frank Norris's best-selling 1901 novel of the same name) out of politics. Wilson remarked that it was not enough to get SP out of politics, it had to be gotten out of the people's pockets, and that there should not be "powerful corporate interests that need to go into politics" in the first place.[65]

The Central Labor Councils of Los Angeles and San Diego endorsed the entire Socialist Party ticket and sent telegrams to San Francisco unions asking them to vote for Wilson, saying, "For God's sake, boys, get in and deliver us from the grip of the Merchants and Manufacturers Association."[66] In San Francisco and Oakland, only a trickle of union endorsements came in for the Socialist Party ticket: Cooks and Waiters Local 31 of Oakland,

Carpenters Union Local 304 of San Francisco, and a few others. More typical was formation of a Wilson-Wheeler Club by the central labor organizations in Alameda County. This allowed endorsement of Wilson for governor and Wheeler for lieutenant governor without severing ties that local unions had to local candidates from the major parties.[67] In San Francisco, Wilson speeches were sponsored by a labor committee that included the president of the Iron Trades Council, heavily involved in backing the Metal Workers strike in Los Angeles; the secretary-treasurer of the Building Trades Council; and officers from twenty union locals—mostly members of the Building Trades Council, with the exception of the Tailors Local 2 and the Janitors Local 1067.[68]

Wilson's campaign was also supported by the Christian Socialist Fellowship. The editor of the *Christian Socialist* did a special September issue on "Stitt Wilson's Message to California and to All America" with a press run of more than 100,000 copies and later reported mailing 78,000 copies to California before the election, mostly in bundles for distribution at campaign meetings and churches. The issue contained excerpts from Wilson's speeches, some from his campaign but mostly from his statements on Christianity and socialism.[69] When the opportunity arose, Wilson spoke to church audiences and presented the "Bible Argument for Socialism." When Wilson was invited to speak in San Luis Obispo by the Rev. Dr. Boller, minister of the Congregational Church in that city and who had known Wilson in Chicago, the *San Luis Obispo Daily Telegram* reported that he gave an "electrifying address."[70]

On September 30th, Wilson received an enthusiastic reception at the fortieth annual convention of the California Equal Suffrage Association. Preceding his talk was one given by John Braly, a wealthy Southern Californian who helped fund women's suffrage organizations. Braly extolled the work of the "good government" forces in Los Angeles in support of women's suffrage as well as in electing a new mayor and city council, which he described as "the best city government in the United States." At that point he was nearly drowned out by hisses from the audience, which included many socialists. Thinking his praise of Los Angeles had offended San Franciscans, he quickly made a reference to San Francisco's virtues. Following him to the speakers' platform, Wilson received "storms of cheers and handclapping." As part of his remarks, he explained the hissing. "It was not for San Francisco. . . . It was for his 'good government,' which has 200 (union) men in jail tonight." Both the Republican and Democratic parties now endorsed voting rights for women, but Wilson argued that "freedom for women at the ballot box" was not sufficient if accompanied by "slavery for women in the shop, factory and mill." He promised to "fight for the political freedom of women at the polls, and for her economic freedom in industry." To great applause, he pledged that "whether the women's suffrage movement supports my candidacy or not I will make Votes for Women one of my main points in my campaign."[71]

The next day an explosion by dynamite and subsequent fire destroyed the *Los Angeles Times* building, killing twenty-one employees and injuring scores more. Publisher Harrison Gray Otis, a leader in the movement to break the unions in Los Angeles, immediately blamed the unions, who denied any connection to the disaster. As a gesture of good faith, the printers union offered to provide enough printers to ensure the *Times* could continue publishing until Otis could hire replacement staff, but he declined.[72] In the already polarized setting of Los Angeles, and the uncertainty about who was responsible, the bombing had little immediate political effect.

Wilson continued to vigorously campaign throughout the state. In mid-October, however, he had to cancel several days of appearances in San Diego and nearby cities due to the death of one of his wife's sisters.[73] Returning to the campaign, he toured forty cities in Northern California, then went south through the Central Valley to San Diego.[74] On November 3rd, he joined a solemn parade through the streets of Los Angeles of 15,000 union men and women carrying small American flags and wearing union badges. Once the marchers arrived at Fiesta Park, a group of them carried Wilson to the bandstand on their shoulders, where he urged them to get out the vote for the Socialist Party ticket on November 8th.[75] He ended his campaign in the Bay Area with three large evening rallies: one in San Jose on the 5th, one in Oakland at the Rice Institute before an audience of 2,000 on the 6th, and one in San Francisco before an audience of several thousand at the Dreamland Rink on the 7th.[76] When the returns came in, the results were mixed.

Governor's race election results, Nov. 8, 1910			
PARTY	**CANDIDATE**	**VOTES**	**% OF TOTAL**
Republican	Hiram Johnson	177,191	45.9%
Democrat	Theodore Bell	154,835	40.1%
Socialist	J. Stitt Wilson	47,819	12.4%
Prohibition	Simeon Meads	5,807	1.5%

Wilson's total was by far the highest that any Socialist Party candidate had ever received in California. It was nearly triple the vote received by

Austin Lewis for governor in 1906 and two-thirds higher than Debs had received in his campaign for president in 1908. But it was only half of what Wilson had hoped for. Far more people heard his speeches than voted for him. On the positive side, most of the people who voted for him voted the straight Socialist Party ticket, at least in statewide races. Wheeler received 45,830 votes and no statewide socialist candidate received less than 40,000 votes, even for obscure offices such as state printer and state surveyor. Agnes Downing, the Socialist Party candidate for superintendent of public instruction and the only woman running for state office, received 40,905 votes.[77] Those people who were persuaded to vote for Wilson were, for the most part, persuaded to vote for the entire Socialist Party ticket and did not simply vote for one charismatic individual and then go back to their usual party allegiances.

Stitt Wilson's best results by county		
COUNTY (MAJOR CITY)	VOTES	% OF TOTAL
Los Angeles	11,129	16.7%
San Francisco	9,476	16.0%
Alameda (Oakland)	5,743	18.0%
San Diego	1,870	19.7%
Humboldt (Eureka)	1,324	21.7%

Wilson won votes throughout California and was most successful in larger urban areas with high levels of union membership. He also received a high percentage of the vote in Humboldt County and San Diego County. Humboldt had a long history of radical movements among lumber workers and small farmers. San Diego was a diverse area with a port, a small but growing city, and one with an active union movement that included about 1,500 union members divided among 25 different craft unions. These unions generally looked to Los Angeles as a model, and several of them, including the Cigar Makers and the Bakers, had socialist leadership.[78]

In the weeks after the election, Wilson gave several talks to socialist and union audiences with the theme, "On with the Battle," arguing that great progress had been made, that the Socialist Party was

Socialist Party button, circa 1910 (from the author's collection).

now seen as a significant political force and not simply a fringe party, and that thousands of new members were joining the party. He urged socialists to redouble their efforts.[79] Indeed, Socialist Party membership more than doubled from 2,900 in 1909 to more than 6,000 in early 1911.[80]

CHAPTER 9

SOCIALIST FOR MAYOR

Once the campaign for governor was over, Wilson needed to consider how he would support himself and his family. He stopped teaching New Thought after his departure for England in 1907 and never took it up again, leaving no indication of why. Perhaps he gradually concluded that while the divine might be immanent throughout the universe, it was not as accessible to the "science" of New Thought as he had hoped. He began holding regular 11 a.m. Sunday meetings at the Central Theater in San Francisco, at which he delivered socialist sermons to a substantial audience and took up a collection.[1] He did paid speaking on behalf of the unions. He also began work on a book he planned to call *The Bible Argument for Socialism*. In it he intended to bring together his past several years of research and lecturing on Moses, the Prophets, and the life of Jesus. Ultimately, he published only an overview in pamphlet form.

Seeing the growing interest in socialism, numerous churches and religious associations invited Wilson to speak, including the San Francisco associations of Presbyterian and Methodist ministers. He also reached out to adherents of alternative spirituality, publishing his speech to the Presbyterians as a series of articles in *Aquarian New Age* magazine.[2] He arranged for the general secretary of the Christian Socialist Fellowship to visit the Bay Area to encourage the organizing of local branches, beginning with a talk at Wilson's Sunday meeting.[3] A few weeks later, an East Bay branch was announced, headed up by ministers from Oakland, Berkeley, and Alameda. Two of the fellowship's three officers were from Berkeley: President Rev. H. J. Loken of the First Christian Church (Disciples of Christ) and Secretary Rev. Philo F. Phelps, an unassigned Presbyterian minister.

Wilson's Sunday talks were inspirational, urging his listeners that "as a man turns to the good of the human race, he becomes the incarnation of God and is living the eternal life."[4] He worked through a range of biblical themes, likely with his proposed book in mind. The texts of two of them were published in the journal of the Journeyman Tailors Union. On April 16, 1911, Easter Sunday, he spoke on "The Resurrection," arguing that capitalism left both individuals and humanity itself morally dead and urging his audience to resurrect themselves and their society:

> Capitalism does not want gentleness . . . Capitalism does not want mercy; its gospel is mercilessness . . . I care not how your soul has been fettered and tied; I say that there is resurrection for you. Come forth from thy tomb; stand forth in the light . . . socialist-minded, for that is the resurrection . . . place humanity above every other value and capitalism will be judged. Peacefully we will bind it in chains and deliver it to its tomb, and gladly we will hail the morning of the resurrection. [Applause][5]

The next Sunday he spoke on "Socialism: the Judgment of Civilization," expounding on Jesus's explanation of God's coming judgment on "the nations of the earth": "I was hungry and ye gave me to eat; I was thirsty and ye gave to me drink; I was naked and ye clothed me; I was sick and ye visited me; I was a stranger and ye took me in; I was in bonds and ye came and delivered me." Wilson pointed out the increasing scope of this basis for judgment, first meeting the necessities of life with food, water, and clothing, next inclusion in the community with care in sickness and loneliness, and finally delivering people from bondage. "Take notice . . . The Christ, the son of man comes to judge the nations—and the socialist program, its purpose, spirit, direction, is the fulfillment of the judgment of Christ."[6]

Later that year, Wilson brought a Japanese minister to his Sunday meeting. We do not know if he was local; there was a Japanese Methodist Episcopal Church in Oakland that the minister might have been connected to or he could have been a visitor from Japan. A member of Wilson's socialist "congregation" wrote a letter of complaint, arguing that the visit was contrary to the exclusion policy.[7] Wilson responded that he was "not under any auspices but my own at these meetings," thanked his correspondent for support of their common cause, and concluded that "each of us is doing his best." This response suggests that Wilson was trying to maintain some distance, in his own mind at least, between his belief that gaining support from white workers required support for racial exclusion and his belief in the socialist principles of international and interracial solidarity as well as his religious belief that all people of all races shared in God's divine nature.

We know about this exchange from Selig Schulberg, a union activist and opponent of racial exclusion policies, who accused Wilson of hypocrisy. He described the person who complained as "a victim held in the clutches of the spiritist dope Wilson peddles on Sundays of each week to the ladies of the species of both sexes [implying that the men in Wilson's audience were effeminate or homosexual] that delight in the gushing nonsense that is a cross between the old-fashioned Methodist revival and the modern mystified new thoughtlessness . . ."[8] Entertaining as the phrase "new thoughtlessness" may be, the sexism and homophobia Schulberg expressed were typical of the hyper-masculinity often adopted by those who considered themselves revolutionaries.

Shortly after the 1910 election, Wilson was the lead speaker at a Socialist Party protest against "political tyranny" in the United States, Canada, and Japan.[9] He had shared the platform with Schulberg, who described the legal lynching of a group of Japanese socialists accused of plotting against the emperor. Wilson's speech, "Shall Fred Warren Go to Jail?," continued a story that dated back to 1906, when Wilson had addressed a meeting to protest the police kidnapping of Charles Moyer and "Big Bill" Haywood.

Fred Warren, editor of *Appeal to Reason*, the leading socialist newspaper of the time, wrote an article describing how, in 1900, gunmen working for William Taylor, the Republican candidate for governor of Kentucky, shot and mortally wounded the Democratic candidate, William Goebel. Goebel lived just long enough to be declared the winner after a recount. Taylor fled to Indiana where the Republican governor there refused to allow his extradition back to Kentucky, and Taylor became an insurance executive. Warren argued that the law should give equal treatment to Republicans and Socialists and offered a reward of $1,000 to anyone who would capture Taylor and return him to Kentucky for trial. Warren was then arrested for sending "threatening" material through the mails, convicted, and sentenced to prison. Warren was still out on appeal in 1910, but in February of 1911 President Taft would commute Warren's sentence to avoid creating a socialist martyr.

On December 30, 1910, Wilson attended the annual meeting of the California Anti-Compulsory Vaccination League, which was held near its headquarters in Berkeley, and agreed to serve as one of its ten vice presidents. There were nine Berkeley residents among the League's twenty officers. Other Berkeley officers included executive committee member John A. Wilson (no relation), owner of a bicycle shop and an active member of the Berkeley branch of the Socialist Party, and vice president Friend W. Richardson, editor and publisher of the *Berkeley Daily Gazette*.[10] Two months later, a compromise measure was passed by the state legislature that allowed parents to opt out of vaccination if a physician signed a statement that it would endanger the health of the child or if the parent signed a sworn statement that they were conscientiously opposed to vaccination.[11] This system remained in place for a century, until conscientious objection was removed from the law in 2016 after an avoidable measles epidemic. The contacts Wilson made in Berkeley through the anti-vaccination campaign would soon be important to him.

"You are nominated for mayor. You must accept."

In February of 1911, Wilson and Job Harriman were retained by the California Labor Federation to spend two weeks giving speeches in the Central Valley to drum up support for labor's legislative agenda. Labor had strong support from legislators from San Francisco, Oakland, and Los Angeles, but needed to pick up additional support from places like Stockton, Modesto, Bakersfield, and Riverside.[12] The trip itself was uneventful, but while Wilson was in Stockton, the local branch of the Socialist Party in Berkeley nominated him for mayor, and his daughter, Viola, decided to get married.

Two months earlier Viola had gotten engaged to John Conway, who had been her leading man in *The Jungle* and now had leading roles with the Bison Moving Picture Company. Without telling their families, the pair went off to the Southern California town of Santa Ana and were married in a private ceremony on February 22nd.[13] Viola was two weeks shy of her 20th birthday and Conway was 23. At the time, Viola was the leading lady in a play called *Is Matrimony a Failure?* She related, "When Mr. Conway begged me to marry him—and he begged hard too—I just made up my mind to find out for myself whether it was a failure or not. Now I know it's not a failure. I am very happy."[14]

The morning after his daughter had married, Wilson received a telegram from Herman Stern, writing on behalf of the Socialist Party's Berkeley branch, which had met the previous evening. "You are nominated for Mayor. You must accept. Great chance for propaganda. Need not neglect the state at large. Answer within two days." Wilson recalled that he was sharing a hotel room with Harriman at the time, and when Harriman saw the telegram he laughed. "Berkeley! Why, Wilson, your vote would be so small it would be a joke. . . . [Bourgeois Berkeley is] the last city in the state, Wilson, that will elect a Socialist. Don't accept it." Wilson told Harriman he agreed and they continued on to their next meeting in Modesto. He had to return to Berkeley for a few days and as he prepared to take the early morning train that Friday, Harriman called out a reminder, "Don't accept."[15]

Upon his arrival in Berkeley, Wilson was met by Stern, who pleaded with him to run. Nominating petitions were due to the Berkeley city clerk by March 1, 1911, for the April 1, 1911, primary election, but Wilson was scheduled to lecture with Harriman until March 2nd, so if he was going to file, he needed to get his petitions signed the next day. Except for his participation in the anti-vaccination effort, he had no previous involvement in local politics and no obvious reason to believe he would do well. The Berkeley chapter of the Socialist Party ran a full slate of candidates for office in 1907 and again in 1909. In 1909, the Socialist candidate for mayor had received only 188 votes out of 5,035 votes cast, compared with the winning candidate's 2,520 votes. Wilson had done much better in the governor's race, getting 813 votes in Berkeley, but still not nearly enough to be elected mayor. Wilson later recalled that he spent a sleepless night at Highland Home and "when day dawned, I had the hunch that I would be elected." He and Stern rushed around town to collect the necessary twenty-five nominating petitions from registered voters.[16] Then Wilson took the train to rejoin Harriman and complete their Central Valley tour before returning to begin his campaign.[17] There is no record of how Harriman reacted to the news that Wilson had entered the race for mayor against his advice.

The City of Berkeley was operating under a new city charter, passed by the voters on January 30, 1909, that placed the city under the commission form of government. The mayor and four city council members were elected "at large" by the whole city, rather than by district. Elections were nonpartisan, with no indication of party membership on the ballot. The primary election was held on the first Saturday in April and if no candidate received an absolute majority a runoff election was held three weeks later. The mayor was elected every two years and served as president of the city council. The four members of the city council were elected for four years, with two coming up for election every two years. Each council member also served as a "commissioner" in charge of one of four departments of the city: finance and revenue, public health and safety, public works, and public supplies. The finance and revenue commissioner also served as an ex-officio member of the five-person school board.

The charter gave the citizens of Berkeley the powers of recall, initiative, and referendum and empowered the city to purchase, own, and operate its own public utilities. Berkeley residents were particularly concerned with the poor quality and high cost of water supplied by the private water company. The new charter set minimum payment standards, required competitive bidding, limited the length of private transit and utility company franchises to 35 years, empowered the city to regulate both safety and cost, and allowed it to buy out the property of the franchise holder based on the value of the "property and plant" without additional payment for the value of the franchise itself.[18] The charter was hailed nationwide as the embodiment of the progressive reform thinking of the day.

At the time, government ownership of utilities was not specifically a "socialist" issue. The private monopolies that controlled water, gas, electricity, and streetcar service in many cities tried to extract as much profit as possible at the least cost to themselves. As highlighted in Lincoln Steffens's bestselling book *The Shame of the Cities*, these private monopolies provided payoffs to local elected officials and jobs to favored constituents in return for the ability to impose high costs on residents and local businesses. Their reluctance to reinvest their profits in capital improvements resulted in poor service, inadequate supplies, and underserved areas. This slowed urban growth and harmed builders, real estate companies, newspapers, and other businesses that benefitted from a growing population.

The first mayor elected under the new charter, Beverly L. Hodghead, was a prominent lawyer with offices in San Francisco. He had served on the board of freeholders, the group elected to develop the new charter, and was one of the leaders in campaigning for its approval. He was a Democrat in a mostly Republican city but the nonpartisan election format made his affiliation less visible, so he simply called his campaign organization the Good Government Club. His major opponent in 1909 had been Charles H. Spear, a local businessman and member of the Alameda County executive committee of the Lincoln-Roosevelt "reform" Republican organization that backed Hiram Johnson for governor. Spear was strongly backed by Friend Richardson and his newspaper, the *Berkeley Daily Gazette*. Richardson objected to Hodghead on several grounds. He was a Democrat. He would not be a full-time mayor and would continue his work as a lawyer in San Francisco, including work for utility companies. His Good Government Club, while made up of good and well-intentioned citizens, was a socially exclusive group that was contrary to the open and democratic spirit of the charter. Despite these objections, Hodghead received a majority of votes in the first round over his three opponents. Following his election as mayor, Hodghead was elected as president of the League of California Municipalities on the strength of Berkeley's new charter.[19]

In 1911, Hodghead announced that he would run for reelection and reactivated his Good Government Club. Spear declined to run again and another Republican businessman who had been expected to run declined at the last minute, saying that Hodghead "had made good" as mayor.[20] This left the mayor's race as a two-man contest between Hodghead and Wilson.

The Socialist Party candidates and program

On March 1st, the Socialist Party local filed papers for a full slate of candidates. If the Socialists could elect their entire slate, including the mayor and the two city council seats that were up for election, they would have a majority. If they won the two school board seats and could select a Socialist as the council member who would also serve on the school board, they would have a majority on the school board as well. The primary election was set for Saturday, April 1st, and in races where no candidate for an office received a majority there would be a runoff election three weeks later. In the race for mayor, with only two candidates, the highest vote-getter would automatically be elected on the 1st. With seven candidates for city council and six candidates for school board, a runoff election would likely be necessary.

The Socialist candidates for city council were Archer F. Waid and John A. Wilson. Archer Waid was a carpenter/contractor and a member of the Carpenters Union and the Socialist Party. John Wilson had a bicycle repair, sales, and rental business that at times served as a meeting place for the Berkeley Socialist Party. He moved to Berkeley after many years in Idaho, where he worked in mining and rose to superintendent of a mine.[21] He had been active in the Socialist Party since at least 1906 and his wife, May Wilson, was a Socialist candidate for school board in 1907. He was also a leader in the movement opposing compulsory vaccination and believed in physical culture and periodic fasting for health.[22] The Socialist candidate for city auditor was John Ogden, who ran a small grocery store and served as the organizer for the Berkeley branch of the Socialist Party.

The Socialist candidates for school board were Mary L. Clifford and Herman I. Stern. Clifford was active for several years in San Francisco's William Morris Club, modeled on Berkeley's Ruskin Club. (In the late 1800s, Morris, famous as an artist-designer, and Ruskin, famous for his art criticism, wrote influential critiques of industrial capitalism, charging that it deadened workers' intellect and creativity.) After moving to Berkeley, where her daughter was a public school teacher, Clifford became active in the Berkeley Socialist local.[23] Herman Stern had been a college teacher and then a minister in the German Reformed (Presbyterian) Church in the Midwest. Searching for a better climate for his wife's health, he moved to Florida, then San Diego, and finally Berkeley, where his wife died in 1909. He was the author of a play criticizing the Mormons for their exploitation of women, as well as a study of Norse mythology that he claimed illuminated the character and culture that made the "Saxon" countries dominant throughout the world.[24] After arriving in Berkeley in 1905, Stern went

SOCIALIST CANDIDATES AND PROGRAM

Primary, April 1, 1911

For Mayor

J. Stitt Wilson

For Councilmen

Archer F. Waid
John A. Wilson

For School Directors

Herman I. Stern
Mrs. Mary L. Clifford

For Auditor

John Ogden

Our program: 1. For Municipal Ownership of all Public Utilities as soon as the legal machinery can be made to effect it. 2. Immediate Regulation of Rates on the basis of the actual investment, physical valuation, franchise values, and gross earnings of the public service corporations. 3. The Additional Taxing of Vacant Land as a source of increased revenue needed for large public enterprises. Decreasing assessments on improvements. 4. In the meantime, bond issues should be for necessary public improvements only. 5. Municipal Lighting Plant, and Incinerator, Reduced Telephone Rates, One Dollar Water Rate; commutation rates on street cars morning and evening, and half rates for children; free text books, kindergartens and playgrounds, "The City Beautiful," and strictest economy of administration consistent with genuine municipal achievements.

Ad for Socialist candidates and program, *Berkeley Daily Gazette*, March 1911 (Berkeley Historical Society collection).

into the real estate business, which gave him a clear understanding of how land speculators manipulated the larger community in order to profit from increased land values.[25] He became a strong advocate of land value taxation.[26] At one campaign rally, he commented that his opponent "is a lawyer and I am a real estate agent and I don't know which is worse."[27]

Stitt Wilson convened meetings of the candidates to develop a program he called "constructive municipal socialism." Berkeley's branch of the Socialist Party was firmly in the "constructive socialist" camp. In 1907 and 1909 it had run a full slate of candidates for municipal office, arguing in 1907 for social ownership of public utilities and in 1909 that it was the only group that could be trusted to implement the provisions of the new Berkeley charter allowing for public ownership of utilities.[28] Municipal ownership was a subject of heated controversy within the Socialist Party. Oakland editor of the socialist paper *The World*, H.C. Tuck, argued that municipal ownership of public utilities was only "municipal capitalism" that would benefit major business interests and divert attention from a revolutionary transformation of the entire economy.[29] Wilson and Berkeley's Socialist Party branch believed that local government should own and operate natural monopolies efficiently for the benefit of all citizens. Doing this would demonstrate the practicality of socialism, increase public support for government ownership of other industries, and develop a cadre of experienced public administrators for the increasingly socialized economy.

The program the branch worked out under Wilson's leadership was similar to the programs set forth by previous progressive and socialist mayors, such as Samuel "Golden Rule" Jones, mayor of Toledo from 1897 to 1904; Hazen Pingree, mayor of Detroit from 1889 to 1897 and governor of Michigan from 1897 to 1901; Tom Johnson, mayor of Cleveland from 1901 to 1909; and the new Socialist administration of Mayor Emile Seidel in Milwaukee. Its program derived in part from Henry George's writings and in part from the women's movement, which played a major role in supporting "social" reform efforts to improve the welfare of all who made the city their home, in contrast with middle-class male reformers who mostly focused on making the city a good place to conduct business through efficient and honest government.[30] The program promoted active local government that provided forms of "collective consumption," such as public parks, gardens and youth recreation programs, and public education through kindergartens, public schools, and libraries. It maintained that the public must own the utility companies that provided street railways, water and sewer service, gas, electricity and, later, telephone service. It espoused good relations with unions and keeping the police neutral in strikes. And it favored land value taxation, although the mayors had never been able to do more than improve the administration of the existing property tax system and reduce corruption.

The Berkeley Socialist program was designed to appeal to the economically diverse Berkeley electorate and focused on three main points. First, the Socialists would move toward public ownership of utilities, especially water, gas, electricity, and telephone service, as rapidly as possible in order to provide better service at lower rates. Second, until public ownership was achieved, the Socialists would regulate for-profit utilities to reduce the excessive rates being charged to the public. Third, the current unfair tax system would be replaced with land value taxation, which would capture the increases in land value created by the public and use them for public benefit. There would also be an additional tax surcharge on vacant land to reduce land speculation and encourage a more compact and economical pattern of urban development.

The Socialist program also called for more parks and playgrounds, payment of union wages to city employees, economy in city administration, and, provided by the school system, universal kindergarten, free books, night classes for working people, and vocational education as well as college preparatory classes. Wilson vowed that hiring for government positions would be based entirely on qualifications, with no preference for members of any political party.[31] The Berkeley Socialists made no mention of "class struggle," instead using the more inclusive language of "the people" against "the plutocracy."

The primary election campaign

Wilson arranged for Carl K. Bronner, a socialist, union activist, and carpenter who had helped manage Wilson's campaign for governor, to come up from Los Angeles and help organize the Berkeley campaign.[32] They established the Socialist Party's headquarters at the Coffee Club on Oxford Street in downtown Berkeley next to the university and kicked off their campaign with a large public meeting in the Berkeley High School auditorium on the evening of Monday, March 13th. This was followed by a series of public meetings held almost every evening in the largest halls available in different parts of the city so that voters could easily walk to a meeting and hear the Socialist candidates.

The Socialist Party invited all candidates for city offices and the school board to appear with them at their meetings. The Good Government Club had put forward a full slate of candidates, but it declined the invitation. Two independent Republican candidates for city council, E. Q. Turner and Francis W. Reid, took the Socialists up on their offer and were given time to speak at each meeting. They realized that the Socialist meetings would draw voters who did not already support the Good Government Club slate and might be open to voting for them. In return they gave credibility to the Socialist Party's commitment to democracy, and their criticisms of the Good Government Club reinforced the socialist message. Men, women, and children filled halls around the city, with dozens and even hundreds left standing outside, to hear Wilson and the other candidates.

In addition to Socialist Party events, Wilson spoke wherever he was invited—at the Berkeley WCTU, to campus organizations, and on street corners—wherever he could attract a crowd. One of the many supporters in his audience was a University of California junior named Earl Warren, a progressive Republican who had supported Hiram Johnson for governor the previous year and would eventually become governor of California and later chief justice of the United States Supreme Court.[33]

In the mayor's race, unlike the governor's race, Socialist Party meetings received extensive local newspaper coverage, often appearing on the front page of the *Berkeley Daily Gazette*. Editor Richardson never directly endorsed Wilson, but he treated him as a serious and reasonable candidate and fully reported the content of his speeches and those of other Socialist Party candidates. He gave space for supporters of Wilson to refute criticisms from the Hodghead campaign and in some cases he refuted them himself.[34] Richardson reassured the public that the Socialist Party platform involved mostly implementing provisions of the recently passed city charter and, in any case, could not be implemented unless the people of Berkeley voted for the necessary bond measures.[35]

It is clear that Richardson was still angry that a Democrat had been elected mayor of a largely Republican city over Richardson's objections in 1909. Stanford Professor Ira Cross claimed that Richardson was trying to "get even" because, after being elected mayor, Hodghead had not reached out to bring Richardson into the administration's inner circle.[36] There were also cultural affinities that likely helped create a good relationship between Richardson, a Quaker, and Wilson, a former Methodist minister who had close relations with Quakers in both the U.S. and England. They were both leaders in Berkeley's anti-vaccination movement, both were interested in "alternative" health measures, and both were strong supporters of prohibition. The masthead of the *Berkeley Daily Gazette* described it as "a clean family newspaper which declines to publish liquor, lottery, racetrack, or other objectionable advertising."

Wilson received few endorsements from established organizations, although the Longfellow Improvement Club endorsed Wilson immediately on March 8th, accusing the Hodghead administration of using part of San Pablo Park as a garbage dump, building "firetrap" schools, and failing to provide playgrounds close to schools.[37] Wilson welcomed support from non-socialists and his campaign manager helped organize independent Wilson Clubs in North Berkeley and South Berkeley, an Independent Businessmen's Wilson Club, and a West Berkeley Independent Businessmen's Club. Both the Socialists and the independent Wilson Clubs organized people to canvass their neighborhoods, in the one case for the entire Socialist slate, and in the other specifically for the Wilson for Mayor candidacy.

The Hodghead campaign started out confidently to the point of complacency, since no one but a Socialist had been willing to challenge the incumbent. Hodghead received endorsements from the *Berkeley Independent*, the *Oakland Tribune*, the *San Francisco Call*, and the *San Francisco Chronicle*, as well as from former President Theodore Roosevelt, who visited Berkeley on March 23rd to speak to the students and faculty of the University of California. The campaign initially planned only two public speeches by Hodghead and did not hold its first public meeting until the evening of March 20th, a week after the Socialists did and only twelve days before Election Day. Once campaign organizers realized that Wilson was a serious candidate, though, they ran a very active campaign in the remaining days.

The Good Government Club set up campaign headquarters in the offices of Mason-McDuffie, a major real estate company, whose owners were strong Hodghead supporters. Mason-McDuffie, likely as a sales tool, had prepared block-by-block card files with information on many of the residents of Berkeley. For the campaign, the Club hired staff to extend this information to include all registered voters, with addresses and phone numbers, where people worked, their church, their lodge memberships, and other information that might help determine how best to reach out to them. It prepared three issues of a newspaper, *Good Government Advocate*, and delivered them to all registered voters on March 21st, 25th, and 28th.[38]

Debating the issues

Over the three weeks of the primary campaign, the Socialist Party and the Good Government Club engaged in a substantive debate over city policies that was well reported by the local newspapers. "Substantive" did not mean devoid of emotion, however. One Socialist meeting began with a moving presentation by J.O. Davis, the father of a girl killed by a streetcar that lacked adequate fenders. He accused the city council of keeping his initiative measure to require improved streetcar safety off the ballot on technicalities. Instead, he said, the council worked with the streetcar company to pass a measure "as insufficient as if they had not passed anything at all."[39]

The Socialists criticized Hodghead and his fellow council members for failing to bring about municipal ownership of any of Berkeley's utilities during the previous two years and for failing to use the city's regulatory powers to lower utility rates. Wilson pointed out that for a modest homeowner the cost of water, gas, light, and telephone service was more than seven times the taxes paid to the city. He pointed to three other cities with municipal utilities that were already saving the public significant amounts. The City of Pasadena had established its own electric company and, despite strenuous opposition from Southern California Edison, had reduced the price of electricity in that city by half. The City of Alameda near Berkeley had established its own electric company and set rates at two-thirds of what Berkeley residents paid and provided power free of charge to the city for street lighting. The City of Los Angeles had purchased the local water company and was supplying water at half the previous price while upgrading its facilities as needed for a rapidly growing city.

Hodghead criticized the Socialist plan as impractical because the City of Berkeley could not possibly raise enough money to bring about public ownership of all of its utilities and transit systems. Wilson said that he knew full well that not everything could be done at once. The Socialist platform called for "immediate regulation" but "ultimate public ownership" of utilities and transit companies. He intended to start with the most urgent issues of water, electricity, and a municipal incinerator for garbage disposal. Virtually every speech Wilson gave included a reminder to his listeners that progress toward public ownership would be fiercely resisted and that all he could promise in a two-year term as mayor was to get the process started.[40]

Hodghead argued that the city's highest priorities were improving its police and fire service; improving its sewers and drainage systems to reduce flooding; and establishing more schools, parks, and playgrounds. In his view the city needed to use its limited bonding capacity on these matters first, before turning to ownership of utilities. Socialists often opposed government borrowing on the grounds that it was simply another way for capitalists to profit from the interest payments. John Wilson, a Socialist Party city council candidate, for example, was opposed to issuing bonds as a matter of principle, although he would make occasional exceptions.[41] Stitt Wilson argued that whenever the city borrowed money, its highest priority should be to invest in public ownership of services such as water and electricity where the service charges could pay off the bonds. With exceptions for urgent situations—and he agreed that Berkeley's rapid growth had created an urgent situation—he believed that capital spending in support of public services such as police, fire, schools, and parks should be paid for through land value taxation because the value of the public services would be reflected in the land value.

Hodghead pointed out that he had already begun studies of what the city would need to do in order to establish public water and electric provision, and that efficient public ownership in many cases required cooperation between Berkeley and its neighboring cities. The Socialists, his supporters said, were blaming Hodghead for failing to accomplish what they themselves could not have done if they had been in office.[42] Wilson described this endorsement of public ownership as a "deathbed conversion" under political pressure, but history would prove Hodghead right. It took until 1923 before Berkeley, Oakland, and other nearby cities were able to form the East Bay Municipal Utility District that now supplies Berkeley's water.[43] As for lowering current water rates through regulation, Hodghead argued that this was risky since the courts were likely to side with the utility companies. Wilson responded that this was simply foot-dragging by a mayor who favored private utilities because he did legal work for the telegraph and telephone company.

Land value taxation played a large part in the Socialist platform and in Wilson's campaign speeches. The Socialist platform pointed out that the growing city was constantly increasing both the value of the land underneath it and the value of the public franchises. (Franchises were city agreements to allow private companies to place water, electricity, gas, and telephone and transit lines on or under city streets and rights of way for an extended period of time in return for an annual payment.) These values, the platform stated, are "socially created by the presence and activities of the whole community" and are a "veritable gold mine" available for taxation.[44] Hodghead and his allies ridiculed the idea of a "gold mine" under the city and dismissed land value taxation as irrelevant because the California constitution required uniform taxation of property and did not allow differential treatment of land and improvements. Wilson would spend a great deal of his time in the coming years trying unsuccessfully to change that.

The Socialists linked their critique of the current property tax system with a strong critique of the Mason-McDuffie company, which was backing Hodghead. Socialist school board candidate Herman Stern, himself a real estate agent, pointed out that a person who bought a lot and built a house on it would immediately pay at a higher rate than the owner of a neighboring vacant lot. As the city extended and improved roads, sidewalks, and sewer lines to serve the families building homes, the value of the vacant lots increased but the public services were largely paid for by the people who had built homes rather than by the speculators who held the vacant lots.

Stern explained that land speculation resulted in an ugly pattern of partial development. Many desirable lots were left vacant in the center of the city and amid surrounding residential neighborhoods while the lot owners waited for the price to go up. Development then sprawled into the outskirts of the city where would-be residents had to go to find available lots for homes. This patchwork development greatly increased the cost to the city to extend streetlights, to provide police and fire protection, and to build more schools. Mason-McDuffie and a couple of other real estate companies owned virtually all of the vacant land on the outskirts of Berkeley, so the audience had no difficulty understanding who benefitted from land speculation. Stern concluded by noting that he himself owned a vacant lot, but he considered a fair tax system more important than self-interest. Socialist council candidate Arthur Waid made a brief but similar argument. Republican council candidate Francis W. Reid, an architect who spoke at all the Socialist meetings, accused the city of wasting money opening up and widening streets for Mason-McDuffie and the Realty Syndicate, another major owner of vacant land.[45]

Trading charges

Mayoral candidate Wilson challenged "the whole Hodghead-Mason-McDuffie club" to join him on the platform for a debate.[46] City council candidate John Wilson described Berkeley as having a two-party system, "one is the Socialist and the other is Mason-McDuffie."[47] Stern called the Good Government Club "the Mason-McDuffie Machine" and described its efforts to create a voter information database as "a machinery of espionage, inquisition and intimidation" that threatened "our American liberty and manhood."[48] Not to be outdone, Francis W. Reid, who said that he had voted for Hodghead two years earlier, promised that "I will not rest until the block card system of tyranny is abolished." Reid described the Good Government Club as a Mason-McDuffie-controlled "ring" whose "dupes and thugs" were trying to "bulldoze," "bluff," and "terrorize" the voters into believing there was no alternative to their rule.[49]

Elinor Carlisle, candidate for reelection to the school board and a strong proponent of free public kindergartens, spoke at the Socialist meeting of March 21st and most of the subsequent meetings. Carlisle was president of the Berkeley Federation of Mothers Clubs (a predecessor of today's Parent-Teacher Associations), president of the Child Welfare League of Alameda County, and a prominent member of the Berkeley Woman's Christian Temperance Union, all of which endorsed her reelection. She had been elected to the school board in 1909 and actively campaigned for women's suffrage, arguing that "the community was only a larger home and it was the duty of women to attend to the business of the municipal home as it was for her to attend to the domestic home."[50] She accused her Good Government Club opponents of being part of a "ring" intent on having a "machine" in the schools. Her opponents claimed that she was a difficult person and that the only "machine" in the schools was the Mothers Clubs she had organized. Carlisle responded that her approach was "fearlessness when I feel that I am right."[51]

Hodghead and his allies attacked socialists in general and Wilson and his supporters in particular. They criticized socialists as impractical and dangerous and argued that the Socialist government in Milwaukee had been a disaster, with growing numbers of unemployed walking the streets. The Socialist refutation of these claims was greatly aided by the *Berkeley Daily Gazette*, which reported that the Milwaukee Socialists were widely praised for honest and effective administration of the city government.[52] The Good Government Club also criticized Wilson's lack of practical business experience. Wilson responded that he would be a full-time mayor, unlike Hodghead, and would be entirely dedicated to the citizens of Berkeley. The

Gazette ran articles on the high esteem in which Wilson was held by prominent people.[53]

The Hodghead forces pointed out that former mayoral candidate Charles Spear and former postmaster George Schmidt had signed Businessmen for Wilson petitions and urged others to vote for him. This, said articles in the *Good Government Advocate* of March 25th and the *San Francisco Call* a few days later, made Wilson an associate of a Spear-Schmidt (or Spear-Schmidt-Richardson) "machine." An irate Wilson responded that he had not talked with Spear or Schmidt for as much as ten minutes in his life and that the Socialists had made no alliances with them.[54] He argued, "It is ill-becoming these men behind the mayor to brand every citizen . . . a 'bad' citizen because they choose to support me. . . . Does the only good citizenship in this city emanate from the Mason-McDuffie office?"

Spear, Schmidt, and Richardson were progressive Republicans at that time, as were many Hodghead supporters. A few years previously, Richardson and Schmidt persuaded August Vollmer, Berkeley's progressive and innovative police chief, to run for the position of town marshall to replace an ineffective and possibly corrupt incumbent.[55] Just the previous year they had supported Hiram Johnson for the Republican nomination for governor. In reality, Berkeley had two competing factions of progressive reformers, each accusing the other of being a "machine," with the "out" faction willing to support a "constructive Socialist" for mayor over a Democrat.

As Election Day approached, the intensity of campaigning increased. Wilson put the Socialist positions and responses to criticisms into a four-page newspaper called *The City for the People*, distributed citywide on March 28th. That same day he spoke in West Berkeley to "a large gathering of working men" on their lunch break at the corner of Third Street and University Avenue after being introduced by Frank Heywood, vice president of the West Berkeley Lumber Company and a member of the Socialist Party.[56] That evening Wilson and the other Socialist candidates spoke to a large crowd in Lincoln Hall in South Berkeley. On the evening of the 29th, the Socialists and their invitees spoke to a large meeting at Finnish Comrades Hall in West Berkeley, preceded by fireworks and music by the Finnish Comrades band.[57] He spent the evening of the 30th being driven around Berkeley in an automobile (the same one used by former President Theodore Roosevelt the previous week), giving speeches on street corners and ending the evening with a talk at the Hillside Club in North Berkeley.[58] On March 31st, the last day before the election, he continued to tour the city by auto and concluded with a speech before a packed house of 2,700 people in the Berkeley High School auditorium, described by the *Berkeley Daily Gazette* as the largest political gathering ever held in Berkeley.[59]

Victory!

Voting took place on Saturday, April 1st. The polls opened at 6 a.m., early enough for commuters to San Francisco to vote before leaving for work, and closed at 6 p.m. The vote count was largely completed by late evening and it was apparent that Wilson had won. The final tally was Wilson with 2,749 votes to 2,468 for Hodghead, a margin of 271 votes.

His victory set off a tremendous celebration among campaign workers and supporters, as described by the *Berkeley Daily Gazette*:

> Men threw their hats in the air and danced and yelled when the result of the election was announced. They carried the victorious candidate on their shoulders from the *Gazette* office to the Socialist headquarters at the Coffee Club and then back to Center Street and Shattuck Avenue where, surrounded by several thousand cheering citizens, Wilson was forced to address the throng. Standing in an automobile, Wilson spoke to the admiring audience which greeted every statement with cheers of approval. He told them of his fight—for it was a fight; of his plans and what he hoped to accomplish for the people of Berkeley. He told them, as he had explained during the entire campaign, not to expect a revolution of affairs, as such was impossible, and he reiterated his promises to do all in his power to carry out the provisions of the charter.[60]

Several hundred cheering supporters then pushed the automobile carrying Wilson around the downtown district, stopping to allow him to speak wherever citizens were gathered.[61]

The next day Wilson received a tremendous welcome when he arrived at the Central Theater in San Francisco to give his Sunday morning talk. Pulling up in a car driven by a supporter, he was greeted by a brass band and picked up and carried into the theater on the shoulders of a group of enthusiastic followers. Once placed on the stage, he faced a packed hall of 2,000 people who had filled all the seats and the available standing room and cheered for a full five minutes. Wilson waited until the audience quieted and in a soft voice that brought complete silence said, "We have had a desperate fight, but we must still keep on fighting." He described the campaign, the Socialist platform and how he had received support from people of every class and promised to work for the good of all—his presentation frequently interrupted by cheers. He then went on to the previously

Front page of the *Berkeley Daily Gazette*, April 3, 1911
(Berkeley Historical Society collection).

announced topic for his morning talk, "Socialism, the Good Samaritan of Human History."[62] A few weeks later, with regular attendance much larger than before, Wilson moved his Sunday talks on socialism to the Valencia Theater, where he regularly brought in audiences of some 1,200 people.[63]

The vote for the entire slate of Socialist candidates increased spectacularly in 1911 from 1909. In the 1909 primary election, Herman Stern received 249 votes for school board. In 1911, he received 1,662 votes and qualified for the runoff election. Also going into the runoff for two school board seats were the incumbent, Elinor Carlisle (2,408 votes) and two independent candidates generally considered close to the Good Government Club, Elmer Nichols (1,926 votes) and Mrs. J. B. Hume (1,845 votes). Both Good Government Club candidates for city council advanced to the runoff election. Incumbent R. A. Berry received 2,400 votes, only 100 short of what he needed to be elected in the first round, and Fred Connor, a former member of the board of trustees (as the city council was called before the new charter), came in third with 1,752 votes. Independent Republican E. Q. Turner was in second place with 1,809 votes, and Socialist John Wilson in fourth place with 1,343 votes, coming in 200 votes ahead of fellow Socialist Archer Waid. In the two-person race for city auditor, the incumbent M. L. Hanscom won easily with 3,243 votes against the Socialist candidate, John Ogden, whose total of 1,753 votes was still quite respectable.[64] Overall, the

Socialist candidates received 25% of the total votes cast for city council and 31% of the votes cast for school board. The Socialists reported spending $760 on the campaign for Mayor Wilson and his comrades (around $20,000 in 2020 dollars), much of it collected by passing the hat at meetings.[65]

Hodghead blamed his loss on non-voters in the areas where his support was strongest, particularly among men who commuted to work in San Francisco. He had almost the same vote as in 1909, when 2,520 votes were enough for a narrow majority, but Berkeley's population and registered voters had increased since then. His strongest vote was in the east of Berkeley, in the hills, and around the campus where university faculty and students and business and professional people were concentrated. In southeast Berkeley and on the south side of the university campus, Hodghead won 863 votes to 256 for Wilson. In Wilson's own precinct, located to the northeast next to the university, Hodghead won 146 votes to 72.[66] The vote was more evenly divided in the central areas of Berkeley, but mostly in Wilson's favor, with his vote percentage increasing in precincts closer to the Bay. In West Berkeley, the area nearest the Bay with most of Berkeley's industry and a heavily working-class population, Wilson won 612 votes to 123 for Hodghead. Pastor A. Y. Skee of the West Berkeley Methodist Church, himself a socialist, said that all the members of his church but two had voted for Wilson.[67] Wilson praised the population of Berkeley for their clear thinking and stated that he was proud to have received support from people of all social classes.

Wilson stated that he had campaigned as a socialist and the people had voted for him as a socialist, but much of the press claimed his election had nothing to do with socialism. The *San Francisco Chronicle* called it "a triumph of all that is indecent and grafting in civic life," a coalition of impractical socialists and a resentful and corrupt machine previously defeated by Good Government forces.[68] A wire service story said it was the other way around, that Wilson's election was a vote for honest government against a "machine" masquerading as a "Good Government Club."[69] The *Oakland Tribune*, whose reactionary owner hated both sides, argued that Wilson's vote tally was not "for" Wilson or the "utopian promises of Socialism" but rather a "rebuke to moral snobbery" and to a "mutual admiration society" that "presented its members as being better than their neighbors."[70]

Austin Lewis agreed that Wilson's victory had little to do with socialism, which could only be brought about by a general strike by the revolutionary proletariat. So-called "constructive municipal socialism," he said, is nothing but a basket of bourgeois reforms and anyone who calls it socialism is "either a fool or a knave."[71] The editor of *The World* was more nuanced; H.C. Tuck congratulated Wilson and noted that while socialism cannot be created in one city, Wilson was now in "a better position than ever to aid in the coming national revolution." He was far more enthusiastic about the election of a socialist mayor and council majority in the working-class mining town of Butte, Montana, two days after the Berkeley election.[72] A few weeks later, Tuck commented that "the so-called Socialist victory in Berkeley was after all only a personal victory for Mayor Wilson and not a victory for the wage-workers' revolt."[73]

The runoff election

One of the arguments made against voting for Wilson was that he would have no real power as mayor because the voters of Berkeley would not elect any other Socialists. Now the voters had a chance to do just that in the general election, by electing John Wilson to the city council and Herman Stern to the school board. If all of the opponents of the Good Government Club candidates were elected, Wilson might even have a working majority, though not entirely Socialist, both on the city council and on the school board. Edward Q. Turner declared that he looked forward to working with Mayor Wilson and that he supported his program. Elinor Carlisle similarly supported the Socialist program's education proposals. Wilson included her denunciation of the "political machine" in his campaign publication, *The City for the People*, making her the only non-Socialist candidate mentioned in a positive light in the issue.

The political difficulty Wilson now faced was that it was contrary to Socialist Party policy to endorse non-Socialist candidates, especially those connected with capitalist political parties, and Turner was a Republican. Herman Stern explained, "We cannot put Mr. Turner's name on our list, or that of Mrs. Carlisle. If we did, we would be put out of the state organization of our party. . . . We cannot endorse any other candidates, but we can vote for other candidates."[74] Wilson endorsed John Wilson and Stern and asked the voters to give him a council majority that would support his program. He stated, "As Mr. Turner is an independent candidate, I don't think it is up to me to boost him. I think that it is up to the people to state their position . . . The question is not whether I endorse Mr. Turner, but whether Mr. Turner endorses me."[75]

Hoping to be part of a working majority on the school board, Stern spent much of his time at campaign meetings speaking in support of John Wilson, who was not much of a public speaker. John Wilson's high school education, while above average for the time, might have been considered a reason to vote for another more highly educated candidate for the city council, especially since that council position could also place the holder of that position on the school board. At the final campaign rally, Stern extolled both John Wilson and Elinor Carlisle, saying that "the school department is a socialist department in any city, and so Mrs. Carlisle and myself are both socialists. . . . [I] hope all the socialists will vote for Mrs. Carlisle."[76] Stern may have felt that he could make such an endorsement because as a woman, Carlisle was not allowed to vote and therefore was not registered with any political party.

A small campaign controversy arose following accusations that John Wilson, when called for jury duty, had stated that he would never convict anyone. He responded that "when I was summoned as a juryman I plainly stated that I believed in the Golden rule, that I looked upon all men as my brothers, that I believed in overcoming evil with good, in short I accepted the teachings of the gentle Nazarene and I believe in putting them in practice." He then explained at some length his belief that criminals should be treated as "moral patients" and that while in prison they should be provided physical and vocational training to help them develop a personal character capable of "self-supporting citizenship" and to enable them to return to society as soon as possible.[77]

The Better Government Club, a coalition of people opposed to the Good Government Club, had endorsed various independent candidates in the primary election and, for lack of any other opponent to Mayor Hodghead, the group endorsed Wilson for mayor. Distribution of its slate card with Wilson at the top had upset the Socialists, who produced their own slate card with a warning that Wilson had not authorized the other slate card and that only the Socialists could be trusted to give him full support. With Turner and Carlisle in the runoff, two of the candidates endorsed by the Better Government Club, the club now endorsed Socialist candidates John Wilson and Herman Stern along with Turner and Carlisle.[78] Council candidate Reid also endorsed the four opponents of the Good Government Club slate.

The Socialists again organized a series of meetings to which all candidates were invited. This time the Good Government Club's council candidates, Berry and Connor, agreed to participate. They both spoke at the first Socialist-sponsored campaign meeting in Lincoln Hall in south Berkeley and pledged to work cooperatively with Mayor-elect Wilson.[79] Berry went to no further Socialist meetings. Connor attended most subsequent meetings and, pressed by Wilson, repudiated the claim in the *Good Government Advocate* that he would be part of a group that would block Wilson's socialist agenda. He released a campaign platform that mirrored much of the Socialist platform.[80]

Victory again!

The April 22nd runoff election results were a triumph for Wilson, the Socialist Party, and the opposition generally. John Wilson was elected to the city council with 2,373 votes, a gain of 1,030 over his vote in the primary. Herman I. Stern was elected to the school board with 2,402 votes, a gain of 740. E. Q. Turner was elected to the city council with 2,548 votes, a gain of 739. And Elinor Carlisle was elected to the school board with 2,846 votes, a gain of 438. The total vote was 4,550, down from 5,217 in the April 21st primary, but Socialist and independent voters had come together around the remaining opposition candidates, while the Good Government Club candidates all received 200 to 400 fewer votes than they had three weeks earlier. Their best showing was the 1,996 votes for R. A. Berry. The geography of the vote was much the same as it had been in the Wilson–Hodghead contest.

In addition to campaigning for his fellow Socialists in the Berkeley runoff election, Mayor-elect Wilson traveled around the Bay Area, giving speeches in Oakland, Vallejo, Petaluma, and San Rafael, where Socialist candidates were running in other municipal elections.[81] He worked particularly hard in support of the Socialist candidates in Oakland, led by mayoral candidate Thomas Booth. Booth owned a machine shop that employed 18 workers and was a longtime member of the British machinists' union, the Amalgamated Society of Engineers, which also had branches in the U.S. He started as a journeyman machinist and went into business for himself following an accident that left him partially disabled. He ran a union shop, where employees worked an eight-hour day at a time when the norm for the industry was nine hours. Shortly after Wilson's election, Booth led a delegation of Oakland Socialists who met with Wilson and asked him to speak on behalf of their campaign. Wilson angrily told them that the "stream of lies and slander" about him from the Oakland local was "almost beyond endurance." (The Oakland local was a stronghold of the revolutionaries in the California Socialist Party.) Booth urged Wilson to set the past aside and consider the benefits of having Socialist administrations in neighboring cities.[82] Wilson agreed and spoke alongside Booth several times in April in advance of the Oakland primary election. On April 18th, Booth came in second and advanced to the city's general election along with two of the four Socialist candidates for city council and five of the seven Socialist candidates for school board.[83]

Once the Berkeley general election was over, Wilson had until July 1, 1911, before he and the newly elected council and school board members would take office. Every day for the week before the May 9th general election in Oakland, he joined Thomas Booth in speaking at campaign rallies. (Austin Lewis spoke twice with Booth at events that Wilson did not attend.)[84] For the Oakland general election campaign, Wilson returned to the strong rhetoric that he had put aside during the Berkeley campaign. He urged Oakland Socialists to work hard for their ticket on behalf of "the millions of little children whose blood has been coined into profit by old King Plutocracy—the exploiter of America."[85] The entire Oakland Socialist slate went down to defeat, but they were encouraged by their best-ever showing. After the Oakland election, Wilson also traveled farther afield to support Socialist candidates in Santa Cruz and Modesto.[86]

The newly elected mayor and council members began to attend meetings of the Berkeley city council, watching as the "lame duck" council approved studies of the water and electric systems, both with a view toward future public ownership and toward rate regulation. The water and electric companies had an incentive to overvalue their plant and equipment so that they could claim that the current high rates were necessary to provide a reasonable return on their investment. In June, the council lowered the water rate by 17% and the electric rate by 6% over protests and threats of lawsuits by the two companies.[87] The mayor-elect and council members-elect held several meetings among themselves to discuss their future roles. They agreed that E.Q. Turner would serve as the commissioner of public works, the position he was best suited for as a former superintendent of streets. John Wilson would serve as commissioner of finance, which would also place him on the school board along with Herman Stern and Elinor Carlisle and potentially give the Socialists effective control over the school system.[88]

Mayor-elect Wilson began to study the water supply issue in detail and decided to combine the issue with a much-needed break.[89] On June 19th, he and Gladstone and some friends left for a week of hiking and camping in the High Sierra, walking from Placerville along the South Fork of the American River, through areas being considered as a potential water supply, to Emerald Bay at Lake Tahoe, where they climbed nearby mountains before taking the train back to Berkeley on the 26th. They followed this excursion with another two-day hiking trip from Fairfax in Marin County north into Sonoma County, returning on the 29th, a couple of days before Wilson would start work as the mayor of Berkeley.[90]

CHAPTER 10

MAYOR OF BERKELEY

On Saturday, July 1st, at 11 a.m., J. Stitt Wilson was sworn in as the mayor of Berkeley, along with new city council members Edward Turner and John Wilson. The new council thanked the outgoing mayor and council members for their service and Mayor Wilson gave a speech outlining the priorities of the new administration. For the most part, he recapped his campaign speeches, saying that the "supreme issue" before the American people is "the people versus the plutocracy." He pledged to move forward on municipal ownership of utilities, city beautification (including parks and "public lavatories at the centers of traffic"), investment in West Berkeley to reduce flooding and create waterfront jobs, and the creation of a bureau of municipal affairs at the university to place local government on a "scientific" basis. He concluded with an appeal for the revenue increases necessary to support the needed improvements, saying, "You can't run a progressive city on a village tax."[1]

The new council then organized itself as the city government. As mayor, Wilson would preside over the city council and oversee the work of the city attorney and city clerk. They voted to appoint E. Q. Turner as commissioner of public works and John Wilson as commissioner of finance and revenue, which also made him the council representative on the school board. This left Christian Hoff to continue as commissioner of public health and safety and, in a gesture of comity between old and new members, he was elected vice chair of the city council, meaning that he would preside in the absence of the mayor. E. B. Norton continued as commissioner of public supplies.

The city council then turned to appointed positions. Wilson had announced two weeks previously that under the new administration most appointed staff would remain in place, but that he and council members John Wilson and E.Q. Turner had agreed to replace the city attorney, assistant city attorney, city treasurer, and building inspector. For building inspector, they appointed Harry Banker, president of the Berkeley Building Trades Council, one of Wilson's few overt gestures toward his supporters.

Overcoming dissension among Berkeley socialists

Wilson considered replacement of the city attorney essential to the success of his program because he did not trust the previous administration on the subject of utility companies. In light of the mayor-elect's views, city attorney B. D. M. Greene resigned and Wilson proposed the appointment of Redmond Staats, who had served as town attorney several years previously. When the appointment came up on the agenda, however, John Wilson objected and after a brief and apparently heated discussion, the mayor postponed consideration of the appointment to the next meeting.[2]

Mayor Wilson and councilman John Wilson had different ideas about the responsibilities of Socialist-elected officials toward the Socialist Party organization and towards the citizens who elected them. While Wilson was away on vacation, a number of active members of the Berkeley local of the party had persuaded John Wilson that it was his duty as a Socialist to be guided by the local executive committee elected by the Party members. For some it was a matter of principle. For others, it was an effort to obtain city jobs. Mayor Wilson felt betrayed. John Wilson had assured the voters that as a fellow Socialist his election would provide support for Stitt Wilson's administration.[3] The mayor explained his opposition to rehiring the former city attorney, even on a temporary basis. John Wilson then suggested appointing Austin Lewis, the revolutionary socialist labor lawyer who had repeatedly attacked Stitt Wilson and municipal socialism. This suggestion was quite unrealistic, since Lewis would never have agreed to serve under Wilson, nor would Wilson have been willing to hire him. The pair's discussion ended without agreement.

At the next city council meeting on Wednesday, July 5th, the mayor again nominated Staats as city attorney, seconded by Turner. John Wilson argued that the Socialist Party executive committee should be consulted about whom to appoint as city attorney and stated that he would follow the Party's direction.[4] The mayor responded that he had been elected to serve the people of Berkeley, not just the Socialist Party, and had promised during the campaign that he would select staff based on their ability to do the job, not on their party affiliation. During the debate, the president of the Longfellow Improvement Club spoke up with a third point of view, arguing that "the people should have something to say about appointments . . . The improvement clubs should be consulted." School board member Herman Stern, speaking as a member of the public, responded that the people active in improvement clubs did not represent all of the people of Berkeley and that the people had spoken by electing the city council.[5] Council member Hoff stated that he would prefer the just-resigned city attorney Greene, but that the mayor should be able to have the city attorney he preferred. Council member Norton agreed, and Staats was appointed with four votes in favor and John Wilson abstaining.

John Wilson also stated that as a representative of the Socialist Party and following Party custom, he had provided the executive committee of the Berkeley organization with his signed, undated letter of resignation to use if they were not satisfied with his work. Mayor Wilson responded that Socialist Party-elected officials had adopted this custom because most localities did not have provisions for recall, but Berkeley's charter did. If Socialists or any other residents of Berkeley were dissatisfied with him, they could file for a recall election.[6] This represented a fundamental difference in views on the role of Socialist Party-elected officials. John Wilson was arguing that a democratic process internal to the Socialist Party should determine how he voted as a member of the city council, with the party deciding how his position could best further the struggle for socialism. The mayor was arguing that the role of socialists was to create a more democratic process for the whole public and to then demonstrate that socialists and socialist policies would best represent the public interest.

Within the Berkeley branch of the party, the issue was soon resolved. The local steering committee called a meeting of the membership that Friday evening "for the purpose of instructing its elected officials." Perhaps assisted by the extensive newspaper coverage of the split between the Wilsons, the meeting had a substantial turnout. John Ogden, former branch organizer; Chester Staley, the campaign manager during the runoff election; and several others demanded that the mayor submit an undated letter of resignation and meet regularly to take direction from the local executive committee. They were overwhelmingly defeated. Instead, the membership passed a resolution presented by Herman Stern and Rev. Philo Phelps, the new branch organizer, that supported Wilson's positions.

"Our instruction to our officials is that they work together as one man in a united effort to work out the Mayor's program for the highest good of the whole city of Berkeley," the resolution stated. It then went on to commend John Wilson for his loyalty but returned his letter of resignation, noting that with the initiative, referendum, and recall in the Berkeley charter there was no need for such letters. The resolution concluded by setting up a monthly meeting for the membership to meet with party-elected officials "to assist them and cheer them on in their arduous duties."[7] John Wilson, having been directed by the local to work with the mayor, proceeded to do so. The outnumbered dissidents formed their own small West Berkeley branch. From there they issued a stream of denunciations of J. Stitt Wilson, with little effect other than garnering coverage in the ultraconservative *Oakland Tribune*.

The small world of city administration

Under the new charter, the mayor and council members had administrative as well as legislative responsibilities. They typically attended at least two and often three or four council meetings every week as well as committee meetings, and council members each ran a department of the city government. Mayor Wilson was paid $2,400 a year (about $65,000 in 2020 dollars) and the Council members $1,800 a year. The city had a total budget of $346,000 for fiscal year 1911–12 and had about 110 full-time employees, with 40 in the fire department and another 27 in the police department. The highest-paid city employee was the city engineer, making $3,600 a year. (Frank Bunker, the superintendent of schools, made $4,000 a year.) Police Chief August Vollmer made $2,400 a year. The lowest-paid fulltime employee was the telephone operator, making only $480 a year. The city also contracted with a great many people who provided such services as keeping the dust down on the major unpaved streets, either by laying down a covering layer of oil, which soaked in and held the street surface together for a few weeks, or by spraying streets with water, which had to be done almost daily during the dry summer months.[8]

With the conflict between John Wilson and himself resolved, Stitt Wilson settled down to the business as mayor and for the next three months every vote taken by the city council was unanimous. Council meetings were filled with administrative minutiae, hearing reports from the departments, referring incoming correspondence to the appropriate department, approving expenditures, etc. At the meeting of July 5th, for example, the council approved bids of $794 for twenty-five bicycles, $232 for a motorcycle, and $110 for stationery for the police department. They authorized the commissioner of public supplies to purchase ten tons of hay for the fire department horses at a cost not to exceed $14 a ton and to purchase a carload of crude oil for the street department at a cost not to exceed 90¢ a barrel.[9] Frequently on the agenda were one or more resolutions approving the extension of sidewalks, often for a block or less, at the request of the residents. A campaign in San Francisco to ensure adequate emergency exits in large halls

The mayor with city council members and staff. Left to right, Mayor J. Stitt Wilson, city attorney R.C. Staats; council member E.B. Norton; city clerk W.J. Seaborn (standing); council members E.Q. Turner, John Wilson, and C. Hoff (Berkeley Historical Society).

and movie theaters led the city council to direct the police and fire departments to check conditions in Berkeley as well.

Not everything the city council did was routine. City ordinances required permits to install boilers over a certain size, and neighbors frequently protested such proposals from businesses on the grounds that they were hazardous. City ordinances regulated the presence of animals within city limits, and there was conflict among residents in parts of Berkeley where some families and businesses owned cows. Street railroad safety was a major issue. Collisions among trains and automobiles and pedestrians crossing the street made deaths and injuries from the commuter rail system a regular item on the front pages of the local newspapers. The city council pressed the railroads to slow down the trains in congested areas, increase the number of flagmen at intersections, add fenders to streetcars, and create safe areas for passengers to wait before boarding. The railroad companies resisted the added expense, and many commuters opposed the reduction in speed.

Wilson wrote to his friend Caroline Severance, reflecting on the change in his life:

> There is a sense in which I am living in a smaller world now
> than I was before in my extensive travels and large meetings

and meeting with public personalities, but I am right at my
work every day and, indeed, every night, and I may say that
I am fanatically devoted to this municipal task and if I fail
it will be because of lack of head and not for lack of heart,
for my very soul is in the matter.[10]

His newfound celebrity brought both larger audiences and revolutionary critics to his regular Sunday "services" in San Francisco. Socialist Labor Party members heckled Wilson as he left the building, and he
angrily responded that he had reached more workers than the whole Socialist Labor Party. His critics told him that he did it by providing "narcotics" in
the form of "immediate demands" at which point his son, Gladstone, pulled
him away to return home.[11]

Building a coalition for a more active city government

As Wilson pointed out in his inaugural address, the active city government
that the Socialists envisioned required the voters to increase taxes. Passing
bond measures to invest in publicly owned utilities and other improvements
needed a two-thirds majority. The Hodghead administration had called a
special election on May 7th to vote on a series of bond measures to raise
money for new schools, fire and police stations, parks, playgrounds, sewers,
and a municipal incinerator. All of the bond measures fell short of the two-
thirds majority needed, with only three of the bonds receiving a majority—
police stations with 53%, fire stations with 55%, and the incinerator with
65%. Opinions were divided as to whether this was meant as a vote of no
confidence in the new administration, no confidence in the old administration, or simply that a third election in six weeks had resulted in a greatly
reduced turnout composed mostly of homeowners with a preference for low
taxes.[12] Wilson hoped to see an amendment to the California constitution
to allow Berkeley to increase taxes on absentee owners of vacant land and
keep taxes low on homeowners, but until that happened, he needed broad
community support for higher taxes.

With his support on the city council apparently consolidated and the
issues of water and power supply being reviewed by the public works department, Wilson looked for ways to mobilize public support. His first step was a
"spotless town" campaign to clean the streets and remove overgrown weeds
and grasses from sidewalk areas and vacant lots, using a combination of city
employees and volunteers working on their own neighborhoods. He had
received many complaints about the condition of the vacant lots scattered
throughout the city and this was both a quick way to be responsive and a

way to begin to mobilize citizens of Berkeley for cooperative action. The city council passed an ordinance allowing the city to fine property owners who failed to maintain vacant lots, but Wilson focused on persuasion and civic pride and tried to involve as many Berkeley residents as possible in the cleanup campaign set for three days early in September.[13]

Wilson also used the cleanup campaign to make some larger points about the inequities of the current economic system and the role of government. Speaking to the Berkeley real estate exchange, he urged that it obtain the cooperation of its clients who owned the vacant lots, saying, "Under the present system whereby landowners keep property off the market awaiting an increase, the least they can do for the public welfare is to keep vacant city lots in tidy condition and prevent their becoming an eyesore in the neighborhood and damaging to the value of other properties."[14] At Wilson's request, the council also increased the budget of the city's charity commission so that it could set up an employment office for unemployed Berkeley residents in preparation for the cleanup campaign. The parks commission allocated money to hire temporary cleanup workers through the employment bureau and Wilson urged property owners to use the new employment office if they planned to hire temporary workers to clean up their lots and sidewalk areas.

Wilson treated the cleanup as if it were a political campaign, which in a sense it was. Early in the evening of September 6th, Wilson led a procession of automobiles from downtown to the commercial centers of neighborhoods around the city, with several cars carrying the drum corps of the Native Sons of the Golden West. Wilson made a brief appeal at each stop and then the auto parade proceeded to Berkeley High School, whose auditorium provided the largest indoor meeting space in the city. After a performance by the high school band, there were brief addresses by local notables including Elinor Carlisle for the suffrage movement and Rev. Philo Phelps for the socialists, along with people from churches, schools, the university, and the parks and charities commissions, after which Wilson gave the main address of the evening urging everyone to cooperate in the cleanup.

The usually hostile *Oakland Tribune* featured a picture of Mayor Wilson in khaki, Chief of Police August Vollmer in uniform, and a number of other city employees taking up hoes and rakes to clean up City Hall Park.[15] The newspapers reported that a great many people had come out and done cleanup work in the early hours of the morning before going to work. Over the weekend, Mayor Wilson, assisted by Gladstone, cut weeds around his own home along with his neighbors and performed a citizen's arrest on a person seen dumping garbage in the street.[16] Letters from the mayor to the city's neighborhood improvement clubs brought in a steady stream of endorsements and promises to continue the cleanup effort. Through the cleanup campaign, Wilson had tried to strengthen a civic commitment to collective action and to illustrate how working together for the common good could strengthen neighborliness and accomplish more than individuals working alone.

Wilson also reached out to the schools and the university to participate in beautification of the city. He arranged for school children to learn about gardening by working as volunteers under supervision of a university agricultural education instructor at the new Codornices Park. This earned Wilson a headline in *Revolt*, the new publication of the revolutionary socialists of San Francisco. In the article, "Making Young Scabs in Berkeley," students were described as "unpaid slaves."[17]

The views of Berkeley's businessmen and professionals would be crucial in obtaining tax increases, especially with the two-thirds requirement for bond measures. Most of them were strongly opposed to socialism, but many were angry at the poor service provided by the People's Water Company and prepared to support public ownership. In early July, the company had begun cutting off the water supply for several hours a day in West Berkeley because it couldn't get enough water into the area. The city quickly set up its own water tank in the area to supply street sprinkling and thus free up company water for household and small business use, but this was clearly a stop-gap measure.[18]

Friend Richardson, editor of the *Berkeley Daily Gazette*, encouraged Berkeley's business organizations to establish common ground with the new mayor. On July 18th, the Chamber of Commerce, the Board of Trade, the Merchants Exchange, and the Manufacturers Association jointly hosted a dinner in Wilson's honor at Berkeley's Masonic Temple. The 300 people present represented the whole range of Berkeley businesses, including a number of small businesspeople who were also union members, along with officials from the city and the university, doctors, lawyers, other professionals, and officers of fraternal organizations.

The dinner was designed to help businesspeople feel comfortable with the idea that there were socialists in their community and there were important areas where they could work together. Among the dinner speakers were friends of Wilson who would help introduce him to the audience. Halvor Hauch, owner of a grocery store in Alameda, was vice president of the Alameda Chamber of Commerce and a fellow member of the Socialist Party and the Ruskin Club. He described how he first heard Wilson speak in Oakland in 1901 and could vouch for him as a friend and a family man of "sterling integrity." Hauch pointed out that the City of Alameda had a successful municipal electric lighting plant and wished Wilson success in developing one in Berkeley. Harry Sully, secretary of the Elks lodge, real estate agent, and an old socialist friend of Wilson (although now a Republican) spoke about how appropriate it was that a Socialist had been elected to implement the "socialistic" aspects of the new city charter. Council member Christian Hoff spoke on the urgent need to raise taxes to provide services to a growing city. Other speakers reviewed the development of Berkeley over the past several decades and portrayed Wilson as a man who would provide honest and capable administration and meet the needs of the city rather than maneuvering for political advantage.[19]

When it was Wilson's turn to speak, he began with his love for the beautiful city of Berkeley and then turned to the meaning of socialism as economic justice, that "what the people socially need, the people must socially own." This he said, was "the twentieth-century proposition of genuine Americanism," of "government of the people, by the people and for the people." He then applied this to Berkeley's need for water and power and concluded with a call for municipal taxes sufficient to meet the many needs of a growing city and improve its quality of life. Most of his audience disagreed with his socialism, but they shared his "boosterism." They were open to his ideas on how best to give Berkeley the public services it needed to grow and appreciated the eloquence with which he promoted Berkeley as a place to live, work, and do business.

Debating municipal socialism

A few weeks later Wilson wrote to a friend that "the only difficulty that I am finding in my administration of the City of Berkeley is with the Extremists in the Socialist Party, who seem to have no patience with anything except something of a radical and impossible nature."[20] Wilson frequently used the language of "the people against the plutocracy" or "the people against the one percent" and described himself as the mayor of all the people of Berkeley. H.C. Tuck, editor of *The World*, argued that in claiming to be mayor of all the people, Wilson was acting as just another "capitalist politician" trying to obscure the class struggle.[21]

Richard Judd's 1989 study of "socialist cities" found that socialist mayors and city councils generally needed support from middle-class reformers as well as from their working-class base in order to gain and hold office. In the period from 1910 to 1915, socialist office holders were remarkably successful at this. In part, this was because many middle-class progressives regarded the socialists as "an ethical, ingenious and somewhat unconventional reform movement." In part, this was because the core strength of the labor movement was among skilled workers, who often went into business for themselves and frequently retained their union membership while self-employed or even while employing others in small businesses. Many socialists ran small businesses, sometimes because they were blacklisted from other employment after a strike or having helped organize a union.

While the short-run goals of the evolutionary socialists were similar to those of the "social reform" progressives, the Socialist Party was much more pro-labor. It appealed to those in the middle class who felt threatened by the rise of giant corporations and monopolies, but when Socialists supported strikes and other forms of class conflict, that frightened the middle class. The result was that Socialists were often defeated for reelection by Democratic-Republican fusion tickets. When Socialists made compromises to keep middle-class support, they faced the second-most-frequent cause of defeat for Socialist-elected officials, expulsion from the Socialist Party by their local chapters.[22]

In the case of Berkeley, there was no large industrial working class whose strikes and protests might be large enough to threaten public order, and there were few capitalists with more than 100 employees. The major industry was the publicly-owned University of California. Berkeley's police chief, August Vollmer, agreed that police should enforce the law evenhandedly and keep the peace rather than help break strikes. On several occasions, Berkeley police arrested strikebreakers for illegally carrying firearms and disarmed them. However the citizens of Berkeley felt about strikes, they did not want violence to spill over into Berkeley and had no problem with the idea that the city should arrest armed men and maintain neutrality.

Nor did Wilson have to worry about internal party opponents as he tried to win over the two-thirds of the Berkeley voters necessary to pass bond measures. Wilson and his allies effectively mobilized his supporters, who constituted the vast majority of Berkeley Socialists, and maintained firm control over the local organization. Constructive socialists had firm control of the state organization as well, and half of the membership had joined in response to Wilson and his allies' statewide campaign the previous year.

Revolutionary socialists, angry at the prestige Wilson's election brought to the "evolutionary" side, launched savage attacks. A month after Wilson's dinner with the Berkeley businessmen, the city received a visit from William "Big Bill" Haywood, a leader in the Western Federation of Miners and the revolutionary wing of the Socialist Party and a founder of the Industrial Workers of the World (IWW). Speaking to an audience of about 500 people, he urged preparation for a revolutionary general strike, argued for sabotage as a form of workers' resistance to capitalism, and denied that electoral politics or municipal socialism had any value. He attacked Wilson in vivid language, saying, "When you break bread with the Merchants and Manufacturers you are eating the quivering flesh of little children. When you drink wine at their banquets you are drinking the blood of the working class." Wilson's administration, then two months old, had done nothing for the working class, Haywood declared. Wilson was present and took exception to these remarks, recounting how he had raised money for Haywood's defense. Wilson called for "intellectual freedom" within the socialist movement. Since the path to victory for labor is unknown, he said, socialists are "groping in the dark" and need to be open to "receive whatever light is available."[23] Two weeks later, Austin Lewis, inspired by the Liverpool general transport workers strike of 1911, told an audience of 500 people in Oakland that Wilson was emblematic of the "socialist parliamentary movement throughout the world" that would be swept away along with capitalism when the workers finally rose up in revolutionary general strikes.[24] (For all his disagreements with Wilson, Lewis too considered himself a proponent of "Christian socialism," and despite his reputation as a defender of free speech, had the editor of the Berkeley Daily Gazette arrested for slander for calling him an atheist.)[25]

Campaigning for women's suffrage

As the "spotless town" campaign came to its conclusion, California was only one month away from an October 10th statewide special election featuring twenty-three ballot measures, one of which was women's right to vote. Governor Hiram Johnson allowed the measure to go to the voters because the Republican Party platform had endorsed it, but he was personally ambivalent and took no public position on the measure. He and his progressive male political supporters focused their own efforts on passing measures they considered more important, the initiative and referendum, recall of elected officials, and railroad regulation. They left the campaign for women's suffrage in the hands of the organized women, who brought in male allies such as Wilson to assist in the campaign.[26] Voting rights for women was a longstanding priority for Wilson. On July 6th, less than a week after taking office as mayor, he spoke at a Berkeley meeting of 1,500 people organized by the College Equal Suffrage League.[27]

Socialist support was generally welcomed by women's suffrage organizations in California, despite opponents' efforts to use that support to discredit the movement. The largely upper-middle-class leadership knew it needed to reach out to working-class women and their organizations.[28] The cross-class relationships were not always easy, especially in San Francisco, where the upper-middle-class women's club organizations infuriated the activist women in the Waitresses Union and the Wage Earners Suffrage League with their support for the use of police to help break the streetcar strike of 1907 and their support for the graft prosecution of the Union Labor Party mayor and council members.[29] The working women's organizations were nonetheless strong supporters of women's suffrage, looking at it as a means to increase working-class voting power. The women's suffrage campaign steering committee managed to bring together the entire range of suffrage supporters, from the club women to the wage earners and the socialists.

A previous women's suffrage measure had failed in 1896, in large part due to overwhelming opposition in San Francisco, the largest city in California. Growing the equal suffrage vote there was critical to the campaign. The city's mayor, Patrick McCarthy, and his Union Labor Party (ULP) supported women's suffrage, a position taken in 1908 when the Building Trades Council took control after the graft prosecutions. But with San Francisco's primary election coming up on September 26, 1911, only two weeks before the statewide special election, the mayor and his party were mostly focused on their unsuccessful effort to maintain control of the city government.[30] The Union Labor Party's contribution to equal suffrage was limited to one joint appearance by Mayor McCarthy with Mayor Wilson.

San Francisco's Socialist Party was fairly weak, due to the success of the Union Labor Party, but it did have a significant core of activist women, which the ULP did not. The socialist women's organization supported the suffrage campaign by organizing public meetings with notable speakers, and the most notable speaker they had available was Wilson. As the mayor of Berkeley, he was automatically a major public figure and the highest-ranking elected official in the California Socialist Party. In addition his background as a well-educated former Methodist minister who supported unions and women's suffrage with equal fervor helped him reach across class lines, appealing to the educated middle class as well as to workers. In the campaign he could speak to the Oakland Council of Churches or a meeting of businessmen in downtown San Francisco and then move on to a meeting in the working-class Mission district under the auspices of the Wage Earners Suffrage League or the Women's Committee of the Socialist Party.

As the statewide election approached, Wilson took on increasingly frequent speaking engagements throughout the Bay Area, with the majority in San Francisco but also in Oakland, Berkeley, Alameda, Hayward, Richmond, and San Rafael. On October 4th, the *Berkeley Independent* reported that "Mayor Wilson is an exceedingly busy man these days. Taking an active interest in the suffrage campaign and being an eloquent speaker, he is in great demand . . . Mayor Wilson spoke three times last evening in different parts of San Francisco. He was hurried from one point to another in an automobile, and several thousand people heard his eloquent addresses."[31] These events typically had multiple speakers and Wilson most frequently shared the platform with Dr. Charles Aked, a prominent Congregational minister; Miss Margaret Haley, founder of the Chicago Teachers Union; and Miss Helen Todd, a Chicago factory inspector associated with Hull House.

When a critic accused him of neglecting his duties to campaign for women's suffrage, Wilson responded, "I am in the fourth month of my official capacity as mayor of the City of Berkeley. During that time I have never missed a council meeting. I have never missed a committee meeting, nor have I ever been late to a single meeting of the council or committee. . . . I have never been away from the city hall but one day since the first day of July."[32] Still, the strain of continuous campaigning while serving as mayor is evident in a letter from Wilson to Hester Harland, leader of the equal suffrage campaign in Berkeley, in which he complained that "everybody seems to press me just a little too hard for various kinds of service . . . but I shall endeavor to see you."[33]

Some historians of the suffrage movement argue that its success was made possible by a change from advocacy of women's political equality with men, based on ideas of justice and natural rights, to advocacy of votes for women on the pragmatic grounds that this would bring women's moral influence to bear on increasingly powerful and active local, state, and national governments.[34] Rebecca Mead argues that "the development of many rationales" for equal suffrage was critical in its success.[35] For Wilson these ideas were not different approaches but an inseparable unity. His speeches are notable for their emphasis on justice and fairness arguments for women's political equality, but underlying this argument is the idea that society needs to give greater importance to values that are held by women, especially women as mothers, in order to realize justice for all. The view that women are essential agents in social transformation pervades Wilson's speeches.

Wilson's speech in Berkeley closing the campaign on the evening of October 9, 1911, presented a forceful statement of his egalitarian views. "Sex is not a determining quality in human rights or responsibilities. A PERSON has rights. Not a male person or a female person." He argued that women were equal or better than men, morally, intellectually, and physically, pointing out that "a larger percentage of men are confined in prisons and the women are the bulwark of the churches," and that women did just as well as men in school. As for physical force, "our mothers have rendered a greater physical service in bearing children than any man has killing them when they reached maturity . . . The ability to carry a gun and shoot the son that some other mother has borne is not the true test of citizenship."[36]

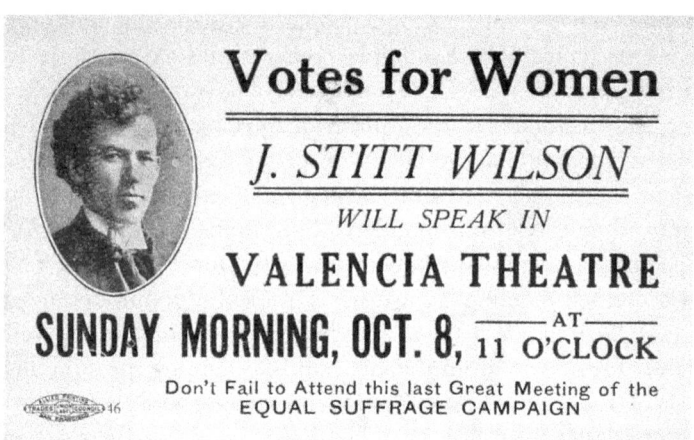

"Votes for Women" advertising card (author's collection).

Many leading male supporters of women's suffrage found it necessary to assert their own masculinity and the importance of "manhood." In 1910–1912, many of the Bay Area's Protestant churches, including those supporting women's suffrage, were engaged in the Men and Religion Forward Movement, reassuring men that "Christianity is peculiarly a man's religion."[37] In the 1912 presidential campaign, equal suffrage would be endorsed in the Progressive Party platform of Theodore Roosevelt, proponent of "the strenuous life," and his vice presidential candidate, California Governor Hiram Johnson. They emblazoned most of their campaign literature with a quote from Kipling: "But there is neither East nor West, Border nor Breed nor Birth, when two strong men stand face to face, though they come from the ends of the earth!"[38]

At times Wilson made appeals to manhood, but they were infrequent and showed no signs of defensiveness. For example, during the women's suffrage campaign he asked voters to "be men at the election and vote as sane men for the sake of your mothers and wives."[39] He was also critical of the rhetoric of masculinity. He described Roosevelt's "strenuous life" as simply another way of saying "every man for himself."[40] At an equal suffrage victory banquet in San Francisco, he advised those present: "Don't imitate the men. The world is saturated with masculinity . . . What the world needs is the mothering instinct in its affairs."[41]

Wilson believed women were both equal and different, that women generally carried a maternal ethic of care, of "human compassion," that would naturally incline women to support a more humane, socialist society and would make voting women into agents of change.[42] Theda Skocpol has suggested that male reformers "may have come to think in more female-centered ways about basic issues of social policy" when they worked in settlement houses where there were strong women leaders.[43] Wilson is clearly an example of this, although in his case the WCTU and the Socialist Party Women's Union were likely more important than Hull House.

On Sunday, October 22, 1911, Wilson opened a packed meeting in San Francisco's Valencia Theater celebrating the victory of the campaign for women's suffrage in California less than two weeks earlier, asking: ". . . how we human beings can secure the physical, mental and moral conditions by which every person in the world can attain to the highest development of his being."[44] For Wilson, of course, the answer was through socialism, and he was extremely optimistic about the socialist movement in California after his own election and the success of women's suffrage. He had been on the winning side of two local and one statewide election campaigns. He had no way to know that he would never see such success again.

Campaigning for home rule in taxation

Along with women's suffrage, the voters at the October 10, 1911, election passed the initiative and referendum, which meant that citizens could gather signatures to bring legislation directly to a vote of the people. Wilson and other proponents of land value taxation immediately began a campaign to have the California constitution amended to remove the requirement for uniform taxation of all real property and allow land value taxation. (Given how quickly they moved, they undoubtedly had prepared in advance of the vote.) Their approach was not to mandate a statewide change, but rather to allow local governments the power to reduce or eliminate taxes on the value of improvements and increase or solely rely on taxes on land value. They were encouraged in this approach by the example of Oregon, where the previous year the voters had passed a measure that combined abolition of the poll tax with language empowering local governments to choose their form of taxation.[45] They may also have been influenced by the California prohibition movement, which had fought for many years for a "local option" to allow citizens to vote on whether or not to allow saloons to operate in their town.[46]

Many socialists supported land value taxation, seeing it as a useful reform and a step towards public ownership of land. The Socialist Party platform called for "the collective ownership of land wherever practicable, and in cases where such ownership is impractical, the appropriation by taxation of the annual rental value of all the land held for speculation and exploitation." They were not "single taxers," however. They agreed with

Henry George that land value reflected the collective contribution of society but saw other forms of socially created value that capitalists took for private profit. A California socialist commented that in addition to land, "knowledge in general, inventions, institutions, etc. are values social in nature and these values should be exploited by and for the collectivity."[47] The Socialist Party program called for an income tax, an inheritance tax, and taxes on corporations as well as on land value.

Despite these differences, socialists and single taxers joined with unions and many progressive reformers to support "home rule in taxation" and open the door to taxing land values. At a meeting of the national single tax leadership in New York City, Wilson described himself as "both a Socialist and a Single Taxer" but he believed that exploitation would continue "even under Single Tax." Even so, a single taxer reported, "He was willing to go our way and work for our way and when we got there, he would continue on his road."[48]

The campaign for home rule in taxation was endorsed by the California Federation of Labor at their annual convention on October 17, 1911, and on October 19th and 20th New York Congressman Henry George, Jr., the son of Henry George, spoke on the single tax at mass meetings in San Francisco and Berkeley. He was accompanied by many local notables including Wilson, who also spoke briefly. The following week, Wilson attended the annual meeting of the League of California Municipalities in Santa Barbara, where he asked the league to support a ballot measure on home rule taxation and made the main speech in favor of the measure.[49]

In his speech to the League of Municipalities, Wilson described the use of land value taxation in Australia, New Zealand, and Canada, particularly Vancouver, in order to argue that this was a practical reform, but his main focus was on the theoretical and moral justification for taxing land values.[50] He explained it thus:

> As the community grows, site values and land values increase. This increase in site values is not made by the industry, skill, labor or forethought of any individual. It is an increase in value arising from the association or coming together of men. It is an outgrowth of his life as a public or social or communal being in competition or association with his fellows . . .
>
> The wealth the individual creates should go to the individual. The values which are created by the social body by its very sociality should go to the social body. . . . The city or the state has great public needs which must be supplied.

If we should personify the city or state, we would say that this Social Mother, in whose household we all live, needs streets and sewers for us all; schools for all our children; peace officers and fire fighters; and social administrators of all these affairs. She, the city, provides or ought to provide social necessities, public utilities, communal enjoyments and civic equipment for all the people. And to do these things she must have money. . . . She has no need to be a pauper, or a beggar, or a thief. The social body, the city or state, should pay its own bills out of that wealth which it has itself socially created. . . . living on her own legitimate earnings . . . [from] taxation on land values.

Clearly influenced by his intense participation in the equal suffrage campaign that had concluded less than two weeks earlier, in this speech Wilson combined the insights of Henry George on the social nature of land values with municipal socialism and the feminist view of city government as a "municipal household." For Wilson, a city government that embodied the maternal ethic of care, a "Social Mother" that provided wide-ranging services to all of the people, provided a model for what a socialist government should be like.

Wilson's approach to Henry George's analysis of urban land value had the potential to overcome a significant gap in socialist theoretical analysis of the role of women. The standard socialist economic theory of the time focused on the exploitation of wage workers and the resulting class conflict. In this view, women as mothers and homemakers had only the indirect role of supporting male family members unless the women were also working in factories and shops and could join unions. George had shown that the city, as a community of both men and women, created economic value that was taken by private landowners. This implied that women as mothers and homemakers still had a significant role in the urban economy and that one of the ways they were exploited was through the private appropriation of the land values they helped create. They therefore had a direct interest in supporting land value taxation to recapture that value, as well as a "maternal" interest in a city government that provided "social necessities" and "communal enjoyments" to its people. Immersed in the practical issues of the campaign and of governing Berkeley, Wilson never followed up on his innovative synthesis of Georgism and feminism.

The League of Municipalities gave the tax measure strong support and Wilson and other representatives lobbied the legislature to place it on the ballot.[51] When the legislative effort was unsuccessful, proponents organized the California League for Home Rule in Taxation and began an initiative campaign, aimed at the November 1912 general election. Former Congressman J. G. Maguire, a prominent Democrat and friend of Henry George, served as president of the league, and Wilson was vice president. The campaign received major financial support from Joseph Fels, a wealthy supporter of the single tax movement nationally, and from the California Federation of Labor and the San Francisco Building Trades Council. The campaign manager, Herman Guttstadt, was a leader of the West Coast Cigarmakers' Union who was a friend of both Henry George and Samuel Gompers, leader of the American Federation of Labor. The measure was quickly endorsed by the California League of Cities, the Assessors Association, the California Democratic Party, the Socialist Party, and the Commonwealth Club, an organization of middle-class progressives.[52]

Wilson also joined and gave speeches on behalf of a newly formed Anti-Capital Punishment and Prison Reform League, which planned to gather signatures for an initiative to abolish the death penalty in California, which was then carried out by hanging.[53]

Job Harriman for mayor of Los Angeles

On Sunday, August 20th, in between city council meetings and equal suffrage campaigning, Wilson made a one-day visit to Los Angeles. There a packed Temple Auditorium heard his urgent plea to support Job Harriman, the Socialist candidate for mayor of Los Angeles. In his talk, "Socialism: Constructive and Administrative," Wilson decried the threat of plutocracy and explained why only socialism could preserve American democracy, then talked about the need for constructive programs and for socialists to "demonstrate to the people our official ability and capacity to carry out these programs," as was now taking place in Milwaukee and Berkeley.[54] A week later in Sacramento he gave a similar speech to another large audience on behalf of the Socialist campaign there.[55]

Wilson's work with Harriman drew fierce criticism from the revolutionaries, both in Berkeley and statewide, who accused the pair of seeking fusion of the Socialists with the Union Labor Party.[56] The revolutionaries launched an unsuccessful campaign to remove F. B. Meriam, the state secretary (equivalent to executive director) of the Socialist Party of California, who worked closely with Harriman and Wilson. Wilson reminded the Berkeley Socialists that, over the past year under his and Harriman's leadership, Party membership had more than doubled and that he had never supported fusion with any other party. He explained that it was thanks to Harriman, among others, that the labor movement in Los Angeles was supporting the

Socialist candidates rather than forming a separate Union Labor Party as had been done in San Francisco.[57]

In Los Angeles, the Socialists had met with leaders of the Union Labor Political Club, the political arm of the Central Labor Council, and agreed on Socialist candidates for municipal office, most of whom were also union leaders and activists.[58] After the defeat of the Union Labor Party in San Francisco, Wilson and Harriman hoped that success in Los Angeles would persuade the unions to back Socialist Party candidates in San Francisco as well and align unions with the Socialist Party throughout California.[59] Bay Area labor unions raised funds for Harriman, knowing that, if he won, that could bring success to union organizing in Los Angeles and empower unions throughout the state by eliminating competition between union and non-union regions. The National Executive Committee of the Socialist Party urged members everywhere to work with their local unions to raise money to support Harriman's campaign.[60]

Knowing that he needed broad support, Harriman campaigned on a platform much like Wilson's in Berkeley. He promised to end the corruption in building the Owens Valley aqueduct and its accompanying land speculation (dramatized in Roman Polanski's movie *Chinatown*). He promised to work for municipal ownership of utilities, public hospitals, parks, and playgrounds and to repeal the anti-picketing ordinance. When the League of California Municipalities meeting in Santa Barbara came to an end on October 28th, Wilson joined Lewis Duncan, Socialist mayor of Butte, Montana, in campaigning for Job Harriman. The result of the primary was a shock to those who had expected the incumbent, Mayor George Alexander, to be easily reelected. Harriman came in first, with 44% of the vote, 20,157 votes out of 45,501. Alexander had 16,790 votes and a conservative Republican received 8,168. This result sent Harriman and Alexander into a runoff in the general election on December 5th.

At the time of the primary election, California had just given women the right to vote but they weren't able to register to vote in time for the election. For the general election, middle-class women's organizations engaged in a major registration campaign, as did socialist and working women's organizations, but with fewer resources. In addition, there is evidence that, despite Wilson's hopes, women voted somewhat more conservatively than men.[61] And unlike Berkeley, Los Angeles was the scene of years of intense conflict over unionization that had likely activated middle-class fears of disorder and class conflict. It is telling that Caroline Severance, despite her Christian Socialism, endorsed Alexander. A few days after the primary, Wilson wrote to her describing the strategic situation as he saw it and pleading for her support:

> . . . stand with us in this battle. . . . It is part of the great
> struggle of humanity for human rights and human justice
> in which your life and influence has been so potent. . . . My
> dear mother . . . with all gentleness & courtesy and love and
> with pride in your noble life & labors, I ask you to give us
> your help.[62]

Wilson served as the keynote speaker for two labor-sponsored fundraisers for Harriman, one in Oakland and the other in San Francisco, then
went to Los Angeles and spent the weekend before the general election
giving speeches for the campaign.[63]

On Saturday, December 1st, four days before the election, the context of the campaign changed dramatically when the McNamara brothers
pleaded guilty to bombing the *Los Angeles Times*. John McNamara was the
secretary-treasurer of the International Association of Bridge and Structural Iron Workers, and James, his brother, was a union staff person. The
Iron Workers was a conservative craft union that had been losing membership since 1906, when employers organized into the National Erectors
Association and began a nationwide open-shop campaign that involved use
of undercover agents to identify and fire union members, accompanied by
injunctions against strikes and picketing. In response, the union's leadership
had taken up the desperate expedient of bombing non-union construction
sites. Prior to the *Los Angeles Times* bombing, they had bombed more than
100 sites over the previous four years, fortunately without loss of life. The
association had decided to intervene in the Los Angeles metal workers strike
by attacking the *Times*, the main anti-labor newspaper. The dynamite blast
set fire to gas lines and to barrels of printers' ink, consuming the entire
building and killing twenty-one employees working the night shift. The
McNamaras' lead attorney, Clarence Darrow, finding the evidence of their
guilt to be overwhelming, engaged in plea bargaining to save their lives,
and one of the conditions imposed by the prosecution was that they confess
before Election Day.

The conventional story of the Los Angeles election is that this confession turned the tide against Harriman, who had also served as an attorney
on the McNamara defense and had believed their professions of innocence.
Certainly, Harriman himself believed that was why he lost. But a look at the
vote suggests the story is more complicated. In the general election, Harriman received 51,796 votes, more than two-and-a-half times as many as
he received in the primary election, clearly reflecting not only the addition
of women voters but increased turnout among his working-class supporters. Alexander received 85,739 votes, more than five times his vote in the

primary election. His supporters had been complacent in the primary, but faced with the prospect of a Socialist who had a serious chance of being elected they came out to vote. Supporters of the conservative Republican who was eliminated in the primary also turned out for Alexander. Despite Harriman's efforts, there was no split among middle-class progressives as there had been in Berkeley. The McNamaras' confession likely increased the turnout among people fearful that socialism meant literal class warfare, despite the entirely peaceful approach of Harriman and Wilson, but it is unlikely that the confession changed the result of the election.[64]

Wilson and Harriman continued to work for an alliance of the unions and the Socialist Party, but Harriman's defeat was a severe blow to their hopes for rapid union and Socialist Party growth. Harriman made another try for mayor in 1913, but received only one quarter of the vote and this time did not even make the runoff election. Instead, Los Angeles capitalists maintained their political power over the city government and used the police and the courts to break strikes and keep unions weak for the next thirty years. San Francisco remained a "union town" for the rest of the decade, but the unions lost both political and bargaining power due to competition from non-union Los Angeles.

The political drama of the Los Angeles mayor's race was accompanied by family drama for the Wilsons. Earlier in the year, their 16-year-old daughter Violette formed an attachment to an older former schoolmate who was on parole for breaking into an apartment. Her mother commented that "I didn't object to their attachment at first, but when the boy's constancy began to interfere with my daughter's school work I insisted that he remain away."[65] Wilson backed up Emma's edict by giving the young man "a thrashing" when he insisted on seeing Violette, and in October the fellow decided to leave town (which violated his parole) and make a new start in Portland, Oregon. The two wrote letters almost daily to each other and the young man decided to return to Berkeley to reunite with Violette and see his family over the Christmas holidays. Upon his arrival, he was arrested and sentenced to a two-year term in reform school, with Violette promising to wait for him.[66] No doubt to the relief of her parents, she instead turned to satisfying her love for drama by acting in plays, writing skits, and creating her own "pictorial" dances. Two years later she coauthored a skit with future playwright Thornton Wilder, a fellow Berkeley High School student, with the two of them playing the leading roles.[67]

The Wilsons' son, Gladstone, graduated from Berkeley High School and entered the University of California, Berkeley, in the fall of 1911. After initial hazing—"College Freshmen Forced to Drink Milk" ran the newspaper headline—he took up acting in student productions and was inducted into the Mask and Dagger Dramatic Society at the end of his first semester.[68] Their oldest daughter, Viola Wilson Conway, spent the summer of 1911 in Yosemite Valley with her husband, where the pair acted as leading man and woman for a series of movies produced by Selig Polyscope Company.[69] Their movies were soon showing in Berkeley, where the New Berkeley Theater had given up vaudeville and switched to the new "motion picture plays."[70]

The recall campaign

After Harriman's defeat in Los Angeles, Wilson returned his focus to the City of Berkeley. In an effort to deal with the immediate financial constraints, Wilson and the city council placed an increase in local property tax on the ballot for a special election on April 26th. It would be accompanied by a measure they strongly opposed. Enough signatures had been gathered to force a vote on creating an exception to Berkeley's prohibition ordinance by allowing retailers from outside the city to deliver sealed packages of alcoholic beverages to homes in Berkeley.

Wilson and the council's effort to lower water rates through regulation failed after the People's Water Company filed suit against the city. The city attorney opined that fighting the suit would be extremely expensive, requiring extensive use of costly expert testimony, and advised settling. In October 1911, the city council, faced with a tight budget, agreed to settle for a return to the old rates, and the company agreed to drop its suit and its request for still higher rates. Significant progress was made on creation of a publicly owned water company, however.[71] In December 1911, the state legislature approved a bill, sponsored by the City of Oakland and supported by Wilson, allowing Oakland and its adjoining cities to form a public water company serving multiple cities. Mayor Mott of Oakland then convened a series of meetings bringing together the mayors and key staff from Oakland, Berkeley, Alameda, Piedmont, Emeryville, Albany, and San Leandro to plan a public water company.[72] Telephone service also became an issue in January 1912. A proposed merger between the Pacific Telephone and Telegraph Company and the Home Telephone Company led Wilson to propose that the cities of the Bay Area should instead purchase both companies. The Berkeley city council voted to support Wilson in this effort and the mayors of Oakland and San Francisco expressed interest and agreed to consider it.[73]

The period of good feelings and relative civic unity did not last. Wilson spent his first seven months as mayor working to build broad support for his vision of an active city. He would spend the next several months in an intense conflict over the school board, during which his apparent majority on the city council fell apart. Unlike the initial harmony on the city council, the change in the school board majority resulted in constant disagreements over policy, personnel, budget, and admissions. Herman Stern became the de facto leader of the board majority with Elinor Carlisle in poor health and John Wilson focused largely on cost savings. In one controversy, two young Chinese men applied for admission to the Berkeley schools. Board president W. C. Morgan objected to having grown foreigners attending classes alongside younger Americans, but the Socialists approved the application over his opposition.[74]

On February 1, 1912, the school board majority decided that it would not renew the contract with Superintendent Frank Bunker when it expired at the end of the school year. Bunker had gained a nationwide reputation as an educator after implementing the junior high school concept in Berkeley. Elinor Carlisle considered him "bureaucratic and autocratic"—a man so taken with his own credentials that he had little patience with differing points of view. She felt he had shown "scant courtesy" in dealing with her and the Federation of Mothers Clubs when they were trying to get kindergartens established in Berkeley. Herman Stern considered him a very able man who had chosen to be "an ambitious self-seeker." Stern wanted a superintendent whose character and manner of dealing with others would provide a good example within the school system. John Wilson agreed and, always concerned with economy in government, felt that there was no need for the superintendent to be the highest-paid public employee in Berkeley.[75]

When Bunker learned that his contract would not be renewed, he refused to leave quietly at the end of his term and take a position elsewhere. Instead, he organized his supporters, who were largely affiliated with the Good Government Club and the university, to attend the next board meeting and he personally confronted the board. He charged the board majority with "politics" and an effort to use the school system for political patronage. He described Elinor Carlisle as "a woman who must dominate" and who sought a superintendent who would allow her to meddle in school administration.[76] Adopting a rhetorical theme of Wilson's, he argued that he was building a modern city school system and the board majority wanted to go back to having a village school system. His supporters, including the two holdover board members, then called a mass meeting at which they selected a steering committee and organized a campaign to recall the board majority and replace them with a slate led by Benjamin Bither, president of the Chamber of Commerce. Over the next month, they gathered more than 4,000 signatures and the city council set the election date for April 30th, three days after the special city election on charter amendments. The

West Berkeley branch of the Socialist Party piled on with a call for Wilson to be removed as mayor and put forward its own slate of three candidates.[77]

Wilson regarded the recall as an attack on his administration and on socialists in government. He pointed out that a recall of John Wilson would deprive him of support on the city council. In response, representatives of the recall campaign offered to drop the recall against John Wilson if Wilson would arrange to put a different council member in charge of the finance department, thus removing John Wilson from the school board. Mayor Wilson indignantly refused this "shameful proposal" to engage in what he considered "political skullduggery."[78] He pointed out that Bunker's supporters could have obtained their objective by recalling any one of the three members of the majority, but instead aimed to recall all three or allow John Wilson to stay on the condition that he and the mayor bow to political threats and abandon their allies. Wilson never stated a personal opinion on Superintendent Bunker. He argued that the recall should be defeated because the decision was within the authority of the school board, which had been elected to make such decisions, and that Berkeley voters should not undo the results of the previous election.

As the recall contest was getting underway, the city council had its first division over a major policy question. Mayor Wilson wanted to prevent the merger of the two telephone companies that provided service in Berkeley and work on making them into publicly owned utilities. Local businesses, which had to subscribe to both services in order to have full coverage of the city, wanted to allow the merger to go ahead and were supported in this by Friend Richardson of the *Berkeley Daily Gazette*, who argued that the city could move to take over the merged service at some later date.[79] Council member Turner voted against the mayor on this one and provided the majority to approve the merger against objections from Stitt and John Wilson.

Mayor Wilson was also presented with a difficult political situation regarding the neighboring city of Oakland. In the wake of Frank Mott's reelection as mayor over Socialist Thomas Booth, the Oakland police began breaking up radical street meetings and using the police to arrest strike pickets and to protect strikebreakers, many of whom were armed. On March 3rd, police chased several members of the Industrial Workers of the World (IWW) off the streets for speaking without a permit and then, when several of them fled to the Socialist headquarters, forced their way in and arrested them. The Socialists met a week later and decided to run a recall campaign against Mayor Mott and two council members. They were joined by the Oakland Building Trades Council and the Oakland Central Labor Council.[80] The combined forces of the Socialists and the trade unions had no trouble gathering enough signatures and a recall election was set for August 6, 1912.

The only real chance Berkeley had to gain public ownership of the water company was by working with Oakland and other nearby cities. Oakland's Mayor Frank Mott strongly supported public ownership and Wilson and Mott were cooperating on the effort. Nonetheless, Wilson attended the initial Socialist meeting to discuss recall and vehemently condemned Mayor Mott's anti-labor policies. Wilson strongly supported free speech, even for groups like the IWW, whose policies he disagreed with, and workers' rights to picket and strike. Both Stitt Wilson and John Wilson refused, however, to support a proposal from the West Berkeley Socialists that the Berkeley city council condemn the actions of the Mott administration, saying it was not appropriate for the city government to officially make such a statement about a neighboring city whatever his opinion might be as a Socialist.[81] Wilson stayed out of the subsequent recall campaign and continued to work with Mott on utility issues during the campaign, even addressing the Oakland city council on telephone rate regulation at Mott's invitation.[82] In the end, Mott and his council allies won easily, with 17,140 votes against his recall and 10,850 in favor.[83]

Proponents of the Berkeley recall were quick to point to Wilson's support for the Oakland recall and charged him with hypocrisy. Both sides campaigned vigorously, with mass meetings in halls around the city and brass bands to liven up the proceedings. The recallers reserved use of the Berkeley High School auditorium for the last few evenings of the campaign, preventing Wilson from using it for a concluding meeting. But as in his previous campaigns, Wilson spent his evenings in the closing days of the campaign being driven around Berkeley speaking at street corners. Advertised in advance by newspapers and fliers, the lead cars would arrive at the scheduled intersection, one with a small brass band and another with Herman Stern and other speakers. The band would play to help attract a crowd and Stern and others would speak until cars with Wilson and additional supporting speakers arrived. Elinor Carlisle had become ill in the early days of the recall and recovery from surgery kept her out of the campaign entirely.[84]

The recall campaigners followed the mayor in their own cars and tried to make their own pitch to the assembled crowds as soon as the mayor stopped speaking. On one occasion, in West Berkeley, the recall cars arrived and pushed into the crowd as Wilson finished his speech. Former City Attorney Greene, who had engaged in constant attacks on Wilson since losing his job, began speaking to the crowd through a megaphone before the next anti-recall speaker could be heard. Wilson denounced their "contemptible politics" for breaking up his meeting; the crowd hissed and shouted so that no one could be heard.

Wilson went on to his next meeting, speaking to a crowd of nearly a thousand people at the intersection of Adeline Street and Alcatraz Avenue in South Berkeley.[85] Again the recall cars moved in as Wilson finished his speech, blocking out the car for the next anti-recall speaker. As recall supporter Professor Thomas Reed started to speak, an irate Wilson returned and shouted to the crowd, "They have no business here. This is our meeting and these people should hold their own meetings." According to the police report of the incident, the crowd then shouted down Reed and Greene as they tried to speak. Someone in Greene's car threw a candy package at the crowd, hitting a bystander. In response, several boys in the crowd threw gravel at them, after which the police officer present stepped in and sent the boys home.[86] The recall campaign claimed that they had been hit with a barrage of rocks and charged Wilson with "inciting to riot" and making an "un-American appeal to violence," charges that were widely reported by the press without reference to Wilson's version of events, supported by the detailed police report, which named names and cited witnesses.[87]

On April 30th, Mayor Wilson won an overwhelming victory, as voters retained his allies, John Wilson, Herman Stern, and Elinor Carlisle, by a wide margin. John Wilson received 5,752 votes to 3,895 votes for Benjamin Bither. The vote count for the other candidates was similar.[88] The West Berkeley Socialists' slate received five votes.[89] Following defeat of the recall, the two minority board members resigned. The board majority then appointed Frank B. Heywood and Dr. Herbert F. Briggs, both of whom had worked hard against the recall. Frank Heywood was vice president of the Berkeley Lumber Company and a member of the Socialist Party.[90] Briggs was a former Methodist minister who was now a lawyer with a practice in San Francisco and president of the Berkeley Board of Trade. He had been appointed to the library board by Wilson and was progressive but not a socialist.[91] The Board of Education now had a clear Socialist majority.

The voters also showed that they were willing to put money into Wilson's vision of an active city government. Three days before the recall election, a much smaller turnout of voters had rejected delivery of liquor to homes in Berkeley and approved three charter amendments, one of which empowered the city council to raise property taxes from $1 per $100 assessed valuation to $1.35.[92]

Socialist delegate

On May 8, 1912, Mayor Wilson left for Indianapolis to attend the annual Socialist Party convention as elected leader of the California delegation. There he had a welcome reunion with his brother Ben, a delegate from

Kansas. Ben had spent the previous year traveling around the U.S. speaking on "The War of the Classes" as part of the Socialist Party "Lyceum Course." This was a set of five lectures given by socialists with high reputations for public speaking, designed to provide a basic socialist education and which locals could sponsor as part of a membership drive. He was also reunited with fellow delegate and former Social Crusader Carl Thompson, who was no longer the city clerk of Milwaukee as Mayor Seidel had just been defeated for reelection by a Democratic-Republican fusion campaign. Thompson was now in charge of the Socialist Party Information Bureau, where he tracked and publicized the accomplishments of elected Socialists. He was also chairman of the committee on municipal and state program, whose report to the convention described the reforms being fought for by elected Socialists around the country.[93]

Wilson was elected to the platform committee, which prepared the Socialist Party Platform in preparation for the presidential election later that year. One of the participants later wrote a detailed description of the process, in which each of the four committee members wrote a draft from which the final platform was pieced together. Wilson's draft was considered too "populistic" but the platform used his "splendid presentation of social conditions" and he helped organize the listing of immediate demands.[94] When the platform was completed and approved by the convention, Wilson called it "the political program of a patriot" and gave a series of talks about it under that title after his return to Berkeley.[95]

The 1910 convention had continued the committee on immigration and elected Wilson as one of its members. As in 1910, Committee Chairman Ernest Untermann had written a report favoring exclusion of Asians from immigration to the United States. For the 1912 report, Untermann not only repeated his previous arguments but added some of the language of "scientific" racism, arguing that "race feeling is not so much a result of social as of biological evolution" and that socialism would reduce but not entirely eliminate racial competition.[96] The majority of the committee—Untermann, Robert Hunter, Joshua Wanhope, and Wilson—all signed on to this report, while the minority of Meyer London, John Spargo, and Leo Laukki endorsed the Stuttgart resolution of the Socialist International, opposing exclusion based on race or national origin.

Wilson tried to distance himself from the majority report when it came up at the convention, pointing out that Untermann and Hunter were not present and saying that he (Wilson) and Wanhope, who were both present, "had the least to do" with writing it. Rather than speaking in favor of it, he proposed to simply "continue the committee with instructions to further investigate and report at the next convention." This left in place as Party policy the 1910 Hilquit resolution, which largely followed the Stuttgart resolution. The delegates seemed eager to avoid the whole debate, which had taken up a great deal of time in 1910, and rather than try to pass a resolution approving one position or the other, they approved the motion to continue the matter without any substantive discussion.[97]

The convention again elected Eugene Victor Debs as the Socialist Party candidate for president of the United States. Debs won a clear majority of 165 votes to 56 votes for Emile Seidel, the former mayor of Milwaukee, and 54 votes for journalist Charles Edward Russell. Wilson voted for Seidel, while Ben Wilson voted for Debs.[98] The delegates chose Seidel as the nominee for vice president. After the convention, Wilson spent a week visiting friends and family in the Midwest and examining the garbage disposal systems, incineration plants, and road paving methods in Milwaukee and in Evanston and Oak Park, Illinois.[99]

One of Wilson's first activities on his return to Berkeley was to join a mass meeting at the Dreamland Rink in San Francisco protesting repression and lynching in San Diego. While he had been away, San Diego banned street speaking to get the IWW (Industrial Workers of the World or "Wobblies"), the socialists, and the Single Taxers out of the central business district. The IWW called for reinforcements to come and speak and hundreds of men were arrested and jailed under brutal conditions for asserting their right to freedom of speech. Local businessmen organized as vigilantes and, in coordination with the police, took the men out of the jail in small groups, kidnapped others as they arrived on trains, beat and tortured them, and dumped them in the desert at the county line to make their way to safety as best they could. Several IWW members were killed. Wilson rejected the charges of anarchy typically leveled against the IWW, saying "We are here to protest against actual anarchy . . . of the respectable mob."[100]

Socialist candidate for Congress

Wilson then turned to his work as mayor, awarding banners to the schools whose children had created the best gardens, restarting the "spotless town" campaign, trying to hold the line on water rates in the face of threatened litigation from the People's Water Company, and keeping the municipal water district effort going. A plan was agreed upon among the seven cities of Northern Alameda County and water district proponents began gathering signatures to place it on the ballot, a task that was not completed until March of 1913.[101] Higher city taxes enabled the city council to buy new police and fire equipment, purchase an ambulance, speed up street improvements, and fund a new municipal incinerator.[102] The city council struggled with the incinerator location, since all the neighborhood improvement clubs wanted it to be placed in some other neighborhood.[103] Realizing that he was unlikely to ever find the time to write his planned book on the Bible argument for socialism, Wilson gathered several hundred copies of his nine Social Crusade pamphlets and had them bound into a book, *How I Became a Socialist and Other Papers*, which he distributed to friends and local libraries.

While carrying out his work as mayor during the day, Wilson began another round of campaigning during the evenings and weekends. On August 20th, Wilson opened his campaign as the Socialist Party candidate for Congress from Alameda County, giving speeches around the county every evening until the primary election on Sept. 3rd. The incumbent congressman was conservative Republican, Joseph R. Knowland, who first won election in 1904 with 68% of the vote and had never received less than 60% in subsequent elections. Democratic opponents typically received about 20% of the vote and in the previous 1910 election, the Democrats had not even put up a candidate against him and Knowland won with 82% of the vote, against 16% for the Socialist. In the Republican primary, Knowland received 23,659 votes and easily defeated a progressive Roosevelt Republican challenger, who received 11,665 votes.

Wilson believed he had a real chance of being elected by picking up votes not only from socialists but from union members, women who had fought for equal suffrage, and disappointed progressives.[104] He pledged the receipts from his weekly socialist sermons in San Francisco to enable the Socialists to rent a campaign office in downtown Oakland. A number of unions formed a J. Stitt Wilson Union Labor Club led by the president of the Alameda County Building Trades Council.[105] A week before the election, the Union Labor Club sponsored a debate between Wilson and the Democratic candidate, Hiram Luttrell. Luttrell emphasized his and Woodrow Wilson's promise to lower tariffs on imported goods, which they argued would lower the cost of living and benefit workers. Wilson derided this claim, saying that his experience in England and Wales had shown him that lowering tariffs made little difference to workers and that only socialism could spread prosperity to all.

Prominent Berkeley women's suffrage supporters organized meetings in support of his candidacy, among them Elinor Carlisle, Hester Harland, and Mary McHenry Keith, the first woman to graduate from Hastings Law School.[106] Wilson and his supporters reminded women, who would be voting for national and statewide offices for the first time, that he had been a leading supporter in the equal suffrage campaign while Knowland had remained silent. Wilson issued an "Open Letter to the Women of Alameda County," printed as a pamphlet and widely distributed by Socialist women.[107] In the letter he urged women to see socialism as the way to apply maternal values to society:[108]

> You have come into this right to vote at an hour when giants of injustice and oppression stalk through the land, and it is your most imperative and sacred duty to use your ballot to undo these wrongs and let the oppressed go free. . . . It is your business—surely it is the business of women as mothers—if little children are forced from the school into the mill and the shop, there to be physically and mentally stunted and morally degraded, only that their nimble fingers and hustling little feet may add greater profits to the already uncounted gold of the plutocracy.

Wilson also had a chance to pick up votes from progressive Republicans. When President Taft was renominated by the Republican Party over Theodore Roosevelt, Roosevelt and his supporters formed the Progressive Party and their platform adopted many of the immediate reforms proposed by the Socialist Party. Having won the California Republican primary, Roosevelt was on the November ballot as the Republican candidate and Taft was reduced to running a write-in campaign. Wilson argued that the Progressive Party platform was "stolen" from the Socialists and pointed out that Knowland was a "standpatter" who opposed any reforms. He did not stop there however, arguing that even progressive reforms would only deal with symptoms and that social ownership of the means of production was the only permanent solution.[109] Several newspapers endorsed Wilson, including the *San Francisco Bulletin* and the *Berkeley Independent*.[110]

The Socialist movement rallied behind Eugene Debs's candidacy for president and the entire Socialist ticket. H.C. Tuck, editor of *The World*, put aside his dislike for Wilson's brand of socialism and again featured Wilson's statements and campaign events on the front page. He even ran a front page column featuring criticism of Knowland from progressive Republicans such as Governor Hiram Johnson and Friend Richardson.[111] When leading socialists spoke in Oakland and San Francisco, Wilson had a prominent place on the agenda. Five thousand people paid admission to hear Debs speak in Oakland; he was introduced by Wilson.[112] Three thousand people paid to hear Congressman Victor Berger speak in San Francisco, followed by a concluding speech by Wilson.[113] (The newspapers regularly expressed amazement that Socialist candidates could charge admission to raise money for their campaign expenses and still bring in crowds equal to those of major campaign figures such as William Jennings Bryan who spoke without charge.) Wilson then went to Nevada, where he met Emile Seidel, vice presidential candidate and former mayor of Milwaukee, and did introductory speeches for him before moving on to the Bay Area, where they spoke to several thousand people in San Francisco and Oakland.[114]

J. Stitt Wilson for Congress button (from the author's collection).

Wilson's daughter, Viola, and her husband, Jack, returned to the Bay Area and raised funds for Wilson's campaign by producing and starring in the Northern California premier of *The Landslide*, a humorous play by the popular playwright, Austin Adams, about the election of a socialist candidate for governor who had expected to lose.[115] (They had gotten to know Adams a couple of months previously, when they starred in another of his plays, *The Bird Cage*, about the future of marriage.)[116]

Nineteen-year-old Gladstone Wilson joined the campaign committee of the Socialist Party of Alameda County as an assistant to the campaign manager and drove his father to most of his speaking engagements. In the last two weeks of the campaign, Wilson kept up his usual frenetic pace, speaking at four and five rallies every evening. Returning from a speech in Oakland one evening, Gladstone drove across the path of a horse-drawn police wagon, which was unable to stop in time. His father was bruised in the collision and the auto was severely damaged, but Gladstone was able to drive it home.[117] This would not be the last occasion when Gladstone's driving made the newspapers, usually for speeding.[118]

On Election Day, Knowland received 34,933 votes (54%) to Wilson's 25,888 (40%) and the Democrat received 3,924 (6%). This was the best showing any opponent had ever made against Knowland and the best showing by any Socialist candidate for Congress that year. Wilson had won the votes of the Socialists, most Democrats, and a substantial number of Progressives. The right-wing *Oakland Tribune* was livid, running an editorial entitled "Who Knifed Joe Knowland?" that accused Roosevelt voters of "treachery."[119] Debs received 9,228 votes in Alameda County, nearly three times his 1908 total. Wilson regarded the election as evidence that the Socialists could break through to major party status.[120] Eugene Debs received more than 900,000 votes nationwide, 6% of the national vote, of which 79,000 votes were from California, just under 12% of the statewide vote. Wilson's brother, Ben, was one of three Socialists elected to the Kansas State Legislature.

Wilson had also helped organize and served as vice president of the California League for Home Rule in Taxation, which gathered signatures and placed the home rule taxation initiative on the state ballot in November of 1912. Once the measure was on the ballot, its opponents organized as well. Statewide, the opposition was led by the State Realty Federation, supported by Chambers of Commerce and farm organizations.[121] Real estate interests feared that land value taxation would destroy profitable real estate speculation and argued that having different tax systems in different areas would create confusion and make it hard to sell local government bonds used to support urban development. Agricultural businesses feared that reducing taxes on buildings and increasing taxes on land value would shift the burden of taxation from urban to rural property owners and force the breakup of large land holdings. They argued that this would harm California's agricultural economy.[122]

At the League of California Municipalities meeting, held in Berkeley that year, Wilson led the supporters during an extensive debate and the League again endorsed the measure.[123] He was unable, however, to gain the endorsement of the Berkeley city council, which voted 3–2 to table the matter on the grounds that the council should not involve itself in political questions.[124] With most of his energies going into his work as mayor and his congressional campaign, he did only limited campaigning for the home rule taxation initiative.[125] On Election Day, the initiative failed, although it received a respectable 41% of the vote statewide, the highest vote yet received by a state initiative on land value taxation. It won majorities in Los Angeles, San Francisco, and most other urban areas, but lost in the rest of the state. In Berkeley, both Wilson and home rule taxation received 44% of the vote.[126]

Wilson celebrated his efforts with the purchase of a new 30 horsepower Regal touring car (list price $950, equivalent to about $25,000 in 2020) to replace the one damaged in the accident the week before the election and returned to his work as mayor.[127] On November 19th, he and the city council directed the city attorney to prepare a January election for bonds to finance sewer improvements, purchase of a playground site, and construction of a municipal lighting plant and a municipal market.[128] Wilson had prepared a detailed report on municipal electric power plants and urged the city council to hire the head of the Pasadena system to prepare plans for Berkeley. A member of the Berkeley branch of the Socialist Party, Frank O'Neil, had developed a plan for a municipal market that would bring farmers in direct contact with consumers. The Socialists argued that cutting out the many wholesalers and distributors would enable farmers to receive more for their produce and still cut prices to the consumer by as much as one-third.[129] Wilson strongly supported this idea.

Family tragedy and its aftermath

The next day the Wilsons' seven-year-old son, Melnotte, came down with diphtheria and doctors quarantined the entire family to prevent it from spreading. Wilson tried to keep working from home, dictating messages to the city council over the telephone.[130] A few days later, Emma Wilson was also diagnosed with diphtheria. Wilson collapsed under the stress and was bedridden for several days amid fears that he too would contract the disease. On November 30th, just nine days after falling ill, Melnotte died. Due to the quarantine, the family was not allowed to attend the funeral services.[131] Both Emma and Stitt recovered a few days later and the quarantine was ended on December 19th. During the last days of his quarantine, Wilson wrote a moving memorial statement expressing his and his wife's grief, remembrances of Melnotte, their belief in the immortality of the soul, and the presence of his spirit in their lives. Wilson also stated his intention to use his life to its highest spiritual value by rededicating himself to the "freedom and fullness of life" for everyone through the socialist movement.[132]

Wilson returned to work as mayor and to giving his Sunday sermons in San Francisco. His friend, Herman Stern, had given the talks during the month Wilson was unable to attend.[133] Shortly after New Year's Day, Wilson gave an address on "Vocational Education" to the California Teachers Association, which was meeting in San Francisco. He described universal public education as essential to the future of democracy. He argued that the current educational system provided little more than basic literacy to the vast majority of students who would not go on to college. He then sketched out his vision of a socialist education system, in which students would spend one half of the day learning agricultural and industrial skills and applying them for decent wages and spend the other half of the day in academic pursuits, taking them as far as desired, secure in the knowledge that they can support themselves as they study.

> I make a plea for a life that never leaves school; for a school that is life; for a school that trains for life, . . . a school where fellowship and brotherhood and justice are not discussed as theories or expounded as rules, but are realized in the actual social co-operation of workers and students . . .[134]

Such a system of education, he argued, would do as much to build a just society as the church, the union movement, or political action.

In January 1913, the United States plunged into another recession, with its accompanying unemployment and hardship. Wilson immediately proposed that the city fund the charity commission to create a municipal labor bureau to help find jobs for unemployed residents of Berkeley and to rent a house for the bureau offices with additional rooms to provide homeless job seekers with a place to sleep. After several revisions to reassure the council majority and the city auditor that the city would not take on liability beyond what it contributed to the commission, the measure was passed. Rev. Norman Pendleton, the young former pastor of the Covenant Baptist Church, a member of the Christian Socialist Fellowship, and a Socialist Party candidate for Congress from San Francisco, was appointed superintendent of the labor bureau. By mid-February he was immersed in helping hundreds of people look for work, providing meals to the hungry and temporary shelter for the homeless, the majority of them residents of Berkeley. The city supported the effort with money and by advertising job openings for street work at the bureau.[135]

As mayor, Wilson was showing distinctly less patience. On one notable occasion, a group of real estate agents presented a request from the Berkeley Real Estate Exchange that the city council repeal the city's real estate license requirement, thus exempting them from the city's business license tax. The exchange between them made all the local newspapers.

Mayor Wilson: "I do not believe in any of the taxes on business, but to remove this tax on the real estate agent and let the grocery man and merchant go taxed would be unjust discrimination . . . We tax the laundries and in my opinion a laundryman is more valuable to the community than a real estate man."

Real estate man George H. deKay: "I personally resent the Mayor's statement. If I didn't think I was more valuable than the Chinese or Jap who does laundry I would move out of Berkeley."

Mayor Wilson: "I welcome the resentment. I believe in taxing real estate, not the real estate man. But I do say that a laundryman is more useful and more of a necessity, an element of the community that you cannot get along without. . . ."[136]

A few days later, Wilson received an invitation to attend a charity fundraising banquet in San Francisco, at a cost of $3 (equivalent to about $75 in 2020). Wilson denounced the banquet as an upper-class society event, "vulgar and ostentatiously pagan," and mirroring the biblical parable of the rich man, Dives, and the impoverished Lazarus who waited outside his door hoping for crumbs from his table.[137] His response was reported in newspapers nationwide.

Wilson declared that the council majority was systematically opposing his efforts, despite past promises to work with him, and he began to prepare for a Socialist campaign against the "reactionary" council members in the upcoming April 1913 municipal election.[138] In his absence, the council had refused to arrange for consultants to prepare a plan for Berkeley to build its own electric power plant that would follow the Pasadena model. The three non-Socialist council members stated that they would support purchase of the existing Berkeley Electric Light Company but did not want to go into competition with it.[139] The council majority decided to move ahead with a sewer bond issue and put aside Wilson's proposals. Wilson responded by dropping his call for a vote on bonds for the electric power plant and municipal market, arguing that even if they passed, proper implementation would require that a Socialist majority replace the current city council. Berkeley Socialists nominated him for reelection, prepared a platform, and selected candidates to run with him. Wilson called on the citizens of Berkeley to give the Socialists a working majority and expressed great optimism about the upcoming campaign.[140]

On February 19th, Wilson suddenly announced that he would not run for reelection as mayor of Berkeley in 1913.[141] He gave two reasons. First, he stated that while he believed he would be reelected, he was unwilling to continue to serve as mayor in the face of a reactionary majority on the city council. He recognized that there was "a bare chance" that the Socialists would secure a majority in the 1913 elections but claimed that the changes he wanted were so sweeping that he would likely need support from not merely three but four out of the five members of the city council, all "animated with moral enthusiasm for the success of such an administration." He was unwilling "to take such a risk" as without a majority he would "feel compelled to resign." Second, he believed that he could help change the state of California and indeed the nation by campaigning throughout the state and by building a "temple of socialism" at which he and other socialist speakers would generate "a spiritual and ethical revival" among the multitudes who would soon attend the Panama-Pacific International Exposition planned for 1915. "I must go out of the honor and comparative ease and comfort of municipal office into the less grateful and more arduous labors of an itinerant herald and apostle of the Social Revolution."[142]

It is hard to reconcile Wilson's belief that socialism was sweeping the state and the nation, supported by the real gains of the Socialist Party during that period and his record of success in Berkeley, with his sudden pessimism about the Berkeley city council election. With John Wilson only halfway through a four-year term on the five-member city council, Stitt Wilson needed only his own reelection and election of one more Socialist council member in the next election to have an outright majority. (As it turned out, the 1913 election did give the Socialist Party three out of five seats on the Berkeley school board.) Only a few days before his withdrawal, Wilson claimed to expect such a victory.[143] No doubt Wilson was more realistic in private than in his public statements, but in his initial campaign for mayor he had warned his supporters that it might take years of effort before the program of public ownership of utilities could be implemented. Now he was leaving the field after only two years as mayor.

His portrayal of an implacably hostile opposition is clearly an exaggeration, perhaps initially made for campaign purposes. In the present day, with no significant socialist or labor party and with electricity, gas and telephone service in the San Francisco Bay Area still almost entirely provided by privately owned companies, it is easy to envision a beleaguered Wilson faced with "reactionaries" who opposed his platform. But there was broad support for public ownership of utilities in Berkeley in 1913.[144] Despite their hesitations, the non-Socialist council members gave at least verbal support to the idea of public ownership. The examples of public ownership Wilson pointed to in Pasadena, Los Angeles, and the City of Alameda were all carried out by progressive reformers, not Socialist Party majorities. The fragmented political structure of the Bay Area added to the difficulties of the task, but just the previous week the effort to create a seven-city public water district had succeeded in gathering enough signatures to bring the measure to a vote. Mayor Wilson and Oakland Mayor Mott had announced that they would present the signatures to the Alameda County board of supervisors on March 3rd and the election was eventually set for July 29th.[145] The change in Wilson's attitude toward his municipal work is not adequately explained by the reasons stated in his letter.

Wilson was a devoted husband and father now living with overwhelming grief over the death of his young son, Melnotte. Under the circumstances, it seems more likely that Wilson was unable to deal with the idea of years more of the minutiae and frustrations of the "smaller world" of day-to-day Berkeley politics and administration. His grandiose plans for a "temple of socialism" at the Panama-Pacific International Exposition suggest that he wanted to return to the deep emotional connection that arose from sharing his socialist vision with large and enthusiastic audiences. There he could merge his grief over the loss of his son with his grief over the many injustices and unnecessary deaths caused by the capitalist system, and transfigure grief into an urgent message of hope for a better day.

Berkeley socialists regroup

Knowing he would be mayor for only a few more months seemed to restore much of Wilson's normal energy. The city council majority set April 12th as the day to hold an election to authorize bonds to pay for an improved sewer system, new fire houses, and acquisition of playgrounds. The citizens of Berkeley would now have three elections in April, a primary election for municipal offices on April 5th, a bond election on April 12th, and the general election on April 26th. Wilson had argued for a bond election after the general election so that the public would know who would implement the bonds if they passed. Despite his disagreements with the majority, Wilson supported the three bond measures and agreed to chair the campaign committee, saying, "I hope I am a good loser . . . now my coat is off for the proposed bond issue . . . Let every patriotic citizen boost for all three proposals."[146] He also took on statewide responsibilities as the acting president of the California League for Home Rule in Taxation, helping to keep the organization together in anticipation of another try in 1914.

Immediately following Wilson's withdrawal from the mayor's race, appointed school board member Herbert Briggs announced his candidacy, to the disappointment of the Socialists who had expected his support.[147] Charles Heywood, president of Berkeley Lumber and more conservative than his socialist brother Frank, was the candidate of the Good Government Club. Charles Spear, who backed Wilson in 1911, announced that he would try again. The Socialists reconvened and selected Philo Phelps as their candidate for mayor. For city council the Socialists nominated James McIndoe and Fedor Alexis Postnikov, and for school board, Elvina S. Beals, Hester Harland, and Frank G. Shallenberger.[148] Berkeley's Socialists also passed resolutions of praise for August Vollmer, Berkeley's chief of police, noting his humane treatment of suspects and respect for free speech, in contrast to the common practices of police in neighboring cities.

Phelps had been selected as the replacement candidate for mayor after Herman Stern refused to run. Phelps was the Berkeley branch organizer, a member of the charity commission, secretary of the Christian Socialist Fellowship, and an unassigned Presbyterian minister. He was not well-known outside of the Socialist Party and lacked Wilson's eloquence. Elvina Beals was a former teacher from Kansas, where she had also served on a teacher certification board. She and her husband, a journalist, had moved to Pasadena and then to Berkeley when their sons entered the University of California. She had run as the Socialist candidate for State Assembly in 1912, with her major issues being opposition to child labor and support for mothers' pensions so that poor widows could properly care for their children rather than being forced to work.[149] Hester Harland was well-known in Berkeley as a longtime women's suffrage activist, having been a state organizer for the 1896 effort and the Berkeley organizer in 1911. Frank Shallenberger worked as a purchasing agent for the Hartford Fire Insurance Company.[150]

Fedor Postnikov was a former lieutenant colonel in the Russian Army in Vladivostok. He started as an officer commanding Cossack cavalry, then obtained a military engineering degree and became a specialist in the design and use of observation balloons. Like many other educated Russians, even in the military, he associated socialism with aspirations for modernization and democracy. When a revolt against Tsarist absolutism followed Russian defeat in its war with Japan in 1905, he anticipated that he would be ordered to help suppress it. To avoid this, he arranged to do further engineering studies at the University of California, brought his family to Berkeley, and then resigned his commission. With his Berkeley degree in hand, he started his own civil engineering business. Soon after receiving American citizenship, he joined the Berkeley branch of the Socialist Party, becoming a delegate to the Alameda County Central Committee in 1911.[151]

Having placed Postnikov, one of Berkeley's most colorful characters, on its election slate, Berkeley's Socialists now welcomed one of the *state's* most colorful characters as he passed through town. Carl Browne was for many years a landscape painter and populist orator. During the depression of 1893 he had helped Jacob Coxey organize several hundred unemployed workers into his "Army of the Commonwealth in Christ," better known as Coxey's Army. They marched from Coxey's hometown of Massillon, Ohio, to Washington, D.C., to demand that the government provide jobs for the unemployed after which Coxey and Browne were jailed for public speaking on the grounds of the Capitol building. After getting out of jail, Browne eloped with Coxey's daughter and went back to California. The marriage soon broke up and Browne took up an eccentric life of political commentary, producing a magazine called *The Silver Sword*, known for its humorous political cartoons of the state's elected officials, and sometimes sleeping in unused rooms in the state Capitol in Sacramento. On public occasions, he would often dress up in a suit of armor to help publicize his magazine.[152] He had recently joined the Socialist Party and campaigned for Wilson for governor in 1910.

In the recession of 1913, Browne decided to reprise his "army" days and organized a march from San Francisco to Sacramento to demand that the state government provide jobs for the unemployed. On March 2nd, Browne and about a hundred men met in San Francisco for a rally and then took the ferry to Oakland, where they were welcomed by local labor leaders and held street corner rallies. Browne and about fifty of the marchers proceeded to Berkeley, where they held another street rally and were welcomed at Socialist Party headquarters with dinner and speeches by Wilson and Philo Phelps. The Berkeley Socialists gave blankets to those without them and the men then marched into the hills to spend the night. The next day, Browne and his group marched to Richmond and continued on, holding demonstrations in each town they passed through. After several days, they arrived in Sacramento, where the legislature did nothing to reduce unemployment, the marchers dispersed, and Browne returned to political cartooning.[153]

Mayor Wilson and the Socialists campaigned vigorously during March and April, holding meetings in houses and halls around the city and distributing a new version of their campaign newspaper, *The City for the People*. Wilson argued that the Socialists offered plans to deal with the important issues of the times, while their opponents had no coherent program beyond a "businesslike" administration. Phelps denounced "industrial slavery" and called for public ownership of utilities. Postnikov stated that he was a man of action who would be a persistent and courageous fighter for the Socialist program. Elvira Beals proposed an extensive program for the schools, including universal kindergarten, school libraries and reading rooms, school gardens, and cooking classes to help provide all students with warm lunches, better connection of vocational classes with workplaces, and ungraded classes for children with special needs.[154] The *Berkeley Daily Gazette* continued to speak warmly of Wilson, but urged that voters select a capable businessman as their next mayor.

The results of the April 5, 1913, primary election were disappointing for the Socialists. Philo Phelps came in third in the mayoral race and did not make the general election. His 1,477 votes were only 20% of the total vote. Wilson felt that without Briggs in the election, Phelps would have drawn votes from non-socialist voters and at least made the runoff.[155] The leading candidate, and eventual winner was Charles D. Heywood. As in 1911, the Socialists placed one school board candidate, Elvina Beals, and one city council candidate, Postnikov, in the general election. In the race for two seats on the city council, Fedor Postnikov came in fourth with 1,462 votes, and the two Socialists together received 19% of the votes cast for city council, a decline of 6% from 1911. Beals came in second among candidates for two four-year seats on the school board, with 2,315 votes, and together, the three Socialists received 36% of all the votes cast for school board, an increase of 5% over 1911.

The following week the bond campaign held three large meetings in North, West, and Central Berkeley, all featuring brief speeches by Wilson, and house meetings every day of the week. Drawing only 5,000 voters, compared with just under 7,500 in the primary election, the sewer and fire department bonds narrowly passed, while the playground bond narrowly failed.[156]

Wilson and the Berkeley Socialists continued their campaign for the general election and received a special assist from Ben Wilson, who had just completed his session as an elected member of the Kansas House of Representatives.[157] The results of the general election on April 26th were a disappointment. Postnikov came in fourth in the council race, with 2,671 votes. Elvira Beals was the only Socialist elected, coming in second in the school board race with 4,027 votes. Beals's vote reflected her educational credentials and also showed that the Socialists had gained broad respect for their work on the school board over the past two years. With John Wilson, Herman Stern, and Elvira Beals all on the school board, the Socialists would have a majority for the next two years.

Wilson steps down

With the Berkeley elections over, Wilson arranged a month-long leave of absence from his duties as mayor to travel, combining a speaking tour, visits with family, and attendance at the Socialist Party National Committee meeting in Chicago, to which he was an elected delegate from California. Ben Wilson had finished his service in the Kansas State Legislature, which met from January to March 1913 for its biannual session, and he and his family traveled from Girard to Berkeley and stayed at Highland Home while Stitt and Emma were away. Ben filled in for Stitt at his Sunday lectures and did a speaking tour of the Bay Area.[158] In leaving Girard, Ben and Leila were also leaving behind the scene of a recent tragedy, the death by suicide of their close friend, Julius A. Wayland, editor of *The Appeal to Reason*. Ben had given the memorial address at his funeral.[159] Ben and Leila's move back to the Bay Area proved to be permanent. Since their family was now too large for the downstairs apartment at Highland Home, they rented a house in Oakland and a few years later moved to a house at 2809 Buena Vista Road in Berkeley, only a few blocks from Stitt and Emma.[160] In subsequent years, Stitt and Emma usually rented out their downstairs apartment for extra income, often to graduate students at the university. The Wilson families would both remain in Berkeley for many years, with the elderly Mrs. Agnew, Emma and Leila's mother, living with one or another of the two households until her death in 1921.[161]

On May 2nd, Wilson and his wife traveled to Sacramento, where he gave a speech supporting the Socialist Party candidate for mayor, then continued on to lecture in Denver, where two of his brothers still lived, and in

Kansas City, where one of Emma's brothers lived. They then crossed over into Canada to visit family in Wingham, Goderich, and other nearby parts of Ontario, where Emma and Stitt had grown up. Always happy to talk about his love for Berkeley, Wilson had brought advertising booklets from the Chamber of Commerce to hand out.[162]

At the Chicago meeting, Wilson was elected as one of the five members of the National Executive Committee, which oversaw the work of the Socialist Party. Also elected were former Congressman Victor Berger; James Maurer, a member of the Pennsylvania legislature and president of the Pennsylvania Federation of Labor; Adolph Germer, an organizer with the United Mineworkers Union from Illinois; and George Goebel, a former national organizer for the party. Wilson was narrowly elected to the fifth spot over Butte, Montana, Mayor Lewis Duncan after several ballots. (Duncan would join Wilson on the Executive Committee the next year.) Following the meeting, Wilson and his wife traveled to New York, where he spoke to the Single Tax Club of Manhattan.[163] The Wilsons then revisited friends and family in Ontario and returned to Berkeley on June 7th, three weeks before Wilson's two-year term as mayor would come to an end.[164]

Wilson spent his last days as mayor preparing his final report and recommendations to the city and trying to support striking workers at the Pacific Gas and Electric Company (PG&E). In late 1912, unions representing employees of PG&E formed the Light and Power Council of California to do joint collective bargaining. PG&E refused to bargain with the council and the workers went on strike in May, a few days after Wilson left Berkeley on his speaking tour. PG&E hired strikebreakers and armed security guards who drove around threatening picketers. Strikers sabotaged power lines. The Light and Power Council effort was severely undercut by a struggle over control of the International Brotherhood of Electrical Workers (IBEW). The California locals had the misfortune to support the losing side in that nationwide conflict, and as a result, were undermined by the national IBEW administration, which expelled the California locals and supplied strikebreakers to PG&E.[165]

On his return to Berkeley, Wilson urged the company to negotiate with the Light and Power Council, demanded that the company meet its contractual obligations to provide power to the city's electric street lights, withdraw armed strikebreakers from the streets, and allow the police to do their jobs in protecting people and property. Wilson and the city council proposed to lower electric rates in Berkeley, based on a study of the company by Professor Corey of the University of California. Over Wilson's strenuous objections, the council majority compromised with PG&E on a modest decrease in rates for a small number of high users of electricity. Wilson reiterated his belief that the city should establish its own electric power plant.[166] A few months after his term as mayor ended, the strike fell apart and the Light and Power Council disbanded.[167]

In his final report, Wilson briefly reviewed the modest accomplishments of the city administration during his past two years as mayor: a municipal incinerator under construction, a municipal ambulance, a municipal bacteriological and chemical laboratory for food safety regulation and public health work, a municipal employment bureau, street improvements, the spotless town campaign and improvements in police, fire, and other municipal buildings and equipment. He expressed pride in having raised the salaries of most city employees. The main part of his report focused on his recommendations for the future, ranging from land value taxation, municipal lighting plant, and municipal market to administrative improvements such as a four-year term for the mayor to match the terms of the council members and an addition to increase the size of the public library. He thanked the citizens of Berkeley, all those he had worked with, socialist and non-socialist, and told them that "I now go forth to what appears to me to be a larger service to my fellowmen."[168]

CHAPTER 11

CAMPAIGNING TAKES ITS TOLL

Suffrage Headquarters, Reno Nevada . . . Cannot possibly
give any other date. Every hour filled.

—J. Stitt Wilson"[1]

For the next seven months, Wilson toured the state of California giving
speeches on behalf of the Socialist Party. After a farewell address as
mayor in the Berkeley High School auditorium on Sunday evening, June
29, 1913, he spoke in San Jose on the following Tuesday, Pacific Grove on
Wednesday, Santa Cruz on Thursday, Paso Robles on Friday, and San Luis
Obispo on Saturday, returning to San Francisco to give his usual Sunday
morning talk at the Scottish Rite Auditorium.[2] Traveling by train and
automobile, he toured throughout California. No town was too small if
local socialist comrades could arrange publicity for a meeting. As the former
mayor of Berkeley, Socialist candidate for governor, and renowned public
speaker, Wilson was a celebrity who drew large crowds even in small towns.

At first, Wilson was assisted by J.S. Cato, state organizer and a former
Baptist minister, but Cato had many other responsibilities that demanded
his time. In August, Rev. Norman Pendleton came to work as Wilson's
organizer and advance man, leaving his position with the Berkeley Municipal Employment Bureau, which would not survive for long under the new
administration. They were joined by Prudence Stokes Brown, the Socialist
Party's women's organizer. (Brown taught the first free public school kindergarten class in the U.S. in 1889 and later went on to study early childhood
education with John Dewey and Maria Montessori.) In November, when
the crusaders reached the town of Selma in Fresno County, they were met
by two socialists with an ingenious campaign contribution. A.M. Salyer, a
piano maker from Los Angeles, and John Coleman, who owned an automobile, had joined forces to build a trailer with a player piano mounted on it.

They drove it through the streets of Selma and other nearby towns, attracting attention to Wilson's upcoming appearances and providing a musical interlude between speeches.[3]

Wilson's usual presentation portrayed socialism as "The New Americanism," or when speaking in a church, he gave his speech, "The Biblical Argument for Socialism." He appealed to the American revolutionary tradition and the radicalism of the abolitionists. "If we will be true to the hungry men of Valley Forge, we will be true today to the hungry men of Los Angeles." He described socialism as industrial democracy, the next step in American ideals and thus true patriotism. "We must take the American flag out of the hands of the plutocracy of America and all their hirelings and retainers. We must take it and hold it as our flag."[4] The state secretary of the Socialist Party credited the Social Crusade with major increases in party membership.

In early September, writer-director Frank E. Wolfe released *From Dusk to Dawn*, a dramatic two-hour silent film in which a deadly industrial accident

J. Stitt Wilson and supporters with car and piano trailer in Selma, CA, November 11, 1913 (left to right: A.M. Salyer at the piano, Martha Salyer of the Socialist Women's Union, J. Stitt Wilson, H. Wells, and Rev. Pendleton) (Photo courtesy of Kent Kanouse, a descendant of A.M. and Martha Salyer).

precipitates a strike, mass protests, and the election of a socialist governor and legislature who pass legislation establishing full employment through a real "right to work" law, all wrapped around a love story. The film included documentary footage shot at strikes, labor parades, Socialist Party picnics, and rallies, and its actors included well-known socialist figures such as Clarence Darrow, Job Harriman, and Wilson, who had a small part. It was released nationally, showing in 28 theaters in Chicago alone.[5] The California Socialist Party purchased a copy and took it to towns around the state where it would not normally have been shown. No copies are known to survive, so we miss out on being able to see, but not hear, several of the great speakers of the time.[6] Wilson had an additional reason to be happy with Hollywood. In October, a new and very successful silent film version of Jack London's novel, *The Sea-Wolf*, was released starring Viola Barry (his daughter's stage name) as Maud Brewster, the female lead.[7] It was the only movie London appeared in; playing a sailor.

Socialism and moralism

Wilson regularly returned to Berkeley to spend a day or two with his family and give his Sunday morning talks in San Francisco. At his September 21st talk, he criticized some of his former allies in the women's suffrage campaign who had now moved on to anti-vice campaigns such as shutting down dance halls.[8] Wilson regarded this as "civic quackery," attacks on symptoms designed to obscure the need for fundamental change. In his address, "The Harlots and the Pharisees: or, the Barbary Coast in a Barbarous Land," Wilson ridiculed those engaged in the current campaign against San Francisco's vice district, the Barbary Coast:

> The order went forth: "The Barbary Coast must go." Shouts of victory! The great task is accomplished—the addresses of some unfortunate women will be changed to some other part of the city—and—over five hundred little sisters—dancing girls—are to be thrown . . . upon the care of the clubwomen of San Francisco.

He called out several of the leaders of the campaign by name, including Rev. Dr. Charles Aked, saying they were simply "making clean the outside of the cup." He pointed out that most prostitutes come from the ranks of the poor and the unemployed, and he recounted in dramatic terms the role of capitalists in holding down women's wages and generating poverty and unemployment. For Wilson, the people engaged in this "clean-up spasm" sustained the problem by supporting a system of exploitation of workers. "At the door of this legalized, church-sanctioned Capitalism I lay the crime of this social rape of woman in the twentieth century."[9]

Rev. Aked was highly offended. He and Wilson had worked together on the suffrage campaign and had mutual friends. Mrs. Philip Snowden, wife of a leading Labour member of Parliament with whom Wilson had worked in England, publicly credited Aked with awakening her social conscience.[10] Aked responded with a widely reprinted newspaper column, describing Wilson's speech as "a sneer in three columns and a rant in the remaining two" and declared himself mystified that Wilson did not support this effort to cleanse the city of "commercialized vice," one of the "crimes of capital— the crime of making profit out of the bodies and souls of women."[11]

The controversy brought a capacity crowd to hear Wilson respond on November 2nd with "Revolutionary Christianity, or the Call of the Christ to the Christian Church." Aked "does not wound me," said Wilson. He reiterated that capitalism was a system for making a profit from destroying bodies and souls and that it would be impossible to eliminate this one particular form of exploitation without the abolition of capitalism itself.[12] Over the years, as new anti-vice campaigns followed the previous ones, Wilson would again argue the necessity of systemic economic change, later making "A Plea for Mary Magdalene."[13]

Hellen Keller, interviewed by Wilson for the *California Social Democrat*, shared his perspective. Already world-famous for overcoming her disabilities to become the first deaf and blind person to graduate from college, she told how she had studied the causes of blindness. She learned that half of the blindness in the U.S. was caused by workplace accidents that would be preventable with proper safety equipment and that much of the rest was caused by diseases that were preventable through good sanitation and a decent standard of living. (Though not included in the published interview, Keller was well aware that the venereal diseases often spread through prostitution were a major cause of blindness.) She talked about having to fight employers "inch by inch, for every safety appliance" and concluded that socialism was the only way to ensure safe workplaces, sanitary conditions, and a decent standard of living for everyone.[14]

The number of unemployed grew substantially that winter, partly the usual effect of the onset of the rainy season but worsened by the economic recession. As the Christmas season approached, Wilson arranged to spend the last three Sundays in December holding Christmas events that would combine socialist rallies with celebrations of true Christianity. Rev. Pendleton, an accomplished singer, put out a call for volunteers for the choir. Wilson sent out a letter to Bay Area ministers denouncing the commercialization of Christmas and asking that they announce his Sunday events. Wilson used the mass meetings to raise funds for food and clothing for the unemployed from the more than 2,000 people who attended each meeting. He was careful to distinguish this from "charity," saying, "Charity is an insult to the working class. We are simply sharing with you what we have, as brothers in a common battle against a common enemy." Working with the San Francisco Socialists, he led repeated marches of several thousand unemployed workers to the city hall to demand both immediate relief and creation of public works jobs and road work to provide employment.[15]

In the new year, 1914, Wilson left for the quarterly National Executive Committee meeting in Chicago, being held January 10–13, then proceeded to Washington, D.C., for the National Single Tax Conference, January 15–17, followed by a speaking tour around the East coast, including New York City, Boston, Philadelphia, and Pittsburg, and then speaking in major cities in the South and Southwest before returning home near the end of January.[16] He told his listeners that with the Democratic Party's surrender to big business under President Woodrow Wilson he expected the workers would now rally to the Socialist Party.[17]

Campaigning for prohibition

That year Wilson focused an increasing amount of his energy on the prohibition of alcoholic beverages. He believed that prohibition was a reform that would help strengthen the workers in the class struggle, not a mere palliative.[18] The prohibition movement in California had begun to take advantage of the potential for citizens' initiatives and Wilson, while serving as mayor of Berkeley, had campaigned for two of them. One, intended to close the saloons in the neighboring town of Albany, failed, and the other, restricting liquor licenses in Modesto, a town in the Central Valley, succeeded.[19] The prohibition movement was largely middle class and well-organized, backed by many Protestant churches. The California Dry Federation reached out to Wilson, as a speaker with proven appeal to working-class voters. Wilson believed in the message, plus he also needed the money he could make giving paid speeches for local ballot measures to close the saloons. Collections at socialist meetings paid expenses, but they hardly made up for his salary as mayor and the contributions made by his Sunday "congregation" that went to replacement speakers when he was touring far outside the Bay Area.

At the end of 1914, a tired Wilson traveled to San Bernardino to speak in favor of a proposed anti-saloon ordinance, then returned home and rested in January and February. His Sunday talks focused on the harm done to the working class by the liquor traffic and the saloon and on the work being done by European socialists to combat them. He urged his audiences to see *John Barleycorn*, the just-released silent film version of Jack London's autobiographical novel about his struggles with alcohol, starring Wilson's daughter, Viola Barry, as Haydee, Jack's first love.[20] Wilson initially planned to take three weeks off, but took an extra week to recover his strength. On February 28th, Wilson returned to touring on behalf of the Socialist Party with a rally at the Temple Auditorium in Los Angeles, followed by daily lectures in different Southern California cities. He also served as the featured speaker at a meeting in Riverside, helping to organize a chapter of California Dry.[21] Two weeks into the renewed speaking tour, he collapsed from physical and nervous exhaustion.

Wilson took several weeks off to recover and for the next several months limited his public speaking to the Bay Area and nearby towns. He later described his recovery process in an uncharacteristically personal Sunday talk on "Human Suffering and Its Amelioration."

> The solution for mental suffering is the most difficult to find, and until one has been stripped of everything, till the heart is broken and pulled apart and you quit stitching to keep it together you will not know the joy of going all to smithereens. Don't stop to stir up, as with a spoon, the mess of complexities in your soul but "leave the poor old stranded wreck and pull for the shore." Once you have got on speaking terms with your soul you have got out of hell. Difficulties will come as before, but you face them with optimism in your soul. Fight pessimism as a devil. Think, talk, act the good. Think good worlds, good civilization, good government, good principles and the abolition of human suffering will be a reality.[22]

As always, Wilson saw his personal suffering as one part of the suffering of all humanity and believed the appropriate response was to get back to work on reducing suffering in the world.

Nearly one hundred local socialist organizations voted to nominate him for governor or senator. He responded in an open letter two months after his collapse, saying that he was feeling better and with more rest he hoped to soon be "ready for the battle" but that he did not have sufficient strength for such a campaign. He also made a vague reference to "other persuasions that I need not recite here."[23]

Emma Wilson was again having serious health problems. She suffered severe pain that made it difficult for her to sleep without drugs administered by a doctor and was bedridden for much of the next two years. The difficulty of the situation was compounded when a person who raised special breeds of roosters rented a flat next door. The crowing kept the Wilsons awake and the neighbor refused to make any accommodation to them. In desperation, Stitt and Emma rented another house in North Berkeley and stayed there for some months until the rooster breeder moved on. Emma's health issues substantially improved after treatment by a chiropractor, Linden McCash, who became a close family friend. A few years later, after having to deal with another tenant who raised chickens, the Wilsons bought the house next door to ensure it was rented to quiet tenants.[24]

Later in March of 1914, just weeks after his collapse, Wilson helped mediate a conflict between the California Dry Federation and the Anti-Saloon League. California Dry had gathered signatures to place prohibition on the statewide ballot in November. As written, the measure would abruptly shut down all production and sale of alcoholic beverages five days after it passed. The more realistic Anti-Saloon League argued that this would doom the measure to defeat because it was clearly unfair to people working in the industry. Three representatives from each group met in San Francisco at the end of March, with Wilson one of the California Dry delegation members. They worked out a compromise in which they agreed to place a second measure on the ballot setting the effective date of the measure fourteen months later, on January 1, 1916.[25] By mid-April, Wilson had recovered enough to do a small tour of three small towns in Northern California—Willows, Lodi, and Red Bluff—where there were anti-saloon measures on the local ballot.[26]

Representing the Socialist Party

Immediately after Wilson finished this speaking tour, he was called on to help the Socialist Party respond to major national and international events. On April 20th, the Colorado National Guard and a mining company's private police opened fire with rifles and a machine gun on a camp where striking miners and their families lived near Ludlow, Colorado. The armed miners fought back but were forced to flee. Company forces burned the camp and murdered the strike leader after he was captured. Two women and eleven children were found dead under one of the burned tents and a total of around twenty miners and family members were killed in what became known as the Ludlow Massacre. Then, the day after the mining camp event, on April 21st, United States Marines seized the port of Veracruz, Mexico, to confiscate a shipload of arms and ammunition purchased by General Huerta, who had made himself dictator of Mexico after murdering the elected president and vice president. The Marines' seizure contributed to the overthrow of Huerta three months later, but the U.S. held the port for an additional four months, creating long-lasting anger in Mexico.

Wilson and the Socialist Party National Executive Committee issued immediate denunciations of the literal class warfare conducted by the mining companies and of the invasion of Mexico. The party supported the Mexican revolutionaries' effort to restore democracy but opposed sending U.S. troops and risking a war. On the evening of Tuesday, May 6th, the Socialist Party sponsored a protest meeting that filled Dreamland Rink in San Francisco with 4,000 people protesting against the Ludlow Massacre and the invasion. The concluding address to the crowd came from Wilson, who followed speeches by a minister, a rabbi, a union official, and Mrs. Cora Older, a noted journalist and novelist.[27]

From May 11th through May 16th, Wilson attended the annual meeting of the national committee of the Socialist Party in Chicago, where he was reelected to another year on the National Executive Committee and won passage of a resolution committing the party to study what to do about the liquor problem. The California branch of the party left it to individual members to determine how they would vote on prohibition and many leading members shared Wilson's point of view. Also speaking in favor of prohibition were Noble Richardson, the candidate for governor that year, and two former Baptist ministers, Rev. Norman Pendleton, the candidate for lieutenant governor, and state organizer J. S. Cato.[28]

After many delays, the proposal for a multicity public water district was scheduled for a vote in Berkeley, Oakland, and the other East Bay cities on June 2nd. In May, while Wilson was at the national committee meeting, proponents of the plan quoted freely from Wilson's previous endorsement. In his statement on leaving the mayor's office, however, he had expressed concern about recent support for the proposal from the People's Water Company, which hoped to sell its lands, reservoirs, and distribution system at an inflated price. Wilson warned that after establishing a public water company the voters would need to elect a slate of directors who would be "champions and guardians of the people's rights" and not "men of capitalistic tendencies." Wilson now retracted his endorsement, saying he was not sufficiently conversant with the current situation.[29]

The measure went down to defeat, capturing just 44% of the vote. There was a very small turnout for this special election and many voters apparently believed that the measure would require purchase of the People's Water Company, rather than simply setting up a special district to determine how best to proceed and then going back to the voters for approval of the bonds necessary to either purchase or build new facilities.[30]

Voter approval of the East Bay Municipal Utility District (EBMUD) would not come until 1923, after which, in 1925, it won approval to build a system that brought water directly from the Sierra rather than purchasing existing water company lands. Public water did not arrive in residents' homes until 1928, when the People's Water Company, now called the East Bay Water Company, capitulated and sold its distribution system to EBMUD.[31] It is doubtful that news reports on Wilson's position made much difference in the result, but if Wilson had continued on as mayor and run an active campaign to get out the vote and elect public-minded board members, he might have brought public water to the East Bay ten years earlier with the Socialist Party receiving much of the credit.

Wilson spent part of June in the state of Washington. The Socialist Party there had split into two competing factions, each claiming to be the legitimate Socialist Party organization.[32] The national committee sent Wilson, Noble Richardson, and Sidney W. Motley, a socialist from Idaho, to re-form the Washington Socialist Party. The state of Washington had established a party primary election system similar to California's, with party candidates and county committees selected by the registered voters of each party. The evolutionary socialists had defeated their revolutionary opponents in the primary elections and thus gained control of the Socialist Party county committees. The revolutionary socialists had a majority among the active membership who attended Socialist Party conventions, however, and expelled their rivals from the party.

Among those expelled was David C. Coates, the populist lieutenant governor of Colorado who had joined the Socialist Party on its founding in 1901. After his term as lieutenant governor he became vice president and then president of the American Labor Union, founded by the Western Federation of Miners, and helped found the Industrial Workers of the World before moving to Spokane in 1906. In 1911 he was elected to the Spokane city council, a nonpartisan office. The revolutionaries decried this as "fusion" and demanded that he submit an undated letter of resignation, which Coates refused to do.[33] These efforts at revolutionary purity undoubtedly repelled Wilson, who had been elected mayor in a nonpartisan election and similarly refused to give the party control over whether he stayed in office or not. The committee spent most of June talking with both sides, wrote a new state party constitution, and then forced the two factions to reunite under threat that the national party would recognize only those who agreed to operate under the new constitution.[34]

At the end of June, Wilson returned to Chicago to speak to the Chicago Methodist Preachers' Association. His speech, "Christianity in Overalls: An Appeal to the Church on Behalf of Socialism," was printed in full as the lead article in a special issue of *The Christian Socialist*.[35] It drew a letter from Professor Walter Rauschenbusch, author of *Christianity and the Social Crisis* and for many years the intellectual leader of the Social Gospel movement, saying he considered "the address by Stitt Wilson one of the best Christian Socialist appeals I have read" and asking that copies of the issue be sent to the entire national membership list of German Baptist preachers and workers (his denomination) at his expense.[36] The speech was one of Wilson's best, recounting his experiences over the twenty-five years since he had begun his studies at Garrett Biblical Institute and drawing from his previous speeches on socialism as applied Christianity. Several critics spoke after him, one of whom compared him to the uncompromising abolitionist, William Lloyd Garrison. Wilson responded that, like Garrison, he called on the church to repent of its complicity in a sinful system. Ever the optimist, he concluded that "I suppose I must give you another twenty-five years to understand . . . and by that time Socialism will have swept on and over you; and the capitalist system for which you apologize will have vanished from the earth."[37]

Against the war

August 1914 was a difficult month for socialists in America and around the world. As the nations of Europe entered a war that all socialist parties opposed, the parties had to make a choice. They could oppose the war, call for strikes, and likely be outlawed and repudiated by their affiliated unions, or they could join in and hope that in the elections after the war their patriotism would be rewarded with control of their national governments. They invariably chose the latter. In the case of France, many thought the personal popularity of the militantly anti-war socialist leader Jean Jaures was such that he might swing the party into opposition, but he was assassinated by a right-wing nationalist.

To his Sunday congregations, Wilson poured out his anger and disgust with the war, with the ruling class that chose war, with the churches who supported that ruling class, with America's willingness to profit from armament sales, and with the capitalist system that led to the war.[38]

> World-tragedy in the name of God is in progress. The working classes of Europe, saturated by lies, instructed in false patriotism, made moral eunuchs by false religion, all are now led to the most colossal wholesale slaughter of each other that the world has ever known. Rivers run red with blood, hell drops from the heavens and hell rises out of the seas, the wounded cry out under the stench of the decaying

> dead and God is at the head of the columns, according to
> all the prayers.

Socialists in Berkeley and San Francisco held demonstrations in favor of peace, with Wilson as a featured speaker, but there was little they could do to influence events in Europe.[39] In September the National Executive Committee issued a call for representatives of all socialist parties to attend a World Peace Conference to try to bring the war to an end.[40] It was a hopeless gesture. In the coming months, the Socialist Party's energy would increasingly go into keeping America out of the war.

Also in September Wilson began active campaigning on behalf of the California Dry initiative which, unlike the Socialist Party, could pay him for his work. Initially he spoke several times a week, staying mostly in and around the Bay Area. In October he increased his pace, campaigning along with Norman Pendleton for the Socialist Party ticket as well as for California Dry.[41] When speaking in the Bay Area he was often accompanied by his son, Gladstone.[42] Now twenty-one and a frequent leading man in collegiate dramas, Gladstone was no longer limited to being the driver or handling out leaflets. In April he had spoken on "Socialism and Youth" to the Young People's Socialist League of San Francisco along with Sun Fo, a fellow UC Berkeley student and the son of Dr. Sun Yat-sen, founding president of the new Republic of China.[43] Gladstone also served as an occasional warm-up speaker for his father and substituted for his father as a speaker when a scheduling conflict prevented the senior Wilson from addressing a Dry rally in Santa Cruz.[44]

The campaigns Wilson supported did not fare well on Election Day. California Dry received only 40% of the vote. Wilson had continued to serve as vice president of the California League for Home Rule in Taxation, largely as a symbol of Socialist support. The state legislature, impressed by the 1912 effort, placed a similar measure on the November 1914 ballot, saving the campaign the task of gathering signatures. It failed again, this time garnering 42% of the vote, just 1% higher than before.[45] A Socialist Party initiative to institute the eight-hour day received only 34% of the vote. Noble Richardson received 50,716 votes for governor, nearly 3,000 more than Wilson in 1910, but with women now voting and a larger state population, this was only 5.4% of the vote compared with Wilson's 12.4%. A rare bright spot, in Los Angeles, George W. Downing was the first Socialist elected to the California State Assembly.

As governor, Hiram Johnson and his progressive majority in the legislature established a railroad commission and then extended their regulatory powers to public utilities more generally. They passed legislation establishing a worker's compensation system for injured workers; set up a commission to regulate the wages, hours of work, and working conditions of women and children; set a minimum wage for work done under contract with the state; and passed a number of other labor reforms. Johnson's support for social insurance and regulation did not extend to support for unions. His opposition defeated legislation to reduce the use of injunctions to ban peaceful picketing, boycotts, and strikes. Nonetheless, his record was sufficient to persuade a substantial number of people who had previously voted Socialist to support him and other "reform" candidates.[46]

With the elections over, Wilson turned his attention back to the war in Europe. The war had mixed effects on working-class Americans. With millions of European workers and farmers now serving in their country's armies, imports from the U.S. rose and unemployment was down. The price of food rose, however, as an increasing amount went to European combatants. Wilson and the Socialists denounced increased food prices and called on the U.S. government to ensure that Americans were fed before food was exported.

But Wilson wanted people to understand the deeper roots of war. At the beginning of 1915 he presented a series of speeches on "Who Shall Be the Master of the World."[47] He explained that within the current world social and economic order, war was understandable and inevitable. One part of his argument was the standard socialist view that war was caused by competition for markets, another part drew on Homer Lea's national-ethnic competition theories, and yet another part drew on Charlotte Perkins Gilman's critique of masculine dominance. Gilman's book, *The Man-Made World; or, Our Androcentric Culture* (1911), argued that "in warfare per se we find maleness in its absurdist extremes" and called for an end to "the present androcracy or rule of the world by men." Homer Lea was a Stanford-educated adventurer and supporter of Sun Yat-sen who became an officer in a revolutionary army fighting to overthrow the emperor of China. Lea described international relations as a competition among the "Saxon" British Empire, the "Teutons" of Imperial Germany, the "Slavs" of Imperial Russia, and the Japanese empire. He predicted that Japan, which had recently taken over Korea and held a sphere of influence in China, would eventually capture Hawaii and the Philippines and invade the U.S.[48] On the West Coast, people often argued for staying out of the European war in order to be prepared for a Japanese invasion, although Wilson did not make that argument in his presentations.

In this series of presentations, Wilson concluded that drastic social changes were necessary to ensure world peace. Well-meaning calls for universal disarmament would fail, given the deep roots of conflict. He said, "It is not our acknowledged wickedness alone that makes war. It is our accepted and imaginary goodness and excellences, our settled and accepted arrangements." He called for a society that did not simply give women equal rights but fully integrated them and the maternal ethic of care into every aspect of society, and for a socialist economy to remove the profit motive for war.[49] Wilson's speeches earned him an invitation from Jane Addams to speak at a national Emergency Peace Conference convening in Chicago at the end of February, but he decided not to go.[50] He was, once again, running for mayor of Berkeley.

Running for mayor a second time

Wilson described his decision to run for mayor as "a party matter and not an individual preference."[51] His friend, Herman Stern, told him that he would not run for reelection to the school board unless Wilson would lead the Socialist slate, plus, a petition signed by 1,200 citizens, including Socialists and non-socialists, asked him to run. On February 15th, the Socialist Party nominating convention chose him as their candidate.[52] The Socialist candidates for city council were John Wilson, running for reelection, and Stitt Wilson's close associate, Norman Pendleton. The school board candidates were Herman Stern, running for reelection, and Mrs. Helen Vail Wallace, both a teacher and a trainer for teachers.[53] The party platform was similar to those in the previous two municipal elections, calling for municipal and regional ownership of utilities and transportation, aid to the unemployed, fair taxation, and efficient administration.[54]

The campaign was similar to those of previous years, with house and street corner meetings around the city and mass meetings, mostly held in the Berkeley High School auditorium. Wilson was opposed by Mayor Charles D. Heywood, who had succeeded him as mayor in 1913, and Samuel C. Irving, the wealthy owner of a paint and roofing materials manufacturing business and president of the Chamber of Commerce. Wilson's opponents criticized the Socialists for bringing partisanship into nonpartisan local elections and described themselves as practical men who would use their business experience to ensure efficient government. Wilson argued that as mayor he had demonstrated that he could run an efficient administration and that public ownership of utilities would cost less over the long run than private ownership.[55] There was extensive argument over whether the municipal incinerator built under Wilson's administration had been a good idea or not.[56]

Mayor Heywood ran a very restrained campaign, arguing that he had made steady improvements in city services, run an efficient administration, and would continue to do so if returned to office. Irving described himself as a practical man whose business made millions. He claimed that Berkeley should both improve its public services and lower its taxes in order to attract people of high social and financial status and bring in more industry. He blamed the two previous mayors for the current inadequacies, yet avoided the issue of how he would pay for the improved lighting, streets, and sewer system that he promised to provide. Heywood, Irving falsely claimed, had reduced the number of polling places, making it harder to vote. He described Wilson and the Socialists in city government as impractical "dreamers" who attracted the "failures, faddists and fakirs who are too lazy to work but are not too proud to feed at the expense of the industrious." Wilson, Irving falsely claimed, "favored (women's) suffrage only when the tide of public opinion made suffrage inevitable."[57]

Wilson replied:

> Yes, Mr. Irving, I am a dreamer. . . . I dream of a city called Berkeley where the unemployed will not wander the streets like vagabond dogs . . . I dream of a Berkeley where the people shall own all their own public utilities. . . . Take the dreamers out of this world and you have a madhouse of selfish interests . . . without a vision, the people perish. Truth, Justice and the good must be demonstrated in our practical civic affairs and they cannot be unless held up as social ideals.[58]

The Socialists distributed a tongue-in-cheek campaign newsletter with the heading, "Public Warning to the Citizens of Berkeley: Beware of the Socialists," describing their "nefarious purposes" of "Economic Justice and Human Brotherhood" and recounting "misfortunes that befell our beloved city" under the Wilson administration, such as paving the streets of West Berkeley and passing bonds for a new sewer system. They also took out a full-page advertisement in the *Berkeley Daily Gazette*, quoting press statements favorable to Wilson's work as mayor and describing the high qualifications of the Socialist candidates.[59]

In the April 3rd primary election, Irving received 4,424 votes and Wilson 3,526; Mayor Heywood, with 2,945 votes, was eliminated from the race. Wilson's 32% of the mayoral vote was much better than Philo Phelps's 20% in 1913, but far from his outright victory in 1911. Socialist Adolphus F. Eddy, an accountant running for city auditor for the second time, also received 32% of the vote, coming in second, but the incumbent received a clear majority and was elected on the first round. In the ten-person race for the two city council seats, John Wilson came in third, only two votes behind the second-place finisher, and moved on to the runoff election, while Norman Pendleton came in fifth and was eliminated. Together they received 26% of the council votes, better than the Socialist candidates in 1913 and comparable to the 1911 result. Herman Stern came in fourth in the six-person race for the school board, moving on to the runoff election, with Helen Wallace coming in fifth, thus out of the running. Together the Socialist candidates received 35% of the school board votes, about the same as the comrades received in 1911 and 1913. The total Socialist Party vote was higher than ever, but so were the Berkeley population and the number of registered voters.

A few days later, on April 9th, Wilson was a featured speaker at the World's Social Progress Congress, a three-day-long event convened by the Federal Council of the Churches of Christ and held as part of the Panama-Pacific International Exposition.[60] Two years earlier Wilson had talked about his plans to create a Temple of Socialism for the Exposition. He settled for serving on the planning committee for the Social Progress Congress and giving a speech on "The Minimum Program of a Militant Christianity," once again making the case for socialism as applied Christianity.[61] After the speech, he quickly returned to the campaign.

The runoff election

Going into the runoff election, the odds were clearly against Wilson and the Socialists. They had a solid base of support from one-third of the electorate, but a path to victory depended on picking up another 15–20%. In 1911 there was an active "progressive" movement starting to emerge within the Republican Party, with its voters searching for alternatives and even willing to vote for "constructive" socialists. The Progressive Party, founded in 1912, had now gained control of the state government. It had strengthened the power of the state to regulate the railroads and local, privately owned utilities in the public interest, and for many progressives, public ownership was not necessary now that there was effective regulation. After the initial burst of reform legislation in Johnson's first term, the Progressive Party seemed largely out of ideas beyond honest government, independent of "the interests," which for them generally included labor as well as the large corporations. In 1915 the Progressives were beginning to drift back toward the Republican Party from whence they mostly came.

Friend Richardson, now a registered Progressive, was elected state treasurer in 1914, having won the Progressive, Republican, and Democratic Party nominations in the primaries. He was still publisher of the *Berkeley*

Daily Gazette, which provided full and fair coverage of the local election, but he was becoming more concerned with economy in government than with reform, and the *Gazette* did not provide support for Wilson as it had done in 1911.[62] Mayor Heywood endorsed Irving, urging unity against the Socialists.

Faced with a man Wilson considered a "capitalist millionaire reactionary," he continued to portray himself not only as a practical reformer but as the candidate who would prevent banks and utility and transportation companies from using municipal government for their own enrichment.[63] In a speech given to members of two fraternities, he said, "I am a Socialist. I stand for a conservative, constructive application of the principle of socialization in our municipal life. . . . I propose to take immediate steps to organize a public utilities district of the east bay cities and thus to proceed to acquire our water, light, power and transportation systems . . . and to safeguard the people's interests against the sinister encroachments of the corporations and their stockholders."[64] He denounced Irving as a tool of the banking and utility companies who had "deluged" the city with money in support of Irving.

Wilson's attack struck a nerve with Irving, who announced that "if J. Stitt Wilson can prove any of these slanderous charges against me to a committee of Judge Waste, Friend Richardson and Mayor Charles D. Heywood, I will withdraw from the mayoralty and forfeit one thousand dollars to public charity. If he cannot I call upon him to be a man and apologize."[65] Wilson happily accepted the challenge and invited Irving to join him at a public meeting at the Berkeley High School auditorium for the evening of April 15th. At this meeting, he announced, 100 seats would be placed on the stage, reserved for representatives of Berkeley's major banks, utilities, and transportation and real estate companies and he would ask them for their endorsement of his candidacy. If they endorsed him, he would apologize, since that would demonstrate that he was wrong in connecting them with Irving. If they failed to endorse him, then since all of these companies were known to be politically active, that would demonstrate that they are in fact supporting his opponent. In that case, he challenged Irving to follow through on his promises, provide a check for $1,000 to the City's Charity Commission, and withdraw from the race.[66]

All three of the people Irving proposed for the committee to review the evidence replied that they had not been asked beforehand and declined to be involved in any way. Irving declined to attend, and none of the companies sent representatives. Several replied that while they promoted their interests as companies doing business with or in the city, they did not get involved in campaigns for specific candidates.[67] On the evening of April

15th, the auditorium was filled to the point where police had to turn people away half an hour before the 7:30 p.m. start of the meeting. In addition to close to 3,000 people inside, there were hundreds more waiting outside, hoping to be able to hear the proceedings. Irving's campaign manager and a number of supporters were present in the audience.

The audience saw a stage with three rows of chairs, divided into sections labeled by company (Key Route, People's Water Company, etc.). Over the next three hours, Wilson provided evidence for his charges. He filled the empty seats with placards showing the names of prominent Irving supporters and detailed their connections to the various banks, utilities, and transportation companies. He showed that all three non-socialist candidates for city council were closely tied to local banks, one being a bank vice president. He reviewed the revenues that the local utilities and transit companies took out of Berkeley, pointing out that their annual revenue was more than five times that of the City of Berkeley, and reviewed the rising values those companies claimed and pointed out that they paid taxes based on much lower revenues and values. He reviewed the Socialist platform of public ownership of utilities and fair taxation. He pointed out that Irving the candidate described Berkeley's taxes as high, but Irving, the Chamber of Commerce president, had described them as low. He mentioned that the people who wanted to open Berkeley to the sale of liquor were backing Irving as well.[68]

Near the end, Wilson's well-structured presentation fell apart. Wilson announced that he had a sworn statement from a person who had heard Irving's campaign manager, Mansell Griffiths, say that he had $5,000 from the Key Route transit company to use for Irving's campaign. Griffiths shouted that it was a lie and he and a number of others demanded to know who made the claim. Wilson said that he had promised to keep the name confidential. Amid uproar and shouting, Herman Stern took center stage and stated that he felt Wilson had made a mistake in making such an announcement without being in a position to give the name of the person behind it but that Wilson needed to stick to his promise. Stern promised to do his best to make the name public and waved for Griffiths to come up to the stage. Norman Pendleton, thinking Griffiths was climbing onto the stage to attack Wilson, pushed him back. Eventually the situation was sorted out, Pendleton apologized to Griffiths, and Wilson brought the meeting to an unsatisfactory end with an appeal for the voters to weigh the issues carefully.[69] John Altman, the author of the statement, a student at the University of California law school, and president of the University Students Stitt Wilson Club, came forward the next day and he and Griffiths traded inconclusive charges.[70] Wilson followed up with a series of street meetings at which he gave shorter versions of his demonstration and described the opposition as "the bankers' ticket." The Socialists distributed the 1915 version of their campaign newspaper, *The City for the People*, putting much of Wilson's speech into print.[71]

On Election Day, April 24th, Wilson was soundly defeated, receiving only 38% of the vote. His total vote count of 4,487 was nearly 1,000 votes higher than on April 3rd, but Irving's total of 7,412 was nearly 3,000 votes higher. Wilson had narrowly won the flatlands of Berkeley west of Shattuck Avenue, but Irving had won the hills and campus area by a wide margin.[72] John Wilson came in third out of four council candidates, with 4,471 votes, and lost his council seat. Herman Stern also lost, coming in fourth out of four school board candidates, although his 4,737 votes were the best among the three Socialists. School board member Elvina Beals, whose term ran until 1917, was the sole remaining Socialist-elected official in Berkeley. Conservative to moderate Republicans would control Berkeley's city government for the next fifty years. Wilson and Stern pointed to the increase in votes for the Socialist ticket over 1913 as a reason for optimism.

Campaigning for women's suffrage and prohibition

In order to campaign for mayor, Wilson had to give up most of his income from public speaking, as any collections went into the Socialist Party campaign fund. With the campaign over, Wilson returned to giving his Sunday socialist sermons in San Francisco. Over the coming months, he would also speak to socialist, labor, church, temperance, and suffrage organizations on socialism as applied Christianity, the need to reconstruct civilization on a new basis after the end of the war in Europe, prohibition of alcoholic beverages, women's suffrage, and a variety of other topics. The women's suffrage and prohibition organizations received increasing amounts of his time, perhaps because they could pay him for his work on their behalf and they were winnable reforms. It may be that his Sunday socialist meetings were declining along with the Socialist Party membership and were not bringing in an income sufficient to support Wilson and his family.

In early May Wilson headed off to Chicago for the annual meeting of the Socialist Party National Committee, where he, Carl Thompson, and the three other members presented the report of the committee on the liquor problem. The report strongly criticized the effects of alcoholism on the working class but recognized that remedies such as restrictions on sale and full prohibition were controversial within the party and concluded that the party should take no position without more extensive discussion and debate in order to preserve party unity. With no established party position, Wilson was free to continue to campaign for restrictions and for full prohibition. At the beginning of June, he was a prominent speaker at the convention of the California Dry Federation, which began a new prohibition campaign aimed at the November 1916 ballot.[73]

In June and July Wilson spoke in Los Angeles and San Diego on the Christian argument for socialism. Several times, the crowd was too large for everyone to fit in the hall and the overflow was addressed by Gladstone Wilson, who had cast his first vote for his father just two months previously.[74] Speaking in Los Angeles provided the senior Wilson with a welcome opportunity to visit his daughter, Viola, son-in-law Jack Conway, and his first granddaughter, Rosemary Conway.

In late May, a national conference on child labor was held during the Panama-Pacific International Exposition with Wilson's friend, Edwin Markham, as a featured speaker. Markham was the celebrated author of the poem, "The Man with the Hoe," as well as a book on child labor, *Children in Bondage*. Markham visited Wilson in Berkeley a few days before the conference and presented him with a signed copy of his new volume, *The Shoes of Happiness and Other Poems*, inscribed "To Stitt Wilson, one of the consecrated, a friend of humanity," and accompanied by an excerpt from one of his earlier poems.

> *There is a destiny that makes us brothers:*
> *None goes his way alone:*
> *All that we send into the lives of others*
> *Comes back into our own.*[75]

In August Wilson spoke again at the Exposition, giving a speech on "The Liquor Problem" to the state WCTU's Annual Congress of Reforms and another speech on land value taxation to the annual Fels Single Tax Conference.[76] At the Exposition, he, his wife, and daughter Violette all attended and graduated from Dr. Maria Montessori's Third International Training Course, a series of twelve lectures on her educational methods.[77]

In mid-September he was one of two men among the featured speakers at a national Woman Voters Conference, also held at the Exposition, and focused on passing a women's suffrage amendment to the constitution.[78] Wilson's speech evidently made a strong impression on the delegates from New York, which had a women's suffrage measure on the ballot in November 1915, and they hired him to come to New York and speak on behalf of their campaign. Wilson traveled throughout New York State, starting in Rochester and continuing on to Syracuse, Schenectady, and many smaller cities upstate, speaking at factories to workers on their noon lunch breaks and in the evening at rallies.[79] As in California, his speeches emphasized human rights and justice for all, as well as reports on the success of woman voters in helping reduce corruption in politics.[80] After two weeks of barnstorming these cities and many smaller towns, he spent the last ten days of the campaign in New York City, speaking in halls and parks. On Election Day, Tuesday, November 2, 1915, unfortunately the women's suffrage measure failed.[81]

Wilson stayed in New York City a few more days to be the featured speaker at a fundraiser for the *New York Call*, one of only two daily socialist newspapers in the nation.[82] He returned to Berkeley via Chicago, where he had the opportunity to talk about rebuilding civilization after the war.[83] The Wilsons rented a house in Los Angeles for the next several months, leaving Gladstone and Violette in Berkeley, where they were both attending the University of California. Wilson rented a large hall on Sundays and gave well-attended speeches on topics such as "The Moral and Spiritual Needs of Our World" and "Jesus Christ and the Property Devil," with additional talks at the Labor Temple, the University of Southern California, the YMCA, and wherever else he could secure an invitation.[84]

He continued to pay the bills with prohibition work. In February of 1916, he spent a week in Bakersfield, then a town of about 15,000 people and located 100 miles north of Los Angeles in the Central Valley, where he was the featured speaker in support of a ballot measure to ban saloons. The *Bakersfield Morning Echo* gave his five speeches front-page coverage the entire final week of the campaign.[85] This was one of the rare occasions when Wilson took a position opposed by labor. The Bakersfield Labor Council argued that several hundred people would lose their jobs if the prohibition measure passed and that taxes on homeowners would increase with the loss of liquor tax revenue.[86] The measure went down to defeat.[87]

Leaving the Socialist Party

Once back in California, Wilson reconsidered his role in the Socialist Party. His two years of membership in the five-person National Executive Committee of the Socialist Party had ended. Selection of NEC members for 1916 was done by a referendum vote of the membership rather than by a vote of the committee and Wilson came in ninth.[88] For the past six years, he had worked to strengthen the Socialist Party in California with a practical, issue-oriented approach, trying to persuade unions, the women's suffrage movement, proponents of land value taxation, and proponents of municipal ownership of utilities to unite in support of the Socialist Party. He had driven himself to exhaustion and helped the California Party reach its highest point in membership and votes. Now workers were leaving the

Socialist Party and the women of California, having won the vote, were no more supportive of socialism than the men. Socialist Party membership in California had reached its high point in March of 1914 at 8,275 and declined precipitously over the next year-and-a-half to only 2,508 in October of 2015.[89] Wilson's hopes for a powerful California alliance between unions and the Socialist Party had gone down to defeat with the failure of Job Harriman's mayoral campaigns. Meanwhile, the socialist parties of Europe joined in their countries' mobilization for what became an increasingly bloody and seemingly endless war.

In January 1916, Wilson wrote "A Letter to the Comrades," published in the *California Social Democrat*. In it, Wilson explained that he had undergone "a deep self-examination in the presence of world-tragedy" and concluded that he must leave the Socialist Party and try another path.

> The social and economic emancipation of the working classes and the abolition of capitalism cannot be achieved without a great and overwhelming Spiritual Awakening, a far-reaching Revival of Pure and Undefiled Religion, a mighty Moral Transformation of the people. . . .
>
> This kind of work cannot be done on the Socialist platform or through the Socialist literature or press. This task involves the proclamation of the purest quality of Spiritual Gospel that the modern soul of man can conceive . . . It will involve the creation of new groups and associations of those who seek to dedicate their lives to this supreme task of holy living and social emancipation. Such work will require a new approach . . . different from the usual Socialist approach. It cannot be done without great love, great tenderness and superb spiritual constructiveness of thought and action.
>
> And I feel, too, that these convictions are so deep and irresistible and unescapable in me, that I conclude they are . . . part of a great universal influence of Divine Light . . .[90]

Wilson believed that creation of a peaceful, comradely, and egalitarian society would require broad public support for a thorough social reconstruction that would end both capitalism and male supremacy. The Socialist Party and the international socialist movement, to which he had dedicated his energies and in which he had placed his hopes, had not risen to the demands of the times. Faced with this, he withdrew from the Socialist Party, although so quietly that few people noticed, especially since he remained registered to vote as a Socialist and continued to work closely with Socialist Party members.[91] He returned to the evangelical aspirations he had brought to his original Social Crusade, but with no apparent idea of what the "new approach" would be or how to create the "new groups and associations" that he hoped for.

A girl of the new type

In March, the Wilsons, still living in Los Angeles, received an unexpected visit from their daughter, Violette. Violette was strongly influenced by the bohemian Berkeley milieu in which the Wilson family lived, where the arts, theater, literature, mysticism, and spiritualism mixed with women's equality and socialism.[92] She had graduated with honors from Berkeley High School in December 1914, giving one of the commencement addresses.[93] Taking several months off before starting school again, she received national publicity for protesting local laws against wearing "clothes of the opposite sex." Since the laws made an exception for "riding pants," she rode her horse

Wilson's daughter, Violette, in riding pants, May 1915 (unattributed newspaper photograph, author's collection.)

around town and on the university campus wearing "a khaki riding habit of closely fitting knickerbockers and puttees."[94]

At the end of August 1915, she entered the University of California, but left the University in mid-March, saying it was stifling her individuality and her ability to write. Rather than being a separate activity, she said, learning should be integrated with the rest of life and bring intellectual, emotional, and physical freedom. Dramatizing her departure, she had a friend take pictures as she left the family home through a large window and got into an automobile. She arranged to have the pictures given to local newspapers along with a written statement on "Education Versus the Soul," then left to join her family in Los Angeles.[95]

The story of the daughter of the Socialist mayor who dropped out of college to "develop her own soul" drew press coverage nationwide.[96] Her father supported her, telling the press, "Violette . . . is a girl of the new type . . . She has rebelled and her mother and I are heartily in sympathy with her."[97] Violette added to the publicity with a press interview the next day in Los Angeles in which she stated that "marriage as we know it today is a terrible mistake! . . . The vast majority of men, especially business men, want a pretty little plaything for a wife. The sweet things . . . have no intellectual interests in common with their husbands. They are toys—pets!"[98] The "toy wives" story was irresistible to the press and reprinted around the country. Violette and her father arranged to give a joint presentation of their views on education at Blanchard Hall on Broadway in Los Angeles, where Wilson was a frequent speaker.[99]

Violette drew additional publicity three weeks later when she announced that she had found her soul in dance, where "the body beautiful, half hidden by the costume, breathes vigor, beauty and strength from nature . . . unhampered by man-made conventions."[100] She returned to Berkeley to present a set of four dance-dramas she had written, one a fairy tale, the second in Greek mythology, the third among primitive cave dwellers, and the last in a mythic India. She arranged to perform them as a benefit for the Berkeley Free Dispensary, which provided medical care to the poor, staging them on the lawn of Highland Home, arranged as an amphitheater with seating for 500 spectators. The event drew a full house. Violette danced as the leading lady in each drama, and Gladstone, now a senior at the university, was the leading man. Twenty of their friends and classmates, many veterans of college dramatics, filled out the cast, provided professional lighting effects for the evening performance, and prepared elaborate costumes. The musical score was by a local orchestra.[101] The *Berkeley Daily Gazette* described a scene of combat between two cavemen played by Gladstone and Thornton Wilder as "fiercely realistic."[102] A news photograph shows Gladstone,

Violette and William Gladstone Wilson in
Prisoner of Ranee, May 26, 1916 (unattributed
newspaper photograph, author's collection).

wearing a turban and short tunic, embracing Violette, wearing a feathered
headdress and diaphanous gown in *Prisoner of Ranee*.

Her celebrity continued with interviews and pictures of the "University
Rebel" in Sunday supplements in the newspapers of San Francisco, Oakland, San Diego, and Seattle among others.[103] Returning to Los Angeles
to visit her sister, Viola, Violette won a position as a leading lady in the
newly formed "Little Theater," which opened in mid-October of 1916. At
years' end, on Sunday, December 31, 1916, the young woman who had been
so dismissive of matrimony just a few months earlier married her leading

Violette as the "University Rebel," June 1916 (unattributed
newspaper photograph, author's collection).

man, Irving Pichel, at the wedding chapel of the Mission Inn in Riverside,
California.[104]

Searching for a path forward amid losing campaigns

After leaving the Socialist Party, Wilson continued campaigning for reforms
he had always supported—women's suffrage, prohibition, land value taxation, and world peace—but with little success, and it was unclear how
any of this was building toward the grand moral and spiritual revival he
believed was necessary. While Violette was turning Highland Home into a
theater, her father was campaigning for women's suffrage in Iowa. His work
in New York State had made a strong impression and the National Woman's
Suffrage Association brought him to Iowa for the five weeks before the June
6th election.[105] Wilson canvassed the state with his characteristic energy,

traveling by train and automobile to cities and small towns, but once again he was on the losing side.

Wilson returned to Berkeley and, after a brief rest, launched into full-time campaigning on behalf of the California Dry Federation, which put him on salary through the election.[106] Accompanied by Gladstone, he spent late June and the month of July touring Northern California, taking turns driving and speaking at up to five meetings a day, with Gladstone serving as the warm-up speaker.[107] Wilson denied claims that drink was the cause of poverty, arguing instead that "the liquor traffic" took what little remained to the poor, demoralized workers, and destroyed families. He moved on to Southern California in September and early October, and then to the Central Valley while Gladstone returned to Berkeley, speaking at meetings in Alameda and Contra Costa Counties and helping to fill in for his father at the Sunday socialist sermon in San Francisco.[108] In the last weeks of the campaign, Wilson returned to speak in Bay Area and Sacramento area cities, but Election Day on November 7th showed that, once again, he had worked on a losing campaign.

President Woodrow Wilson successfully campaigned for reelection on his record of keeping the U.S. out of the war. Eugene Debs refused to run for president again and the Socialist nomination was won by Allan Benson, a virtual unknown until he wrote a popular series of anti-war, anti-preparedness articles in the socialist press. He received only 3% of the vote. In the privacy of the voting booth, Wilson likely voted for Woodrow Wilson although he did publicly endorse the Socialist candidate for State Assembly from Berkeley. Two weeks later, on November 22, 1916, Jack London died at the age of 40 at his spread in Glen Ellen. The next day his family and a small group from the Ruskin Club, including the poet George Sterling and Stitt and Ben Wilson, held a cremation ceremony in Oakland, after which his ashes were buried on his ranch.[109]

Wilson joined a local branch of the American Neutral Conference Committee, a group that hoped to persuade President Wilson to convene a conference of neutral nations to mediate an end to the war. The committee had broad support, ranging from the Alameda County Central Labor Council and Building Trades Council to leading businessmen including Berkeley Mayor Samuel Irving.[110] On December 12, 1916, and again on January 25, 1917, Wilson spoke to the Women's Peace Party, which supported a similar plan to end the war.[111] These appear to be his last public statements against U.S. participation in the war.

In December 1916, Wilson started another effort at unifying the single tax movement in California. After the local option measure to allow cities to choose land value taxation failed to pass in 1914, the single tax movement had split into two wings, one favoring local option and the other favoring an immediate change to a land value tax. The group supporting an immediate land value tax were led by Luke North, who argued that a Land Taxation ballot measure would generate far more public enthusiasm than a modest technical reform like local option and urged supporters to join what he called the Great Adventure. Early in 1916, Wilson had convened meetings to try to find a compromise, but instead each group gathered signatures for the November 1916 ballot. Land taxation drew the financial support of the Fels Fund and most of the single tax movement volunteer signature gatherers and qualified for the ballot.[112] (The land taxation measure did allow use of income and inheritance taxes to fund "old age pensions, mothers' endowments, and workingmen's dis-employment and disability insurance," a compromise necessary to win support from labor and the Socialist Party.) In November 1916, the land taxation initiative failed, with support from only 31% of the voters. Although this was a loss of votes compared with the local option's 42%, it was the best statewide showing ever made by a measure that would directly institute land value taxation. It made Great Adventure leader, "Luke North," the pen name of James H. Griffes, famous throughout the single tax movement.[113]

In December 1916 and January 1917, Wilson again brought together representatives of the different California single tax organizations to try to gain agreement on a 1918 ballot measure. Those present agreed on a measure that would switch city and county governments entirely to land value taxation, while leaving the state to be funded through the inheritance tax and the gross receipts tax on railroads, utilities, and financial corporations. The unions, socialists, and progressives who supported land value taxation were unwilling to abandon the corporation tax, passed by the voters in 1910. They argued that within the framework of Henry George's analysis it was appropriate to tax railroads and utilities until they were brought under public ownership, since as natural monopolies they would extract monopoly rents from the public. At the conference, the new Equity Tax League of California was formed, with Wilson as chair and campaign manager.[114]

Luke North refused to attend the January 1917 conference or to support the equity tax measure. He proposed a measure that would shift all forms of government in California to land value taxation and eliminate all other state and local taxes. In language that mirrored the revolutionary critique of the evolutionary socialists, North argued that "single tax is not an evolutionary drift, but the Bed Rock of Freedom" and characterized Wilson and the Equity Tax League as "designing politicians and job hunters."[115] North appealed for support from the California and nationwide single tax movement and once again the volunteers and financial contributors turned out for the more comprehensive single tax measure. Wilson and other leaders in the Equity Tax League lobbied the legislature to place their measure on the ballot but in April the measure failed to get out of committee and toward the end of 1917 the Equity Tax League collapsed.[116]

In November 1918, the Great Adventure ballot measure received 24% of the vote. After North's death in 1919, his supporters continued to gather signatures to place identical measures on the ballot. In 1920 it received 25% of the vote, and in 1922 it received 19% of the vote, after which the Great Adventure no longer had enough support to get on the ballot. Wilson had only minor involvement in the single tax movement after the failure of the Equity Tax League effort. In 1934 he would join an advisory committee regarding a proposed single tax initiative campaign, an effort that culminated in 1938 when the final initiative measure for land value taxation appeared on the California ballot and received just 17% of the vote.[117]

CHAPTER 12

MAKING AMERICA SAFE FOR DEMOCRACY

On February 7, 1917, Wilson announced his candidacy for mayor of Berkeley as an independent, making public his year-old break with the Socialist Party. Wilson is often listed among those who left the Socialist Party to support the war effort, but this is a misunderstanding of the timing of his changing views on the party and on the war.[1] After he left the party in 1916, he continued to work closely with it, particularly in opposition to preparedness and American entry into the war. It was only after the U.S. declaration of war on April 6th that he declared his support for the war effort, two months after beginning his campaign for mayor.

In his mayoral campaign announcement, Wilson called for public ownership of utilities, economy in spending, fair taxation, and civility. The incumbent, Mayor Samuel Irving, had promised to bring "business" methods to the running of the city. As mayor he acted as if he owned the city government, showing no tolerance for differences of opinion. In his annual report as mayor, Irving described people who disagreed with his policies as "mental cripples, human failures and disgruntled politicians" and described criticism of his policies as the "howl of a coyote."[2] Wilson denounced Irving and his city council allies as "arbitrary," "extravagant," and "ruthlessly autocratic." He promised open, respectful government and supported amendments to the city charter to provide easier citizen access to the recall, initiative, and referendum.[3]

In addition to Wilson and Mayor Samuel Irving, two other candidates entered the race. Charles Spear was a partner in the Berkeley Building Company and a leader in local Republican politics who had run for mayor unsuccessfully in 1909 and 1913 and supported Wilson in 1911.[4] The

Socialist Party ran publisher Herbert Coggins for mayor and school board member Elvina Beals for city council, the first woman to run for that office.[5]

During his campaign, Wilson pointed out that the cost of food and other necessities was rising due to the war and that it was essential for government to keep its costs down. He reminded the voters that Irving had promised he would not raise taxes when he ran in 1915 and then raised them to the maximum allowed under the city charter. This, Wilson said, was in part the result of excessive expenditures and in part because land in Berkeley was assessed at less than its real value. He criticized Mayor Irving for appointing Duncan McDuffie of the Mason-McDuffie Real Estate Company to oversee creation of Berkeley's new zoning ordinance. According to one account of early city planning, this ordinance was "primarily designed to protect the developers and owners of large and expensive homes on the East side of the City and the developers and owners of factories and railroad property on the West side."[6]

Many Berkeleyans had become more conservative since Wilson's successful 1911 campaign, but he received strong support from Elinor Carlisle and a new Mothers Club leader, Mrs. W. T. Cleverdon. Cleverdon organized campaigns against the rising price of food and served as the chair of the Citizens Committee of Berkeley, which argued that prices were rising due to illegal price-fixing in the food industry. She promoted a ballot measure to have the City of Berkeley establish a municipal bakery, modeled on the military bakery at the Presidio in San Francisco, which sold bread for less than half the price of Berkeley's for-profit bakeries.[7]

Irving vigorously defended his administration and criticized Wilson. In his annual report, Irving had described taking over a city in which its business had been handled in "a satisfactory and efficient manner," but now he denounced Wilson and Heywood's previous administrations, arguing that the amount of money spent conducting city business and improving streets and schools was made necessary by the serious deficiencies he found when he took office.[8] Wilson in turn agreed that sewer, school, and road improvements were necessary but pointed out that most of the accomplishments claimed by Irving had actually been done or set in motion by previous administrations. In the 1915 campaign, Irving criticized Wilson for building an unnecessary municipal incinerator. By 1917, however, Berkeley was using the incinerator because it was no longer able to dump its waste in the ocean. Irving now claimed the credit since, while he was mayor, city staff had discovered that separating dry and wet waste allowed the incinerator to run more economically.[9] Irving also supported the ongoing effort to establish a publicly owned water company. If the back-and-forth exchanges demonstrated anything, it was that, despite drastic differences between the two men's visions of a good society and their personal styles, the differences in how they would govern a growing city within the existing constraints of state law were actually fairly minor.

Campaigning in a nation at war

On Election Day, April 7, 1917, Mayor Irving received only 41% of the vote, followed by Stitt Wilson with 36%, Spear with 20%, and Coggins with 3%, sending Irving and Wilson into a run-off election, scheduled for April 28th. Elvina Beals was the only Socialist candidate to advance to the runoff. Irving had won easily in the hills and campus area and the well-to-do home-owner neighborhoods of Northeast Berkeley. Wilson had won the central flatlands, and the two candidates split the mixed industrial and residential areas near the waterfront. Wilson had held the working-class and socialist voters who supported him in previous elections, despite having a Socialist opponent this time. Clearly a majority of Berkeley voters were unhappy with Mayor Irving. Wilson's challenge for the runoff was to win over most of those who had voted for Spear.

Mayor Irving and his allies were shocked at the result of the primary election. They called an "emergency meeting" at the Hotel Shattuck "to thwart the attempts of J. Stitt Wilson to seize the reins of government." Wilson responded that this demonstrated "how the autocratic methods of the Irving administration turn into comedy,"[10] further stating:

> It sounds like the summons of the Czar Nicholas . . . As the aforesaid J. Stitt Wilson marches to the city hall to seize the reins of government will he approach with a troop of cavalry or will he just walk down Center Street, past the Foss lumber yard, greeting his fellow citizens with a kindly good morning?

But when he made this light-hearted response, Wilson already knew he was about to face a smear campaign that would treat his previous hopes for peace and his opposition to social injustice as disloyalty to his country in a time of war. During the runoff campaign, Wilson pointed to the rising cost of basic consumer goods resulting from the war and re-emphasized the need for economy in government, promising to "go very slowly in any improvements that involve the citizens in special assessments against their property."[11] He spoke to the WCTU and other temperance groups and reminded them of his work for California Dry.[12] He reviewed the accomplishments of his years as mayor in upgrading fire and police services and rebuilding the sewer system. He reminded the public of Irving's exaggerated claims and vicious attacks on those who disagreed with him. All of this was overshadowed by the drama accompanying American entry into the war.

On January 31, 1917, Germany declared that it would resume unrestricted submarine warfare and would sink any ships that appeared to be heading towards hostile nations, regardless of the nature of their cargo or the nationality of their crew and passengers. This horrified many Americans and on February 3rd, Woodrow Wilson broke off diplomatic relations with Germany. At that point, it was widely recognized that U.S. entry into the war was only a matter of time. This was followed by the February revolution in Russia, which overthrew the tsar and temporarily established a democratic government. There now appeared to be a clear divide between the relatively democratic Allies (Great Britain, France, and Russia) and the autocratic Central Powers (the German, Austro-Hungarian, and Ottoman Empires).

On April 2nd, after several U.S. ships were sunk by German submarines, Woodrow Wilson called on Congress to declare war against Germany. On April 6th, the day before Berkeley's first-round election, the House and Senate voted to declare war. President Wilson stressed idealistic, democratic motives, declaring that:

> A steadfast concert for peace can never be maintained except by a partnership of democratic nations. No autocratic government could be trusted to keep faith within it or observe its covenants. . . . The world must be made safe for democracy. Its peace must be planted upon the tested foundations of political liberty.

President Wilson called on Americans to "observe with proud punctilio the principles of right and of fair play we profess to be fighting for," both in the conduct of the war and in dealing with U.S. residents of German nationality or descent. But he also fed a rising war hysteria, saying that "disloyalty . . . will be dealt with a firm hand of stern repression."

The Socialist Party had consistently opposed both American involvement in the war and "preparedness"—building up the army and navy to be ready for war. The many opponents of preparedness believed it would encourage militarism at home and increase the likelihood that America would enter the war. As the war continued in Europe, some socialists left the Socialist Party because they wanted America to join with England and France against what they regarded as German militarism and autocracy. After the U.S. declaration of war, the party held an emergency convention April 7–14 in St. Louis and adopted a strong anti-war resolution. The party urged opposition to the war and all preparations for war, including the draft, sale of war bonds, and military training in the schools and opposed any measures to restrict freedom of speech, assembly, organization, and the right to strike. The minority of socialists who supported the war left the party.[13]

Wilson immediately disassociated himself from the anti-war position. This was likely eased by his close ties to the British Labour Party. The majority of the Labour Party had supported the British declaration of war against Germany and the party leader, Arthur Henderson, was now a cabinet minister in the wartime national unity government. Wilson contacted Police Chief August Vollmer to apply to join the newly formed Berkeley Home Defense Corps, made up of people who could not serve in the military due to age or family obligations.[14] (The Home Defense Corps was intended to replace the Berkeley Company of the California National Guard, which was going to be mobilized into the U.S. Army.)

In an "Open Letter from J. Stitt Wilson to Mayor Irving," published in the *Berkeley Daily Gazette*, Wilson expressed his admiration both for President Woodrow Wilson's past efforts to stay out of the war and for the ideals that now motivated American entry, saying President Wilson "has spelled the word 'Democracy' in letters of living light." Wilson argued that through serving their country Americans would also be serving the cause of "a free humanity." He urged unity in service to the United States and to its democratic ideals and pledged his "utmost cooperation" with the mayor in the national defense.[15] Wilson also followed up with an advertisement in the *Gazette*, stating that he was running an independent campaign and was not associated with any of the other candidates for city council, disassociating himself from the Socialist candidate, Elvina Beals.[16]

American wartime "neutrality" had allowed sale of munitions and food to both sides, which in practice meant sales to the Allies, since the British, French, and Italian navies were blockading ports serving the Central Powers. (Starting in 1917 a group of Japanese destroyers also provided the Allies with anti-submarine assistance in the Mediterranean.) In response, the Germans conducted a sabotage campaign in the U.S. against U.S. military production and shipping. By 1917, parts of the German network had already been exposed and most of the rest left the U.S. when it entered the war, so there was actually very little in the way of sabotage or spying against the U.S. after it declared war. There was widespread fear, however, that the declaration of war would lead to a major new sabotage campaign.[17]

Throughout the U.S., state and local officials began to organize "Home Guard" or "Home Defense" units, made up of men who would be unlikely to serve in the Army due to age or family status. The purpose of these units was to replace the mobilized National Guard, and they took on duties ranging from encouraging conservation of food and other necessities to guarding essential public works and industries from potential sabotage.[18] In addition, as the U.S. neared its declaration of war, federal officials in the Justice Department's Bureau of Investigation (later the F.B.I.) and the War Department's Military Intelligence Office encouraged formation of private "secret service" organizations for the purpose of identifying spies, preventing sabotage, and reporting people who did not support the war effort.[19] These were quasi-official domestic surveillance organizations, in which people spied on neighbors and co-workers, reporting and inventing signs of "disloyalty." They often became vigilante groups that used claims of patriotism to justify campaigns of fear and intimidation against both American and foreign citizens whose beliefs they disagreed with, including members of the Industrial Workers of the World (IWW) and the Socialist Party.[20] The best-known of these organizations was the American Protective League, which had headquarters in Washington, D.C., and a membership of 250,000 people by the end of the war. Another such organization was the citizen secret service organization, the Nathan Hale Volunteers, head-quartered in Berkeley.

As soon as the U.S. declared war, Mayor Irving convened meetings in his office to organize what he described as a Home Guard and Secret Service Corps. The characterization of the Berkeley Home Guard as, in part, a "Secret Service Corps" set off great concern, especially among foreign-born residents of Berkeley. The group quickly changed its name to the Berkeley Defense Corps, and Mayor Irving issued a proclamation assuring foreign-born residents, including citizens of other countries, that their rights would be protected so long as each person "goes peaceably about his business and conducts himself in a law abiding manner" and calling for "a calm and considerate attitude" on the part of the citizenry.[21] Once the Berkeley Defense Corps was organized, with an initial membership of thirty men, Mayor Irving called for a mass meeting in the Berkeley High School auditorium on the evening of Tuesday, April 17th, to introduce the organization and encourage more people to join.[22] Mayor Irving arranged for his address to be accompanied by other speakers, including Frederic S. Hughes, head of the newly formed Nathan Hale Volunteers.[23]

The Nathan Hale Volunteers

The Nathan Hale Volunteers was founded by the husband-and-wife team of Frederic Sumner Hughes and Irma Drew Hughes. The Hughes were modestly successful organizational entrepreneurs, and the story of the Nathan Hale Volunteers is a case of what might be called "entrepreneurial patriotism." Understanding their motivation for intervening in the Berkeley mayoral election and the way they went about it requires a close look at their background.

The Hugheses had been claims agents for streetcar companies in Los Angeles, dealing with people injured in streetcar accidents and with the families of those who died. The main role of claims agents at that time was to identify fraudulent claims and to try to keep payments for valid claims low by offering quick cash settlements so that the injured or the families of the dead would not go to court, where sympathetic juries often approved large compensation payments. In a number of cities around the U.S., people had begun to use public education to try to prevent accidents.[24] In 1909 Frederic and Irma Hughes persuaded streetcar companies in Los Angeles to fund them to provide safety education to school children and adult civic organizations, explaining how to safely board and exit and otherwise behave safely around streetcars.

Building on their Los Angeles campaign, in 1910, the couple founded the American Safety League, with Frederic, then 35 years old, as field director and Irma, 33, as a lecturer. The Hugheses moved to Portland, organizing local Safety League branches in Portland and Seattle, and then to Berkeley to work in the San Francisco Bay Area with the support of the Key Route, Oakland Traction, and United Railroads companies. From their home in Berkeley, they traveled throughout the U.S., speaking to schools and civic groups and setting up statewide and local league affiliates. They spent time in New Jersey in 1912 and Wisconsin in 1913, going wherever local transit companies would pay them to organize safety leagues.[25] Their

Safety League buttons. Slogan "Better Safe than Sorry" on the back. (author's collection).

work was a genuine public service, but it was also designed to give transit companies good publicity for supporting rider safety. The message that 98% of streetcar accidents were preventable if people exercised sufficient caution was welcomed by the companies. It helped them deflect public pressure to take the more expensive approach of redesigning and replacing streetcars and streetcar stops.

Frederic Hughes had lived in the East Bay before, but apparently no one connected him with the Rev. Ural S. Hughes, who had fled the area in 1898. The front page photograph of Frederic Sumner Hughes in the November 19, 1911, edition of the *Oakland Tribune* showed a 36-year-old balding, clean-shaven, round-faced man who was teaching the public about streetcar safety. The front page drawing of Rev. Ural Sumner Hughes in the August 2, 1898, edition of the *Oakland Tribune* showed a handsome 23-year-old, curly-haired clergyman with an elegant mustache who was charged with bigamy. In truth, they were one and the same.

In March 1894, at the age of 18, Hughes was in Evanston, Illinois, studying for the ministry. Claiming to be 23 years old, he married a woman whom he abandoned soon afterward. He moved to California and obtained an annulment of the marriage in January 1896, arguing that he had been too young for proper consent. He enrolled in the Pacific Theological Seminary in Oakland and served as pastor for a small Methodist congregation in San Jose. He also attended the Methodist Church in Oakland, where he met and in 1898 married his second wife. Shortly afterward he was expelled from the Theological Seminary, and his first wife, having finally located him, charged him with bigamy and fraud in obtaining the annulment. Taking his second wife with him, Hughes fled to British Columbia, having raised some ready money by subleasing his apartment and taking the rent money in advance without paying the landlord. They then moved to Washington, D.C., where their daughter was born in 1899 and soon afterward, Hughes abandoned his second wife and their daughter. He moved back to California, where he met and married Irma Drew, apparently without bothering to divorce his previous wife, settled down in Los Angeles under the name of Frederic Sumner Hughes, and worked as a claims agent before founding the American Safety League.[26]

As World War I raged in Europe, Frederic and Irma Hughes joined and became West Coast representatives of the Defense Reports Committee shortly after it was formed on May 7, 1916.[27] The Defense Reports Committee claimed to be a business-sponsored group that would advocate preparedness and assist the U.S. government with research and information. It was actually organized by and operated out of the offices of John Duval Gluck, Jr., who turned out to be a highly successful con man.[28]

John Gluck gained prosperity and a measure of celebrity by founding the Santa Claus Association of New York in 1913. The association donated Christmas gifts to poor children in New York City who had written letters to Santa Claus. It became a popular charity and enabled Gluck to draw a substantial income from the public's contributions. In its early years at least, the Santa Claus Association did actual charitable work, but after repeated investigations, the U.S. Post Office eventually refused to forward letters to it and the association closed down in 1928. Gluck also had a leadership role in fundraising for the United States Boy Scout. Once intended as a competitor of the Boy Scouts of America, U.S. Boy Scout had come to exist entirely to raise money that went into the pockets of its officers and fundraisers. The group took a strong "preparedness" position, claiming to ready boys for military service in case America went to war. After America entered the war, U.S. Boy Scout fundraisers, under Gluck's leadership, would call on companies and owners with German names and threaten those who declined to donate with public accusations of disloyalty.[29]

The initial press releases of the Defense Reports Committee announced plans to investigate claims that Germany had purchased land on the Massachusetts coast and then to broadly review ownership of land along the East and West Coasts. A month later, it proposed to make films publicizing the danger of a Japanese invasion of the West Coast, despite the fact that in World War I Japan was allied with Great Britain against Germany.[30] None of these Defense Reports Committee plans was actually carried out. Their main purpose was to encourage people and businesses to contribute funds to the organization.

Another project of the Defense Reports Committee was the Citizenry Secret Service, also operating out of Gluck's Santa Claus Association offices.[31] In June 1916, it placed ads in newspapers around the U.S. asking for 1,000 "additional" volunteers to "offset the activities of foreign secret services in this country," offering volunteers a photographic identification card with the inscription, "Citizenry Secret Service, Defense Reports Committee," and making the nonsensical claim that it would be "recognized by United States Consuls everywhere."[32] After visits from actual Secret Service agents of the U.S. government, Gluck changed the name of the organization to the Citizenry Information Bureau.

With the coming of war, there was less demand for the Hugheses' safety education services, and they needed something new to offer their funders. Involvement with the Defense Reports Committee provided Frederic and Irma Hughes with a model for creating two new organizations of their own, the American Safety League—Secret Report Service, and, as a project of the Secret Report Service, the Nathan Hale Volunteers. They arranged with

Gluck that his Citizenry Information Bureau would operate on the East Coast and the Nathan Hale Volunteers would operate on the West Coast and that the two organizations would cooperate.[33] (It is not clear if the Hugheses understood that Gluck was running paper organizations.)

The Secret Report Service may have been an effort to use American Safety League contacts with transit companies to persuade them to fund the creation of a network of informants to protect against sabotage.[34] It left few traces, however, and the Nathan Hale Volunteers soon became the Hugheses' main activity. Investigative work was part of the job for a claims agent, and while living in Portland, Irma had reported her occupation as manager of a "Pacific Coast Secret Inquiry Service," so the idea of doing investigative work for patriotic purposes came easily to the couple.[35] Their work for the American Safety League had given them connections with police departments and school systems, especially on the West Coast.

Frederic Hughes claimed that the Nathan Hale Volunteers were founded on Nathan Hale's birthday, June 6, 1916, but its actual inception appears to be in March 1917, when the expectation of American entry into the war opened up opportunities for official government recognition. As it happened, the chief intelligence officer for the U.S. Army in the Western States, Lieutenant Rufus W. Putnam, was a fellow Berkeley resident. With the approval of his commanding officer, Putnam worked with Hughes to prepare a "plan of organization and cooperation" establishing a "Nathan Hale Volunteers Bureau of the Intelligence Office, Western Department, U.S. Army," with Hughes as the chief of the bureau reporting to Putnam.[36]

According to the plan, the Nathan Hale Volunteers was a "secret organization for patriotic service," whose purposes were surveillance of foreign nationals, "foreign sympathizers," and members of groups suspected of "disloyalty." Its members would investigate and report on people who engaged in "hostile acts or utterances." The results of investigations by the volunteers would go to Field Secretary Hughes, who would pass them on to the U.S. government. The existence of the organization was to be kept "absolutely secret" until "actual hostilities," at which point the field secretary was authorized to announce its existence.[37]

As soon as President Wilson called for a declaration of war, Hughes recruited a number of Berkeley residents to provide the nucleus of his organization. After meetings at Putnam's house and the Hughes' residence, Berkeley Police Chief August Vollmer was placed in charge of "Identification and Police Matters."[38] L. J. Richardson, an associate professor of Latin at the University of California, would be in charge of the "Bureau of Translations." George Martin, owner of Martin's Camera Shop, would head the "Photographic Department," and Z. P. Smith, president of the Berkeley Business College, would direct clerical work.[39] Immediately upon congressional approval of the declaration of war, Chief Vollmer joined Hughes in calling for volunteers and encouraged Berkeley police and fire-fighters to join. Using initial funding from the Army, Hughes opened up a headquarters office at 1910 Kittredge Street in downtown Berkeley using office furniture and equipment donated by local businesses.[40]

Hughes persuaded the Oakland Chamber of Commerce and the superintendent of schools to propose creation of a "juvenile secret service," organized along the lines of the Boy Scouts and affiliated with the Nathan Hale Volunteers. Hughes grandly envisioned that the Oakland organization would become a model for a nationwide youth organization, with Oakland as its national headquarters.[41]

From his Berkeley headquarters, Hughes sent press releases to news-papers throughout the western United States urging all American citizens to join. "Every Person May Be Secret Agent, Vast Interstate Intelligence Organization is in Course of Formation" was the headline of the story in the *Portland Oregonian*.[42] "Berkeley to be Sleuth Center," was the headline in the *Oakland Tribune* report, which stated that Berkeley "has been selected by the Intelligence Office of the Western Department of the United States Army as one of ten division headquarters of the new citizens' interstate secret service organization known as the Nathan Hale Volunteers." The article reported that the organization covered California, Oregon, Washington, Nevada, Utah, Montana, and Idaho and that Army Intelligence Officer Rufus Putnam was the head of the organization, with Frederic Hughes as bureau chief.[43] Newspapers around the Western states ran these claims as news stories the day after the declaration of war.[44]

Nathan Hale Volunteers photo identification card (author's collection).

In his announcements, Hughes stated that the identity of members of the Nathan Hale Volunteers would be kept secret, communications with it would be confidential, and members would receive photo identification cards for use on missions for the Volunteers. There were no membership fees to join, but members were requested to contribute up to $1.00 (equivalent to $20 in 2020) toward the cost of producing the identification cards and patriotic pins and for mailings.[45] Unlike most such organizations, a special effort was made to recruit women as well as men.[46] An exciting role as a wartime secret agent was available without having to leave home.

Hughes versus Wilson

Wilson's campaign for mayor created an unexpected challenge for Hughes. Wilson's chances looked good since, as the primary election results showed, Mayor Irving had made himself unpopular with many Berkeley voters. Although Wilson supported the American war effort and had left the anti-war Socialist Party, Wilson was still a socialist and known as such throughout the West Coast. Hughes feared that the election of Wilson would harm the credibility of his Nathan Hale Volunteers. How would he persuade "patriots" to join an organization intended to provide surveillance of "disloyal" elements, which for many Americans meant socialists as well as German immigrants, if the mayor of its headquarters city supported socialism? Hughes may have also hoped for financial support for his organization from Mayor Irving, the wealthy owner of a paint manufacturing company.

On the evening of Sunday, April 15th, Hughes sent a courier with a letter to Wilson asking Wilson to meet him at his home office near downtown Berkeley on Monday morning. Wilson agreed and the next day Hughes urged him to quit the race for mayor for the greater good of the war effort. Hughes told Wilson that he was one of the "great men" of California, "a perfect dynamo of power" who should not be wasted on a routine job as mayor of Berkeley but rather should be used for greater service in a time of national crisis. Hughes offered to use his influence, wiring the president of the United States and the governor of California, to find a position in which Wilson could render great service to the nation. Wilson assured him that if, on the morning of April 29th, he was not elected mayor he could pack in 24 hours and be ready to set about any task the president might summon him to. Even if he were elected, if the president called him for some greater task, he would go and the citizens of Berkeley would select a replacement as mayor. But, said Wilson, "The people have rights . . . Mr. Irving is not their choice. They have a right to a new choice as Mayor."[47]

The two men met again at Hughes' office on Tuesday morning, and this time Hughes told Wilson that if he refused to withdraw from the mayor's race in favor of Irving, then Hughes would use his position as the head of an important government-sponsored organization to publicize Wilson's past opposition to the war and to preparedness as evidence that he was unfit for leadership in wartime. He would publicly attack Wilson as unpatriotic, a "disgrace to the proud city of Berkeley" and, as a long-time socialist, "a menace to the national welfare." Wilson pointed out that it was President Woodrow Wilson who had said that "we are too proud to fight" and that just as the president had changed his mind, so had Stitt Wilson. As the threats continued, Wilson allowed Hughes to think that he was being intimidated and asked him what he had in mind. Hughes outlined the melodrama that he wanted Wilson and Mayor Irving to act out that very evening, Tuesday, April 17th.

Mayor Irving was holding a mass meeting in the Berkeley High School auditorium that evening to recruit volunteers for the new Berkeley Home Defense Corps.[48] Along with the mayor, speakers would include Frederic Hughes.[49] According to Hughes's scenario, Wilson would join them on the platform, throw his arms around Irving, and announce that he had heard the call of higher service and was withdrawing from the race. The press would be present and would spread far and wide the news of Wilson's sacrifice for the greater good, creating "a thriller to stir the patriotic heart." Wilson was deeply offended.[50]

> While inwardly carrying out the role of a contemptible coward, I was outwardly to make a great show of the most exalted patriotism. I was to lie down like a lickspittle beneath the threats of this man, cringe like a whipped cur, and yet I was to walk to the platform of my city where I had lived for sixteen years and in which I have been Mayor with an unchallenged record for honesty, integrity and devotion and there I was to wrap the flag around me, so to speak, and with the pretense of devotion to my country surrender the city to Mayor Irving.

Wilson declined to give an immediate answer and returned home thinking of how he might turn the tables on Hughes. He arranged for prominent supporters to speak in his place at two house meetings scheduled for that evening. Then, he later related, "I telephoned Mr. Hughes that I was going to the meeting. And I went—and enlisted in the Home Defense Corps. . . . The little drama did not come off."[51] Wilson believed that Hughes had told others of his expected triumph and hoped he had embarrassed Hughes by his refusal to follow the script.

Hughes immediately followed through on his threats. He sent an open letter to Wilson and to Elvina Beals, published in the *Berkeley Daily Gazette*, urging them both to withdraw from the races for mayor and for city council. It was, he declared, a time for national unity and not for those who created division with their talk of "the people versus privilege" and who supported "the red flag of revolt." He argued that if a socialist or a person widely known as a socialist were elected in Berkeley, a city known throughout the world for its university and as the headquarters of the Nathan Hale Volunteers, it would send a harmful message across the U.S. and even in "war-smitten England." He described those supporting Wilson as "disgruntled politicians" and "the well-meaning weak-kneed sisters of the male-biped class" and concluded with the hope that the voters would save Wilson from himself so that he could go on to a larger service to the nation.[52]

Hughes followed up the next day with another open letter making the transparently false claim that Wilson had said privately that he had no real interest in being mayor, would neglect his duties if elected, and wanted the position only because it would open up more opportunities for public speaking. He also attacked Wilson for having criticized the preparedness movement and attached a copy of a newspaper article about Wilson's telegram of support to an anti-war rally in July 1916.[53]

Elvina Beals responded that "I have taken my oath to support the Constitution and the Government of the State and Nation" and described Hughes as a "little political wire-puller" who "wants to wave the flag for political capital."[54] Hughes did not bother to answer. His purpose in calling for her to withdraw was simply to link a current Socialist Party member with Wilson.

Wilson responded that all of the Allies that the U.S. was joining had brought socialists into their wartime national unity governments. Socialists had overthrown the tsar and brought democracy to Russia and he hoped that the socialists of Germany would bring democracy to Germany as well. Furthermore, as part of its war mobilization, the U.S. government was planning to place much of the economy under "government supervision," a "socialistic proposal" already adopted by the warring countries of Europe. Hughes's attack on socialism and his claims that the election of socialists would demoralize our European allies or harm the U.S. war effort, said Wilson, showed "colossal ignorance."[55] Wilson invoked Woodrow Wilson's calls for civility and democracy and argued that it was Hughes who was being divisive and undermining American democracy. In an election pamphlet he coauthored with Mrs. Cleverdon and in his speeches, Wilson asked the citizens of Berkeley, "Do you want a city government that is defended and elected by the assistance of the espionage of a man who has been either the voluntary or paid detective and sleuth of the Oakland Traction company?"[56]

Hughes responded that Wilson had proved Hughes' point by endorsing socialism and socialist revolutions.[57] His wife, Irma, sent a lengthy letter to the *Berkeley Daily Gazette* in which she recounted at length their good works for child safety through the American Safety League, denied that Frederic Hughes was a detective for the Oakland Traction Company, and claimed that the company was simply one of the Safety League's funders.[58] In saying this, she concealed the existence of the American Safety League—Secret Report Service and her own past work as manager of the Pacific Coast Secret Inquiry Service. Perhaps Wilson had pegged the wrong Hughes as the detective.

Wilson called on Mayor Irving to repudiate Hughes's attacks, but Irving was evasive, saying, "The newspaper controversy between J. Stitt Wilson and F. S. Hughes is entirely between themselves. Neither I nor my campaign committee have any connection with either of the parties to this dispute."[59] Fourteen prominent Berkeley women who supported Irving followed Hughes's example and sent a letter assuring voters that Mayor Irving had "no political creed which will prevent him from whole-heartedly supporting the President," implying that Wilson did.[60]

The *Berkeley Daily Gazette* joined in the attack. Initially the *Gazette* ran a very civil editorial that described Wilson as "an able, talented gentleman" but endorsed Irving as "the better business man . . . more capable of managing the affairs of the office."[61] The day before the election, editor James Wales ran an editorial entitled "Business vs. Socialism," asking, "Do you, voters of Berkeley, want a Socialist administration while our nation is at war with Germany?" In language nearly identical to that of Hughes, he suggested that the election of Wilson as mayor of Berkeley would weaken the American war effort.[62] Irving, said Wales, "is not and never has been affiliated with an organization opposed to the government."[63] (Actually, they both were. The *Gazette* was a Republican newspaper and Irving a conservative Republican and they had both opposed reelection of Woodrow Wilson as president.)

Wilson angrily denounced efforts to denigrate his patriotism and to divide the community into patriots and non-patriots. He urged his fellow citizens to reject such anti-democratic tactics, but on Election Day, April 28th, Irving was narrowly reelected with 6,271 votes to 6,147 for Wilson, a margin of just 124 votes.[64]

After the election, many of the women who had signed the letter opposing Wilson formed a Mobilized Women's Organization of Berkeley to support the war effort by encouraging donations of socks to the Red Cross,
collecting magazines and books for the troops, and encouraging frugal-
ity to save food.[65] In contrast, Mrs. Cleverdon and the Berkeley Citizens
Committee, after supporting Wilson, continued to assist the war effort by
campaigning against wartime profiteering and speculative hoarding by food
companies.[66]

The Nathan Hale Volunteers collapse

By Election Day, the Nathan Hale Volunteers claimed to have gone from
100 members in ten cities, to 2,000 members "in nearly every branch of
public and private life."[67] A few weeks later, Hughes claimed that the organization now included "Rangers, Motor Scouts, and Safety Guards" who
worked out in the open to protect vital defense industries from sabotage,
while the secret "Nathan Hale Volunteers never betray their identity."[68]
There is no evidence that these "open" organizations ever existed. Hughes
also claimed that there were another 6,000 volunteers on the East Coast
under the leadership of John Gluck in New York City.[69]

Unlike Gluck, for whom a citizen secret service was just one of a number
of money-raising scams, Hughes needed to build an organization capable
of paying his salary and expenses. But the Nathan Hale Volunteers ran into
immediate organizational problems. Hughes' advertisements drew random
members of the public as volunteers. Hughes would then send the volunteers a letter asking them to send membership information to his post office
box in Berkeley, to send a "secret report" on loyalty in their community to
Rufus Putnam's post office box in San Francisco, and to recruit additional
volunteers. Hughes' operational model was "Six-point Star Clusters," unit
chiefs with six assistants who would cover a "zone of protection." Each unit
was assigned to a "district" and each district to a "division." He then had to
select unit, district, and division chiefs based on possible past acquaintance
through the American Safety League, phone conversations, or the quality
of written reports. Volunteers, even district leaders, would join based on
passing enthusiasm and then move on to other things without bothering to
send any notice to Hughes.[70]

An active volunteer later described how he became involved and his
assignment as Division Chief for the Los Angeles area:

> Immediately upon the declaration of war by the United
> States in 1917, the first thing that came to my mind was,

"what can I do to help my country win the war?" Being
physically somewhat stout, close to forty years of age
and . . . somewhat lacking in ability for "hiking" . . . on
account of my feet and poor circulation. . . . A few days later
a notice in the papers gave me the clue . . . shortly after I
was empowered to take charge of the Southern half of the
State of California and organize it . . . for the Nathan Hale
Volunteers.[71]

While Frederic Hughes tried to bring organization out of chaos from
his headquarters in Berkeley, Irma Hughes traveled around the West Coast
meeting with local "leaders" to provide some personal contact and encour-
agement. An April 18th press release announced that "a woman who will
be known as courier 67" would go on a "secret journey" around the Pacific
Coast to "test the efficiency of the information system of the Nathan Hale
Volunteers." In addition to meeting local leaders of the organization, Irma
contacted local newspapers to encourage coverage of her "secret" mission
and get publicity for the Nathan Hale Volunteers.[72]

By the end of May 1917, Frederic Hughes was floundering in the use-
less minutiae of wartime paranoia. He wrote to Chief Vollmer, temporarily
working in San Diego to reorganize that city's police department, telling the
chief that the volunteers were sending in hundreds of reports of "suspects"
but that they lacked the skills and organization necessary to follow up with
"investigations of real value."

A young member of the Nathan Hale Volunteers who was "very much
enthused" about serving his country as an investigator looked into an explosion that occurred several months earlier in a plant in Stockton, California,
that manufactured Caterpillar tractors—possibly sabotage or possibly an
industrial accident. The volunteer heard accusations that an employee at
the plant was a member of the IWW, a German, and a dangerous man who
"was experimenting with chemicals." The volunteer made his acquaintance
and reported that the employee was anti-draft and "has in his possession
a bottle of liquid, (and) a small jar that may contain powders or paste."[73]
There were no apparent results from this report, which, while no doubt
exciting for the eager volunteer, risked having serious consequences for the
employee if put under suspicion on such tenuous grounds.

It appears that most of what the Nathan Hale Volunteers reported was
neighborhood gossip. Scattered reports from NHV members, preserved in
Justice Department files, inform the authorities that an individual living in
Spokane, Washington, "is extremely pro-German" and that another "pro-
German" individual told his son to leave the house when the son enlisted in

the U.S. Army. The Justice Department often passed such routine reports on to the American Protective League for further investigation.[74] Recognizing the limitations of his organization, Hughes encouraged volunteers living near Berkeley to take an upcoming summer school course in criminology and planned to take the course himself and obtain a private investigator's license.[75]

Around the end of April, Army legal counsel advised that it was contrary to law and Army regulations to provide direct funding for a civilian organization such as the Nathan Hale Volunteers and funding for the group was discontinued.[76] Hughes asked members of the Nathan Hale Volunteers to contribute voluntary dues of one dollar a month and appealed to the public for contributions but had little success.[77] The potential for raising money from the public was further limited when the Volunteers lost their official connection with the Army.[78] At the end of May, Lieutenant Rufus Putnam was sent to France. His replacement, Captain H. Evans, directed Hughes to stop using materials that described the Nathan Hale Volunteers as a "Bureau of the Intelligence Office." Hughes changed his stationery to read "Nathan Hale Volunteers Bureau of the U.S.A., American Safety League—Secret Report Service."[79] After seeing Hughes' new stationery, Captain Evans sent him another letter, copied to Chief Vollmer, directing him to remove the "U.S.A." from his stationery to avoid giving any impression that the Nathan Hale Volunteers were affiliated with the Army. Vollmer showed the letter to the *Berkeley Daily Gazette*, which ran a story to alert people in Berkeley who believed otherwise. Hughes responded with the disingenuous claim that "U.S.A." stood for "Universal Safety Alliance" and for "Unity, Security and Amity."[80]

Hughes' American Safety League had depended on business funding, but this was blocked by the success of the American Protective League (APL), now the largest of the citizen secret service organizations. Formed in March 1917 by the vice president of an advertising company, its leaders were successful businessmen and professionals who recruited additional members directly from their own social circles and subordinates. This approach gave the APL access to significant resources and an organization based on America's existing economic hierarchy.[81] Immediately following the declaration of war, the APL had selected a Northern California coordinator who recruited local units in San Francisco, Oakland, Berkeley, Richmond, and other Bay Area cities and set up a network of informants in major Bay Area industries, including telephone and telegraph, gas and electric, and meat packing companies, and the railroads, which otherwise might have funded the Hugheses' organization.[82] In June 1917, the Justice Department formally recognized the American Protective League as its civilian partner and discouraged cooperation with other organizations.

Without public funding and without Army sponsorship to encourage private funding, the Nathan Hale Volunteers collapsed. Captain Evans was assigned a group of enlisted men to serve as investigators, and local police and detectives, including Police Chief Vollmer, provided them with training.[83] Evans took over some of the contacts from the Nathan Hale Volunteers and organized a "Volunteer Intelligence Corps" operating under his direct authority.[84]

The Hugheses moved out of Berkeley, renting a series of apartments in Oakland. In late 1917 and early 1918, Hughes made unsuccessful efforts to create a new organization, describing himself as the "Executive Secretary of the I.F.A. and N.H.V. of the U.S. Alliance."[85] By the middle of 1918, however, he and Irma had gone back to working as claims agents for transit companies.[86] After the war, Irma spent some time as the secretary of an organization that sponsored training in music, song, and spoken arts. Frederic, who was said to have a very fine singing voice, sang at some of their events.[87] In 1920, they moved back to Los Angeles, where he reverted to using his birth name, Ural, and worked as a claims agent for several more years. Eventually they went into real estate. Hughes died in 1939.[88]

The Nathan Hale Volunteers were not the worst of the World War I vigilance organizations. Unlike California's Knights of Liberty, they did not kidnap, whip, and tar and feather Americans they considered "disloyal."[89] They accomplished nothing of value during the organization's short life, but one could hardly say that the apparently successful American Protective League accomplished much either. The APL's activities nationwide included investigating reports of food hoarding and profiteering on wartime food shortages, helping round up people suspected of failing to register for the draft, conducting background checks on people applying for positions in government and overseas, and investigating suspected German agents or sympathizers and opponents of the war. These investigations often involving illegal searches of peoples' homes and offices, so members were supplied with an official-looking badge saying, "American Protective League—Secret Service," later changed to "American Protective League—Auxiliary to the U.S. Department of Justice," in case they were stopped by the police.[90]

At the time it was disbanded at the end of the war, the APL had units throughout California with thousands of members. In Berkeley, Police Chief Vollmer provided them with free space in the police department offices.[91] The league's major accomplishment in the San Francisco Bay Area, proudly reported in its official history, came when the Oakland branch reported to the authorities that a group of seventeen German-American business and professional men drank a toast to the Kaiser. This was sufficient to have them convicted of "disloyalty" under the Sedition Act of 1918 and the judge sentenced each of them to three months in jail and $250 fines (around $4,250 in 2020 dollars). This assured the voters of the judge's own patriotism but failed to provide them with an example of the democracy America was supposedly making the world safe for.[92]

The Institute of Democracy

After the mayoral election, Wilson moved on. Perhaps wanting to get away from Berkeley for a while, he spent the rest of the war doing speaking tours in Southern California and the Central Valley. He had left the Socialist Party because he believed what was needed was a "moral transformation." He now hoped that intense wartime patriotism might lay the foundation for a post-war democratic reconstruction of European and American society.[93] Along with individual talks, he created a week-long, six-part lecture series on the purpose and meaning of the war, which he called an "Institute of Democracy."

He now described democracy, rather than socialism, as applied Christianity, the war as a conflict between "Kaiserism," based on the Nietzschean morality of might, and democracy, based on Jesus's morality of love. He expounded on the importance of cooperation over self-seeking and denounced those who used the war for personal gain. These included land speculators who were withholding usable farmland from production and businesses profiteering from wartime shortages. Said Wilson, "Any IWW blustering on the street corner is a tiddlywink compared to the man who is raising prices in this crisis."[94] The "Bible Argument for Socialism" became the "Bible Argument for Democracy." "Jesus, Hero of the Common People," was now "Jesus, Hero of World Democracy."[95] Democracy was America's great contribution to the world, and, Wilson urged, it should be extended to industry as well as government.

At the beginning of September, Stitt and Ben Wilson traveled to Minneapolis for the founding convention of the American Alliance for Labor and Democracy. Funded by the U.S. Committee on Public Information and controlled by Samuel Gompers, head of the American Federation of Labor, it brought together pro-war socialists, progressives, and labor leaders to support the war effort. Many of the participants had been preparing to launch a new, pro-war socialist party and to Gompers's dismay they used the Minneapolis conference to set up another conference in Chicago a month later at which former socialists, including the Wilsons, the remnants of the

Progressive Party, and some of the Prohibition Party formed a new National Party.[96] Ben Wilson was placed on the new party's national advisory committee and employed as an organizer and lecturer. He spent the remainder of the war touring the U.S., giving speeches that combined support for the war with trying to build the National Party into a viable organization, but it collapsed in 1919 shortly after the war ended.[97]

At the end of September 1917, Wilson's son, Gladstone, was drafted into the Army, saying he was "glad to do my bit."[98] He completed artillery training, then was reassigned to the Signal Corps and sent to the University of California School of Military Aeronautics.[99] Wilson's daughter, Violette, and her husband, Irving Pichel, were also doing their bit. Over the summer they helped stage *Caliban*, a giant spectacle with a volunteer cast of thousands, in New York City and at Harvard Stadium in Boston, both times as a fundraiser for the Red Cross. They returned to Berkeley to stage four new dance-dramas written and choreographed by Violette, also as fundraisers for the Red Cross.[100]

Wilson returned to lecturing in Southern California, where he had a new granddaughter, Virginia Conway, born while he was in Minneapolis. His talks drew people by the thousands; during his talks, he encouraged contributions to the Red Cross and purchase of bonds to help finance the war. After a speech at Pershing Square in Los Angeles, he proudly recalled, the audience bought $100,000 in war bonds (equivalent to about $1,700,000 in 2020).[101] He also spoke to soldiers at various bases around California, under the auspices of the YMCA, which had charge of providing for the social and educational needs of the troops.[102] Most of his Institute of Democracy series of talks and individual speeches were given in mid size and small cities such as Bakersfield, Corona, Fresno, La Jolla, Pasadena, Riverside, San Bernardino, San Diego, San Dimas, and Santa Ana, and drew people from the surrounding countryside as well. An evening speech in Fresno drew 4,000-plus people, more than 10% of the city's population.[103] A Sunday event in Riverside, featuring military music and a speech by Wilson, also drew 4,000-plus people, more than 20% of the city's population.[104] A noontime speech to shipyard workers in San Pedro drew 6,000.[105] In Los Angeles he was one of many people speaking on the war at any given time, but in smaller cities he was the main attraction and his talks were reported extensively in the local newspapers.

The crowds showed that people were eager to hear an idealistic and religious motivation for the war and to believe that the war would lead to a better world. His statements of the democratic ideal were made at a high level of abstraction but could be pointed nonetheless. In one typical speech he said:

> The preservation and perpetuation and perfection of democracy— that is our only business. If that is gone— everything is gone. If that is preserved—everything is possible. Autocracy in religion is humbug; in the state it becomes tyranny; in business it is black injustice.[106]

Wilson implored his audience to ensure that America would not only "whip Germany decisively" but continue to build democracy once the war was over.[107]

> After the war, intelligent, spiritually-minded people will understand that the program of Christianity is to establish the Kingdom of God on earth. . . . You can't any longer use this world for mere gratification of your selfish and personal interests. This is God's world, for the humanity that's on it. If you as much as live and breathe you are a debtor to the human race. Pay your debt—with the best of your ability. We're all drafted—not for the war alone—but for the time when the boys come home . . . When the war is over then we shall begin to build a spiritual world as never before.[108]

His talks were sponsored and paid for by local committees formed to organize support for the war effort, usually led by businessmen and elected officials who would not normally have lent their names to speeches on democracy by a well-known socialist. His previous work on behalf of California Dry had given him a strong reputation with the "respectable" citizens in most of these cities. And, as with the Dry campaign, they recognized the need to bring in someone who had credibility with the working class to compete with Socialist Party opposition to the war. Nonetheless, there was concern about his message in conservative circles. The editor of the *Riverside Daily Press* felt it necessary to remind his readers that the star that heralded the birth of Jesus shone for the wise men who were "rich and highly educated" as well as for the poor shepherds.[109] The *San Diego Union* gave detailed accounts of Wilson's Institute of Democracy but then ran a series of editorials on the theme of "Democracy or Socialism?" The editor told his readers that Wilson had previously espoused socialism of the "Marxian" variety that followed the "Prussian" idea of subordinating "the individual to the rule of the impersonal state" and challenged him to clarify whether his version of democracy was Marxian or Jeffersonian.[110]

Wilson was one of many pro-war socialists and progressives who hoped that wartime solidarity could advance the cause of labor and the working class.[111] John Dewey, America's most prominent philosopher and public intellectual, argued that the war had made visible the process of "manipulating property rights to take a private profit out of social needs" and that this public recognition of "profiteering" might lay the groundwork for a "social reconstruction" of the economy along democratic lines.[112] Prominent attorney and reformer Frank P. Walsh, soon to be appointed co-chair of the National War Labor Board, asked, "Why should industry be made safe for autocracy while soldiers are dying on a thousand battle fields to make the world in general safe for democracy?"[113]

Mixed in with his speeches on the moral basis for the war, Wilson gave speeches sponsored by the WCTU on behalf of new prohibition measures on the ballot for November 1918, with titles such as "Over the Top against the Liquor Traffic and Win the War."[114] The arguments for prohibition gained renewed force during the war, since consumption of alcohol by soldiers and workers could be portrayed as hindering the war effort and food shortages provided an argument against the use of grains for production of alcoholic beverages.

While Wilson toured Southern California, his son, Gladstone, graduated from aviation school in June 1918 and began pilot training at Mather Field near Sacramento. At the beginning of September, with a few days leave, he visited his parents in Berkeley and talked about the feelings he had while flying high above the California countryside, over towns where he and his father had campaigned for temperance, knowing that he was working for the progress of humanity.[115] He returned to Mather Field and his father returned to speaking in Southern California. On Saturday, September 7th, Gladstone and another pilot in training were practicing maneuvers when they collided head-on. Both were killed instantly.[116] Upon being informed of his death, Gladstone's father and sisters rushed to Berkeley from Southern California to help comfort his mother and each other. Wilson preached at the memorial service at the Trinity Methodist Church, attended by family, hundreds of friends, and 700 cadets from the University of California aviation school. Wilson spoke of his pride in his son as a patriot, for making the supreme sacrifice for the sacred cause of democracy, and of his pride as a father, his son having been "the most complete and satisfying personality we have ever known."[117]

In response to the hundreds of condolence letters they received from family, friends, and organizations, Stitt and Emma and their daughters wrote a letter, which they had printed. In it they eulogized Gladstone, assured the writers that they were "comforted and consoled" by the "great tide of human fellowship" they had received, and that they felt a "strange exaltation of spirit" in which they were comforted by the "Eternal Heart of Divine Love and by the Unseen Presence of our darling lad," since "Is it not written that 'Christ abolished death'? And that he 'brought Life and Immortality to Light'?"[118]

A mere two days after the memorial service, Wilson was back on the road, speaking in Pasadena, then moving on to San Diego and Riverside, believing that the best way to honor his son was to continue his efforts to support the war to make the world safe for democracy. While on the road, he poured out his grief in a long letter to Emma. Emma responded with a letter stating her belief that Gladstone was alive and happy in another plane of existence and that when she "let my spirit go to him" she could feel his presence. Her response moved him so deeply that he printed it (with the personal endearments edited out) along with a brief comment for distribution to their friends. His concluding words were "As I write this, the Great War is over. May history so fruit that none of these noble boys shall have died in vain. We shall live to fulfill their holy sacrifice."[119]

CHAPTER 13

FROM SOCIALISM TO THE NEW DEAL

At the end of the war, Wilson took time off to grieve and consider what to do next. He wanted to find a way to work for the religious and moral revival he considered necessary to broaden American democracy and, of course, he needed to make a living and support his family. He found both in the International Student Department of the Young Men's Christian Association (YMCA). With the war ending, the Student Department was looking for ways to transition from supporting the troops to persuading college and university students to work towards Christian democracy in America. Wilson's Institute of Democracy initiative was a natural fit, with its emphasis on democracy as applied Christianity. For the next ten years, Wilson visited more than fifty colleges and universities a year promoting his vision of Christian democracy.

The YMCA of that time was a quite different organization from the "Y" that people today know mostly as a local gym, swimming pool, and place to take exercise classes. It was an active, non-denominational Protestant movement working to engage people in living a "Christian life." Of the approximately 1,000 colleges and universities in the U.S. at the end of the war, three-quarters of them had an active chapter of the YMCA and together the chapters had nearly 100,000 members among the 600,000 students attending college. The Student Department was run by proponents of the Social Gospel, influenced especially by Walter Rauschenbusch and by George Coe, with whom Wilson had done graduate studies. The international secretary of the YMCA was Sherwood Eddy, nationally renowned for his years of missionary work in India and overseeing missions throughout Asia. He had come to have a deep respect for the people he worked with and supported national independence from the colonial powers. He strongly opposed racial discrimination and wanted to eliminate the root causes of poverty. On his retirement from the YMCA in 1931, Eddy immediately joined the Socialist Party.[1]

YMCA workers were required to be members of an evangelical church, so in January 1919, Wilson returned to the Methodist Church and remained a member for the rest of his life.[2] As he pointed out in an open letter explaining his return, the church had moved a long way toward his own views in the previous twenty years.[3] One of the major changes was led by his classmate from Northwestern University, Rev. Harry Ward, who helped organize the Methodist Federation for Social Service (MFSS) in 1907, along with Rev. Worth Tippy, who had hosted the Social Crusaders at his church in Indiana. The following year Ward wrote the Social Creed of the Churches, which included calls for an end to unsafe working conditions and child labor and support for social insurance for old age and disability, a "living wage" and "an equitable division of the products of industry." In 1912 Ward became executive secretary of the MFSS and it was officially recognized as an "executive agency of the church."

Now there was an organized arm of the Methodist Church that proposed to reconstruct society and the economy along social Christian lines, but what this meant exactly was contested. During the 1910s and 1920s, many church leaders used the Social Creed to give credibility to efforts to draw workers away from socialism and toward church-led self-improvement and management-led "cooperation" at the workplace.[4] Others, like Wilson and Ward, treated the Social Creed as a reason for the church to support workers' efforts at organizing for structural changes, keeping a radical version of the Social Gospel alive until it could gain renewed strength in the 1930s.

In February 1919, under the auspices of the Student Department of the YMCA, Wilson toured California colleges and universities, giving a lecture series he called "Constructive Christian Democracy." In this adaptation of his Institute of Democracy, he spoke of those who had died for the ideal of democracy during the war and of the sacredness of every human being as exemplified in the life and death of Jesus. He urged the social reconstruction of the industrial order from "strife for profits" to "cooperation and mutual service" that would support democracy and incorporate the sacredness of each person into the life of American society. He ended with an appeal to his listeners to become "consecrated heroes of Christ" and dedicate themselves to the cause of Christian Democracy. By the end of April, Wilson had spoken in California, Arizona, Texas, Louisiana, Georgia, Missouri, Arkansas, and Kansas, and then went on to speak at YMCA summer leadership encampments in Colorado and Massachusetts.[5]

Especially in the first few years, Wilson was an immensely popular speaker and some colleges shut down classes to allow the entire student body to attend his lectures. Students, faculty, and administrators all sought to find meaning in the death and destruction of World War I and were moved by the emotional intensity of Wilson's presentations, clearly based on his pain at the death of Gladstone and his desire to bring their shared ideals to a new generation. At one summer encampment, after Wilson delivered "an unusually powerful address even for that eccentric and saintly prophet," an influential YMCA leader was moved to say, "These talks by Sherwood Eddy and Stitt Wilson are not usual talks. There is a new greatness about them; such speaking only comes when great issues are up . . . (as) in the days before the Civil War in the anti-slavery fight."[6] A report on "Religion among American Students" referred to Wilson and Eddy as "the most widely heard and deeply influential" proponents of the Social Gospel.[7] David Porter, the executive secretary of the National Student Association of the YMCA, described Wilson as "one of the most authentic spiritual prophets of our generation."[8] Wilson was credited with inspiring a new wave of socially conscious YMCA student leaders, including Powers Hapgood, later a leader in the Congress of Industrial Organizations in the Midwest, and Jerry Voorhis, later a member of Congress from California.[9]

During the summer, Wilson took a few days to visit in New York with his daughter Violette, who was starring in a Broadway production called *A Lonely Romeo* while her husband, Irving, worked as a stage director.[10] Wilson then returned home to Berkeley for the latter part of the summer, taking time out to speak at a rally in San Jose in support of striking women telephone switchboard operators.[11] Before getting back on the road for the YMCA, he took time out for yet another campaign. In November 1919, the United States Senate would decide whether to ratify the treaty forming the League of Nations and commit the U.S. to working together with its allies and former enemies to create a durable peace. As the vote neared, treaty opponent Senator Hiram Johnson toured California urging the public to join him in opposition. Wilson trailed Johnson around the state, giving speeches in support of the League of Nations, under the auspices of the California League for the Adoption of the Peace Treaty.[12] Ratification of the treaty required approval by two-thirds of the U.S. Senate and with Woodrow Wilson rejecting compromise proposals to ratify it with certain reservations, it was voted down in November 1919 and again in March of 1920.

As America moved into the 1920s, wartime hopes of progressive social transformations collapsed. During the war, wages and union membership had increased. By 1920, union membership had nearly doubled to 5.0 million from 2.7 million in 1917. But as war production came to an end, unemployment rose, employers reduced wages, and workers responded with a wave of strikes in an effort to maintain their incomes. Europe was the scene of attempted revolutions in Germany and Hungary, inspired by the October Revolution in Russia that replaced its short-lived democracy with a "dictatorship of the proletariat," which turned out to mean dictatorship of the Communist Party leadership. American politicians saw the opportunity to win business support by linking labor and communism and launched a "Red Scare," treating strikes as precursors to attempted revolution. By 1923, union membership had fallen to 3.6 million.

The Socialist Party of America, already weakened by wartime repression of anti-war organizations, split into three groups, the Socialist Party, the Communist Labor Party, and the Communist Party. Socialist Party membership fell from 108,000 in 1919 to 27,000 in 1920 and to 13,000 by 1921.[13] Even some socialists who supported the war would not escape the Red Scare. Fedor ("Fred") Postnikov, Socialist candidate for the Berkeley city council in 1913, joined the U.S. Army as soon as America entered the war. It was a way to show patriotism for his adopted country and to support then-democratic Russia against the German invasion. He was made a captain and assigned to train soldiers in the use of observation balloons. After the war, he considered joining the Communist Labor Party and visited their office in Oakland. There he found three plainclothes Oakland police officers confiscating literature. Postnikov, thinking they were vigilantes, told them to stop and that their actions were "not Americanism." The police pushed him through a glass door and beat him so severely on the head with their clubs that he suffered migraine headaches for the rest of his life. He was acquitted of interfering with the police but lost his suit for damages for mistreatment and false arrest. The publicity linking him to the Communist Labor Party harmed his engineering business, and in 1928 he moved to Mena, Arkansas, to teach at Commonwealth College, which prepared students for work in social justice movements. After a few years, he left his teaching position but remained in Arkansas until his death in 1952, working as an engineer and promoting and teaching Esperanto in the hope that this international language would contribute to world peace.[14]

Wilson had found a satisfying role with the YMCA, but after the first year it did not provide him with a regular salary. Instead, the YMCA chapters that invited him had to raise the money to cover his stipend and expenses. Wilson's presentations in the summer student leadership encampments introduced him to the student YMCA leaders who would then invite him to speak at their schools the following year. Wilson grouped his invitations to keep travel expenses down and used higher payments from larger schools to subsidize speaking at smaller schools whose payments often did not even cover his expenses. He was also able to obtain infrequent contributions of $100 or $200 at a time from a few wealthy supporters. He made a modest living after covering his travel expenses. In the 1923–24 school year, he reported that he cleared somewhat under $200 a month (about $3,000 a month in 2020 dollars) and this came at a real cost to his family life.[15] He was home consistently only in July, August, and September after the encampments were over and before the student YMCAs had organized themselves for the new school year. When home in Berkeley, he was a frequent speaker at local churches, but he never sought to resume his ordination or take a position as a pastor, which would have offered a much easier life.

In the summer of 1920, his son-in-law, Irving, accepted a position as assistant director for his former Harvard classmate, Sam Hume, now in charge of the University of California's Greek Theatre.[16] Violette and Irving moved into the downstairs rooms in Highland Home, where their first child was born in September, and then into a flat in the house the Wilsons owned next door. For the next several years, while Stitt was on the road, Emma had her daughter and first one and then two grandchildren nearby and her sister and nieces down the street.

Along with his work at the Greek Theatre, Irving started a Berkeley Playhouse in which he directed the plays and he and Violette often played the leading roles. They especially favored plays with strong, complex female leads, such as George Bernard Shaw's *Man and Superman* and *Pygmalion*, Molnar's *Liliom* (from which the musical, *Carousel*, was adapted) and Eugene O'Neill's *All Gods Chillun Got Wings* and *The Great God Brown*.[17] Violette began work on designing a new home in Berkeley and received national publicity for being a mother of two who cooked for her family while also working as an actress and, now, as an architect.[18] Before the house was built, conflict between Irving and his Berkeley Playhouse board of directors resulted in his taking a new position as director of the Pasadena Playhouse in 1927.

After moving to Pasadena, the Pichels continued to visit Berkeley regularly. On one of their visits, a reporter for the *Oakland Tribune*, having been assigned to follow up on the state of Violette's soul, learned that her views had evolved since she left the university. "My soul? It's in my children and my home, the two most precious things in the world. If women could only know where happiness lies, they would forget all this talk about their independence and cast aside all these ultra-modern theories as just mere nothings of an unreal world." Had she cast aside all feminist self-assertion, or was she just playing another role? The next month she had the lead in

George Bernard Shaw's *St. Joan* and continued to act alongside her husband for several more years, until his growing success as a movie actor, beginning in 1931, and later as a director left him little time for the theater.[19]

In the early 1920s, Wilson's lectures emphasized "the just and Christian use, and control and administration of property," denounced "economic oligarchy," and made the case for an economy based on cooperation and the dignity of all human beings. His recommended readings featured *The Acquisitive Society* by the English Christian socialist, R. H. Tawney, who called for replacement of capitalism with worker control over industry without explicitly calling for socialism.[20] But the 1920s was not a period in which critiques of the structure of private property rights would gain much traction.

For the 1920–21 school year, Wilson added material on the importance of reducing international and interracial conflict to his calls for economic and social justice. In a new lecture, he appealed for an end to war by making two contradictory arguments. First, war would fatally weaken European and American civilization and destroy the leadership position of the white race. Second, to prevent war, race prejudice must be abolished. The people of Asia and Africa were following the example of Japan and "all of the peoples we used to consider unimportant have developed into mighty forces" who must be respected. "In this day when God is planning more than ever to make the world one, it [race prejudice] is pure hell."[21]

The following year he abandoned this racially oriented approach to international issues. In its place, he took up the socialist analysis presented by Leonard Woolf in *Economic Imperialism* (1920), which described colonialism as economic exploitation, and he returned to the socialist view of war as the outcome of competition for markets.[22] At the YMCA conference at Asilomar in Pacific Grove, California at the end of 1921, students from China and other countries expressed their deep appreciation for Wilson's internationalist appeal for world brotherhood.[23]

Materials on Wilson's views on race are thin and contradictory. In his YMCA talks, he apparently upheld the equality of blacks and whites, but, as with women, he had an essentialist approach to equality. While he regarded women's equality as necessary for creation of a cooperative society, he treated racial equality as secondary. He urged men to respect women's contributions to society, but there is no similar record of his urging white audiences to respect Black or Asian American contributions to society, although he urged respect for African and Asian nations. So there was a clear note of condescension when, in a YMCA speech at a Black college, he urged his audience to "be true to your genius" and suggested that in religion, music, oratory, and the "soulful things of life," they had "a contribution to make that the white race cannot make."[24] It is unclear what he believed that contribution might be.[25] Soon after, the noted theologian Reinhold Niebuhr suggested that Black Americans' "peculiar spiritual gifts" would enable them to successfully use Gandhian nonviolent resistance, such as boycotts against racially discriminatory businesses.[26] The YMCA Student Division was racially "liberal" in the South, but its statements on race, including one whose list of signers included Wilson, were appeals to whites to treat Black Americans decently and to help "uplift" their race, yet avoided any challenge to segregation.[27]

As the possibilities of post-war social transformation slipped away, Wilson's talks aligned more with the traditional YMCA concern for developing Christian character. He criticized modern education for leaving out spiritual and moral development and offered a three-step technique reminiscent of his previous New Thought teaching. He first asked students to commit themselves to God, then to engage daily in silent prayer or meditation in which students would place themselves in touch with all-encompassing God and "the Life of the Infinite as revealed in us." Finally, he asked that they commit themselves to the service of humanity, following the life and message of Jesus.[28] He argued for the compatibility of science and religion, noting that not all of the Bible should be taken literally. He illustrated this with a lengthy criticism of Social Darwinism, arguing that it was based on a misunderstanding of evolutionary theory and that cooperation, mutual aid, and "Christ-spirit" better enabled species to survive than individualism and competition.[29] His religious critique of the current institutions of property continued, but with much less emphasis.

Independent and third-party campaigns

Wilson was briefly drawn back into California politics in 1922 by personal connections and his ties to the union movement. Dr. Linden McCash, the Wilson family chiropractor, had become a close family friend. McCash was married at Highland Home in a ceremony conducted by Rev. Herman I. Stern and assisted by Ben Wilson, with the rest of the Wilsons as witnesses.[30] In January 1920 and again in February 1921, McCash was arrested for practicing medicine without a license. Emma and Leila Wilson posted bail and Stitt Wilson testified in his defense. In both cases, McCash was convicted and chose to serve brief jail terms rather than pay a fine that would help support the state medical board.[31]

Wilson denounced this as persecution of chiropractors by medical doctors, described how chiropractic treatment had saved Emma Wilson from a life of pain, and argued that a free people had a right to the medical treatments of their choice. He accompanied delegations of chiropractors and their supporters to the state legislature, asking for a separate state licensing board for chiropractors, but their efforts failed due to opposition by the medical board. In September 1921, Wilson spoke to a mass meeting to kick off a signature-gathering campaign that succeeded in placing the matter before the voters for the November 1922 election. The state medical board continued its enforcement efforts, and in May 1922, three chiropractors were jailed in Stockton, an agricultural city east of the Bay Area in the Central Valley. Just back from lecturing at colleges in Pennsylvania, Wilson led a protest parade of several hundred automobiles from Oakland to Stockton, where he urged support of the initiative. In September, he spoke to a major chiropractic rally in Sacramento.[32] Wilson enjoyed a political success when the initiative to establish a Board of Chiropractic Examiners passed in November.

On July 1, 1922, there was a nationwide strike of railroad maintenance and repair workers opposing wage cuts at a time of rising prosperity. A few days later, Wilson was a featured speaker to 6,000 delegates at the annual meeting of the California Christian Endeavor Union, held in Oakland that year. He applauded the strike and warned that America must not allow a "plutocracy drunk with power" to place civilization at risk. In his conclusion, however, he urged only careful study on to how to apply the Sermon on the Mount to the institutions of property rather than appealing for an economy based on cooperation.[33] Both Stitt and Ben Wilson followed up with speeches to the striking railroad shop workers in which the pair denounced the post-war effort by business to break the unions. After the president of the Sacramento local was shot and killed by a strikebreaker, a memorial parade was held with some 9,000 area unionists and their families marching, followed by an address by Wilson.[34] The show of union strength was unavailing against railroad companies backed by the power of the Federal government. In September, the strike collapsed after a federal judge issued a sweeping, unconstitutional injunction against striking, picketing, and even assembling to hear speeches supporting the strike.[35]

After the war, employers in San Francisco organized an Industrial Association that coordinated efforts to reduce wages in San Francisco to the same level as other cities with much weaker unions and to eliminate provisions in union contracts that required employees to join a union. This effort to weaken the unions was largely successful.[36] Partly as a result, in statewide politics, Governor Stephens, who was relatively friendly to labor, was defeated in the Republican primary by State Treasurer Friend W. Richardson, who had become hostile to progressivism of any sort, and the Democratic candidate was also very conservative. Impressed by Wilson's support for the railroad workers and desperate for a pro-union alternative, a coalition of unions asked him to run for governor again as an independent and he agreed.

Wilson announced his candidacy on September 15th, with a platform focused on democracy and human rights over property rights. He proposed to convene "a convention of the plain people of California and set them to write their own State platform," since neither farmers nor workers had any influence on the major party platforms. He and his supporters had only three weeks in which to gather nearly 10,000 qualifying signatures, and they had to be from people who had not voted in the primary election. He toured Southern California holding rallies and gathered well over 10,000 signatures, but too many of them were disqualified and the effort failed.[37] Instead of running for governor, Wilson headed east to lecture at colleges in New England.

On Monday, September 17, 1923, Wilson was on his way home from a Methodist conference in Cleveland, where he had given a series of talks on the application of Christianity to industry. While he was still en route, a grass fire in the hills northeast of the university swept downhill and burned much of the residential area north of the university, all the way to a small section of Shattuck Avenue, the main north-south street through downtown Berkeley. Several thousand people were made homeless in the worst natural disaster in Berkeley history, although miraculously no one was killed. Its path came within just two blocks of Highland Home, but it destroyed Ben and Leila Wilson's house and a four-unit apartment building that Stitt and Emma had built as a source of retirement income. They had paid for it with their savings and by mortgaging their home, and while the insurance paid off the mortgage on the apartment building, the Wilsons were left continuing to pay off the mortgage on their home for years afterward.[38] Ben and Leila were fortunate to find temporary quarters and then built a new home on the north edge of town.[39]

Ben had only recently returned home himself. He and his family had traveled to England in the summer of 1923, where he gave speeches on behalf of the Labour Party as he had done back in 1909 and 1910.[40] The parliamentary elections in December 1923 gave Labour its best result ever. With support from the Liberal Party, the Labour Party formed a minority government under Ramsey McDonald, which lasted only nine months until October 1924. No doubt inspired by the welcome given his brother and by the chance to see a Labour government in action, Wilson arranged to travel and lecture in Great Britain over the summer. The plan fell through when he was unable to obtain a passport, something that had not been necessary for foreign travel before the war. He could not find his citizenship papers and the Chicago office that had originally issued them was unable to find copies. Wilson decided that the easiest course was to reapply for citizenship, which then required a two-year waiting period.[41]

In October 1924, Wilson took a break from lecturing at colleges to campaign in Southern California for Republican Senator Robert La Follette of Wisconsin, the presidential candidate of a coalition of progressives, unions, and socialists.[42] Ben Wilson toured Colorado and Wyoming as a campaign organizer.[43] In most of the U.S., La Follette was the candidate of the Progressive Party, but the Socialist Party endorsed him and in order to get a ballot line in California, La Follette was nominated as the Socialist Party candidate. This was a new direction for the Socialists.

The older party leaders, Eugene Debs, Victor Berger, and Morris Hilquit, had stayed with the Socialist Party rather than joining the Communists, but party membership had fallen to only 11,000 by 1922.[44] The Socialists now sought alliances with local Farmer-Labor and Labor parties, which they had previously scorned as being capitalist. There were a number of left, liberal, union, and agrarian efforts to create an explicitly liberal nationwide third party, and in 1924 all these fragments of the non-revolutionary left briefly came together in the La Follette campaign. Faced with two conservative major-party candidates, the American Federation of Labor joined in supporting La Follette. Nationwide, he received 17% of the vote, winning only his home state of Wisconsin. In California he received one-third of the vote, coming in second to Republican Calvin Coolidge. La Follette and the American Federation of Labor refused to continue support for the Progressive Party and make it a permanent organization after the campaign, disappointing those who hoped for a major left-wing third party.

After the 1924 election, Wilson returned to YMCA lecturing, starting with a month giving talks at colleges in Iowa. Helped by a friendly YMCA state secretary, he arranged for his brother Ben to join the lecture series. Stitt would do three days of two or three lectures a day and Ben would follow with another two days of lectures to sociology, economics, and history classes on the principles, program, and people of the British Labour Party. After Iowa, the brothers were not able to sustain their joint presentations, and Ben struggled to find work during the rest of the 1920s. He continued to lecture to colleges and civic organizations interested in hearing about this new force in British politics and then moved on to other topics. He lectured for a time for the Berkeley-based Anti-Rodeo Cruelty Association before taking a position in 1929 as minister of the Unitarian Church of Erie, Pennsylvania. This kept him away from home for much of the year until he finally became minister of the Unitarian Church in San Jose in 1933.[45]

Now in his late 50s, Wilson was feeling tired and wanted to move on from lecturing at colleges. He wrote to a longtime friend and supporter, Dr.

John Randolph Haynes, that his most recent lecture tour had taken him to fifteen states over eleven weeks and the travel was now "too hard and too strenuous" and "most of all my heart is almost broken with these long, long absences from home, with which my whole life has been filled." Haynes had supported the Social Crusade when Wilson first came to California; over the years the doctor provided financial support to many progressive and socialist causes and individuals, including the Public Ownership League run by former Social Crusader, Carl Thompson.[46] He and other wealthy supporters had talked about going beyond occasional small donations and creating a fund to support Wilson's work. Hoping this might allow him to slow down and be more selective in his speaking engagements, Wilson asked them to follow through, but without success. One supporter sent a letter confessing his embarrassment, saying, "It is an easy matter to talk generalities but when it comes to 'talking turkey' it is different."[47] Another effort some years later was similarly unsuccessful.

Revisiting the British Labour Movement

La Follette died in 1925; Herman I. Stern, Wilson's old friend and neighbor, died in July 1926; and Eugene Debs died soon after, in October 1926. The older generation was passing and the American left seemed less influential than ever. The state of the left was much more hopeful in Great Britain. There, Conservative economic policies had led to stagnation and high unemployment throughout the 1920s and helped motivate increasing support for the Labour Party. In the summer of 1927, with new citizenship papers in hand, Wilson joined the staff of the annual YMCA and YWCA tour, led by Sherwood Eddy. The tours took leading Protestant church people from around the U.S. to Great Britain and Europe to learn about Christian social welfare programs and international relations. After they arrived in London, Wilson took a small group of those staying at the Toynbee Hall settlement house on a weekend trip to Cardiff, Wales, where he introduced the group to old friends from the Independent Labour Party and spoke to a crowd of 3,000 people who gathered in the Cardiff city square to hear the famous American orator. He did a similar side trip to Bradford, Yorkshire. Wilson then continued on with the tour to visit the Netherlands, Germany, Czechoslovakia, Austria, France, and Switzerland, where they spent a week studying and observing the League of Nations.[48] His old comrades from Bradford and Cardiff urged him to return and, inspired by his reception, Wilson agreed to come the next summer.

Shortly before Wilson was to leave for England in the summer of 1928, his Independent Labour Party sponsors told him that in the worsening

British economy their resources were feeding the families and helping pay the rent for their many unemployed members and they could not pay his travel expenses. Wilson decided to go anyway, telling the comrades that he would "trust in the Lord."[49] Wilson asked Dr. Haynes for $100 (about $1,500 in 2020 dollars) to help cover expenses, which Haynes duly forwarded.[50]

That June, Wilson boarded a ship in New York City, joining that year's Sherwood Eddy tour, which paid his way to England and, after a month with the tour, he began work with the Cardiff Independent Labour Party.[51] A.W. Hunt, president of the Cardiff Trades and Labour Council, had been deeply impressed by Wilson's speeches in 1908–1909 and served as chair of a Social Crusade Committee that organized weekly mass meetings in which Wilson was the featured speaker. Wilson was again well received, beginning with a speech to 4,000 people in a large park at the end of July and concluding his time in Wales a month later with an address to at least 2,000 people at the Cardiff Hippodrome.[52] He and the Cardiff comrades produced a four-page "Souvenir Edition" of *The Social Crusader: A Messenger of Brotherhood and Social Justice*, with articles and quotations from Wilson and statements from local Labour candidates for Parliament.[53] Wilson then moved on to Bradford for two weeks of speeches and visiting old friends.[54]

Wilson returned home in mid-September of 1928, energized by the possibilities in Great Britain. Resting up in Berkeley, Wilson told a University of California student forum on the coming elections that while he was a registered Democrat he intended to vote for the candidate of the Socialist Party, Norman Thomas. He warned that "we are sailing along on what we think to be an eternal prosperity. This is a tragic illusion . . . our little house of cards will crash. . . . Workers, farmers and middlemen will walk poor in a civilization run by an oligarchy of money. When that time comes, America may learn something from the struggles of British Labor."[55] The stock market crash on Wall Street was just a little more than a year away as he spoke.

In Great Britain, the Conservative government was approaching its fifth year and would soon have to call a parliamentary election, with the exciting prospect of a Labour Party government. Wilson decided to close out his work with the YMCA at the end of the year and return to Great Britain to campaign on behalf of the Labour Party. To come up with money for his trip, Wilson took every speaking engagement he could obtain. Starting with Oregon, Washington, and Idaho, he continued on to Oberlin College in Ohio, and in December he was lecturing at North Carolina State University in Raleigh. With limited funds for his next trip to England and Wales, Wilson stayed on the East Coast, far from his family, for the Christmas holiday.[56]

In early January, Wilson sailed to England, accompanied by his 18-year-old niece, Leila Wilson.[57] From February through April they stayed in Cardiff, Wales, where A.W. Hunt again chaired a Social Crusade committee that organized mass meetings and published an edition of the *Social Crusader*. As always, Wilson emphasized the religious case for a society that would place human rights over property rights.[58] Unlike his YMCA lectures, Wilson's speeches for the Labour Party were again explicitly socialist, but he did not profess to know exactly what socialism would look like.

> This Social Calamity of Poverty that engulfs millions and endangers civilization cannot be cured by any mere "ism," any mere recipe. . . . Socialism is not a thing to put into lectures or books. Socialism is a thing to be done . . . society must arise and abolish the exploitation of the people and organize a just economic order where poverty is no more.[59]

In mid-March, Wilson was laid low by severe leg pains, initially diagnosed as sciatica and then as arthritis. This kept him bedridden, lying on his side, unable to read or write and unable to sleep without pain-reducing drugs. Wilson declined surgery and in desperation turned to a Christian Science healer. After six weeks the pain vanished as mysteriously as it had come. The examinations and care had cost him $300 (close to $4,500 in 2020 dollars) so he was quite grateful that, after several letters, Haynes sent him $200 towards his expenses.[60]

Wilson now resumed campaigning for Labour Party candidates, with the Election Day set for May 30, 1929, and he moved on from Cardiff to Bradford, Leeds, Derby, and other nearby areas. A high point for Wilson came shortly before the election when he served as a warm-up speaker for Ramsay McDonald before a crowd of 5,000 people in Bradford.[61] The Labour Party won 37% of the vote and elected 47% of the members of Parliament, while the Conservatives won 38% of the vote and 42% of the M.P.s. The Liberal Party held the balance of power again, with 24% of the vote but only 10% of the members of Parliament. Having campaigned on a platform of public works to generate employment, the Liberals chose to support formation of a Labour government under Ramsey McDonald. Wilson remained in England for another two weeks, speaking at a series of conferences on religion and citizenship in Leeds, Sheffield, and Bradford. Set up by his friend, David Blythe Foster, now lord mayor of Leeds, the conferences were intended to reinvigorate Christian socialism in England and counteract the rise of materialist and Marxist socialism. In Wilson's view, "In the Bible there is a ground and basis for the most revolutionary thing ever accomplished. Karl Marx is but a pale pink pamphlet compared with the might and force of the Bible."[62]

On June 15th, Wilson and his niece, Leila, sailed back to New York and then took the long cross-country train ride back to Berkeley. He spent the next few weeks resting and giving talks to Bay Area churches and civic organizations on the larger meaning of the Labour Party victory for modern civilization, and he accepted an invitation from D.B. Foster to return to England later in the year and join him in a renewed Social Crusade. Wilson visited Dr. Haynes in Los Angeles and received a promise of financial assistance if it was needed. This time Emma would go to England with him.[63]

Stitt and Emma Wilson headed off to England in November 1929, right after the stock market crash that precipitated the Great Depression in the U.S. In the coming months, the already depressed economic conditions in Great Britain worsened dramatically. D.B. Foster had stepped down as lord mayor, although he remained an alderman, and set up a series of meetings on "Religion and Citizenship" to which he invited clergy and civic leaders. At their initial meeting in Leeds on December 1st, Foster explained that their goal was to "pour spiritual vitality into the common life" so that religious teachers were not left out of the process of governing. Wilson and Foster spent the rest of the week holding follow-up meetings in Leeds, then moved on to spend a week in Bradford and a week in Sheffield. They received invitations from clergy in London, Glasgow and, Cardiff, but the effort failed to generate enough interest to support an active campaign.[64] D.B. Foster continued to hold Social Crusade meetings in Leeds Town Hall for some years and spent the rest of his life urging unity between religion and citizenship.[65]

In March, Stitt and Emma moved on to Cardiff, where he had many friends and supporters.[66] From March 9th to April 6th, he conducted a strenuous campaign of near-daily meetings in churches and halls, preaching his Social Gospel and distributing a four-page "Stitt Wilson Campaign" pamphlet in which he called for "a True Social System, where the rights of human beings shall be first and the institutions of property shall be made the servants of a free humanity."[67] The campaign was not a success. The depression was deepening, unemployment was higher than ever, money was scarce, and a Labour government was in power. Religious and moral appeals to support socialism were no longer so urgent. The best Wilson could say was that "a quiet and serious interest has followed my work." As he had said during the campaign the previous year, "Socialism is not a thing to put into lectures . . . Socialism is a thing to be done." Seriously in debt, having borrowed $500 (about $7,500 in 2020 dollars) to cover living expenses, he wrote to Dr. Haynes to request the promised support, presumably receiving the $500 necessary to pay off his debts, and the Wilsons returned home from what would be their last visit to England and Wales.[68]

California socialism in the Great Depression

After some rest at home, the Wilsons traveled south to Pasadena to visit their daughters and their now-numerous grandchildren. The Pichels had three children and Gladys Viola (stage name Viola Barry) now had five. She and Jack Conway divorced in 1918 after having two children, and in 1921 she married screenwriter Frank McGrew Willis, with whom she had three more children. While visiting Viola, Stitt was stricken by a reoccurrence of the severe pain he had suffered in England. He was hospitalized and had major surgery, after which he came down with pneumonia.[69] Thinking he was near death, Wilson had a vision of an "angel of light" who told him to "arise and serve humanity" and carry the urgent message that the great advances of materialistic science must be balanced by a renewed spirituality and a society engineered for the benefit of all humanity.[70] After this vision telling him to continue what was already his lifelong mission, Wilson gradually recovered, returning home to Berkeley and then returning again to Pasadena to spend the early winter with his children and grandchildren.[71] After more than six months with only the income from renting the downstairs portion of his home and the house next door, Wilson fell back on the YMCA and spent January through March of 1931 making a nationwide tour that took him to North Carolina, Pennsylvania, Ohio, Michigan, Oregon, and Washington.

The Great Depression worsened by the month. In 1929, the unemployment rate was only 3%. In 1930 it was 9% and by 1931 it had reached 16%. That summer he wrote up a "twenty-five-year plan" to transform the economy from its current "anarchy" to a planned economy designed to provide economic security for all. Like many others, Wilson pointed to the success of economic planning during World War I as a model. He proposed a set of local, regional, and federal economic councils that would bring together business executives, labor leaders, and technical experts to organize and coordinate production, continuing private ownership of industry but placing control of the production process with the economic councils and eventually moving to some form of social ownership of key industries. In addition, he stated that the U.S. government should issue "Public Welfare Bonds" to provide immediate relief and employment to the unemployed and their families.[72]

The details of Wilson's proposal were not reported, but his views were likely similar to those of a group led by Sherwood Eddy for the YMCA student division. They argued that "the profit motive must be supplanted by the motive of service or production for use, which in turn means that ownership . . . should rest in the hands of the community and that control should rest jointly with the producers and consumers." They called for a national economic planning commission and support for all forms of social ownership, including worker and consumer cooperatives, government ownership, and corporate governing boards that would include workers, consumers, and representatives of the public.[73]

As the Depression dragged on, the rhetoric of liberal Democrats sounded more and more similar to that of the Socialists, but without the call for social ownership. New York Governor Franklin D. Roosevelt talked about the economic "chaos" and "lack of plan." As a candidate for president, he proclaimed that the U.S. must become not only a "nation of independence" but also a "nation of interdependence." In 1933, immediately after his inauguration as president, he instituted the National Recovery Administration (NRA), an effort at national economic coordination that established industry councils with representatives of business and labor along with technical experts. Big business quickly came to dominate these industry councils and the Socialist Party expressed fears that the NRA might turn in the direction of fascism.[74]

Wilson attended various student conferences and recruited several students to join him in a new Social Crusade, giving speeches around the San Francisco Bay Area calling for a planned economy based on the teachings of Jesus.[75] In July and August of 1931, his speaking invitations included the First Methodist Episcopal Church of Oakland, the First Congregational Church of Alameda, the Berkeley Society of Friends, the Kiwanis Club of Alameda, the Commonwealth Club in San Francisco, the Alameda County Building Trades Council, and the Oakland branch of the American Legion.[76] He briefly drew national attention when *The New York Times* reported that church leaders from thirteen states attending a conference in Buckhill Falls, Pennsylvania, were "Stirred by Stitt Wilson." He challenged the churches to lead the way to creating a planned economy, advocating, in addition, reduced hours of labor, a public works program, unemployment and sickness insurance, old-age pensions, and the abolition of child labor.[77]

He followed up with a Social Crusade tour through the cities of the Central Valley and Southern California, using the model he developed for his Institute of Democracy series during the war. He spent the first week of November in Bakersfield, where he gave an introductory public talk on Sunday evening at the First Methodist Church and spoke there every evening thereafter, introduced variously by the mayor, the president of the local labor council, and prominent business and professional men. In addition, he conducted a "School of the Social Gospel" in four afternoon meetings with ministers and religious leaders and spoke to the Boosters Club, the Lions Club, the Rotary Club, and the Kern County Ministerial Union.[78] Wilson and his student assistants were unable to sustain the new Social Crusade, but his enthusiasm and sense of the possibilities of the time remained high.

Describing the YMCA Asilomar conference at the end of 1931, an observer remarked that Wilson had "all of his usual fire and enthusiasm; Sir Galahad on his way to the shining City of God by way of the oppressed of the slums."[79] Wilson spent most of his time at home in the Bay Area and in Southern California where he could stay with his daughters in Pasadena, but did some traveling to Eastern and Midwestern states, speaking to church conferences and church-affiliated colleges on "The Worldwide Depression and the Way Out," "The Responsibility of the Church in the Present Worldwide Economic Crisis," "Wanted: a Christian Crusade for Economic Justice," "Our Economic Revolution," and similar themes.[80]

Wilson's enthusiasm for economic planning would soon be widely adopted by mainstream Protestant churches. Over the next several years, to cite a few notable examples, the Federal Council of Churches strengthened its Social Creed to include "social planning and control of the credit and monetary systems and economic processes for the common good." The Northern Baptist Convention stated that "the people have the natural right to hold, and can safely be entrusted with, the power of democratic control over their economic life." The General Council of the Congregational Church went so far as to pass a resolution "to work toward the abolition of . . . our present profit-seeking economy."[81]

In 1932, the Depression continued to worsen, with unemployment passing 23%. Wilson returned to the Socialist Party, and urged on by an enthusiastic group of Young Socialists at the University of California, Berkeley, he declared his candidacy for Congress. A newly formed congressional district represented Northern Alameda County (including Berkeley and the northern half of Oakland) and Southern Contra Costa County. These were areas where he had done well twenty years previously and where he had maintained an ongoing speaking presence in local churches. Wilson called for "national planning . . . in the interest of all the people."[82]

Wilson was immediately brought into the leadership of the party. He gave the keynote address at the California Socialist Party annual convention and was elected to chair the state central committee.[83] He campaigned as hard as he had twenty years earlier, speaking in high school auditoriums, churches, and street corners, renewing his ties with unions and working with former comrades despite past conflicts. When Socialist presidential candidate Norman Thomas arrived in the Bay Area in October, Wilson presided at his rally in San Francisco and was one of the speakers at his Oakland rally, with his old rival, Austin Lewis, presiding. Also among the speakers were officers of the "Union Labor J. Stitt Wilson Club" from the Machinists Union and the Sheet Metal Workers.[84]

On Election Day, Wilson came in third, with 23% of the vote, behind the Democrat with 32% and the Republican with 45%. He was one of only three Socialist Party congressional candidates to receive more than 20% of the vote, but it was more a personal than a party accomplishment. The other two Socialist candidates ran in long-time socialist strongholds, the area of Milwaukee where Victor Berger had been elected to Congress several times and the area around Reading, Pennsylvania, which had elected Socialist Party candidates as mayor and sent Thomas Maurer, the Socialist vice presidential candidate, to the state legislature.

By 1933, one quarter of the workforce was unemployed. Many engaged in self-help efforts, such as labor exchanges and barter exchanges where people would trade goods and services with each other. Some of the organized exchanges traded with farmers in outlying areas, helping to harvest crops in return for a percentage of the crop that they would bring back and distribute to the exchange membership. The most successful of these efforts were able to bring small manufacturing facilities back to life to serve their

J. Stitt Wilson for Congress campaign flier (Berkeley Historical Society).

membership. Some distributed their own money or "scrip" based on hours of work. Wilson helped organize a short-lived Pacific Coast Barter Exchange and did outreach for the Pacific Coast Cooperative League (PCCL). Headquartered in West Berkeley, the PCCL operated a labor exchange, store, garage, lumber yard, flour mill, and canning and weaving projects.[85]

As the nation waited out the four months between Election Day in November 1932 and inauguration day in March 1933, which would bring in the new Roosevelt administration, the Socialist Party tried to organize and take leadership of a broad coalition of workers, farmers, and unemployed organizations. Drawing on the language of the American Revolution, it created local "Committees of Correspondence" and called for a "Continental Congress of Economic Reconstruction" to meet in Washington, D.C., on May 6–7, 1933.[86] Wilson led a delegation from Alameda County representing the Socialist Party, the unemployed, and cooperative self-help organizations.[87] The congress drew around 4,000 people, many of them leaders of local unions, farmers resisting foreclosure, self-help organizations of the unemployed, and some small third-party or would-be third-party organizations. The League for Independent Political Action sent a delegation led by Professor (later Senator) Paul Douglas, hoping to persuade the Socialist Party to join in creation of a broad-based Farmer-Labor Party.[88]

The congress approved a "Declaration of Independence," drafted by Wilson and two other prominent Socialists, Paul Blanshard, a former Congregationalist minister, journalist, and lecturer, and Harry Laidler, an economist and head of the League for Industrial Democracy. They declared that "since the first Declaration of Independence the American people have discovered and created the means of unheard of wealth. . . . But today the nation starves in the midst of plenty." They called for "a new economic system based upon the principles of co-operation, government ownership and democratic management" and for an end to planlessness, waste, and exploitation.[89]

The Continental Congress called for state congresses to be held around the country as the next step in forming a permanent national organization. Wilson was selected to convene the California group, and the California Congress of Workers and Farmers met in Sacramento on July 22–23, 1933.[90] It brought together 350 delegates representing 150 groups, "farmer, unemployed, barter, union, fraternal, political, youth, student, etc." and had another 250 observers.[91] The organizing committee had very little money and many of the delegates were unemployed and in extreme poverty. They held the congress in the cattle barn at the state fairgrounds, with one section used as the convention hall and committee meeting spaces, another section closed off as men's and women's dormitories, and another area used for the kitchen and dining room.[92] Wilson had appealed for the loan of rugs for the delegates to sleep on—they brought their own blankets.[93] The congress passed a series of resolutions calling for immediate improvements and long-term economic reconstruction and set up regional meetings to arrange support for local actions and organizing.[94]

Wilson was the keynote speaker for the Southern California regional meeting, held on September 9th in Pomona, a small city 30 miles east of Los Angeles in an area specializing in growing oranges and lemons. There, several hundred people from throughout Southern California proposed to use the union provisions of the new National Recovery Act to organize a union of unskilled laborers and agricultural workers, groups largely ignored by the American Federation of Labor.[95] Local organizers followed up with the creation of a Pomona Valley Congress of Workers and Farmers and Wilson spoke at several of their meetings.[96] Wilson described the participants in the organizations represented by the congress as "new recruits . . . the majority of them have no experience in mass action of the workers or farmers on the economic field and none whatever of mass action on the political field." Against proposals to immediately form a third party, he argued that "the supreme task before us right now is to promote every possible organization of the workers and farmers to face their dire economic situation and to let this process develop into a solidarity of interest that must inevitably fruit in corresponding solidarity on the political field."[97]

Wilson claimed that more than 4,000 orchard workers had been organized by groups affiliated with the congress. It is not clear what role the Socialist Party or the congress may have played in agricultural labor organizing in California. During the 1933 harvest time, a major agricultural strike wave went through Northern and Central California in response to successes by workers affiliated with the Communist-run Cannery and Agricultural Workers Industrial Union (CAWIU). Even when workers organized themselves, they usually sought out the CAWIU for advice. Previous agricultural workers' strikes in California had been met with systematic violence and repression by vigilantes and local law enforcement. This time, after vigilantes murdered several strikers, representatives of the Roosevelt administration stepped in and threatened to withdraw the benefits provided by the Agricultural Adjustment Act from farmers who refused to accept federal mediation.[98] The strike wave won wage increases for most agricultural workers in California, but agribusiness refused to recognize their unions and since most of the workers moved from crop to crop the workers' organizations fell apart once the harvest was completed. The Communist Party's *Western Worker* happily reported that membership in the Socialist-sponsored

Union of Workers and Farmers had fallen from 5,000 to only 200 in October 1933.[99]

Socialists and Communists were bitter enemies. Under the direction of Soviet dictator Joseph Stalin, the Communists asserted that democratic socialist and labor parties worldwide were "social fascists" who must be destroyed in order to set up a direct confrontation between capitalism and the Communist Party. When Communists joined mass organizations, they did so to take them over and recruit members. The Socialist Party's 1933 Continental Congress in Washington, D.C., excluded Communists. When four delegates representing the Communist Party showed up at the California Congress in Sacramento, Wilson denied them speaking privileges and they got no support from the other delegates.[100]

Socialists generally considered the Soviet Union to be a continuation of a long-standing authoritarian Russian culture whose experience did not apply to the U.S. Even so, many socialists had great respect for the way the Soviet Union had established a national planning process and put its entire population to work. Ben Wilson, now a Unitarian minister, visited the Soviet Union during the summer of 1932 with a group called the American Social Sciences Commission and gave many talks about his experience, often accompanied by movie footage shot by a member of the group. He spoke under the auspices of both the Communist-controlled Friends of the Soviet Union and the Socialist Party as well as churches and civic groups, so his overall presentation must have been favorable. Stitt introduced his brother for one such talk at the Unitarian church in Berkeley, but there is no record of his own views on the Soviet Union.[101]

Organizing against foreclosures

Soon after his return to Berkeley from the Washington, D.C., Continental Congress, Wilson began working with the Sonoma County branch of the Farmers Protective League, an organization of small farmers fighting foreclosures. The league focused its initial campaign on James L. Case, a 70-year-old retired minister who lived with his wife and two daughters on a 50-acre Gravenstein apple and cherry orchard in Forestville, about 60 miles north of Berkeley. A local bank had already seized and sold his apple crop and had arranged for the county sheriff to auction off the farm. League chairman Wilford Howard asked Wilson to attend a protest meeting, which Wilson was happy to do. "Paul Revere Riders" from the league posted signs along area roads calling for farmers and farm hands to join in protesting the foreclosure. On Sunday, July 9th, more than 1,000 men and women rallied at the Case ranch and heard a series of speakers call for them to come and protest the foreclosure auction scheduled to be held the next Friday at 10 a.m. on the county courthouse steps in Santa Rosa.[102]

The keynote speaker was a very emotional Stitt Wilson. Case's situation likely evoked Wilson's earlier effort to retire to a small ranch and orchard in Hemet and his recent years worrying about his own retirement.

> This nation now faces an emergency in which the letter of the law should be discarded in favor of the welfare of humanity. . . . President Roosevelt has urged that foreclosures be delayed and in fighting this sale we are only backing up the President. . . . We showed them in Iowa (where protesting farmers had blocked roads leading to courthouses) and we will show them here. It may be necessary to drag any bidders off the courthouse steps. Are you willing?

The assembled farmers shouted promises to come and some said they would bring their pitchforks.[103] Fearing violence, Governor James "Sunny Jim" Rolph urged the bank to "carry Mr. Case until better times. . . . Mortgage holders who are lenient now will gain later." The bank president refused, saying, "This affair has evolved into a matter of principle—whether mob rule or law shall prevail." The county sheriff promised to carry out the sale and the Santa Rosa Police Chief canceled all leaves previously granted for the coming Friday.[104]

On Friday morning at 9 a.m., an hour before the auction was scheduled, 1,500 people supporting Case gathered in front of the courthouse— no pitchforks were visible—along with a large contingent of police and sheriff's deputies, and listened to a series of speakers, while lawyers for the Farmers Protective League made a last-ditch effort to persuade a judge to cancel the sale. The size of the crowd had grown to about 2,500 when Wilson launched into his speech. Wilson assured the audience that the protest would be entirely peaceful and expounded on how the finance industry oppressed small farmers. The Depression had caused deflation and lowered wages and prices, with the result that borrowers like Rev. Case were being forced to repay far more than the value of what they had borrowed. "This isn't a fight for James Case," he shouted, "It's a fight for all the farmers from San Francisco Bay to Plymouth Rock."

With the auction only minutes away, the chairman of the Farmers Protective League came out and whispered to Wilson, who announced that the judge had granted a one-week injunction against the sale. This success, Wilson said, "would echo across the entire United States in this battle of the farmers against the oppression of financial interests." He then led the crowd in singing "John Brown's Body" and they dispersed peacefully.[105] Ten days later the injunction was made permanent, on the grounds that when the bank had seized and sold Case's crop it had accepted a payment and would have to restart any foreclosure proceedings. In January 1934, with the assistance of a federal mediator, the bank negotiated a revised loan agreement with Case that lowered the interest rate on his loan and gave him three years to get current on his loan.[106]

J. Stitt Wilson, James L. Case, and Case's wife in Santa Rosa
after the Cases' foreclosure sale is blocked (unattributed
newspaper photograph, author's collection).

The Roosevelt Administration created a Federal Land Bank for the purpose of assisting farmers with loans and refinancing to reduce foreclosures. One of the twelve regional offices was located in Berkeley. Two days before Thanksgiving, Wilson, Wilford Howard, and fifty farmers picketed the bank, urging faster action on the loans necessary to fend off foreclosures. After an hour of picketing, the bank president invited them in, talked over the problems, and met individually with many of the picketing farmers, promising to notify mortgage holders that they must cease foreclosure proceedings while the Land Bank reviewed their cases.[107] Wilson continued speaking to groups representing small farmers. His main topic was foreclosures and how to stop them, drawing upon the law, federal agencies, and the political power of organization.[108] In July of 1934, he spoke to another large rally at the courthouse in Santa Rosa, protesting foreclosure against a blind 76-year-old retired farmer, proposing that most of the farm be sold to repay the mortgage but that Mr. and Mrs. Goddard be allowed to keep the small section with their home, a proposal that was apparently successful.[109]

The EPIC campaign

The gains made by workers in the first year of the Roosevelt administration were modest. Unemployment continued to rise in 1933, reaching nearly 25%. But the gains were real and they weakened the effort to create a coalition to the left of the New Deal. By the end of 1933, the Continental Congress had collapsed back into the work of the Socialist Party.[110] One recent history of the Socialist Party argues that it was a mistake for the Socialist Party to keep its distance from the League for Independent Political Action and the Farmer-Labor Political Federation it formed shortly after the Continental Congress.[111] The two groups were eager for Socialist participation and the delegates to the conference that founded the Farmer-Labor group even elected Wilson to their National Committee in absentia. Wilson declined and explained that in his view "any effort to launch a new radical political party in California at this time . . . would (bring together) small groups of genuine radicals to be sure, and a few progressives and liberals, but *no mass action* and no backing by large and important organizations of either workers or farmers."[112] The Minnesota Farmer-Labor Party was the only left-wing third party to develop real strength, electing its candidates for governor throughout the 1930s, but the Minnesota party had been building strength and electing candidates to office since 1918.[113]

A number of prominent Socialists tried a different strategy and left the Socialist Party to join campaigns within the established parties that they believed would move the New Deal to the left. Paul Blanshard, one of the coauthors of the Continental Congress' Declaration of Independence, left the Socialist Party to support Fiorello LaGuardia's 1933 race for mayor of New York as a candidate of the Republican and Fusion parties. Upton Sinclair, Socialist candidate for governor of California in 1930, took a more direct route. In September 1933, he changed his party registration and announced that he would run for governor in the Democratic primary.

In classic Upton Sinclair fashion, a month later he followed this announcement with a sixty-eight-page booklet, "I, Governor of California, and How I Ended Poverty: A True Story of the Future." Sinclair decided that the American people could be won over to a socialist message if they were approached through the political parties they already identified with, using language that was easy to understand and that could be identified with American traditions. Sinclair's EPIC Plan (End Poverty in California) drew on the experience of the unemployed workers' self-help cooperatives and proposed that the State of California acquire unused land and factories so that the unemployed could produce and exchange the food, goods, and services they needed.[114] The sales tax would be repealed, modest homes and small farms would be exempted from property tax, and instead there would be taxes on high incomes, inheritances, and stock transfers, as well as an increase in taxes on banks, private utility companies, and unused land. This would fund pensions for the elderly, the disabled, and widows with dependent children.

Norman Thomas, the Socialist Party leader and successor to Eugene Debs as its perennial presidential candidate, told the party and Sinclair that he was doomed to failure—that without an organization of workers committed to taking power and taking over industry, the forces of capitalism would defeat EPIC and ruin any EPIC producer cooperatives. Socialist Party membership in California was about 1,200. Thousands of California voters organized themselves and formed hundreds of EPIC clubs supporting a campaign whose slogan was "production for use," a longstanding way of describing socialism.[115]

Wilson stayed with the Socialist Party and spoke out against violations of civil liberties in California, along with Austin Lewis, who had helped found and was now a leader in the California chapter of the American Civil Liberties Union.[116] Wilson gave a series of talks on the spread of fascism in America.[117] His recent work supporting agricultural laborers, as well as experiences twenty years earlier, had given him a close familiarity with the repression by law enforcement and armed vigilantes that was typical of agricultural areas in California. His new talk for church groups, "The Gospel of Property and Poverty," reminded his listeners that the earliest Christians shared all their property.[118]

At the Socialist Party's annual convention in Detroit in June of 1934, the party declared that if there was an effort to bring the U.S. into a war it would be opposed by "massed war resistance . . . a general strike (that would) convert the capitalist war crisis into a victory for Socialism." A similar promise was made that if there was an effort to prevent an elected Socialist majority from governing the country "we shall not hesitate to crush, by our labor solidarity the reckless forces of reaction . . . true democracy must be created by the workers of the world."[119] This was strong talk for a party whose membership nationwide was still only about 21,000 after four years of economic depression. Wilson considered these "grandiloquent threats" from the tiny party to be "ridiculous." He was offended by the "poor lip service" given to the defense of democracy. "Democracy is in danger. All the more crying necessity to rally the whole soul of democracy . . . and renew the confidence of the despairing masses in the ways of democracy." Instead the party mimicked the bombastic, revolutionary language of the Communists.[120]

A disgusted Wilson re-registered as a Democrat and went to work campaigning for Upton Sinclair. Wilson and Sinclair had been friends for a long time. Sinclair was a resident of Pasadena and Wilson likely visited him occasionally while visiting the Pichels, who were also enthusiastic Sinclair supporters. Sinclair initially proposed that Wilson run for state controller but the campaign committee opposed this, concerned about having too many former Socialists on the EPIC slate, and Wilson declined the offer.[121]

He threw himself into the EPIC campaign with his characteristic energy, traveling up and down the state, describing the current misery and asking people to unite behind "a man and a plan who is going in the right direction."[122] On several occasions, he spoke along with Sinclair. At other times, he spoke alongside Jerry Voorhis, who had been inspired by Wilson's YMCA talks at Yale. Voorhis had moved to Pasadena in 1927 to found a racially integrated residential school for orphaned boys and he had helped organize the Pomona Valley Congress of Workers and Farmers.[123] Like Sinclair and Wilson, Voorhis left the Socialist Party and was running in the Democratic primary as the EPIC candidate for state assembly in the Pasadena area.[124] The August 28th primary showed Upton Sinclair the victor with more than 400,000 votes, more than all the other Democratic candidates combined. Voorhis and many other EPIC candidates also won their primaries.

Virtually all of the longtime Democratic leadership refused to support Sinclair in the general election. Some endorsed Merriam, the Republican. Others, like Senator William Gibbs McAdoo, made generic statements that they supported all Democratic candidates. Sinclair argued that the EPIC program was simply an advanced version of the New Deal and tried, unsuccessfully, to gain Roosevelt's endorsement. The campaign against Sinclair that followed was groundbreaking in the amount of money spent and in its use of film—fake newsreels were shown in movie theaters throughout the state purporting to show hobos with Russian accents heading for California. Major newspapers drew on Sinclair's copious writings, including statements by fictional characters in his novels, to portray him as anti-religion, anti-family, a communist, and so on, while largely blacking out news of Sinclair's campaign events.[125]

EPIC relied on people-power, concentrated mostly in the Los Angeles area and the San Francisco Bay Area. Wilson again traveled up and down the state, calling EPIC "a campaign to start a great revival of Americanism" and using his background to refute claims that Sinclair was against religion.[126] His brother, Ben, gave speeches in the Bay Area and son-in-law Irving Pichel gave speeches in Pasadena and acted in a benefit performance of a Sinclair melodrama called *Depression Island*. As he had in so many campaigns, Wilson ended his tour in Berkeley, speaking the Monday evening before Election Day, November 6, 1934, in the auditorium of the Veterans Memorial Building.[127] This time Sinclair lost, receiving 38% of the vote to 49% for Merriam and 13% for an independent candidate. His 879,537 votes were almost as many as Norman Thomas had received nationwide in 1932.

With the election over, Sinclair went home to write his book, *I, Candidate for Governor: And How I Got Licked*, while the EPIC candidates and activists worked to continue the EPIC legacy. Although at first their differences were not apparent, they gradually split into two factions. One group, which received backing from Sinclair, worked to make EPIC a permanent organization called the End Poverty League, with an elected board rather than leaders appointed by Sinclair. The league focused on supporting the cooperative self-help movement and candidates for political office committed to "production for use" in California and in other states. They considered themselves a movement, separate from any political party. The newly elected EPIC members of the state legislature, led by State Senator Culbert Olson, proposed that the EPIC clubs become Democratic clubs and work to move the New Deal to the left. Many EPIC clubs did this, with the result that Olson was elected chair of the State Democratic Party Central Committee, and ongoing conflict began within the party between Olson supporters and McAdoo supporters.

In 1935, Wilson worked with both sides and traveled around the state speaking both to Democratic Clubs controlled by EPIC activists and to EPIC Clubs.[128] In March, he played a prominent role in the creation of the statewide Production for Use Congress, which brought together representatives of cooperatives, EPIC Clubs, the Technocracy Society, the Utopian Society, and Democratic Party activists and unionists who had supported the EPIC campaign. Wilson gave the keynote address, thanking Sinclair for his great educational campaign and urging support for the cooperative movement. He was chosen as chair of the steering committee, which also included Jerry Voorhis, a board member of the End Poverty League who was also on the State Democratic Party Central Committee, and Wilfred Howard of the Farmers Protective League of Sonoma County.[129] They immediately began planning for a series of mass meetings around the state, to be followed by a larger statewide convention in July.

At the July conference, the EPIC forces had a bitter struggle with the Communist Party. The Communists had denounced EPIC as social fascism in 1934, but in 1935 there was a new party line. After Stalin realized that Communist attacks on the German Social Democratic Party had helped pave the way for Hitler to take power and destroy the Communist Party as well, he called for a broad "popular front" against fascism. A delegation from the California Communist Party asked to have representatives at the Production for Use Congress. Wilson, as conference chair, oversaw a vote that denied representation to the Communist Party on the grounds that they were an anti-democratic organization. Many party members still participated as representatives of other organizations. As a result, Sinclair and his supporters spent a great deal of energy trying to prevent the Communist Party from taking over EPIC and its related organizations.[130]

The Roosevelt administration created a number of programs to support consumer and farmer co-ops, but it refused to allow work within self-help organizations to qualify for pay under its emergency employment programs. This drew workers away from the self-help worker cooperatives. Despite some support from the State of California, based on the idea that producer cooperatives could save money over conventional relief payments, between 1934 and 1936 participation in the self-help movement declined by more than two-thirds. With a declining co-op movement and ongoing conflict over Communist influence, the Production for Use Congress soon collapsed.[131]

Roosevelt or Fascism!

Late in 1935, concerned that division among California Democrats might hand the state to the Republicans in the next presidential election, EPIC Democrats and McAdoo Democrats began efforts at reconciliation. Speaking at a Roosevelt rally in Oakland that brought together leaders of both groups, Wilson declared to much applause that "the people of California don't want any more sweet words . . . the people want action. We'll go along with the President of the United States if he marches forward."[132] By the end of 1935, Wilson, along with many others on the left, were feeling much more positive about the Roosevelt administration. In what is often called the Second New Deal, Congress passed Social Security, which would provide old age pensions; the National Labor Relations Act, which put real teeth into workers' right to organize independent unions; and the Works Progress Administration (WPA), which provided government-funded employment to millions of unemployed.

Wilson undoubtedly noted the contrast between Roosevelt's accomplishments and the failure of most European socialist and labor parties to deal effectively with the Great Depression. In Great Britain, Prime Minister Ramsey McDonald and Philip Snowden, Chancellor of the Exchequer (Secretary of the Treasury) had maintained strict fiscal orthodoxy, cutting government programs to balance the budget as revenue declined during the Depression. This made unemployment worse, and Snowden's actions were opposed by a majority of the Labour Party members of parliament. McDonald left the Labour Party and created a "national" coalition government with the Conservative and Liberal Parties along with Snowden and a few other Labour MPs. McDonald's supporters were immediately expelled from the Labour Party. The result of this debacle was that the Labour Party was decimated in the 1931 elections.[133]

Most European socialist parties, with the exception of the Swedish Social Democrats, also maintained capitalist fiscal orthodoxy, taking the attitude that little could be done until capitalism was replaced by socialism. This paralysis of the socialist and labor movements, combined with the Communist Party's attacks on the noncommunist left, left the door wide open for the rise of fascism in Germany and elsewhere in Europe.[134] The fascists were not constrained by capitalist economic orthodoxy, and preparing for war provided effective employment programs. The conclusion that Wilson drew was that the United States had a simple choice, "Roosevelt or Fascism!"[135]

With the 1936 Democratic National Convention coming up in June, the EPIC Democrats submitted a list of proposed Roosevelt delegates to be part of the administration-approved slate of candidates in the upcoming Presidential primary election. The EPICs had pledged both to support Roosevelt and to propose "production for use" as part of the national Democratic platform. They were dismayed when Roosevelt approved a slate of 49 candidates that included 32 McAdoo "regulars" and only 10 EPICs, including Olson, Voorhis, and Wilson. Since this was far fewer than their proportional support within the Democratic Party, all ten agreed to resign from the slate.[136] At the EPIC conference that followed a few days later, Sinclair and his supporters decided to run a slate of candidates pledged to vote for production for use and to vote for Sinclair for president. This was too much for Wilson and he and one of the other EPIC supporters agreed to return to the Roosevelt slate.[137] Wilson made the break with Sinclair complete by denouncing Sinclair as undemocratic because he had required that no criticism of him ever appear in the *EPIC News*.[138] In the May 5th primary, the administration slate was overwhelmingly elected and the EPIC movement in California never recovered from its break with Roosevelt.

The filing deadline was coming up for the August primary election to determine candidates for state and federal offices. Berkeley and North Oakland now had a Democratic congressman. The neighboring district, covering southwest Contra Costa County and the remainder of Oakland, was represented by a Republican, Albert Carter. He was first elected in 1924 and since then had run unopposed in every general election, winning both the Republican and Democratic primaries, as was then allowed under California's open primary system. At the urging of the Democratic Party leadership in the area, who were looking for someone with sufficiently broad appeal to win back the Democratic Party ballot line, Wilson rented an apartment in Oakland and filed to run for Congress in the Democratic primary, declaring his complete loyalty to Franklin D. Roosevelt. Two other Democrats also filed, including an EPIC Democrat, who denounced Wilson as a "political opportunist" and a tool of a reactionary Democratic machine whose intention was supposedly to split the Democratic vote and reelect a Republican.[139]

In late June, Wilson flew east to the Democratic National Convention in Philadelphia, having been appointed to the Platform Committee and the Resolutions Committee, stopping off in Lakeside, Ohio, to speak to the Christian Youth Conference of North America to give his usual call for youth to follow Jesus and help build a moral economic system. On his return to Berkeley, he began a round of speeches at Democratic meetings and picnics. The primary election results gave Carter 43% to Wilson's 41%, with the remainder going to the two other Democrats. Carter easily won the Republican nomination and even won the Progressive Party nomination with write-in votes.[140] He would not see opposition in a general election until he was finally defeated in 1944.

Conflict between "regular" and "progressive" Democrats continued, with Wilson trying to play a neutral role and appeal for unity. When the Alameda County Democratic Committee met in an Oakland courtroom to elect officers, the progressives, who had one-third of the delegates, demanded a secret ballot. The temporary chair, a regular, refused, the progressives shouted down the proceedings, and a fist fight started that was broken up by dragging the participants outside. At that point, Wilson, showing real agility for a man of 68, jumped up on the judge's bench, demanded "fair play," and insisted that the delegates vote on the motion to use a secret ballot. The chair finally agreed, but when the secret ballot was voted down 22 to 12, most of the progressives walked out.[141] Things were far more amicable the following week at the California Democratic convention. The McAdoo and Olson forces settled on a joint slate of delegates to the convention, including Wilson, and declared unity in their campaign for Roosevelt and the Democratic congressional candidates. Wilson spent the ensuing six weeks until the general election campaigning for Roosevelt and for Jerry Voorhis, who was now running for Congress.[142]

After his reelection, Roosevelt turned his attention to protecting his legislative accomplishments. The U.S. Supreme Court had spent the previous forty years overturning progressive economic legislation, including much of the first New Deal legislation, and he had every reason to believe that the current members would uphold challenges to the Second New Deal. After four years as president without getting the chance to appoint a justice to the Supreme Court, in February 1937 he proposed Federal court reform legislation that included provisions allowing him to appoint an additional judge to the Supreme Court for each judge who remained on the court after reaching the age of 70 rather than retiring. This would have allowed him to appoint six new justices. The plan was vehemently opposed not only by Republicans but by more conservative Democrats.

In California, the Democratic Party organized to support Roosevelt with a statewide petition drive and employed Wilson to speak in support of the proposed court reform legislation. From March through May, Wilson toured the state, giving hard-hitting speeches. He reviewed the horrors of the Great Depression, the failure of the Hoover administration to act, and the accomplishments of Roosevelt and the New Deal. He described how the courts, packed with reactionary servants of the plutocracy, had systematically laid waste to legislation that was passed by large and democratically elected legislative majorities. This was, he argued, a fight "to place human rights above the rights of property and privilege" and to vindicate democracy against a dictatorial exercise of power by five judges on behalf of "economic royalists." He concluded by describing President Roosevelt as "a wise, a humane man, a fearless champion of human rights, the outstanding leader of the principle of democracy in the world" and insisted that "we are not going to be thwarted or turned aside from our march to economic freedom."[143] In March of 1937, the Supreme Court began issuing decisions

that were more favorable to the New Deal, and in May one of the most conservative justices announced his retirement. This made Roosevelt's Supreme
Court proposal unnecessary and allowed Congress to pass court reforms
without the sections that would change rules governing the Supreme Court.

With Roosevelt safely in the White House and the Supreme Court willing to uphold most New Deal legislation, California Democrats returned to
their internal conflicts, looking forward to the 1938 elections for governor
and for U.S. senator. In October, Wilson helped organize and gave the keynote address to a "California Committee of 100 for Political Unity," which
hoped to unify liberals and progressives against "reactionaries" of both the
Republican and Democratic parties. The group brought together both former EPIC Democrats and union leaders from both the American Federation of Labor and the new Congress of Industrial Organizations. Within a
few months, the group was moribund, split between those who wanted to
unite behind liberals in the Democratic primary and those who wanted to
use the shell of the old Progressive Party to start a third-party movement
in California.[144]

Wilson was now firmly in the Democratic Party camp and supported
the successful primary and general election campaigns of former EPIC
leader Culbert Olson for governor. Wilson also continued to be active in
support of the cooperative movement. For a time he was the state organizer
for the newly formed California Cooperative League, which tried to bring
together farmer and consumer cooperatives for mutual support.[145] After taking office in 1939, Governor Culbert Olson appointed Wilson to the State
Social Welfare Commission, which had oversight of the state Department
of Social Welfare (DSW) and its programs for assistance to the elderly, disabled, and children and to the State Relief Commission, which oversaw the
State Relief Administration (SRA) and its programs for the unemployed.
These appointments provided him with a modest income in addition to
what he and Emma received from renting out the downstairs portion of
Highland Home and the house next door that they had purchased in the
1920s. Wilson was an active commissioner, chairing or participating in small
subcommittees that investigated whether appointments to jobs in the SRA
had been subject to undue personal influence, evaluated re-employment
programs, and made various other studies and reports.[146]

In April of 1938, Wilson spoke alongside Lillian Hellman at a rally
held at the University of California's Sather Gate and sponsored by the
Student Peace Conference and the Committee for the Anti-War Strike,
calling for America to stay out of European wars. By November, with the
Spanish Republic collapsing under the attacks of General Franco's fascists,
assisted by troops and weapons provided by Hitler and Mussolini, Wilson

had changed his mind. He was one of several speakers at a Friends of the Abraham Lincoln Brigade dinner and rally honoring Fred Keller, who was wounded fighting in defense of the Spanish Republic and returned to the U.S. to campaign for American intervention.[147]

In early 1940, in preparation for the Democratic National Convention in Chicago that would select a candidate for president, Governor Olson organized to elect a slate of delegates, including Wilson, who were committed to support a third term for Roosevelt. Wilson campaigned at Democratic Party events and house meetings, although to do so he had to resign from his commission appointments, due to a state law banning political activity by state employees. In the May primary, the Roosevelt slate received three-quarters of the vote, overwhelming a slate supporting Roosevelt's vice president, John Nance Garner, a conservative Texas Democrat who opposed most New Deal legislation and was running for president against FDR, and a slate headed by Lieutenant Governor Patterson, who argued that Roosevelt was too conservative.[148]

The remainder of 1940 was a difficult time for Wilson. He became too ill to attend the Democratic National Convention in July. Shortly after he recovered, on August 28, 1940, he had the sad duty of conducting the memorial service for his brother Ben Wilson, who died of a heart attack at age 66.[149] Despite his illnesses, Wilson was reappointed to the State Social Welfare Commission in April of 1941 and continued to do some public speaking on issues of social welfare and the war.[150] By mid-1940, Hitler had conquered continental Europe and was bombing Great Britain. Wilson helped organize a Berkeley branch of the Committee to Defend America by Aiding the Allies and spoke at meetings and signed newspaper advertisements to support Roosevelt's Lend-Lease bill and other U.S. aid to Great Britain.[151]

A week before the bombing of Pearl Harbor brought America into the war, Wilson told an audience that "Hitler and the wicked gangsters who support him . . . have butchered, slaughtered, bombed and murdered hundreds of thousands of human beings in countries where people were sitting waiting, even as our isolationists are waiting, crying peace, peace when there was no peace."[152] Wilson went on to say that "the greatest achievement of the human race is not invention, not the production of wealth, not the building of great cities—Man's greatest achievement is liberty, incorporated into law. This liberty is so sacred . . . that life is cheap compared to the loss of that sacred right."[153] Back in the 1920s, Wilson had several reinforced concrete garages built into the hillside below his home to serve his family and tenants. With American entry into the war, he offered them as bomb shelters for the neighborhood in case the Japanese attacked the Bay Area.[154]

Confronted by his own mortality and continuing to suffer from frequent illnesses, in the spring of 1941 Wilson began work on his autobiography with characteristic energy. His manuscript, which reached 210 typed pages, gives remarkably detailed descriptions of the area he grew up in, his extended family, his youth, and his courtship of Emma, but it offers only passing comments about his life beyond the day of his marriage at the age of 21. On several different occasions he remarked on his current state.

> It is springtime as I write. . . . At the moment I am convalescent from a recent illness. Day after day I have looked out of my bedroom window at the trees and the shrubbery and the flowers with the almost hourly change of tone and color, and away up through the tree tops to the green hills and on to the panorama of cloud effects in the distant blues or grays of the sky. Time and again, during these days, I have been moved to tears at the unpretentious glory of it all.[155]
>
> Today I lay down in the tall green grass away up on the hill and as I opened my eyes the most perfectly formed and radiant little California poppy looked straight into my heart. . . . All lives are sacred. Too sacred for our dull minds to comprehend.[156]
>
> Last week, while lying here on my bed, not feeling so good, as usual in my convalescence, my beloved daughter Violette unexpectedly romped up the upstairs hallway and broke into my door and leaped onto my bed and seized me in her arms before I knew it (and) I forgot my illness as the spirit of that visit enveloped me.[157]

One of his last talks was at the Fellowship of Humanity on May 30, 1942, on the subject of "The War—The Victory—The Peace."[158] In it he no doubt called for thoroughgoing social reconstruction after the war. By that time he doubted he would live to complete his autobiography, so he wrote a brief five-page overview intended to accompany his now-lost papers, concluding:

> This is 1942. I am still on the battle line, fighting for Freedom and Justice and Humanity, as I have been down through my crowded years—and so shall I fight to the end, The Lord being my helper.[159]

J. Stitt Wilson died at his beloved Highland Home on August 28, 1942.[160]

A visionary life

At the time of Wilson's death, the outcome of World War II was very much in doubt, and with it the future of democracy. During his lifetime his adopted country, the United States, had endured constant economic cycles, with a few years of prosperity always followed by disastrous economic collapses. When Wilson was 25 years old in 1893, the United States plunged into what was, up to that point, its worst depression, and when he was 61 in 1929, the country plunged into an even worse depression whose effects lasted for nearly the rest of his life. Yet despite the difficult, ever-changing nature of his times, he lived his life with great energy and optimism for the future. Faced personally, as a minister, with dramatic extremes of wealth and poverty and their attendant suffering, he became determined to persuade his fellow citizens to create a society based on caring, cooperation, and democracy; a society that would embody Jesus's message of love and sacrifice for one another.

He took great joy in communicating his vision of a better world. Often he worked himself to the point of collapse, and he endured endless personal attacks, both from those who defended the existing social order and from those who believed in revolutionary shortcuts. He drew strength from his family, but he and his wife Emma were haunted by the deaths of three of their beloved children. In spite of all the heartbreak in his personal life, he took an open and experimental approach to building a better world, and as mayor of Berkeley proved himself a capable administrator and politician. He made mistakes, changed his mind, moved on, and never stopped fighting for his ideals. Always, he returned to his visionary teachings and as his life came to an end, he was content in believing that he had done what he could.

BIBLIOGRAPHY

A partial list of pamphlets, articles, texts of speeches, and unpublished biographical material written by J. Stitt Wilson.

1898

"Ethical Aspect of the Labor Problem," *New Time: A Magazine of Social Progress*, November 1897. Reprinted as a pamphlet, 1898.

"The Social Crusade," *New Time: A Magazine of Social Progress*, April 1898. Reprinted in part in *The Social Gospel*, May 1898.

Christ's Solution of the Labor Problem, pamphlet (no date), 1898.

1898–1902: Articles in *The Social Crusader*

Wilson founded and wrote for the monthly magazine *The Social Crusader* (Evanston and Chicago) from September 1898 to February 1901, and again from February 1902 to possibly September 1902 (Los Angeles). For the year 1902, only the February issue is known to survive.

"Five Fundamental Truths of the Social Crusade," September 1898.

"An Analysis of Social Conditions," December 15, 1898.

"Christ's Solution of the Labor Problem," revision of the 1898 pamphlet, January 15, 1899.

"An Appeal to the Working Classes: What We Must Do to Be Saved," February 15, 1899.

"Social Crusade Program: Definite Objects of Our Work," July 1, 1899.

"Individual and Social Salvation," September 1899. Reprinted with minor revisions in *Christian Socialist*, 4, no. 11, 1907.

"Labor Day Address," October 1, 1899. Originally an address delivered in Terre Haute, Indiana, on September 4, 1899.

"The Ideal Reformer," November 1, 1899.

"The Free Man," December 1, 1899.

"Our Convictions," May 1900.

"The Whole Task," June 1900.

"The New Continent of Thought," July 1900.

"The Competitive System vs. Socialism, or Animal Ignorance vs. Human Intelligence," September 1900.

"The New Social Apostolate formed by Prof. Geo. D. Herron, It Includes the Brothers of the Social Crusade," January 1901.

"The Spiritual, Moral and Social Elements of the New Gospel," February 1901. Reprinted in the February 1902 issue.

"The Objects of Our Work," February 1902.

1901–1902

"The Present Moral Conflict," *International Socialist Review*, 1, no. 7, January 1901, 385–394.

"The Revolution of Revolutions," excerpt, *The Challenge*, June 12, 1901.

"Christianity and Paganism (A Reply)," *International Socialist Review*, 2, no. 1, July 1, 1901, 1–13.

"Labor's Politics," *Advance*, San Francisco, October 12, 1901, 2–3.

"The Impending Social Revolution or the Trust Problem Solved," *Social Crusade*, Berkeley (no date), mid-1902. Excerpt printed as "An Economic Exposition" in *Wilshire's Magazine*, November 1902. Entire pamphlet reprinted as "The Impending Social Revolution or the Labor Problem Solved," 1904. Note: This pamphlet is completely different from "The Impending Social Revolution," with no subtitle, published in *The Social Crusade Series* in 1909 and 1911.

"A Strike in Colorado," *The Socialist*, Seattle, October 26, 1902.

1902–1904: Articles in *The Path-Finder*

Published by Edgar Wallace Conable, Path-Finder Publishing, Conable, Arkansas. From November 1902 to October 1904, Wilson wrote a column under the heading "Socialism and Life" in *The Path-Finder* (after January 1904, the periodical was called *Conable's Path-Finder*). The journal titled itself the *Path=Finder*, but it is unclear whether this was a metaphysical equivalence or a design statement.

"Socialism and Life," introduction to column, November 1902.

"Life," December 1902.

"Perpetual Opulence," January 1903.

"Can New Thought Talk Abolish Poverty?" February 1903.

"New Thought and Poverty Again," March 1903.

"Socialism—A Great Social Idea," April 1903.

"The Law of Suggestion and Socialism," May 1903.

"Socialism Is a Remedy," June 1903.

"Socialism Is Democracy in Industry," July–August 1903.

"A Study of Liberty," September 1903.

"Animal Ignorance vs. Human Intelligence," excerpt from September
1900 edition of *The Social Crusader*, January 1904.

"Socialism and Government," March 1904.

Untitled, excerpt from "The Impending Social Revolution," May
1904.

Untitled, June 1904.

"The Morals of the Competitive System," August 1904.

"Socialism and Disease," October 1904.

1904–1906

"An Open Letter to William Jennings Bryan and His Followers," *Appeal to
Reason*, Aug. 20, 1904.

The Message of Socialism to the Church. Berkeley: published by the author,
Sept. 15, 1904, and May 1, 1906. Originally an address delivered
before the Bay Association of Congregational Churches and
Ministers, Oakland, California, on September 13, 1904. Republished
in *The Social Crusade Series*.

The Three Great Hypnotisms. Westwood, MA: Ariel Press (no date), circa
1905.

Life Lesson—The Mission of Jesus to Our Time. Westwood, MA: Ariel Press.
Note: no surviving copies—based on "Inspired Life" classes, circa
1905.

The Tragic Game of Capitalism. Berkeley: published by the author, May
1906.

"The Moral and Spiritual Significance of Socialism," *Conable's Path-Finder*,
July 1906.

1907–1908: Articles in *Ariel*

Published by George E. Littlefield, Ariel Press, Westwood, MA. Wilson published under the heading "The Life Message."

"Follow the Inward Urge," March 1907, 16–25.

Untitled, February 1908, 4–8.

"Capitalism Analyzed," March 1908, 9–14.

"The Moral and Ideal Element in Socialism," March 1908, 14–17.

"Socialism: The Cry for Life," August 1908, 6–10.

1907–1908

*The New Theology and Socialism, or Social Evolution in the Light of the Divine
Immanence*. Bradford, Yorkshire, England: published by the author,
1907. Originally an address delivered to the Summer School of
Theology and Applied Religion, Penmaenmawr, Wales, August 3–9,

1907. Republished in *The Social Crusade Series* as "The Kingdom of God and Socialism."

The Social Crusader, a 4-page tabloid, published by the author monthly from August 1907 to at least July 1908. The only known surviving issue is no. 13, published July 1908 in Cardiff, South Wales. It contains "A Morning Meditation" and "Socialism Will Destroy Private Property!"

1907–1913: The Social Crusade Series (SCS)

Self-published pamphlets derived from speeches delivered in 1904, 1907, 1908, 1909, 1910, 1913. Many editions with varying numbering.

How I Became a Socialist and Other Papers. Berkeley: published by the author, September 1912. (Note: includes *The Social Crusade Series* 1–9 collected in book form with pages numbered separately for each pamphlet/chapter.)

The Impending Social Revolution, SCS no. 1, also as no. 8. U.K.: 1909; Berkeley: 1911. See also "Agenda for Discussion on 'The Impending Social Revolution'," *Christian Socialist*, October 15, 1910. (Note: This presentation on Christian socialism is entirely different from the 1902 presentation on political economy with the subtitle "The Trust Problem Solved.").

The Messiah Cometh: Riding Upon the Ass of Economics, SCS no. 2. Originally an address to the Summer School of Progressive Theology, Aberystwyth, Wales, in September 1908. Reprinted in part in *The Christian Socialist*, September 15, 1910.

The Kingdom of God and Socialism, SCS no. 3. Bradford, Yorkshire, England: 1907. Originally an address to the Summer School of Theology and Applied Religion, Penmaenmawr, Wales, on August 3–9, 1907.

The Message of Socialism to the Church, SCS no. 4. Cardiff, Wales: 1909. Originally an address to the Bay Association of Congregational Churches and Ministers, Oakland, California, on September 13, 1904.

Moses: The Greatest of Labour Leaders, SCS no. 5. Cardiff, Wales: August 1, 1908, and Huddersfield, Yorkshire, England: April 1909. Originally an address in Halifax, Yorkshire, in June 1908.

The Hebrew Prophets and the Social Revolution, SCS no. 6. Originally an address to the Summer School of Progressive Theology, Aberystwyth, Wales, in 1908.

How I Became a Socialist, Part I, SCS no. 7, also nos. 1 and 4. Bradford, Yorkshire, England: December 3, 1907; Oxford: July 1, 1908; and

Berkeley: July 1911. Reprinted in part in *The Christian Socialist*, September 15, 1910.

How I Became a Socialist, Part II, SCS no. 8, also no. 2. Bradford, Yorkshire, England: January 4, 1908; Cardiff, Wales: May 1909; and Berkeley: July 1911.

The Bible Argument for Socialism, SCS no. 9. Berkeley: January 2, 1911. Originally an address to Methodist ministers, San Francisco, on December 12, 1910.

The Harlots and the Pharisees: or the Barbary Coast in a Barbarous Land; also *The Story of a Socialist Mayor, Letter Declining Mayoralty Nomination*, SCS no. 10. Berkeley: October 20, 1913. Originally an address given at the Scottish Rite Auditorium, San Francisco, on Sunday, September 21, 1913, along with other material relating to his work as the mayor of Berkeley.

Vocational Education, Appeal to Women, Story of a Socialist Mayor and Other Papers, SCS no. 11. Berkeley: November 1, 1913. Originally an address to the California Teachers Association in San Francisco, in January 1913, along with other material.

1910

"The World Issue Stated," *Christian Socialist*, Sept. 15, 1910.

Articles in *The World*, Oakland, California

"To the Working Class of California," June 25, 1910.

"Open Letter to Comrades," June 25, 1910.

"To the Organized Labor of California," July 2, 1910.

"The Message of the 'Red Special'," July 23, 1910.

"A Message to Labor—Just Where We Stand," August 27, 1910.

"Socialist and Labor Policies," September 3, 1910.

"The Tide Is Turning," October 15, 1910.

"To the Workers of California," October 29, 1910.

"People of California," October 29, 1910.

1911

"Modern Socialism: Its Moral and Spiritual Significance," *Aquarian New Age* (Part I) March 1911, 161–165; (Part II), April–May 1911, 193–196; (Part III) July 1911, 257–263. From an address to the Presbyterian Ministers Association of San Francisco.

The City for the People, March 28, 1911. Contained mayoral, council, and school board campaign statements.

"The Resurrection," *The Tailor: Official Organ of the Journeymen Tailors'*

Union of America, May 1911, 1–4. Originally an address at the Central Theater, San Francisco, on Sunday, April 16, 1911.

"Socialism: The Judgment of Civilization," *The Tailor: Official Organ of the Journeymen Tailors' Union of America*, July 1911, 1–4. Originally an address at the Central Theater, San Francisco, on April 23, 1911.

"Socialism: Constructive and Administrative," *California Social Democrat*, September 2, 1911. Originally an address at the Temple Auditorium, Los Angeles, on August 20, 1911.

"Some Suggestions for Reform in Taxation," *Proceedings: Fourteenth Annual Convention: League of California Municipalities*, Santa Barbara, California, October 23–28, 1911, 152–159. Originally an address on October 25, 1911.

1912

"Open Letter to the Women of Alameda County," *World*, August 24, 1912. Reprinted in SCS no. 11. Reprinted in part as "An Appeal to Women," *Progressive Woman*, November 1912, and reprinted in part as "After Suffrage—What?" *California Social Democrat*, June 13, 1914.

"Message to Non-Socialist Voters," *California Social Democrat*, October 19, 1912. Address given at Dreamland Rink, San Francisco, on September 25, 1912.

"To the Socialists of Alameda County," *World*, September 14, 1912.

"The Labor Problem," *World*, October 26, 1912.

"In Memoriam—A Message to My Comrades," *California Social Democrat*, December 21, 1912.

1913

"Mayor Wilson Urges Closing of Saloons," *Berkeley Daily Gazette*, February 7, 1913. Reprinted in SCS no. 11, November 1913.

"Letter Declining Mayoralty Nomination," *Berkeley Daily Gazette*, February 19, 1913. Reprinted in SCS no. 10, October 1913.

"The Christ Spirit and the Social Revolution," *California Social Democrat*, March 22, 1913.

The City for the People, April 3, 1913. Contained mayoral, council, and school board campaign statements.

"Social Revolution in Moses and the Prophets," *California Social Democrat*, July 12, 1913. Excerpt from a speech given to B'nai B'rith, San Francisco.

"Letter to Governor Hiram Johnson," *California Social Democrat*, August 16, 1913.

"The Story of a Socialist Mayor," *Western Comrade*, September 1913,
186–187, 196. Reprinted in SCS no. 10, October 20, 1913, and SCS
no. 11, November 1, 1913.

"The Mission of Labor," *California Social Democrat*, September 13, 1913.
Originally a Labor Day address given to the Alameda County Central
Labor Council, Piedmont Park, Oakland, on September 1, 1913.

"Revolutionary Christianity, or the Call of the Christ to the Christian
Church," *California Social Democrat*, November 8, 15, 22, 29, and
December 6, 1913, and *New York Call*, March 12, 1916. Originally an
address at the Scottish Rite Auditorium, San Francisco, on November
2, 1913.

1914

"Christianity in Overalls: An Appeal to the Church on Behalf of
Socialism," *Christian Socialist*, July 15, 1914. Originally an address to
the Chicago Methodist Preachers' Association, on June 29, 1914.

"Human Suffering and Its Amelioration," excerpt in *Marin Journal*, San
Rafael, August 6, 1914. Originally an address at the Scottish Rite
Auditorium, San Francisco, on August 2, 1914.

"Socialism, Labor and The Liquor Traffic: Some Reflections," *Out West*,
October 1914, 182–186.

"Will Those Who Pray for Peace Stop the Industrial War Which Hatches
Out in Universal Hell? *American Socialist*, Chicago, October 3, 1914.

"Socialist Solution" in "What Shall We Do with Our Unemployed This
Winter?" *Oakland Tribune*, December 5, 1914.

1915–1916

"The Minimum Social Program of a Militant Christianity," *World's
Social Progress Congress: Addresses*, 22–34. William M. Bell, ed., Dayton:
Otterbein Press, 1915. Originally an address to the World's Social
Progress Congress, Civic Auditorium, San Francisco, convened April
1–11, 1915, by the Federal Council of the Churches of Christ at the
Panama-Pacific International Exposition.

The City for the People, April 21, 1915. Contained mayoral, council, and
school board campaign statements.

"Social Values in Land," *The Rebel*, Hallettsville, Texas, December 11,
1915.

"A Letter to the Comrades," *California Social Democrat*, January 15, 1916.

"Full Text of Stitt Wilson's Address [on the Saloon]," *Morning Echo*,
Bakersfield, Feb. 5, 1916.

"A Radical Prophet," *Day Book*, April 1, 1916.

"Why Women Should Be Given the Ballot," *Railway Carmen's Journal*, April 1916, 214–215.

"Social Righteousness," *The Rebel*, Hallettsville, Texas, April 22, 1916.

"Stitt Wilson on Referendum No. 8," *California Social Democrat*, June 19, 1916.

1917–1918

Open Letter to the Citizens of Berkeley, 4-page pamphlet, no date; library stamp, March 27, 1917.

"Open Letter from J. Stitt Wilson to Mayor Irving," *Berkeley Daily Gazette*, April 14, 1917.

"Reply to Frederic S. Hughes," *Berkeley Daily Gazette*, April 21, 1917.

"Open Letter from J. Stitt Wilson to Mrs. Samuel C. Haight [and list of 13 others]," *Berkeley Daily Gazette*, April 26, 1917.

J. Stitt Wilson to the People of Berkeley, 4-page pamphlet, no date, April 1917.

"Why Germany Must Be Defeated," *San Bernardino News*, March 20, 1918, and *Riverside Daily Press*, March 26, 1918.

1919–1921

Constructive Christian Democracy: An Outline of Fundamentals in the Message and Movement of Applied Christianity. Berkeley: published by the author, April 1919.

"The Johnson Amendment," *Riverside Press Enterprise*, October 25, 1919.

"Medical Board Is Denounced by J. Stitt Wilson" *Berkeley Daily Gazette*, August 5, 1921.

1922–1923

Constructive Christian Democracy: An Outline of Fundamentals. Berkeley: published by the author, January 1922.

"Property Has No Rights," *World Tomorrow*, April 1922, 112–113.

"Jesus in the Labor Movement," *Intercollegian*, November 1922, 40, no. 2, 1–3.

The Militant Church and Property, The Militant Church and Public Opinion. Berkeley: published by the author (no date), likely 1923. Originally addresses to the National Council of Cities of the Methodist Episcopal Church, Chicago, in February 1922, and Cleveland, in February 1923.

The Christ-Spirit in the Animal World. Berkeley: published by the author, June 1923. Published in three parts in *Methodist Review*, 1923.

1928–1930

"A Meditation on Life," *The Social Crusader*, Cardiff, Wales, July and August 1928.

"Merrie England! Merrie England!" *The Social Crusader*, Cardiff, Wales, July and August 1928.

"The Meaning of Prayer," *The Social Crusader*, Cardiff, Wales, February and March 1929.

"Poverty—That Is the Enemy," *The Social Crusader*, Cardiff, Wales, February and March 1929.

"A Constructive Criticism of Modern Education" in *Am I Getting an Education?* George A. Coe, et al. Garden City, NY: Doubleday, Doran & Co., 1929, 47–60.

"Some Sidelights on the British Labor Movement," *Berkeley Daily Gazette*, July 16, 1929.

"How the Social Gospel came to me," *The Stitt Wilson Campaign*, Cardiff, Wales, March 9 to April 6, 1930.

1934–37

"Stitt Wilson Sees Danger to Party in Declaration," *New Leader*, June 30, 1934.

"The President and the Supreme Court," Appendix to the *Congressional Record*, April 15, 1937, 879–882. Originally an address given in March 1937.

Unpublished biographical material

"Dear Friends," a printed letter regarding the death of William Gladstone Wilson, from Mr. and Mrs. J. Stitt Wilson, Gladys (Wilson) Conway, and Violette (Wilson) Pichel, September 1918.

"Postscript," a second printed letter on Gladstone, by Stitt and Emma Wilson, November 11, 1918.

Autobiography/My Life Story/Sweet Auburn, 1942. Note: multiple titles were given to Wilson's unfinished autobiography by family members when they circulated copies.

The Zetland Schoolmaster Falls in Love, 1942.

My Crowded Years, 1942.

Works by other authors

Albanese, Catherine L. *A Republic of Mind and Spirit: A Cultural History of American Metaphysical Religion*. New Haven: Yale University Press, 2007.

Anderson, Douglas Firth. "The Reverend J. Stitt Wilson and Christian

Socialism in California," 375–400, in *Religion and Society in the American West*, Carl Guarneri and David Alvarez, eds., Lanham, MD: University Press of America, 1987.

Anderson, Douglas Firth. "'An Active and Unceasing Campaign of Social Education': J. Stitt Wilson and Herronite Socialist Christianity," 41–64, in *Socialism and Christianity in Early 20th Century America*, Jacob H. Dorn, ed. Westport, CT: Greenwood Press, 1998.

Anderson, Douglas Firth. *Religious Borderlands of the Urban West: Protestant Anglophone Culture and Institutions in Metropolitan San Francisco, 1900–1920*. Orange City, IA: published by the author, 1998. Accessed June 19, 2020. https://www.dropbox.com/sh/567r22qltfm14b6/AAC8vHu29vXNIsbsOmk58ktYa?dl=0

Archer, Robin. *Why Is There No Labor Party in the United States?* Princeton: Princeton University Press, 2007.

Barton, Stephen. "This Social Mother in Whose Household We All Live": Berkeley Mayor J. Stitt Wilson's Early Twentieth-Century Socialist Feminism," *Journal of the Gilded Age and Progressive Era*, 13, no.4, October 2014, 532–563.

Barton, Stephen. "Berkeley Mayor J. Stitt Wilson: Christian, Socialist, Georgist, Feminist," *American Journal of Economics and Sociology*, 75, no. 1, January 2016, 193–216.

Bean, Walton. *Boss Ruef's San Francisco: The Story of the Union Labor Party, Big Business, and the Graft Prosecution*. Berkeley: University of California Press, 1972.

Beck, Frank O. *Hobohemia*. Chicago: Charles H. Kerr Publishing, 2000.

Bell, Daniel. *Marxian Socialism in the United States*. Ithaca: Cornell University Press, 1996 (1952).

Berman, David R. *Radicalism in the Mountain West, 1890–1920*. Boulder: University Press of Colorado, 2007.

Binyon, Gilbert Clive. *The Christian Socialist Movement in England: An Introduction to the Study of Its History*. London: Society for Promoting Christian Knowledge, 1931.

Bissett, Jim. *Agrarian Socialism in America: Marx, Jefferson, and Jesus in the Oklahoma Countryside, 1904–1920*. Norman: University of Oklahoma Press, 2002.

Bordin, Ruth. *Frances Willard: A Biography*. Chapel Hill: University of North Carolina Press, 1986.

Brands, H. W. *Traitor to His Class: The Privileged Life and Radical Presidency of Franklin Delano Roosevelt*. New York: Random House, 2008.

Briggs, Mitchell P. *George D. Herron and the European Settlement*. Stanford: Stanford University Press, 1932.

Buhle, Mari Jo. *Women and American Socialism, 1870–1920*. Urbana: University of Illinois Press, 1983.

Bullock, Paul. *Jerry Voorhis: The Idealist as Politician*. New York: Vantage Press, 1978.

Burke, Robert E. *Olson's New Deal for California*. Berkeley: University of California Press, 1953.

Burns, David. *The Life and Death of the Radical Historical Jesus*. Oxford: Oxford University Press, 2013.

Bussel, Michael R. *From Harvard to the Ranks of Labor: Powers Hapgood and the American Working Class*. University Park: Penn State University Press, 1999.

Cardwell. Kenneth H. *Bernard Maybeck: Artisan, Architect, Artist*. Salt Lake City: Peregrine Smith, 1977.

Carter, Heath W. *Union Made: Working People and the Rise of Social Christianity in Chicago*. Oxford: Oxford University Press, 2015.

Carter, Paul A. *The Decline and Revival of the Social Gospel: Social and Political Liberalism in American Protestant Churches, 1920–1940*. Ithaca: Cornell University Press, 1956.

Carwardine, Rev. William H. *The Pullman Strike*. Chicago: Charles H. Kerr & Co., 1894.

Cherny, Robert W., Mary Ann Irwin, and Ann Marie Wilson, eds. *California Women and Politics: From the Gold Rush to the Great Depression*. Lincoln: University of Nebraska Press, 2011.

Clark, Thomas Ralph. *Defending Rights: Law, Labor Politics, and the State of California, 1890–1925*. Detroit: Wayne State University Press, 2002.

Cobb, Stephen G. *Reverend William Carwardine and the Pullman Strike of 1894: The Christian Gospel and Social Justice*. Lewiston, NY: Edwin Mellen Press, 1992.

Cord, Steven. *Henry George: Dreamer or Realist?* Philadelphia: University of Pennsylvania Press, 1965.

Cormode, D. Scott. "Faith and Affiliation: An Urban Religious History of Churches and Secular Voluntarism in Chicago's West Town: 1871–1914." PhD diss., Yale University, 1996.

Craig, Robert H. "The Underside of History: American Methodism, Capitalism and Popular Struggle," *Methodist History*, 24, no. 2, January 1989, 73–88.

Craig, Robert H. *Religion and Radical Politics: An Alternative Christian Tradition in the United States*. Philadelphia: Temple University Press, 1992.

Cray, Ed. *Chief Justice: A Biography of Earl Warren*. New York: Simon & Schuster, 1997.

Critchlow, Donald T., ed. *Socialism in the Heartland: The Midwestern*

Experience, 1900–1925. Notre Dame: University of Notre Dame Press, 1986.

Cross, Ira B. "Socialism in California Municipalities," *National Municipal Review*, 1, 1912, 611–619.

Curl, John. *For All the People*. Oakland, CA: PM Press, 2009.

Daniel, Cletus E. *Bitter Harvest: A History of California Farmworkers, 1870–1941*. Berkeley: University of California Press, 1981.

Daniels, Roger. *The Politics of Prejudice: The Anti-Japanese Movement in California and the Struggle for Japanese Exclusion*. New York: Atheneum, 1973.

Debs, Eugene V. "Jesus, the Supreme Leader," *Progressive Woman*, March 1914. Reprinted in *Labor and Freedom: The Voice and Pen of Eugene V. Debs*. St Louis: Phil Wagner, 1916, 22–29.

Deverell, William. *Railroad Crossing: Californians and the Railroad, 1850–1910*. Berkeley: University of California Press, 1994.

Dietiker, Debra N. "A History of the First Unitarian Church of San Jose, California." MA thesis, San Jose State University, 1966.

Dubois, Carol, and Richard Candida Smith, eds. *Elizabeth Cady Stanton: Feminist as Thinker*. New York: New York University Press, 2007.

Dunlap, E. Dale. "The United Methodist System of Itinerant Ministry" in *Perspectives on American Methodism: Interpretive Essays*, Russell E. Richey, Kenneth E. Rowe, and Jean Miller Schmidt, eds. Nashville: Kingswood Books, 1993, 415–425.

Echols, James. "Jackson Ralston and the Last Single Tax Campaign," *California History*, 58, no. 3, Fall 1979, 256–263.

England, Christopher William. "Land and Liberty: Henry George, the Single Tax Movement and the Origins of 20th Century Liberalism." PhD diss., Georgetown University, 2015.

Englander, Susan. "We Want the Ballot for Very Different Reasons: Club Women, Union Women and the Internal Politics of the Suffrage Movement, 1896–1911," in *California Women and Politics*, Robert W. Cherny, Mary Ann Irwin, and Ann Marie Wilson, eds. Lincoln: University of Nebraska Press, 2011, 209–235.

Epstein, Barbara Leslie. *The Politics of Domesticity: Women, Evangelism and Temperance in Nineteenth Century America*. Middletown, CT: Wesleyan University Press, 1981.

Evans, Christopher H. *The Kingdom Is Always but Coming: A Life of Walter Rauschenbusch*. Grand Rapids: William B. Eerdmans Publishing Co., 2004.

Evans, Christopher H. *Histories of American Christianity: An Introduction*. Waco: Baylor University Press, 2013.

Evans, Christopher H. "The Social Gospel, the YMCA, and the Emergence of the Religious Left After World War I," in *The Religious Left in Modern America*, Leila Danielson, Marian Mollin, and Doug Rossinow, eds. London: Palgrave, 2018, 41–60.

Ferrier, William Warren. *Berkeley, California: The Story of the Evolution of a Hamlet into a City of Culture and Commerce*. Berkeley: published by the author, 1933.

Flanagan, Maureen A. *Seeing with Their Hearts: Chicago Women and the Vision of the Good City, 1871–1933*. Princeton: Princeton University Press, 2002.

Flanagan, Maureen A. *America Reformed: Progressives and Progressivisms, 1890s–1920s*. New York: Oxford University Press, 2007.

Foner, Philip S. "From Slavery to Socialism: George Washington Woodbey, Black Socialist Preacher," in *Socialism and Christianity in Early 20th Century America*, Jacob Dorn, ed. Westport, CT: Greenwood Press, 1998, 65–92.

Freudenheim, Leslie M. *Building with Nature: Inspiration for the Arts & Crafts Home*. Salt Lake City: Gibbs Smith, 2005.

Freudenheim, Leslie M., and Elisabeth Sussman. *Building with Nature: Roots of the San Francisco Bay Region Tradition*. Santa Barbara: Peregrine Smith, 1974.

George, Henry. *Progress and Poverty*. New York: Robert Schalkenbach Foundation, 1992 (1879).

George, Henry. *The Science of Political Economy*. New York: Doubleday, 1898.

Gilkey, Charles W. "Religion Among American Students," *Journal of Religion*, 4, no. 1, January 1924.

Gilman, Charlotte Perkins. *The Man-Made World; or, Our Androcentric Culture*. New York: Charton Co., 1911.

Ginger, Ray. *Eugene V. Debs: A Biography*. New York: Collier Books, 1962 (1949).

Green, James R. *Grass-Roots Socialism: Radical Movements in the Southwest, 1895–1943*. Baton Rouge: Louisiana State University Press, 1978.

Gullett, Gayle. *Becoming Citizens: The Emergence and Development of the California Women's Movement, 1880–1911*. Urbana: University of Illinois Press, 2000.

Gutman, Herbert G. "Protestantism and the American Labor Movement: The Christian Spirit in the Gilded Age," *American Historical Review*, 72, no. 1, Oct. 1966, 74–101.

Handy, Robert T. "George D. Herron and the Social Gospel in American Protestantism," PhD diss., University of Chicago Divinity School, 1949.

Handy, Robert T. "George D. Herron and the Kingdom Movement," *Church History*, 19, no. 2, June 1950, 97–115.

Handy, Robert T. "Christianity and Socialism in America, 1900–1920," *Church History*, 21, no. 1, March 1952, 39–54.

Hanika, Michael. "J. Stitt Wilson: California Socialist," MA thesis, California State University, East Bay, 1972.

Harris, Leon. *Upton Sinclair: American Rebel.* New York: Thomas Y. Crowell, 1975.

Herny, Ed, Shelley Rideout, and Katie Wadell. *Berkeley Bohemia: Artists and Visionaries of the Early 20th Century.* Salt Lake City: Gibbs Smith, 2008.

Herron, George D. *The Message of Jesus to Men of Wealth.* New York: Fleming H. Revell Co., 1891.

Herron, George D. *The New Redemption: A Call to the Church to Reconstruct Society According to the Gospel of Christ.* Boston: Thomas Crowell & Co. 1893.

Herron, George D. *The Christian State: A Political Vision of Christ.* Boston: Thomas Crowell & Co., 1895.

Herron, George D. *Why I Am a Socialist.* Charles H. Kerr & Co., Chicago, 1900.

Herron, George D. "A Menacing Friendship," *Wilshire's Magazine*, November 1901.

Hoffmann, Charles. *The Depression of the Nineties: An Economic History.* Westport, CT: Greenwood Press, 1970.

Hollingsworth, James H. "A Word from Mr. Hollingsworth," *The Social Crusader*, March 1899.

Hollingsworth, James H. *Eugene Debs: What His Neighbors Say of Him.* Published by the author likely in Terre Haute, circa 1914.

Hopkins, Charles Howard. *The Rise of the Social Gospel in American Protestantism, 1865–1915.* New Haven: Yale University Press, 1967 (1940).

Hopkins, Charles Howard. *History of the YMCA in North America.* New York: Association Press, 1951.

Hopkins, Mark. "No Undue Familiarity: Gender, Vice and the Campaign to Regulate Dance Halls, 1911–1921," in *California Women and Politics*, Robert W. Cherny, Mary Ann Irwin and Ann Marie Wilson, eds. Lincoln: University of Nebraska Press, 2011, 289–307.

Hough, Emerson. *The Web: The Authorized History of the American Protective League.* Chicago: Reilly & Lee, 1919.

Howe, Frederic C. *The City: The Hope of Democracy.* New York: Charles Scribner's Sons, 1906.

Hurley, Teresa, and Jarrod Harrison. "Awed by the Women's Clubs:

Women Voters and Moral Reform, 1913–1914," in *California Women and Politics*, Robert W. Cherny, Mary Ann Irwin, and Ann Marie Wilson, eds., Lincoln: University of Nebraska Press, 2011, 237–261.

Ignatiev, Noel. *How the Irish Became White*. New York: Routledge, 1995.

Issel, William, and Robert W. Cherny. *San Francisco, 1865–1932: Politics, Power, and Urban Development*. Berkeley: University of California Press, 1986.

James, David. "'Our Philip': The Early Career of Philip Snowden," *Bradford Antiquary*, 3, 1987, 39–47 (Third series). http://www.bradfordhistorical.org.uk/snowden.html

Jensen, Joan M. *The Price of Vigilance*. Chicago: Rand McNally, 1968.

Johnson, Daniel J. "'No Make-Believe Class Struggle': The Socialist Municipal Campaign in Los Angeles, 1911," *Labor History*, 41, no. 1, 2000, 25–45.

Johnston, Robert D. *The Radical Middle Class: Populist Democracy and the Question of Capitalism in Progressive Era Portland, Oregon*. Princeton: Princeton University Press, 2003.

Jones, Derek C., and Donald J. Schneider. "Self-Help Production Cooperatives: Government-Administered Cooperatives During the Depression," in *Worker Cooperatives in America*, Robert Jackall and Henry M. Levin, eds. Berkeley: University of California Press, 1984.

Jones, Marnie. *Holy Toledo: Religion and Politics in the Life of "Golden Rule" Jones*. Lexington: University Press of Kentucky, 1998, 57–84.

Jones, Peter d'Alroy. *The Christian Socialist Revival, 1877–1914: Religion, Class, and Social Conscience in Late-Victorian England*. Princeton: Princeton University Press, 1968.

Jones, Samuel M. *The New Right: A Plea for Fair Play Through a More Just Social Order*. New York: Eastern Book Concern, 1899.

Johnson, Neil Wharrier. "'So Peculiarly Its Own': The Theological Socialism of the Labour Church." PhD diss., University of Birmingham, United Kingdom, 2015.

Judd, Richard W. *Socialist Cities: Municipal Politics and the Grass Roots of American Socialism*. Albany: SUNY Press, 1989.

Katz, Sherry J. "Dual Commitments: Feminism, Socialism and Women's Political Activism in California, 1890–1920," PhD diss., University of California, Los Angeles, 1991.

Katz, Sherry J. "A Politics of Coalition: Socialist Women and the California Women Suffrage Movement, 1900–1911" in *One Woman, One Vote: Rediscovering the Suffrage Movement*, Marjorie Spruill Wheeler, ed. Troutdale, OR: Newsage Press, 1995, 245–262.

Katz, Sherry J. "Redefining 'The Political': Socialist Women and Party Politics in California, 1900–1920" in *We Have Come to Stay: American Women and Political Parties, 1880–1960*, Melanie Gustafson, Kristie Miller and Elisabeth Perry, eds. Albuquerque: University of New Mexico Press, 1999, 23–32.

Kazin, Michael. "The Great Exception Revisited: Organized Labor and Politics in San Francisco and Los Angeles, 1870–1940," *Pacific Historical Review*, 55, no. 3, August 1986, 371–402.

Kazin, Michael. *Barons of Labor: The San Francisco Building Trades and Union Power in the Progressive Era*. Urbana: University of Illinois Press, 1987.

Kennedy, David M. *Over Here: The First World War and American Society*. Oxford: Oxford University Press, 2004.

Kerr, Clark. "Productive Enterprises of the Unemployed, 1931–1938," PhD diss., University of California, Berkeley, 1939.

King, William McGuire. "The Emergence of Social Gospel Radicalism: The Methodist Case," *Church History*, 50, no. 4, December 1981, 436–449.

Kipnis, Ira. *The American Socialist Movement, 1897–1912*. New York: Columbia University Press, 1952.

Knight, Robert. *Industrial Relations in the San Francisco Bay Area, 1900–1918*. Berkeley: University of California Press, 1960.

Kraditor, Aileen. *The Ideas of the Woman Suffrage Movement, 1890–1920*. New York: W. W. Norton & Company, 1965.

Kraft, James P. "The Fall of Job Harriman's Socialist Party: Violence, Gender and Politics in Los Angeles, 1911," *Southern California Quarterly*, 70, no. 1, Spring 1988, 43–68.

Kreuter, Kent, and Gretchen Kreuter. *An American Dissenter: The Life of Algie Martin Simons, 1870–1950*. Lexington: University of Kentucky Press, 1969.

Laybourn, Keith, and Jack Reynolds. *Liberalism and the Rise of Labour, 1890–1918*. London: Croom Helm, 1984.

Lea, Homer. *The Valor of Ignorance*. New York: Harper and Brothers, 1909.

Lea, Homer. *The Day of the Saxon*. New York: Harper and Brothers, 1912.

Leader, Leonard. "Upton Sinclair's EPIC Switch: A Dilemma for American Socialists," *Southern California Quarterly*, 62, no. 4, Winter 1980.

Lipset, Seymour Martin, and Gary Marks, *It Didn't Happen Here: Why Socialism Failed in the United States*. New York: W.W. Norton, 2000.

Lloyd, Henry Demarest. *A Strike of Millionaires against Miners: Or, The Story of Spring Valley*. Chicago: Belford-Clarke Co., 1890.

Lough, Alexandra Wagner. "The Last Tax: Henry George and the Social Politics of Land Reform in the Gilded Age and Progressive Era." PhD diss., Brandeis University, 2013.

May, Henry F. *Protestant Churches and Industrial America*. New York: Harper & Brothers, 1949.

McCartin, Joseph A. *Labor's Great War: The Struggle for Industrial Democracy and the Origins of Modern American Labor Relations, 1912–1921.* Chapel Hill: University of North Carolina Press, 1997.

McIntosh, Clarence F. "Upton Sinclair and the EPIC Movement, 1933–1936." PhD diss., Stanford University, 1955.

McKanan, Dan. "The Dialogue of Socialism," *Harvard Divinity Bulletin*, 38, nos. 3 & 4, Summer/Autumn 2010.

McKanan, Dan. "The Implicit Religion of Radicalism: Socialist Party Theology, 1900–1934," *Journal of the American Academy of Religion*, 78, no. 3, September 2010, 750–789.

McKanan, Dan. *Prophetic Encounters: Religion and the American Radical Tradition*. Boston: Beacon Press, 2011.

McQuaid, Kim. "The Businessman as Reformer: Nelson O. Nelson and Late 19th Century Social Movements in America," *American Journal of Economics and Sociology*, 33, no. 4, October 1974, 423–435.

Mead, Rebecca J. *How the Vote Was Won: Woman Suffrage in the Western United States, 1868–1914*. New York: NYU Press, 2004.

Miller, Donald L. *The New American Radicalism: Alfred M. Bingham and Non-Marxian Insurgency in the New Deal Era*. Port Washington: Kennikat Press, 1979.

Miller, Donald L. *City of the Century: The Epic of Chicago and the Making of America*. New York: Simon & Schuster, 1996.

Miller, Sally M. *Victor Berger and the Promise of Constructive Socialism*. Westport, CT: Greenwood Press, 1973.

Mills, Bill. *The League: The True Story of Average Americans on the Hunt for WWI Spies*. New York: Skyhorse Publishing, 2013.

Mohun, Arwen P. *Risk: Negotiating Safety in American Society*. Baltimore: Johns Hopkins University Press, 2013.

Moore, R. Laurence. "Flawed Fraternity—American Socialist Response to the Negro, 1901–1912," *The Historian*, 32, no. 1, November 1969, 1–18.

Mowry, George E. *The California Progressives*. Berkeley: University of California Press, 1951.

Niebuhr, Reinhold. *Moral Man and Immoral Society*. New York: Scribners, 1932.

Noble, John Wesley. *Its Name Was M.U.D.* Oakland: East Bay Municipal Utility District, 1970.

North, Diane M. T. *California at War: The State and the People during World War I.* Lawrence: University Press of Kansas, 2018.

Oliver, Willard M. *August Vollmer: The Father of Professional Policing.* Durham: Carolina Academic Press, 2017.

Ostrander, Gilman M. *The Prohibition Movement in California, 1848–1933.* Berkeley: University of California Press, 1957.

Palmer, Alex. *The Santa Claus Man: The Rise and Fall of a Jazz Age Con Man and the Invention of Christmas in New York.* Guilford, CT: Lyons Press, 2016.

Parkinson, George H. "Intercollegiate Debates" in *Northwestern University: A History, Volume 2,* Arthur H. Wilde, ed. New York: University Publishing Society, 1905, 141–154.

Pettitt, George Albert. *Berkeley: the town and gown of it.* Berkeley: Howell-North Books, 1973.

Phillips, Clifton J. "The Indiana Education of Charles Beard," *Indiana Magazine of History,* 45, no. 1, 1959, 1–15.

Quint, Howard H. *The Forging of American Socialism: Origins of the Modern Movement.* Indianapolis: Bobbs-Merrill, 1953.

Reynolds, J., and K. Laybourn. "The Emergence of the Independent Labour Party in Bradford," *International Review of Social History,* 20, no. 3, 1975, 313–346.

Rogin, Michael P., and John L. Shover. *Political Change in California: Critical Elections and Social Movements, 1890–1966.* Westport, CT: Greenwood Publishing Corp., 1970.

Ross, Jack. *The Socialist Party of America: A Complete History.* Lincoln: University of Nebraska Press, 2015.

Ross, Steven J. "Struggles for the Screen: Workers, Radicals and the Political Uses of Silent Film," *American Historical Review,* 96, no. 2, April 1991, 333–367.

Ryan, Frederick. *History of the San Diego Labor Movement.* San Diego: San Diego State College Bureau of Business and Economic Research, 1959.

Salvatore, Nick. *Eugene V. Debs: Citizen and Socialist.* Urbana: University of Illinois Press, 1982.

Saxton, Alexander. *The Indispensable Enemy: Labor and the Anti-Chinese Movement in California.* Berkeley: University of California Press, 1971.

Saxton, Alexander. *The Rise and Fall of the White Republic.* New York: Verso, 1991.

Schwartz, Richard. *Earthquake Exodus, 1906: Berkeley Responds to the San Francisco Refugees.* Berkeley: RSB Books, 2005.

Setran, David P. *The College "Y": Student Religion in the Era of Secularization.* London: Palgrave MacMillan, 2007.

Shaffer, Ralph Edward. "A History of the Socialist Party of California," MA thesis, University of California, Los Angeles, 1955.

Shaffer, Ralph Edward. "Radicalism in California, 1869–1929." PhD diss., University of California, Berkeley, 1962.

Shannon, David A. *The Socialist Party of America: A History.* New York: MacMillan Co., 1955.

Shedd, Clarence P. *Two Centuries of Student Christian Movements: Their Origin and Intercollegiate Life.* New York: Association Press, 1934.

Sinclair, Upton. *I, Candidate for Governor: And How I Got Licked.* Berkeley: University of California Press, 1994 (1935).

Sitton, Tom. *John Randolph Haynes: California Progressive.* Stanford: Stanford University Press, 1992.

Skocpol, Theda. *Protecting Soldiers and Mothers: The Political Origins of Social Policy in the United States.* Cambridge: Harvard University Press, 1992.

Stanton, Elizabeth Cady. "The Equilibrium of Sex," *Commonwealth,* June 24, 1897.

Stave, Bruce M., ed. *Socialism and the Cities.* Port Washington: Kennikat Press, 1975.

Steeples, Douglas, and David O. Whitten. *Democracy in Desperation: The Depression of 1893.* Westport, CT: Greenwood Press, 1998.

Stewart, Jr., George. *Life of Henry B. Wright.* New York: Association Press, 1925.

Stimson, Grace Heilman. *Rise of the Labor Movement in Los Angeles.* Berkeley: University of California Press, 1955.

Struthers, David. "'The Boss Has No Color Line': Race, Solidarity, and a Culture of Affinity in Los Angeles and the Borderlands, 1907–1915," *Journal for the Study of Radicalism,* 7, no. 2, 2013, 61–92.

Sturm, Douglas. "Martin Luther King Jr. as Democratic Socialist," *Journal of Religious Ethics,* 18, no. 2, Fall 1990, 79–105.

Sturmthal, Adolf. *The Tragedy of European Labour, 1918–1939.* London: Victor Gollancz, 1944.

Thomas, John L. *Alternative America: Henry George, Edward Bellamy, Henry Demarest Lloyd and the Adversary Tradition.* Cambridge: Harvard University Press, 1983.

Thompson, Carl D. *The Principles and Program of Socialism.* Denver: Social Crusade (no date), late 1902 or early 1903.

Tucker, Cynthia Grant. *Healer in Harm's Way: Mary Collson, a Clergywoman in Christian Science*. Knoxville: University of Tennessee Press, 1994.

Tygiel, Jules. *Workingmen in San Francisco, 1880–1901*. New York: Garland, 1992.

Valelly, Richard M. *Radicalism in the States: The Minnesota Farmer-Labor Party and the American Political Economy*. Chicago: University of Chicago Press, 1989.

Van Rensselaer, James T. *The Church and Scientific Socialism*. Boston: Church Social Union, March 15, 1899.

Van Wienen, Mark W. *American Socialist Triptych: The Literary-Political Work of Charlotte Perkins Gilman, Upton Sinclair, and W.E.B. Du Bois*. Ann Arbor: University of Michigan Press, 2012.

Waldron, Caroline A. "Lynch-law Must Go!: Race, Citizenship and the Other in an American Coal Mining Town," *Journal of American Ethnic History*, 2, no. 1, Fall 2000, 50–77.

Weinstein, Dave. *It Came from Berkeley: How Berkeley Changed the World*. Salt Lake City: Gibbs Smith, 2008.

Weinstein, James. *The Decline of Socialism in America, 1912–1925*. New York: Vintage Books, 1969.

Weiss, Marc A. "Urban Land Developers and the Origins of Zoning Laws: The Case of Berkeley," *Berkeley Planning Journal*, 3, no. 1, 1986, 7–25.

Willrich, Michael. *Pox: An American History*. New York: Penguin, 2011.

Wise, William H. "Mr. Wise's Witness," *The Social Crusader*, March 1899.

Wollenberg, Charles. *Berkeley: A City in History*. Berkeley: University of California Press, 2008.

Young, Arthur Nichols. *The Single Tax Movement in the United States*. Princeton: Princeton University Press, 1916.

Zipser, Arthur, and Pearl Zipser. *Fire and Grace: The Life of Rose Pastor Stokes*. Athens: University of Georgia Press, 1989.

ENDNOTES

Chapter 1. "Socialism Is Applied Christianity"

1   *The Challenge* (later *Wilshire's Magazine*), July 31, 1901, 10.

2   *Berkeley Daily Gazette*, August 14, 1912.

3   Kurt Vonnegut, "Prologue" in *Jailbird: A Novel* (New York: Delacorte, 1979), 11–13; *A Man Without a Country* (New York: Random House, 2007), 13; *If This Isn't Nice What Is: Advice for the Young* (New York Seven Stories Press, 2014) 33–34.

4   Michael R. Bussel, *From Harvard to the Ranks of Labor: Powers Hapgood and the American Working Class* (University Park: Penn State University Press, 1999), 17.

5   J. Stitt Wilson, *How I Became a Socialist: Part II*, 1 in *How I Became a Socialist and Other Papers* (published by the author: Berkeley, 1912).

6   *World* (Oakland), August 26, 1911.

7   Eugene V. Debs, "Jesus the Supreme Leader," in *Eugene V. Debs and Jesus of Nazareth* (Winnipeg: Winnipeg Labor Church, no date); David Burns, *The Life and Death of the Radical Historical Jesus* (New York: Oxford University Press, 2013), 162–197; Nick Salvatore, *Eugene V. Debs: Citizen and Socialist* (Urbana: University of Illinois Press, 1982).

8   David A. Shannon, *The Socialist Party of America: A History* (New York, McMillan Co., 1955), 59.

9   Jim Bissett, *Agrarian Socialism in America: Marx, Jefferson, and Jesus in the Oklahoma Countryside, 1904–1920* (Norman, University of Oklahoma Press, 2002) includes useful overviews of the relevant literature on 210–211, 239–240. James R. Green, *Grass-Roots Socialism: Radical Movements in the Southwest, 1895–1943* (Baton Rouge, Louisiana State University Press, 1978).

10   Bissett, *Agrarian Socialism in America,* 97.

11   Mari Jo Buhle, *Women and American Socialism, 1870–1920* (Urbana, University of Illinois Press, 1983), 108. See also Dan McKanan, "The Implicit Religion of Radicalism: Socialist Party Theology, 1900–1934," *Journal of the American Academy of Religion,* 78 no. 3 (September 2010), 750–789.

12   J. Stitt Wilson, *The Impending Social Revolution or the Trust Problem Solved* (Berkeley and Denver: Social Crusade, no date, circa mid-1902).

13 Daniel Bell, *Marxian Socialism in the United States* (Ithaca, Cornell University Press, 1996 (1952)), xli, 5, 199.

14 Seymour Martin Lipset and Gary Marks, *It Didn't Happen Here: Why Socialism Failed in the United States* (New York, W.W. Norton, 2000), 200. See also Robin Archer, *Why Is There No Labor Party in the United States?* (Princeton, Princeton University Press, 2007).

15 Douglas Sturm, "Martin Luther King Jr. as Democratic Socialist," *Journal of Religious Ethics*, 18:2 (Fall, 1990), 79–105.

Chapter 2. The Education of a Minister

1 This section is largely based on unpublished documents by J. Stitt Wilson, an unfinished "Autobiography," an additional chapter, "The Zetland Schoolmaster Falls in Love," and a brief overview, "My Crowded Years." Citations are limited to quotes and to other sources.

2 Wilson, "Autobiography," 39.

3 Wilson, "Autobiography," 27.

4 Wilson, "Autobiography," 7.

5 Wilson, *How I Became a Socialist (Part 1)*, Berkeley, 1911, 1.

6 Wilson, "Autobiography," 24.

7 Wilson, "Autobiography," 31.

8 Wilson, *How I Became a Socialist (Part 1)*, Berkeley, 1911, 1. Wilson, "Autobiography," 128.

9 Wilson, *How I Became a Socialist (Part 1)*, 1 and *(Part 2)*, 7 (Berkeley: published by the author, 1911).

10 Wilson, "Autobiography," 55–56.

11 Wilson, "Autobiography," 78, 123.

12 Wilson, "How I Became a Socialist," (Part 2), 7; "Autobiography," p.103.

13 Wilson, "Autobiography," 151.

14 Wilson, "The Zetland Schoolmaster," 7–8.

15 Wilson, "The Zetland Schoolmaster," 7.

16 Wilson, "The Zetland Schoolmaster," 8.

17 Wilson, "The Zetland Schoolmaster," 16–17.

18 Wilson, "The Zetland Schoolmaster," 22.

19 Wilson, "The Zetland Schoolmaster," 23.

20 Wilson, "The Zetland Schoolmaster," 49–50.

21 Wilson, "Autobiography," 31.

22 Wilson, "The Zetland Schoolmaster," 30–31.

23 Wilson, "Autobiography," 86–87.

24 Wilson, "How I Became a Socialist" (Part 2) p. 7; "Autobiography," 86–87; "My Crowded Years," 2. Northwestern University, *Alumni Record of the College of Liberal Arts*, 1903.

25 Archer, *Why Is There No Labor Party in the United States?* 180.

26   Wilson, "Autobiography," 58.

27   Hanika, "J. Stitt Wilson: California Socialist," (MA thesis, California State University, East Bay, 1972), 38; Evanston, IL City Directory, 1891, 1892; *Minutes of the Fifty-Fourth Session of the Rock River Conference of the Methodist Episcopal Church*, October 5–10, 1892, 95; *Proceedings of the Rock River Conference of the Methodist Episcopal Church*, 1893, 90.

28   Wilson, *How I Became a Socialist (Part 1)*, 6.

29   *Chicago Daily Tribune*, June 13, 1893; *The Northwestern*, June 16, 1893, p. 203; Jackson Stitt Wilson, "Northwestern University, College of Liberal Arts, Matriculation Paper," September 18, 1893.

30   *Minutes of the Fifty-Fifth Session of the Rock River Conference of the Methodist Episcopal Church*, October 4–9, 1893, 42.

31   Wilson, *How I Became a Socialist (Part 1)*, 3–4.

32   Wilson, *How I Became a Socialist (Part 1)*, 3–4.

33   Charles Hoffmann, *The Depression of the Nineties: An Economic History* (Westport: Greenwood, 1970). Douglas Steeples and Whitten, David O., *Democracy in Desperation: The Depression of 1893* (Westport: Greenwood, 1998).

34   Donald L. Miller, *City of the Century: The Epic of Chicago and the Making of America* (New York: Simon & Schuster, 1996), 457, 531.

35   J. Stitt Wilson, "Jesus in the Labor Movement," *Intercollegian*, November 1922.

36   Wilson, *How I Became a Socialist (Part 1)* 5.

37   Wilson, "*How I Became a Socialist (Part 1)* 7.

38   J. Stitt Wilson, "Christianity in Overalls," *Christian Socialist*, July 15, 1914.

39   Wilson, *How I Became a Socialist (Part 1)* 11.

40   Wilson, *How I Became a Socialist (Part 1)* 12.

41   *The New Hampshire* (Durham, NH), January 28. 1920.

42   Henry F. May, *Protestant Churches and Industrial America* (New York: Harper & Bros, 1949).

43   May, *Protestant Churches*, 93, 101.

44   Herbert G. Gutman, "Protestantism and the American Labor Movement: The Christian Spirit in the Gilded Age," *American Historical Review*, 72 no. 1 (October 1966) 74–10; Robert H. Craig, "The Underside of History: American Methodism, Capitalism and Popular Struggle," *Methodist History*, 24 no. 2 (January 1989) 73–88.

45   Heath W. Carter, *Union Made: Working People and the Rise of Social Christianity in Chicago* (New York: Oxford University Press, 2015).

46   Rev. William H. Carwardine, The Pullman Strike (Chicago: Charles H. Kerr & Co., 1894), 128; Stephen G. Cobb, *Reverend William Carwardine and the Pullman Strike of 1894: The Christian Gospel and Social Justice* (Lewiston: Edwin Mellen Press, 1992).

47   Charles Howard Hopkins, *The Rise of the Social Gospel in American Protestantism, 1865–1915* (New Haven: Yale University Press, 1967), 171–183.

48   Alexandra Wagner Lough, *The Last Tax: Henry George and the Social Politics of Land Reform in the Gilded Age and Progressive Era* (PhD diss., Brandeis University, 2013) has a useful discussion of George and the Social Gospel.

49   John L. Thomas, *Alternative America: Henry George, Edward Bellamy, Henry Demarest Lloyd and the Adversary Tradition* (Cambridge: Harvard University Press, 1983).

50 George, Henry, *Progress and Poverty* (New York: Robert Schalkenbach Foundation, 1992 (1879)), 240–241.

51 George, Henry, *The Science of Political Economy* (New York: Doubleday, 1898), 382–396.

52 Ruth Bordin, *Frances Willard: A Biography* (Chapel Hill, University of North Carolina Press, 1986), 146–8; Frances E. Willard, address to the National Convention of the W.C.T.U., 1897, excerpted in "Why Miss Willard Was a Socialist," *Commonwealth*, April 1902.

53 Barbara Leslie Epstein, *The Politics of Domesticity: Women, Evangelism and Temperance in Nineteenth Century America* (Middletown: Wesleyan University Press, 1981).

54 Frances Willard to Susan B. Anthony, January 26, 1898, quoted in Aileen Kraditor, *The Ideas of the Woman Suffrage Movement, 1890–1920* (New York: W. W. Norton, 1965), 68.

55 Mari Jo Buhle, *Women and American Socialism*, 49–103.

56 Elizabeth Cady Stanton, "The Equilibrium of Sex," *Commonwealth*, June 24, 1897, 12. See also Ellen Carol Dubois and Richard Candida Smith, ed., *Elizabeth Cady Stanton: Feminist as Thinker* (New York, 2007).

57 Rev. George D. Herron, *The Message of Jesus to Men of Wealth* (New York: Fleming H. Revell Co., 1891), 29.

58 Robert T. Handy, "George D. Herron and the Kingdom Movement," *Church History*, 19 no. 2 (June 1950) 97–115.

59 George D. Herron, *The New Redemption: A Call to the Church to Reconstruct Society According to the Gospel of Christ* (Boston: Thomas Crowell & Co. 1893), 30–31.

60 George D. Herron, *The Christian State: A Political Vision of Christ* (New York: Thomas Crowell & Co., 1895).

61 J. Stitt Wilson, "The Story of a Developing Fellowship," *The Social Crusader*, January 1901, 13–14.

62 Wilson, "The Story of a Developing Fellowship," *The Social Crusader*, January 1901, 13.

63 *Daily InterOcean* (Chicago, IL) September 6, 1895, 8. *Chicago Tribune*, January 21, 1899.

64 *Chicago Tribune*, May 6, 1895; *American Manufacturer Iron World*, May 3, 1895; *Chicago Journal of Commerce*, April 25, 1895.

65 *Daily InterOcean* (Chicago, IL) June 17, 1895.

66 Henry Demarest Lloyd, *A Strike of Millionaires against Miners: Or, The Story of Spring Valley*, 1890.

67 Waldron, Caroline A., "Lynch-law Must Go!: Race, Citizenship and the Other in an American Coal Mining Town," *Journal of American Ethnic History*, 20 no.1 (Fall 2000), 50–77.

68 W.H. Wise and Benjamin F. Wilson, "A Word from the Comrades," *The Social Crusader* (January 1901), 19–20.

69 *Daily Inter Ocean* (Chicago, IL) November 24, 1895, 8.

70 *Daily Inter Ocean* (Chicago, IL) December 7, 1895, 3

71 *Daily Inter Ocean* (Chicago, IL) December 7, 1895, 3; *Evening Post* (Fort Wayne, IN) December 10, 1895; *Chicago Tribune*, December 5, 1895, January 3, 1896.

72   Nick Salvatore, *Eugene V. Debs*, 151.

73   Wilson, "The Story of a Developing Fellowship," 15.

74   *Minutes of the Fifty-Seventh Session of the Rock River Annual Conference of the Methodist Episcopal Church*, Held in Embury Church, Freeport, Illinois, September 30–October 6, 1896, 106, 111, 123.

75   Wilson, "How I Became a Socialist," (Part 2), 3–4.

76   *Daily InterOcean* (Chicago, IL) March 30, 1896, p.8; *Chicago Daily Tribune*, March 30, 1896.

77   *Daily InterOcean* (Chicago, IL) March 30, 1896, p.8; *Chicago Daily Tribune*, March 30, 1896.

78   *Chicago Tribune*, "Debs Makes Three Addresses," April 11, 1896; *Chicago Tribune*, "Eugene Debs in the City," April 23, 1896; unidentified clipping, "Field of Labor," April 11, 1896, Scrapbook III, folder 508, JAMC, Special Collections, University Library, University of Illinois at Chicago.

79   *Evening Post* (Charleston, SC) June 5, 1896; *Lowell Daily Sun*, June 16, 1896.

80   *Daily InterOcean* (Chicago, IL) September 26, 1896, 13.

81   *Northwestern* (Evanston, IL) January 14, February 4, March 7, 11, April 8, 1897. George H. Parkinson, "Intercollegiate Debates" in *Northwestern University: A History*, Volume 2, Arthur H. Wilde, ed. (New York: University Publishing Society, 1905) 149.

82   Ray Ginger, *Eugene V. Debs* (New York: Collier, 1962) 208–9.

83   *Minutes of the Fifty-Seventh Session of the Rock River Conference of the Methodist Episcopal Church*, September 30–October 6, 1896; *Minutes of the Fifty-Eighth Session of the Rock River Conference of the Methodist Episcopal Church*, October 6–13, 1897; *Minutes of the Fifty-Ninth Session of the Rock River Conference of the Methodist Episcopal Church*, October 5–11, 1898.

84   In "My Crowded Years," Wilson mentions a "long letter to the Church authorities" preserved in a scrap book that no longer survives.

Chapter 3. The Social Crusade

1   J. Stitt Wilson, "The Ethical Aspect of the Labor Problem," *The New Time*, November 1897.

2   Howard H. Quint, *The Forging of American Socialism: Origins of the Modern Movement* (Indianapolis: Bobbs-Merrill, 1953), 131–134.

3   E. Dale Dunlap, "The United Methodist System of Itinerant Ministry," in *Perspectives on American Methodism: Interpretive Essays*, Russell E. Richey, Kenneth E. Rowe and Jean Miller Schmidt, eds. 415–425 (Kingswood Books, Nashville, 1993). Christopher Evans, *Histories of American Christianity: An Introduction* (Waco: Baylor University Press, 2013), 112–120.

4   J. Stitt Wilson, "The Story of a Developing Fellowship," *The Social Crusader*, January 1901, 15–16.

5   *Social Crusader*, September 1900, 11. J. Stitt Wilson, "The Social Crusade," *The New Time*, April 1898, 235.

6   J. Stitt Wilson, "The Social Crusade," *New Time*, April 1898, 232–236.

7   Northwestern University Settlement, *Circular No. 7*, September 1897, 2.

8   *Berkeley Daily Gazette*, April 5, 1911.

9   J. Stitt Wilson, "The Story of a Developing Fellowship," *The Social Crusader*, January 1901, 16.

10 *Social Gospel*, May 1898, 26.

11 J. Stitt Wilson, "The Social Crusade," *The New Time*, April 1898, 235.

12 *Social Crusader*, October 1898.

13 *Marshall News*, May 6, 1898, 1.

14 *Depauw Palladium*, January 17, 1898 quoted in Clifton J. Phillips, "The Indiana Education of Charles Beard," *Indiana Magazine of History*, 45 no.1 (1959) 1–15. Beard was more positive when George Herron visited in April.

15 Web site: "The Koreshans: Cyrus Teed and the New Jerusalem," http://mwweb. org/koreshan/blog/.

16 *The Social Gospel*, May 1898, 28.

17 Bruce Pennington, *King Koresh: The Man from Inside the Earth*. Accessed June 19, 2020 at http://mwweb.org/koreshan/blog/.

18 *Flaming Sword*, September 9, 1898, 10.

19 Wallace gave his occupation as "Koreshian missionary" in the 1900 Census. Wilson would not have worked with him unless he hid his membership and intentions.

20 *Flaming Sword*, January 6, 1899, 13; January 27, 1899, 12–13.

21 "Koreshan Genealogy: William Ross Wallace," Accessed June 19, 2020. http:// koreshan.mwweb.org/gene/new/np135.htm#iin671.

22 *Daily Inter Ocean* (Chicago, IL) August 29, September 7, 1896; *Evening News* (Benton Harbor, MI) Sept 2, 1898.

23 *The Nineteen Hundred Syllabus· Published for the Junior Class of the College of Liberal Arts, Northwestern University* (Chicago: Blakely Press, 1899), 29.

24 *Evening News* (Benton Harbor, MI) August 9, 10, 1898.

Judge Orville W. Coolidge, *A Twentieth Century History of Berrien County, Michigan* (Chicago: Lewis Publishing Co. 1906), 230, 242.

25 *Evening News* (Benton Harbor, MI) September 2, 1898.

26 *Evening News* (Benton Harbor, MI) September 2, 1898; *Daily Palladium* (Benton Harbor, MI) September 3, 1898.

27 *Social Crusader*, October 15, 1898, 10–11.

28 J. Stitt Wilson, "Short Story for the Month," *Social Crusader*, October 1900, 1. Wilson placed these events in September, but the September issue of *The Social Crusader* was clearly published in August, so they must have occurred in July or early August.

29 *Social Crusader*, February–October 1900.

30 *Daily Palladium* (Benton Harbor, MI) September 2, 1898.

31 J. Stitt Wilson, "To the Officers and Students of the University of California," undated open letter used in his campaign for Congress, November 1912. Bancroft Library, Berkeley politics, box 2, folder 10.

32 J. Stitt Wilson, "Analysis of Social Conditions," *Social Crusader*, October, November December 1898.

33   Kent and Gretchen Kreuter, *An American Dissenter: The Life of Algie Martin Simons, 1870–1950*, Lexington: University of Kentucky Press, 1969.

34   Algie Martin Simons, "Socialism: A Philosophy of Social Development," *Social Crusader*, January 1899.

35   Wilson called for people to support the "International Socialist Labor Party," but in context this seems to mean supporting socialist and labor parties around the world rather than the Socialist Labor Party in the U.S.

36   J. Stitt Wilson, An Appeal to the Working Classes," *Social Crusader*, February 1899.

37   *Social Crusader*, January 1901, 18–19.

38   William H. Wise, "Mr. Wise's Witness," *Social Crusader*, March 1899, 4–5.

39   James H. Hollingsworth, "A Word from Mr. Hollingsworth," *Social Crusader*, March 1899, 3–4.

40   *Social Crusader*, March 15, 1899.

41   *Brotherhood*, March 1899, 167. *Social Crusader*, March 15, 1899.

42   J. Stitt Wilson, Autobiography, 12.

43   *Social Crusader*, March 15, 1899, 9.

44   *Social Crusader*, May 1, 1899, 11–15.

45   Daily Mail (London), March 18, 1899; Social Crusader, May 1, 1899, 9–10.

46   *Glasgow Herald*, April 5, 1899; *Social Crusader*, May 1, 1899, 8–9; *Leeds Mercury*, April 5, 1899.

47   Naomi Clayton and Raj Mandair, *Cities Outlook, 1901*, Center for Cities, London, 2012. https://www.centreforcities.org/wp-content/uploads/2014/08/12-07-11-Cities-Outlook-1901.pdf. Accessed June 19, 2020.

48   Neil Wharrier Johnson, "'So Peculiarly Its Own': The Theological Socialism of the Labour Church," PhD diss., University of Birmingham, U.K. May 2015.

49   A. Thomas Lane (ed) Biographical Dictionary of European Labor Leaders, Vol. 1 (Westport: Greenwood Press, 1995), 464.

50   *Greencastle Banner*, August 25, 1899, 1; *Indianapolis Journal*, September 12, 1899, 5.

51   *North Judson News* (Indiana), October 12, 1899.

52   *Marshall County Independent*, September 8, 1899

53   *Social Crusader*, January 1, 1900, 14–15.

54   *Social Crusader*, October 1899, 13. Frank O. Beck, *Hobohemia* (Chicago: Charles Kerr Publishing, 2000), 73.

55   *Social Crusader*, February 1900, 15.

56   *Social Crusader*, September 1899.

57   Beck, *Hobohemia*, 73–78.

58   *Chicago Tribune*, July 22, 29, 1899; *The Public*, July 29, 1899.

59   *Social Crusader*, June 1, 1899, 3–4.

60   James Hollingsworth, "Christianity and the Competitive System: A Word to the Church," *Social Crusader*, August 1, October 1, 1899.

61   J. Stitt Wilson, "Individual and Social Salvation," *Social Crusader*, September 1, 1899.

62   J. Stitt Wilson, "The Ideal Reformer," *Social Crusader*, November 1899.

63   Catherine L. Albanese, *A Republic of Mind and Spirit: A Cultural History of American Metaphysical Religion* (New Haven: Yale University Press, 2007).

64   J. Stitt Wilson, "The New Continent of Thought," *Social Crusader*, July 1900.

65   For example, Mitch Stephens, "Gordon blending mental, physical," *San Francisco Chronicle*, February 17, 2017, B2.

66   Albanese, *A Republic of Mind and Spirit*, 323–25.

67   J. Stitt Wilson, "The Free Man," *Social Crusader*, December 1, 1899.

68   W.H. Wise, "The New Enthusiasm," Social Crusader, January 1, 1900, 3–8.

69   Albanese, *A Republic of Mind and Spirit*, 315–322.

70   Albanese, *A Republic of Mind and Spirit*, 324.

71   Wallace D. Wattles, "The Needed Reformation," *Social Crusader*, February 1900, 14.

72   Jones to Wilson, September 6, 1899, Samuel Milton Jones papers, Columbus: Ohio Historical Society.

73   Marnie Jones, *Holy Toledo: Religion and Politics in the Life of "Golden Rule" Jones* (Lexington: University Press of Kentucky, 1998), 67–69.

74   Samuel M. Jones, *The New Right: A Plea for Fair Play Through a More Just Social Order* (New York: Eastern Book Concern, 1899), 238–239.

75   Jones, *The New Right*.

76   Marnie Jones, *Holy Toledo*.

77   Quint, *Forging American Socialism*, 328.

78   *Social Crusader*, December 1, 1899, 14–15.

79   Jones, April 1, 1901, Samuel M. Jones Papers, Ohio Historical Society.

80   *The Social Forum*, January 1900, 4; Quint, *Forging American Socialism*, 261–270.

81   Social Reform Union letterhead, 1899, Samuel M. Jones papers.

82   *Social Crusader*, January 1901, 16.

83   *Social Crusader*, February 1900, 15, March 1900, 1. *Brotherhood*, February 1900, 159.

84   *Chicago Daily Tribune*, April 15, 1900.

85   *Social Crusader*, March 1900, 4–8, April 1900, 3.

86   *Social Crusader*, March 1900, 3–8.

87   *Kent and Sussex Courier*, March 23, 30, 1900.

88   J. Stitt Wilson, Autobiography, 13.

89   *Social Crusader*, May 1900, 2.

90   *Daily News* (Des Moines) August 23, 1900.

Chapter 4. The Herron Fiasco

1   *Social Crusader*, July 1, 1899, 15.

2   *Social Crusader*, February 1900, 10–11.

3   *Social Crusader*, March 1901, 7. *Midweek News Times* (Goshen, IN) August 23, 1901; *Marshall County Independent* (Plymouth, IN) September 20, 1901.

4   *Star Press* (Greencastle, IN), October 4, 1902; *Warren Review* (Williamsport, IN) October 2, 1902, 1.

5   *Saturday Spectator* (Terre Haute, IN) December 11, 1909.

6   James H. Hollingsworth, *Eugene Debs: What His Neighbors Say of Him* (Terre Haute? published by the author? circa 1914).

7   Theodore Debs to Hellen Hollingsworth Bart, March 11, 1943, Eugene Victor Debs Collection, Indiana State University, Terre Haute, Indiana.

8   For a good overview of the process that resulted in the creation of the Socialist Party of America, see Quint, *The Forging of American Socialism*, 319–389.

9   J. Stitt Wilson, "The Political Situation," *Social Crusader*, August 1900, 4–7; *Workers Call* (Chicago), August 18, 1900.

10   *Social Crusader*, October 1900, 4–7.

11   Quint, *Forging American Socialism*, 138; *Social Democratic Herald*, October 27, 1900, 2.

12   *Kalamazoo Gazette*, October 23, 24, 1900.

13   *Workers' Call* (Chicago), October 27, 1900; Cynthia Grant Tucker, *Healer in Harm's Way: Mary Collson, a Clergywoman in Christian Science* (Knoxville: University of Tennessee Press, 1994), 46–49.

14   George D. Herron, *Why I Am a Socialist* (Chicago: Charles H. Kerr & Co., 1900).

15   J. Stitt Wilson, "The Present Moral Conflict," *International Socialist Review*, 1 no. 7 (January 1901): 365–394; "The Spiritual, Moral and Social Elements of the New Gospel," *Social Crusader*, February 1901, 9–12.

16   *Social Crusader*, January 1901. *Social Crusader* was not published in November or December 1900.

17   *Workers' Call* (Chicago), November 24, 1900.

18   *Evening News* (Benton Harbor, MI) December 27, 1900; *Cleveland Leader*, December 28, 1900; *Evansville Courier*, December 28, 1900; *Dubuque Herald*, December 29, 1900; *Hagerstown Exponent* (Indiana), January 3, 1901; *Carlisle News* (Indiana), January 4, 1901; *Atchison Daily Globe*, January 29, 1901; *Newark Daily Advocate* (Ohio), February 1, 1901; *Lawrence Journal* (Kansas), February 1, 1901; and many more.

19   *Social Crusader*, February 1901, 3–5.

20   *Social Crusader*, February 1901, 27–29.

21   *Evening News* (Benton Harbor, MI) January 16, 1901.

22   *Social Crusader*, February 1901, 5; March 1901, 2.

23   *Social Crusader*, February 1901, 5–6.

24   J. Stitt Wilson, "Social Value of the Religious Work of a Section of the City of Chicago," MA thesis, Northwestern University, 1902. This work became the basis for a section of D. Scott Cormode, "Faith and Affiliation: An Urban Religious History of Churches and Secular Voluntarism in Chicago's West Town: 1871–1914." PhD diss., Yale University, 1996.

25   Wilson, "Autobiography," 137.

26   *Starke County Democrat*, March 14, 1901.

27   *Starke County Republican* (Knox, Indiana) March 21, 1901, 1.

28   J.S. Wilson to S.M. Jones, May 29, 1901, Samuel M. Jones Papers, Ohio Historical Society.

29   Robert Theodore Handy, "George D. Herron and the Social Gospel in American Protestantism, 1890–1901." (PhD diss., University of Chicago Divinity School, 1949), 157.

30   Starke County Democrat (Knox, Indiana), March 14, 28, 1901.

31   *Social Crusader*, July, August 1901.

32   D. Scott Cormode, "Faith and Affiliation," 17.

33   Northwestern University–College of Liberal Arts, Registration for Graduate Studies, Jackson Stitt Wilson.

34 *Challenge* (later *Wilshire's Magazine*), July 31, 1901.

35 Wilson to Jones, April 12, 1901, Samuel M. Jones Papers, Ohio Historical Society.

36 *Omaha World Herald*, April 28, May 1, 1901.

37 Wilson, "My Crowded Years," 3; *Social Crusader*, May 1901.

38 *Omaha World Herald*, May 1, 1901; *Courier* (Lincoln, Nebraska), May 4, 1901; *Rocky Mountain News* (Denver), May 6, 1901.

39 Jones to Wilson, May 23, 1901, Samuel M. Jones Papers, Ohio Historical Society.

40 Wilson to Jones, May 29, 1901. Samuel M. Jones Papers, Ohio Historical Society. The (?) is in the letter.

41 *Daily Journal*, June 7, 10, 1901.

42 J. Stitt Wilson, "Christianity and Paganism: A Reply," *International Socialist Review*, 2:1, July 1, 1901, 1–13.

43 *San Francisco Call*, June 17, 1901.

44 Robert Knight, *Industrial Relations in the San Francisco Bay Area, 1900–1918* (Berkeley: University of California Press, 1960), 66–71. Jules Tygiel, *Workingmen in San Francisco, 1880–1901* (New York: Garland, 1992), 300–304.

45 Wilson to Jones, May 29, 1901, Samuel Milton Jones Papers, Ohio Historical Society. *Daily People*, May 17, 1901, 2.

46 *Social Crusader*, July 1900.

47 *Los Angeles Herald*, January 2, 1900; *San Francisco Call*, February 24, 1902.

48 *Los Angeles Herald*, May 26, 1899.

49 *Los Angeles Herald*, June 6, 12, 19, 21, 22, 23, 25, 26, 1899.

50 *Forward Movement Herald*, June 23, 1900.

51 *The Forward Movement: Origin, Nature and Scope of Work* (Los Angeles: Forward Movement, 1900); *Forward Movement Herald*, June 23, 1900.

52 *Los Angeles Herald*, January 24, 27, February 23, 1900.

53 *Los Angeles Herald*, August 2, 1899; July 19, 1900; April 2, 1901.

54 *Los Angeles Herald*, August 2, 1899; July 19, 1900; April 2, 1901.

55 Radcliff College Library catalog record, Volume VII of the "Sacred Records of the Forward Movement" for July 3–August 8, 1903.

56 *San Francisco Call*, August 11, 1907.

57 *Los Angeles Herald*, October 20, 1907.

58 *Denver Post*, January 17, 21, 31, 1909; *Daily News* (Denver), February 21, 1909; *San Francisco Call*, March 7, 1909.

59 *San Francisco Call*, May 17, 1911, 1; *San Francisco Chronicle*, May 19, 1911, 11.

60 *San Francisco Chronicle*, January 1, 1916, 4.

61 *Los Angeles Herald*, September 26, October 9, November 16, 27, 1900; January 2, 6, 13, 27, 1901; July 27, August 17, 24, 1903; Quint, *Forging American Socialism*, 119.

62 *Los Angeles Herald*, February 27, 1901.

63 J. Stitt Wilson, "The Present Moral Conflict," *Challenge*, June 12, 1901.

64 Undated post card addressed to Caroline Severance, author's collection.

65 J. Stitt Wilson, "The Revolution of Revolutions," *Challenge* (later *Wilshire's Magazine*), June 12, 1901; *Challenge* June 19, July 3, 31, August 21, 1901.

66 *Los Angeles Socialist*, February 8, 1902.

67   J. Stitt Wilson to John Randolph Haynes, July 8, 1928, Stitt Wilson folder, Haynes Papers, University of California, Los Angeles.

68   *Social Crusader*, July 1901, 13–14.

69   *Riverside Independent Enterprise*, July 10, 11, 1901.

70   *San Francisco Call*, July 16, 1901.

71   *Los Angeles Herald*, July 19, 1901; *Riverside Independent Enterprise*, July 20, 1901.

72   Jones to Wilson, July 26, 1901, Jones Papers.

73   *San Diego Union*, July 21, 22, 24, 25, 26, 1901; *San Diego Evening Tribune*, July 22, 24, 1901.

74   *Sun* (San Diego), July 25, 1901, reprinted in *Social Crusader*, August 1901, 29.

75   *Sun* (San Diego), July 25, 1901, reprinted in *Social Crusader*, August 1901, 29.

76   *Los Angeles Herald*, July 30, 1901.

77   *Social Crusader*, August 1901, 3–5.

78   *Indianapolis News*, August 28, 1901, 9.

79   George D. Herron, "A Menacing Friendship," *Social Democrat* (London), October 15, 1901 and *Wilshire's Magazine*, November 1901, 29–31.

80   Robert Handy, "George D. Herron and the Social Gospel," 172.

81   Mitchell P. Briggs, *George D. Herron and the European Settlement* (Stanford: Stanford University Press, 1932).

Chapter 5. The Social Crusade in the West

1   *Challenge* (later *Wilshire's Magazine*), August 21, 1901.

2   *Daily News* (Denver) August 9, 19, 1901.

3   *Denver Post*, September 8, 1901, 3.

4   *Rocky Mountain News* (Denver) August 9, 1901.

5   Undated post card in Stitt Wilson file, Caroline Severance Papers, San Marino: Huntington Library.

6   *Denver Post*, October 5 & 13, 1901; *Daily News* (Denver), October 6, 12, 13, 1901. *Social Crusader* (Los Angeles), February 1902, 12, 14.

7   *San Francisco Chronicle*, October 14, 1901.

8   *The Worker* (New York), November 24, 1901.

9   *The Worker*, December 1, 1901; Local San Francisco also charged that Stitt Wilson was not a dues-paying member of the Socialist Party and in 1902 or 1903 a hostile member of the State Executive Committee wrote to Wallace Conable making a similar claim. (*Conable's Path-Finder*, November 1904). The *Los Angeles Socialist* routinely referred to Wilson as "Comrade Wilson," which implied membership, and it seems unlikely the State Executive Committee would employ a non-member to lecture on behalf of the Party. Wilson always spoke of the Socialist Party as if he was a member. *Colorado Springs Gazette*, October 23, 1902.

10   *Los Angeles Herald*, "Notable Ministers Here to Advocate New Cause: Rev. J. Stitt Wilson and His Co-Workers Are to Be Heard in Every Large Place in Southern California," November 3, 1901; "Truth Makes Perfect Life, J. Stitt Wilson Talks on Christian Socialism," November 4, 1901; "Four Clergymen Who Are Noted Social

Evangelists," November 5, 1901; "Social Problems Are Discussed, Many Speakers at Economic Club Dinner, Noted Divines Explain the Tenets of Scientific Socialism and Its Practical Use as a Solution of the Social Problems of Modern Times," November 6, 1901.

11 *Social Crusader* (Los Angeles), February 1902, 16.

12 *Los Angeles Herald*, December 7, 1901.

13 *Los Angeles Herald*, November 4, 1901.

14 *San Diego Union*, December 9, 1901, "Mission of Inspired Life: Address by J. Stitt Wilson at the First Lutheran Church, Yesterday Forenoon." See also *Los Angeles Herald*, November 11, 1901.

15 *Los Angeles Socialist*, December 14, 1901.

16 *Los Angeles Socialist*, December 21, 1901.

17 *Los Angeles Herald*, December 29, 1901; *Path-Finder*, November 1902, 15.

18 *Los Angeles Herald*, November 6, 1901.

19 *Los Angeles Herald*, November 4, 1901.

20 Carl D. Thompson, *The Principles and Program of Socialism*, Social Crusade, Denver, no date (late 1902 or early1903) 6–7.

21 J. Stitt Wilson, *The Impending Social Revolution: or The Trust Problem Solved*, Berkeley: Social Crusade, no date (1902).

22 *Los Angeles Herald*, February 14, 1902; *San Francisco Call*, November 23, 1902.

23 Mari Jo Buhle, *Women and American Socialism*. Sherry J. Katz, "Dual Commitments: Feminism, Socialism and Women's Political Activism in California, 1890–1920," (PhD diss., University of California, Los Angeles, 1991), 100–152.

24 Katz, "Dual Commitments," 62, 65–66, 319.

25 Grace Heilman Stimson, *Rise of the Labor Movement in Los Angeles* (Berkeley: University of California Press, 1955), 225.

26 *Los Angeles Socialist*, January 12, 1902.

27 *Los Angeles Socialist*, November 9, 16, 23, 30, December 28, 1901.

28 *Los Angeles Socialist*, January 11, 1902.

29 *Los Angeles Herald*, January 24, 1902; *Los Angeles Socialist*, February 1, 1902.

30 *Daily Register Gazette* (Rockford, IL) January 20, 1902.

31 J. Stitt Wilson, "Socialism and Life," *Path-Finder*, November 1902, 15; Social Crusade post card, undated, Severance papers, Huntington Library.

32 James T. van Rensselaer, *The Church and Scientific Socialism* (Boston: Christian Social Union, March 15, 1899). The Christian Social Union was a Christian Socialist organization within the Episcopal Church.

33 *Social Crusader*, February 1902. *Los Angeles Socialist*, February 8, 1902.

34 *Path-Finder*, November 1902, 3.

35 Wilson, "My Crowded Years," 1942, 3. Here and in his autobiography, Wilson mistakenly recalled moving to Berkeley in 1901, but it is clear from newspaper reports of his travels that it was 1902.

36 *Berkeley Daily Gazette*, April 5, 1911.

37 *Berkeley Daily Gazette*, March 7, 1902; Wilson, "My Crowded Years," 3. In 1902 the address of Highland Home was "Highland Place near Ridge Road." It

subsequently went through a number of different Highland Place addresses, all in the 1700s, before being finally designated as 1745. The house was demolished in 1956 and replaced with an apartment building.

38   Leslie M. Freudenheim, *Building with Nature: Inspiration for the Arts & Crafts Home* (Salt Lake City: Gibbs Smith, 2005), 92–100. The address is incorrectly given as 1945 Highland Place.

39   Kenneth H. Cardwell. *Bernard Maybeck: Artisan, Architect, Artist* (Salt Lake City: Peregrine Smith, 1977).

40   Leslie M. Freudenheim and Elisabeth Sussman, *Building with Nature: Roots of the San Francisco Bay Region Tradition* (Santa Barbara, Peregrine Smith, 1974).

41   *Berkeley Daily Gazette*, April 5, 1911.

42   Douglas Firth Anderson, *Religious Borderlands of the Urban West: Protestant Anglophone Culture and Institutions in Metropolitan San Francisco, 1900–1920*, 432, unpublished manuscript, https://www.dropbox.com/sh/567r22qltfm14b6/AAC8vHu29vXNIsbsOmk58ktYa?dl=0. Cites data as drawn from Keven J. Christiano, *Religious Diversity and Social Change: American Cities, 1890–1906* (Cambridge: Cambridge University Press, 1987).

43   *Daily Sun* (San Bernardino), March 12, 1902.

44   Kim McQuaid, "The Businessman as Reformer: Nelson O. Nelson and Late 19th Century Social Movements in America," *American Journal of Economics and Sociology*, 33 no. 4 (October 1974) 423–435.

45   Los Angeles Herald, March 16, 1902; Michael Cooney, "The Downfall of Alfred Dolge," on web site: Upstate Earth, February 1, 2011, https://upstateearth.blogspot.com/2011/02/downfall-of-alfred-dolge.html, accessed on June 20, 2020.

46   Marnie Jones, *Holy Toledo*, 207–8; Los Angeles Herald, March 12, 1902.

47   Kim McQuaid, "The Businessman as Reformer," 423–435, 431; J. Stitt Wilson to Caroline Severance, January 21, 1904, March 21, 1904, Wilson file, Severance Papers, Huntington Library.

48   *The Worker* (New York), April 20, 1902.

49   *Los Angeles Socialist*, April 19, 1902; *Rocky Mountain News*, April 7, 16, 1902; *Denver Post*, April 8, 12, 21, 1902.

50   *World Herald* (Omaha), April 23, 1902; *Denver Post*, April 27, 1902.

51   *Berkeley Daily Gazette*, May 8, 1902; Wilson, "Autobiography," 145.

52   *Oregonian* (Portland), May 5, 19, 23, 25, 29, 31, 1902.

53   *Anaconda Standard*, September 24, 1902, 3.

54   *Berkeley Daily Gazette*, August 21, 1902.

55   *Herald Democrat* (Leadville, CO) October 2, 1902.

56   *Rocky Mountain News* (Denver), October 20, 1902.

57   *An Address by Teller County Locals of the Socialist Party to the Socialists of Colorado*, July 26, 1903. Ira Kipnis. *The American Socialist Movement, 1897–1912* (New York: Columbia University Press, 1952), 180–182; David R. Berman, *Radicalism in the Mountain West, 1890–1920* (Boulder: University Press of Colorado, 2007), 105.

58   Eugene V. Debs, "The Crusaders," *American Labor Union Journal*, February 19, 1903,

also quoted in Nick Salvatore, *Eugene Debs: Citizen and Socialist* (Urbana: University of Illinois Press, 1982), 212.

59   Walton Bean, *Boss Ruef's San Francisco* (Berkeley: University of California Press, 1972), 19–22.

60   Ralph Edward Shaffer, "A History of the Socialist Party of California," MA thesis, University of California, Los Angeles, 1955, 30–33; Shaffer, "Radicalism in California, 1869–1929," PhD diss., University of California, Berkeley, 1962, 156–158.

61   Wilson to Severance, February 18, 1903, Severance Papers, Huntington Library.

62   *Conable's Path-Finder*, November 1904, 4.

63   *Fort Worth Star-Telegram*, August 26, September 1, 1904; *Dallas Morning News*, September 1, 1904, June 5, 1905; *Socialist Voice*, August 26, 1905.

64   *Albert Lea Enterprise* (MN), May 25, 1904; *Montana News* (Lewiston) August 9, 1905.

65   Hopkins, *The Rise of the Social Gospel*, 237.

66   Editor's note, *Christian Socialist*, June 1, 1907, 1.

Chapter 6. Socialism and New Thought

1   *San Francisco Call*, March 6, 1903.

2   *Philosophical Journal* (San Francisco), August 16, 1902, 8.

3   *San Francisco Chronicle*, October 18, 1903 lists a Sunday lecture with an admission fee of 25 cents.

4   *Christian: A Journal for the Individual* (Denver, CO), September 1903, 2.

5   Charles Wollenberg, *Berkeley: A City in History* (Berkeley: University of California Press, 2008).

6   J. Stitt Wilson. *The Three Great Hypnotisms* (Westwood: Ariel Press, no date). *Denver Post*, April 21, 1902.

7   *The Essene* (Denver), June 1903, 27.

8   As published the excerpt is all run together, but the content follows the common New Thought format.

9   *The Essene* (Denver), June 1903, 28.

10   *The Essene* (Denver), June 1903, 29–30.

11   *Path-Finder*, November 1902, 15, 18.

12   *Los Angeles Herald*, April 6, 1903.

13   J. Stitt Wilson, "Christianity and Paganism," *International Socialist Review*," 2 no.1 (July 1, 1901): 9.

14   Wallace D. Wattles. *The Science of Getting Rich* (Holyoke: Elizabeth Towne, 1910), 50.

15   *Path-Finder*, February 1903, 17.

16   *Path-Finder*, November 1902, 16–17.

17   *Path-Finder*, March 1903, 16.

18   *Path-Finder*, March 1903, 15–16.

19   *Los Angeles Herald*, April 6, 1903.

20   *Evening Tribune* (San Diego), October 27, 1903, 3. *Blue Grass Blade* (Lexington, KY) November 15, 1903.

21   Wilson to Severance, February 18, 1903, Severance Papers, Huntington Library.

22 "Affidavit of Mrs. J. Stitt Wilson," June 3, 1905 in Nellie Beighle, *Book of Knowledge: Psychic Facts* (3rd edition) (San Francisco: Hicks-Judd Co., 1911), 544–545.

23 Dr. Nellie Beighle, ed. *Compliments of Dr. Nellie Beighle*, San Francisco, California, 1905, Accessed June 20, 2020 at http://www.iapsop.com/ssoc/1905__beighle___compliments_of_nellie_beighle.pdf.

24 *Daily Chronicle* (Spokane) November 9, 1903.

25 J. Stitt Wilson, "In Memoriam—A Message to My Comrades," *California Social Democrat*, December 21, 1912.

26 Wilson, "In Memoriam," December 21, 1912.

27 *Philosophical Journal* (San Francisco) March 26, 1904, 8.

28 "Spiritualists in Convention," *San Francisco Call*, March 28, 1904.

29 Wilson to Severance, March 21, 1904, Severance Papers, Huntington Library.

30 *Oakland Tribune*, February 13, 1904, 5.

31 *Pacific* (Publication of the Congregational Churches of the Pacific Coast), February 18, 1904, 8. *Berkeley Daily Gazette*, March 9, 1904, 1.

32 For example, a letter to *Socialist Voice* (Oakland) August 12, 1905 happily lists as prominent members Job Harriman, J. Stitt Wilson, Ben Wilson, Jack London and Austin Lewis without regard to their very different views.

33 *Berkeley Daily Gazette*, April 8, 1904, 3.

34 Nelson and Wilson to Jones, April 7, 1903, Samuel M. Jones papers, Ohio Historical Society.

35 "Proceedings of the Convention," *International Socialist Review* (1904) 697–698.

36 Wilson to Severance, June 27, 1904, Severance Papers, Huntington Library.

37 *Berkeley Daily Gazette*, August 12, 17, 19, 1904; *Oakland Tribune*, August 26, 1904.

38 Michael Willrich, *Pox: An American History* (New York: Penguin, 2011).

39 J. Stitt Wilson, "Socialism and Disease," *Conable's Path-Finder*, October 1904, 15–18.

40 *Berkeley Daily Gazette*, January 13, 1905; *Riverside Daily Press*, January 25, 1905, 1; Michael Willrich, *Pox*, 280.

41 *San Francisco Call*, July 18, 1905; *Oakland Tribune*, July 18, 1905; *Berkeley Daily Gazette*, July 21, 1905; "Mass Meeting at Golden Sheaf Hall," flier, in Berkeley Politics box, Bancroft Library, University of California, Berkeley.

42 *San Jose Mercury News*, August 21, September 5, 1904.

43 J. Stitt Wilson, *The Message of Socialism to the Church: An Address delivered before the Bay Association of Congregational Churches and Ministers, Oakland, September 13, 1904* (Berkeley: published by the Author, 1904). Number published reported on page 2 of the 1909 Cardiff, Wales edition.

44 *Los Angeles Herald*, October 9, 23, 30, 1904; *San Diego Union*, October 25, 27, 1904; *Hemet News*, October 21, 1904; *Riverside Daily Press*, October 18, 1904; *Corona Courier*, October 15, 1904.

45 Wilson to Severance, October 20, 1904, Severance Papers, Huntington Library.

46 *Now* (San Francisco), November 1904, 187.

47 *Los Angeles Herald*, November 27, December 4, 11, 18, 25, 1904, January 1, 1905.

48 *Conable's Path-Finder*, January 1905, 10–11.

49 *Los Angeles Herald*, January 8, 1905.

50   *Oakland Tribune*, August 5, 1906, 13.

51   *Los Angeles Herald*, February 26, March 5, 1905.

52   Wilson to Severance, September 14, 1905, Severance Papers; *Hemet News*, August 25, 1905.

53   William Walker Atkinson, "Chips from the Old Block," *New Thought*, September 1, 1905, 210.

54   *Conable's Path-Finder*, August 1905, 11.

55   *Hemet News*, August 25, 1905. April 25, 1906.

56   Wilson to Severance, September 14, 1905, Severance Papers.

57   Wilson to Severance, September 14, 1905, Severance Papers.

58   *Hemet News*, November 17, 1905; December 14, 1906; *Riverside Daily Press*, April 25, 1906.

59   Wilson to Severance, January 30, 1906, Severance Papers.

60   *Hemet News*, February 2, 1906.

61   *Hemet News*, March 9, 1906.

62   *Riverside Daily Press*, December 22, 1906.

63   *Berkeley Daily Gazette*, February 17, 1906; *Now* (San Francisco) March 1906.

64   *Daily People*, March 23, 1906, 1.

65   Richard Schwartz, *Earthquake Exodus, 1906, Berkeley Responds to the San Francisco Refugees*, RSB Books, Berkeley, 2005.

66   *Riverside Daily Press*, May 2, 4, 5, 1906; *Riverside Independent Enterprise*, May 5, 1906; *Berkeley Daily Gazette*, May 8, 1906; *Socialist Voice*, May 12, 19, 26, June 16, 1906.

67   This is a composite based on material from: *Riverside Daily Press*, May 5, 1906; *Riverside Independent Enterprise*, May 5, 1906; *Berkeley Daily Gazette*, May 8, 1906; *Socialist Voice*, June 16, 1906.

68   Arthur and Peal Zipser, *Fire and Grace: The Life of Rose Pastor Stokes* (Athens, University of Georgia Press, 1989), 48, 58.

69   *San Francisco Chronicle*, August 12, 19, 26, September 2, 30, 1906.

70   *San Diego Union*, July 16, 17, 18, October 29, 1906; *Los Angeles Herald*, August 5, 1906; *Evening News* (San Jose) October 16, 17, 1906; *San Jose Mercury News*, October 21, 1906.

71   J. Stitt Wilson, *The Tragic Game of Capitalism: Being an Open Letter to the People of the United States concerning the Injustice of the Present Social Order* (Berkeley: published by the Author, May 1906). The conclusion echoed a book by William Stead that had impressed Wilson when it came out in 1894, *If Christ Came to Chicago! A Plea for the Union of All Who Love in the Service of All Who Suffer.*

72   Emma A. Wilson to Constance Severance, October 11, 1906, Severance Papers, Huntington Library.

73   *San Francisco Call*, July 26, 1906; Oakland Tribune, July 26, 1906, 4.

74   *Oakland Tribune*, August 5, 1906, 13.

75   *Oakland Tribune*, January 5, 1907, 4. *Berkeley Daily Gazette*, Jan 26, 1907, 1. *San Francisco Call*, January 26, 1907.

76   *Socialist Voice*, July 28, 1906.

77   *Riverside Daily Press*, December 22, 1906.

78   *Socialist Voice*, August 26, 1905. *Socialist Woman*, August 1908, 14.

Chapter 7. With the Labour Party in Great Britain

1   J. Stitt Wilson, *The New Theology and Socialism or Social Evolution in the Light of the Divine Immanence* (Bradford: published by the author, 1907).

2   *Shipley Times and Express*, February 28, 1908.

3   J. Reynolds and K. Laybourn, "The Emergence of the Independent Labour Party in Bradford," *International Review of Social History*, 20 no.3 (1975) 313–346.

4   Keith Laybourn and Jack Reynolds, *Liberalism and the Rise of Labour, 1890–1918* (London: Croom Helm, 1984), 115, 152, 169; Wikipedia, "Fred Jowett," accessed March 31, 2017 at https://en.wikipedia.org/wiki/Fred_Jowett; Municipal Dreams (web site), "Bradford's Pre-1914 Council Housing: a 'victory in one of the earliest of conflicts between property and life," January 3, 2017, accessed March 31, 2017, https://municipaldreams.wordpress.com/2017/01/03/bradfords-pre-1914-council-housing/.

5   *Berkeley Daily Gazette*, March 20, 1913, 1; David James, "'Our Philip': The Early Career of Philip Snowden," *Bradford Antiquary*, 1987, 39–47.

6   J. Stitt Wilson, *The Social Crusader*, Cardiff, South Wales, No. 13, July 1908.

7   J. Stitt Wilson, *How I Became a Socialist and Other Papers* (Berkeley: published by the author, 1912). See "A Word," on page following title page.

8   J. Stitt Wilson. *The New Theology and Socialism*, 1907.

9   F. G. Howe, "Socialism and the Christians," *The New Age*, May 27, 1909, 106.

10   *Yorkshire Evening Post*, April 8, 1908, 5.

11   Peter d'Alroy Jones, *The Christian Socialist Revival, 1877–1914, Religion, Class and Social Conscience in Late-Victorian England* (Princeton, Princeton University Press, 1968), 409.

12   "The Lives and Actions of Suffragettes and Suffragists," accessed June 20, 2020 at http://www.uncoveryourancestors.org/blog/archibold-to-armstrong-5-suffragettes-united-by-a-cause.

13   Email from Anna Sander, Archivist & Curator of Manuscripts, Balliol College, Oxford, March 22, 2017.

14   J. Stitt Wilson to Prof. Thomas J. Holgate (Northwestern University), April 30, 1907, John Randolph Haynes Papers, J. Stitt Wilson file, University of California, Los Angeles; Wilson, *The New Theology and Socialism*.

15   *San Francisco Call*, July 21, 1908; *Berkeley Daily Gazette*, December 9, 1909, 5; *Los Angeles Herald*, October 30, 1910.

16   *Los Angeles Herald*, December 6, 1910.

17   *Broad Ax* (Chicago), April 15, 1916, 6. I have not found direct reference to Gladstone attending Bedales, but it seems likely that he would have attended the same school as his sister.

18   *Brotherhood*, November 1910, 472.

19   J. Stitt Wilson, *Moses: The Greatest of Labor Leaders*, 2nd edition (Huddersfield, published by the author, April 1909).

20   *Brotherhood*, July 1908, 297–298.

21   *Brotherhood*, July 1908, 297.

22   *Brotherhood*, July 1908, 297–298; November 1910, 472.

23 J. Stitt Wilson, *The Messiah Cometh: Riding on the Ass of Economics* (Huddersfield, published by the author, 1908), 18–19.

24 *New York Times*, September 21, 1908, 5; *New York Tribune*, September 21, 1908, 9.

25 *Sun* (N.Y.C.), September 21, 1908; *Trenton Evening Times*, September 23, 1908, 4.

26 *Los Angeles Herald*, October 10, 1908.

27 *Los Angeles Herald*, October 15, 17, 18, 19, 1908; *San Diego Union*, October 15, 1908, 2, 6; *San Francisco Chronicle*, October 20, 1908, 16. *San Francisco Chronicle*, August 6, 1908.

28 *Republican Atlas* (Monmouth, IL), October 29, 1908.

29 Sun (N.Y.C.) November 2, 1908, 4.

30 *Sun* (N.Y.) November 2, 1908, 4.

31 *Worker* (N.Y.), December 5, 1908.

32 Leila Wilson, "A Little Journey and a Visit to the Home of Bobby Burns," *Progressive Woman*, July 1909, 13.

33 *Manchester Courier*, April 7, 1909.

34 *Greenock Telegraph & Clyde Shipping Gazette*, April 10, 1909.

35 Keith Laybourn and Jack Reynolds, *Liberalism and the Rise of Labour*, 117.

36 Rev. Gilbert Clive Binyon, M.A. *The Christian Socialist Movement in England: An Introduction to the Study of Its History* (London: Society for Promoting Christian Knowledge, 1931), 184.

Chapter 8. Socialist for Governor

1 Wilson, "Autobiography," 83.

2 *Berkeley Daily Gazette*, December 9, 1909, 5, "Miss Wilson Wins Honors in England." U.S. Census, 1910.

3 Ralph Edward Shaffer, "A History of the Socialist Party of California," 82–83.

4 Ira Kipnis, *The American Socialist Movement*.

5 Kipnis, *The American Socialist Movement*, pp.118–119. Sally M. Miller, *Victor Berger and the Promise of Constructive Socialism* (Westport: Greenwood Press, 1973).

6 *World* (Oakland) June 25, 1910, 1, 2.

7 Thomas Ralph Clark, *Defending Rights: Law, Labor Politics, and the State of California, 1890–1925* (Detroit: Wayne State University Press, 2002).

8 Michael Kazin, *Barons of Labor: The San Francisco Building Trades and Union Power in the Progressive Era* (Urbana: University of Illinois Press, 1987), 150–162, 301.

9 Robert E. L. Knight, *Industrial Relations in the San Francisco Bay Area, 1900–1918* (Berkeley: University of California Press, 1960), 221.

10 Stimson, *Rise of the Labor Movement in Los Angeles*.

11 Knight, *Industrial Relations*, 224–228.

12 Alexander Saxton, *The Rise and Fall of the White Republic* (New York: Verso, 1991).

13 Alexander Saxton, *The Indispensable Enemy: Labor and the Anti-Chinese Movement in California* (Berkeley: University of California Press, 1971); Roger Daniels, *The Politics of Prejudice: The Anti-Japanese Movement in California and the Struggle for Japanese Exclusion* (New York: Atheneum, 1973).

14   Michael Kazin, *Barons of Labor*, 157–159, 164–165, 223.

15   See, for example, Noel Ignatiev, *How the Irish Became White* (New York: Routledge, 1995).

16   David Struthers, "'The Boss Has No Color Line': Race, Solidarity, and a Culture of Affinity in Los Angeles and the Borderlands, 1907–1915, *Journal for the Study of Radicalism*, 7 no. 2 (2013) 61–92.

17   Salvatore, *Eugene V. Deb*, 226–228.

18   William English Walling, J. G. Stokes, editors, *The Socialism of Today* (New York: Henry Holt and Company, 1916), 496–497.

19   For overviews of the debates, see Ira Kipnis, *The American Socialist Movement*, 276–288, and William English Walling, *Progressivism—and After* (New York: MacMillan Co., 1914), 377–389.

20   R. Laurence Moore, "Flawed Fraternity—American Socialist Response to the Negro, 1901–1912," *The Historian*, 32 no. 1 (November 1969) 1–18.

21   Michael Kazin, "The Great Exception Revisited: Organized Labor and Politics in San Francisco and Los Angeles, 1870–1940," *Pacific Historical Review*, 55 no. 3 (August 1986) 392.

22   *California Social Democrat*, February 15, 1913.

23   *California Social Democrat*, January 18, 1913.

24   *California Social Democrat*, May 16, 1914.

25   Philip S. Foner, "From Slavery to Socialism: George Washington Woodbey, Black Socialist Preacher," in *Socialism and Christianity in Early 20th Century America*, Jacob Dorn, ed. (Westport: Greenwood, 1998) 65–92.

26   *Socialist Voice* (Oakland), Dept. 8, 1906, "State Convention Resolutions."

27   Wilson, "The Free Man," *Social Crusader*, December 1, 1899, 7. *Moses: Greatest of Labour Leaders*, 1908, 2.

28   National Congress of the Socialist Party, Chicago, Ill, May 15 to 21, 1910, Stenographic Report by Wilson E. McDermut (Chicago: Socialist Party, 1910), 22.

29   National Congress of the Socialist Party, 1910, 75–77. Full debate, 80–169.

30   National Congress of the Socialist Party, 1910, 77–80.

31   National Congress of the Socialist Party, 1910, 168.

32   National Congress of the Socialist Party, 1910, 290, 301–302, 308, 318–319.

33   Eugene V. Debs, "A Letter from Debs on Immigration," *World* (Oakland) July 16, 1910.

34   National Congress of the Socialist Party, 1910, 179–181

35   National Congress of the Socialist Party, 1910, 181–211.

36   National Congress of the Socialist Party, 1910, 206–207.

37   National Congress of the Socialist Party, 209–211.

38   *Los Angeles Herald*, May 30, 1910; *Daily People* (N.Y.), July 2, 1910.

39   *Los Angeles Herald*, May 30, 1910.

40   *Los Angeles Herald*, May 30, 1910; *World*, June 25, 1910, 3; *Daily People* (N.Y.), July 2, 1910.

41   William Deverell, *Railroad Crossing: Californians and the Railroad, 1850–1910* (Berkeley: University of California Press, 1994), 166.

42 J. Stitt Wilson, "The Message of the 'Red Special'," *World* (Oakland) July 23, 1910, 1–2.

43 J. Stitt Wilson, "To the Organized Labor of California," *World* (Oakland), July 2, 1910, 1.

44 *Daily People* (N.Y.) July 5, 1910, 1; August 25, 1910, 1.

45 *Christian Socialist*, October 1, 1910.

46 *Los Angeles Herald*, July 1, 1910.

47 *International Socialist Review*, August 1910, 107–109.

48 *Sacramento Union*, June 25, 1910.

49 J. Stitt Wilson, "J. Stitt Wilson Writes to the Comrades," *World* (Oakland), July 23, 1910, 1; November 22, 1910.

50 The Red Flag was and still is the official song of the British Labour Party.

51 *World* (Oakland), July 16, 1910, 1.

52 *Los Angeles Herald*, July 9, 1910.

53 *World* (Oakland), July 16, 1910, 1; August 6, 1910, 1; *San Luis Obispo Daily Telegram*, July 26, 1910, 1.

54 *San Jose Mercury News*, July 31, 1910, 5.

55 *Daily People* (N.Y.) August 25, 1910, 1.

56 J. Stitt Wilson, "Socialist and Labor Policies," *World* (Oakland), September 3, 1910, 1–2.

57 *San Francisco Call*, September 6, 1910; *World* (Oakland) September 17, 1910, 1.

58 *Berkeley Daily Gazette*, December 9, 1909, 5; *Los Angeles Herald*, October 30, 1910.

59 *Los Angeles Herald*, November 2, 10, 1910; *Evening Tribune* (San Diego), November 22, 23, 24, 26, 1910.

60 *Los Angeles Herald*, December 1, 6, 1910.

61 *World* (Oakland), September 17, 1910, 1–2.

62 *Labor Clarion* (San Francisco) September 30, 1910.

63 World (Oakland) September 24, 1910.

64 World (Oakland) October 8, 1910.

65 *Fresno Morning Republican*, September 21, 1910, 16; *World* (Oakland), October 1, 1910; Socialist Party, "To the Workingmen of San Francisco," 1910, flier in Huntington Library

66 "To the Workingmen of San Francisco," 1910, flier, Huntington Library; *Los Angeles Herald*, September 25, 1910.

67 *World* (Oakland) October 8, 22, 1910.

68 "To the Workingmen of San Francisco," 1910, Huntington Library; *World* (Oakland), October 1, 1910.

69 *Christian Socialist* (Chicago), September 15, November 1, 15, 1910.

70 *San Luis Obispo Daily Telegram*, October 3, 1910, 2.

71 *San Francisco Call*, October 1, 1910; *Christian Socialist*, October 1, 1910.

72 Grace H. Stimson, *Rise of the Labor Movement in Los Angeles*, 348.

73 *San Diego Union*, October 12, 1910, 10.

74 *Sacramento Union*, October 14, 15, 1910. *San Diego Union*, November 3, 1910 3.

75 *Los Angeles Herald*, November 4, 1910.

76 *Evening News* (San Jose), November 5, 1910, 7; *World* (Oakland) November 5, 1910; Oakland Tribune, November 7, 1910.

77 *Sacramento Union*, December 12, 1910.

78 Frederick Ryan, *History of the San Diego Labor Movement*, San Diego State College Bureau of Business and Economic Research, San Diego, 1959, 9–20.

79 *World* (Oakland) November 22, 1910; *Oakland Tribune*, January 25, 1911.

80 Ralph E. Shaffer, "Radicalism in California," 163, 166.

Chapter 9. Socialist for Mayor

1   *World* (Oakland), February 4, 1911; *San Francisco Chronicle*, April 3, 1911.

2   J. Stitt Wilson, "Modern Socialism: Its Moral and Spiritual Significance," *Aquarian New Age*, March 1911, 161–165; April–May 1911, 193–196; July 1911, 257–263 (address to the Presbyterian Ministers Association of San Francisco); *San Francisco Chronicle*, December 13, 1910, 7.

3   *World* (Oakland), February 4, 1911.

4   *Daily People*, April 16, 1911.

5   J. Stitt Wilson, "The Resurrection," *The Tailor: Official Organ of the Journeymen Tailors Union of America*, 21:10 (May 1911) 1–4.

6   J. Stitt Wilson, "Socialism: The Judgement of Civilization," *The Tailor: Official Organ of the Journeymen Tailors Union of America*, 21:12 (July 1911) 1–4.

7   Selig Schulberg, "Irresponsible Free Lance," *Revolt* (San Francisco), December 30, 1911, 1.

8   Selig Schulberg, "Irresponsible Free Lance."

9   Socialist Party, San Francisco, December 16, 1910, "Political Tyranny in United States, Canada and Japan," flier, author's collection.

10 *Berkeley Daily Gazette*, December 31, 1910.

11 *Berkeley Daily Gazette*, February 7, March 8, 1911.

12 J. Stitt Wilson, "The Story of a Socialist Mayor," *Western Comrade*, September 1913; *Bakersfield Californian*, February 25, 1911; *Riverside Daily Press*, February 27, 1911, 5.

13 *Oakland Tribune*, February 28, 1911.

14 *San Francisco Call*, February 28, 1911.

15 Wilson, "The Story of a Socialist Mayor"; *Oakland Tribune*, February 22, 1911.

16 Wilson, "The Story of a Socialist Mayor" *San Francisco Call*, February 26, 1911; *Oakland Tribune*, February 26, 1911, 32.

17 *World* (Oakland), February 4, 1911; *Oakland Tribune*, March 1, 1911.

18 *Charter of the City of Berkeley* (Berkeley: Lederer, Street & Zeus Co., July 1, 1909).

19 *Berkeley Daily Gazette*, April 24, 26, 29 30, May 2, 1909.

20 *Oakland Tribune*, March 6, 1911, 10; *Berkeley Daily Gazette*, February 18, 21, 1911.

21 Letter from John A. Wilson to Robert E. Bush, March 8, 1914. Author's collection.

22 *Berkeley Daily Gazette*, April 9, 1902, January 26, 1907, 1, October 31, 1911; *Socialist Voice*, October 20, November 24, 1906; *Oakland Tribune*, August 26, 1904, 7.

23 *Oakland Tribune*, September 30, 1906, 15. *Berkeley Daily Gazette*, January 23, 1909, February 27, 1913.

24 Herman I. Stern, *Evelyn Gray, or, The victims of our western Turks: a tragedy in five acts* (New York: Alden, 1890); *The Gods of Our Fathers: A Study of Saxon Mythology* (New York: Harper, 1898).

25 *Berkeley Daily Gazette*, April 14, 1905; March 30, 1909; September 13, 1909; July 3, 1926.

26 *Berkeley Daily Gazette*, March 6, 1915, October 19, 1916.

27 *Berkeley Daily Gazette*, April 22, 1911.

28 "Socialist City Platform of Berkeley," *World* (Oakland), April 17, 1909; "Berkeley Socialist Ticket," *World* (Oakland) March 16, 1907.

29 "Municipal Ownership of Public Utilities a Part of the Capitalist Program," *Socialist Voice* (Oakland) April 15, 1905.

30 Maureen A. Flanagan, *Seeing with Their Hearts: Chicago Women and the Vision of the Good City, 1871–1933* (Princeton: Princeton University Press, 2002) and *America Reformed: Progressives and Progressivisms, 1890s–1920s* (New York: Oxford University Press, 2007); Frederic C. Howe, *The City: The Hope of Democracy* (New York: Charles Scribner's Sons, 1906), 175.

31 *Berkeley Daily Gazette*, March 8, 1911.

32 *Oakland Tribune*, March 6, 1911, 10.

33 Ed Cray, *Chief Justice: A Biography of Earl Warren* (New York: Simon & Schuster, 1997), 28.

34 *Berkeley Daily Gazette*, March 30, 1911.

35 *Berkeley Daily Gazette*, March 31, 1911, 4.

36 Ira B. Cross, "Socialism in California Municipalities" *National Municipal Review*, 1 (October 1912) 616.

37 *Berkeley Daily Gazette*, March 9, 1911.

38 *Berkeley Daily Gazette*, March 30, 31, 1911.

39 *Berkeley Daily Gazette*, March 18, 1911.

40 *Berkeley Daily Gazette*, March 31, 1911.

41 John A. Wilson to Robert E. Bush, March 8, 1914. Author's collection.

42 *San Francisco Call*, April 1, 1911.

43 John Wesley Noble, *Its Name Was M.U.D.* (Oakland: East Bay Municipal Utility District, 1970).

44 *Berkeley Daily Gazette*, March 8, 1911.

45 *Berkeley Daily Gazette*, March 15, 16, 1911.

46 *Berkeley Daily Gazette*, March 28, 1911.

47 *Berkeley Daily Gazette*, March 15, 1911.

48 *Berkeley Daily Gazette*, March 31, 1911, 7.

49 *Berkeley Daily Gazette*, March 14, 21, 22, 31, 1911.

50 *San Francisco Call*, July 20, August 26, 1909.

51 *Berkeley Daily Gazette*, March 22, 1911; *The City for the People*, March 28, 1911, 3; Oakland Tribune, March 31, 1911.

52 *Berkeley Daily Gazette*, March 30, 31, 1911.

53 *Berkeley Daily Gazette*, March 31, 1911; *San Francisco Call*, April 1, 1911.

54 *Berkeley Daily Gazette*, March 27, 1911.

55   Willard M. Oliver, *August Vollmer: The Father of Professional Policing* (Durham: Carolina Academic Press, 2017), 138–156.

56   *Berkeley Daily Gazette*, March 29, 1911.

57   *Berkeley Daily Gazette*, March 30, 1911.

58   *Berkeley Daily Gazette*, March 30, 31, 1911.

59   *Berkeley Daily Gazette*, April 1, 1911.

60   *Berkeley Daily Gazette*, April 3, 1911.

61   *Oakland Tribune*, April 2, 1911.

62   *Daily People* (N.Y.), April 16, 1911.

63   *Berkeley Daily Gazette*, July 1, 1911, 1.

64   *Berkeley Daily Gazette*, "Official Returns: General Municipal Election, City of Berkeley," April 1, 1911, April 5, 1911.

65   *Berkeley Daily Gazette*, April 17, 1911.

66   Precincts grouped by area: South-East Berkeley 1–3; Telegraph (South side of campus) 13–14; West Berkeley 9, 10, 19. Wilson lived in precinct 22.

67   *Berkeley Daily Gazette*, April 8, 1911.

68   *San Francisco Chronicle*, "The Berkeley Election," April 4, 1911.

69   *Washington Herald* (Washington, D.C.), "Socialists Elect Mayor: Machine Politicians Lose to Reformer in Berkeley Campaign," April 3, 1911; same article in *Evening Post* (Frederick, MD) and other newspapers.

70   *Oakland Tribune*, "The Election in Berkeley," April 3, 1911.

71   *Daily People* (N.Y.) May 8, 1911.

72   *World* (Oakland), April 8, 1911.

73   *World* (Oakland), July 22, 1911.

74   *Berkeley Daily Gazette*, April 21, 1911.

75   *Berkeley Daily Gazette*, April 15, 1911.

76   *Berkeley Daily Gazette*, April 22, 1911.

77   *Berkeley Daily Gazette*, April 15, 1911.

78   *Berkeley Daily Gazette*, April 12, 1911.

79   *Berkeley Daily Gazette*, April 10, 1911.

80   *Berkeley Daily Gazette*, April 20, 21, 1911.

81   *Berkeley Daily Gazette*, April 6, 7, 8, 1911.

82   J. Stitt Wilson, letter to the editor dated July 9, 1911, *The World* (Oakland), July 29, 1911.

83   *San Francisco Call*, April 20, 1911.

84   *The World* (Oakland), April 15, 29, 1911; *San Francisco Call*, April 12, 1911.

85   *The World* (Oakland), May 15, 1911.

86   *San Francisco Call*, May 16, 1911; *San Luis Obispo Daily Telegraph*, June 9, 1911.

87   *Berkeley Daily Gazette*, June 16, 27, 1911; *Oakland Tribune*, June 2, 20, 1911; *San Francisco Call*, June 1, 28, 1911.

88   *San Francisco Call*, June 1, 17, 1911.

89   *Oakland Tribune*, June 2, 1911.

90   *Oakland Tribune*, June 16, 29, 1911; *San Francisco Call*, June 20, 28, 1911; *Berkeley Daily Gazette*, June 27, 1911.

Chapter 10. Mayor of Berkeley

1   *Berkeley Daily Gazette*, July 1, 1911.

2   *San Francisco Call*, June 17, July 2, 1911.

3   *California Social Democrat*, July 22, 1911.

4   *Berkeley Daily Gazette*, July 5, 1911; *San Francisco Call*, July 6, 1911.

5   *Berkeley Daily Gazette*, July 5, 1911.

6   *Berkeley Daily Gazette*, July 5, 1911; *San Francisco Call*, July 6, 1911; *Oakland Tribune*, July 9, 1911.

7   *World* (Oakland), July 15, 1911; *San Francisco Call*, July 8, 1911.

8   *Berkeley Daily Gazette*, August 30, 1911, Berkeley City Council minutes of August 31, 1911.

9   Berkeley City Council minutes for July. 5, 1911.

10 Wilson to Severance, August 26, 1911, Severance collection.

11 *Daily People*, August 9, 1911.

12 *San Francisco Call*, May 8, 1911.

13 *San Francisco Call*, July 27, 1911.

14 *Berkeley Daily Gazette*, September 1, 1911.

15 *Oakland Tribune*, September 6, 1911, 4.

16 *Berkeley Daily Gazette*, September 9, 1911, 1.

17 *Oakland Tribune*, August 21, 1911; *Revolt* (San Francisco), August 26, 1911, 3.

18 *San Francisco Call*, July 12, 1911.

19 *Berkeley Daily Gazette*, July 19, 1911; *California Social Democrat*, July 29, 1911; *World* (Oakland), July 22, 1911.

20 Wilson to Severance, August 26, 1911, Severance Papers, Huntington Library.

21 "Reformers and 'Municipal Socialism'," The *World* (Oakland), July 15, 1911

22 Richard W. Judd, *Socialist Cities: Municipal Politics and the Grass Roots of American Socialism* (Albany: SUNY Press, 1989), 16.

23 *World* (Oakland), August 26, 1911.

24 *World* (Oakland), September 9, 1911.

25 *Oakland Tribune*, August 25, 1911, 15.

26 Gayle Gullett, *Becoming Citizens: The Emergence and Development of the California Women's Movement, 1880–1911* (Urbana, University of Illinois Press, 2000), 173–175. Rebecca J. Mead, *How the Vote Was Won: Woman Suffrage in the Western United States, 1868–1914* (New York: NYU Press, 2004), 129.

27 *Berkeley Daily Gazette*, July 7, 1911. The meeting was chaired by Anita Whitney, who joined the Socialist Party a few years later and then became a leader in the Communist Party of California.

28 Sherry J. Katz, "A Politics of Coalition: Socialist Women and the California Women Suffrage Movement, 1900–1911" in *One Woman, One Vote: Rediscovering the Woman Suffrage Movement*, ed. Marjorie Spruill Wheeler (Troutdale: NewSage, 1995), 245–262. Sherry J. Katz, "Redefining 'The Political': Socialist Women and Party Politics in California, 1900–1920" in *We Have Come to Stay: American Women and Political Parties: 1880–1960*, eds. Melanie Gustafson, Kristie

Miller and Elisabeth Perry (Albuquerque: University of New Mexico Press, 1999), 23–32

29 Susan Englander, "We Want the Ballot for Very Different Reasons: Club Women, Union Women and the Internal Politics of the Suffrage Movement, 1896–1911," in *California Women and Politics*, Cherny, Irwin, Wilson, eds. 209–235.

30 Michael Kazin, *Barons of Labor. San Francisco Chronicle*, September 1, 1911.

31 See also Sherry J. Katz, "Dual Commitments: Feminism, Socialism and Women's Political Activism in California, 1890–1920," (PhD diss., UCLA, 1991), 341.

32 *Berkeley Independent*, October 6, 1911.

33 J. Stitt Wilson to Hester Harland, August 16, 1911. Hester Harland papers, Bancroft Library, University of California, Berkeley.

34 Aileen Kraditor, *The Ideas of the Woman Suffrage Movement*, 43–74; Gullett, *Becoming Citizens*, 151–200.

35 Rebecca J. Mead, *How the Vote Was Won*, 5, 136–7.

36 *Berkeley Independent*, October 10, 1911, "Final Plea for Votes for Women: Record Breaking Crowd Hears Mayor Wilson, Miss McLean and Others." *The Sun and the Letter* (Berkeley), October 14, "Suffragists Fill Hall at Last Rally."

37 Anderson, "In the Religious Borderlands of the Urban West," 361–2.

38 Theodore Roosevelt, *Theodore Roosevelt's Confession of Faith before the Progressive National Convention* (New York: Progressive Party, 1912); C.H. Congdon, *Progressive Battle Hymns* (New York: Progressive Party, 1912).

39 *San Francisco Call*, October 10, 1911. See also Wilson, *The Tragic Game of Capitalism*, 13.

40 J. Stitt Wilson. *The Message of Socialism to the Church*, Ruskin Institute, Cardiff, Wales, 1909, 18.

41 *San Francisco Call*, November 19, 1911.

42 *Berkeley Daily Gazette*, September 2, 1911 "Suffrage is Defended by Mayor Wilson."

43 Theda Skocpol, *Protecting Soldiers and Mothers: The Political Origins of Social Policy in the United States* (Cambridge: Harvard University Press, 1992), 350.

44 *San Francisco Call*, "Triumph of Suffrage is Celebrated," October 23, 1911.

45 Robert D. Johnston. *The Radical Middle Class: Populist Democracy and the Question of Capitalism in Progressive Era Portland, Oregon* (Princeton: Princeton University Press, 2003), 163.

46 Gilman M. Ostrander, *The Prohibition Movement in California, 1848–1933* (Berkeley: University of California Press, 1957).

47 Dr. J.E. Pottenger, "Socialism and the Single Tax," *Western Comrade*, December 1913, 305. Similar criticisms of George were made by Bellamy and Veblen according to Steven Cord, *Henry George: Dreamer or Realist?* (Philadelphia, University of Pennsylvania Press, 1965), 96–97.

48 John T. McRoy, "Fels Fund Dinner of the Manhattan Single Tax Club," *Single Tax Review*, January-February 1914, 53.

49 *California Social Democrat*, October 21, 1911; *Berkeley Independent*, October 20 & 21, 1911; *Proceedings: Fourteenth Annual Convention: League of California Municipalities*, Santa Barbara, California, October 23–28, 1911; *Berkeley Daily Gazette*, December 16, 20, 1911.

50 J. Stitt Wilson, "Some Suggestions for Reform in Taxation," in *Proceedings: League of California Municipalities*, 154–156.

51 *Proceedings: League of California Municipalities. Berkeley Daily Gazette*, December 16, 20, 1911.

52 Michael Kazin, *Barons of Labor*, 159; *California Social Democrat*, June 22, 1912; *Single Tax Review*, 12:2 (March–April 1912) 49; November–December 1912, 59.

53 *Oakland Tribune*, January 15, 1912.

54 *California Social Democrat*, September 2, 1911.

55 *Oakland Tribune*, September 28, 1911.

56 These accusations are taken at face value by Ralph Shaffer, who relied almost entirely on publications of the revolutionary wing of the Socialist Party.

57 *Berkeley Daily Gazette*, August 3, 1911; *Oakland Tribune*, August 2, 1911; *World* (Oakland), August 5, 1911.

58 Grace Stimson. *The Rise of the Labor Movement in Los Angeles*, 362–3.

59 Wilson to Severance, November 15, 1911, Severance Papers, Huntington Library.

60 Grace Stimson. *The Rise of the Labor Movement in Los Angeles*, 363.

61 James P. Kraft, "The Fall of Job Harriman's Socialist Party: Violence, Gender and Politics in Los Angeles, 1911," *Southern California Quarterly*, 70 no. 1 (Spring 1988) 43–68.

62 Wilson to Severance, November 15, 1911, Severance Papers.

63 *California Social Democrat*, December 9, 1911; *San Francisco Chronicle*, November 27, 1911, 9; *Oakland Tribune*, December 4, 1911, 7.

64 Daniel J. Johnson, "'No Make-Believe Class Struggle': The Socialist Municipal Campaign in Los Angeles, 1911," *Labor History*, 41 no. 1 (2000) 25–45.

65 *Oregonian* (Portland), January 4, 1912, 5.

66 *Oregonian* (Portland), January 4, 1912, 5; *Day Book* (Chicago), January 17, 1912.

67 *San Francisco Call*, April 13, September 20, 1912, March 16, 1913; *Oakland Tribune*, January 6, March 18, April 19, 1914; *Olla Podrida* (Berkeley: Berkeley High School, June. 1914), 48–49.

68 *San Francisco Call*, August 22, September 18, November 1911, March 7, 1912; *Berkeley Daily Gazette*, October 19, 1911, 2.

69 *San Luis Obispo Daily Telegram*, August 7, 1911, 6.

70 *Berkeley Daily Gazette*, October 5, 1911, 3.

71 *San Francisco Call*, September 30, October 21, 22, November 1, 1911.

72 *Oakland Tribune*, January 12, 1912; *San Francisco Call*, December 2, 26, 1911.

73 *San Francisco Chronicle*, January 24, 1912; *Oakland Tribune*, January 26, 1912; *San Francisco Call*, January 26, 27, 31, 1912.

74 *Berkeley Daily Gazette*, January 31, 1912.

75 *Berkeley Daily Gazette*, February 21, 1912.

76 *Oakland Tribune*, February 7, 1912.

77 *San Francisco Call*, March 1, 1912; *Oakland Tribune*, February 29, 1912.

78 *San Francisco Call*, February 28, 1912.

79 *Berkeley Daily Gazette*, March 8, 9, 1912.

80 *San Francisco Call*, March 11, 14, 18, April 1, 1912.

81 *Berkeley Daily Gazette*, March 12, 1912.

82   *Oakland Tribune*, May 1, 1912, 11.

83   *Oakland Tribune*, August 7, 1912.

84   *Oakland Tribune*, April 6, 1912.

85   *Berkeley Daily Gazette*, April 25, 1912.

86   *Berkeley Daily Gazette*, April 26, 1912.

87   *San Francisco Call*, April 26, 1912; *San Francisco Chronicle*, April 25, 1912; *Oakland Tribune*, April 25, 1912, 8.

88   *Oakland Tribune*, May 1, 1912.

89   *Oakland Tribune*, May 2, 1912, 9.

90   *San Francisco Call*, September 6, 1912.

91   *San Francisco Call*, May 8, 1912.

92   *San Francisco Call*, April 28, 1912.

93   "Appendix K: Report of the Committee on Municipal and State Program," *Proceedings, National Convention of the Socialist Party* (Chicago, 1912), 214–217. (Held in Indianapolis, May 12–18, 1912).

94   A.W. Ricker, "Who Wrote the Socialist Platform of 1912?," *California Social Democrat*, September 28, 1912

95   *Oakland Tribune*, May 27, 1912, 2.

96   "Appendix J: Report of the Majority and Minority Committees on Immigration," in *Proceedings, National Convention of the Socialist Party* (Chicago, 1912), 209–211.

97   *Proceedings, National Convention of the Socialist Party*, 1912, 166–167.

98   *Proceedings, National Convention of the Socialist Party*, 1912, 140–142.

99   *Oakland Tribune*, May 27, 1912, 2; *San Francisco Chronicle*, May 28, 1912.

100 *California Social Democrat*, June 15, 1912.

101 *Oakland Tribune*, August 30, September 7, 1912; *San Francisco Call*, November 29, 1913.

102 *Oakland Tribune*, August 27, 1912; *San Francisco Call*, July 14, 1912.

103 *San Francisco Call*, July 18, 1912.

104 J. Stitt Wilson, "Comrades of California We Need Your Help Now," *California Social Democrat*, September 21, 1912.

105 *Berkeley Daily Gazette*, October 28, 1912, "Stitt Wilson is Confident"; *Oakland Tribune*, October 27, 1912, 22.

106 *San Francisco Call*, October 9, November 2, 1912; *Berkeley Daily Gazette*, October 31, 1912, 1.

107 Prudence Stokes Brown, "A Call to Every Socialist Woman," *World* (Oakland), September 7, 1912.

108 J. Stitt Wilson, "Open Letter to Women of Alameda County," *World* (Oakland), August 24, 1912.

109 "Wilson's Great Message to Non-Socialist Voters," *California Social Democrat*, October 19, 1912.

110 "Bulletin Touts for Stitt Wilson," *Oakland Tribune*, October 31, 1912, 6.

111 *World* (Oakland), September 7, 21, 28, October 26, November 2, 1912.

112 *San Francisco Call*, September 4, 1912.

113 *San Francisco Call*, September 26, 1912; *Riverside Independent Enterprise*, September 28, 1912.

114 *Oakland Tribune*, October 21, 1912; *San Francisco Call*, October 21, 1912; *Reno Evening Gazette*, October 22, 1912.

115 *World* (Oakland), December 14, 1912; *Oakland Tribune*, September 17, 20, 1912; Mila Tupper Maynard, "A Socialist Play—The Landslide," *The Coming Nation*, December 7, 1912, 9.

116 *San Diego Union*, August 21, 29, 30, 1912.

117 *Oakland Tribune*, October 29, 1912; *San Francisco Call*, October 30, 1912.

118 *Oakland Tribune*, February 14, 1913; *Berkeley Daily Gazette*, July 8, 1913, 5.

119 *Oakland Tribune*, November 5, 1912.

120 *World* (Oakland), November 9, 1912, "Stitt Wilson's Words of Cheer."

121 *Single Tax Review* (Nov–Dec) 1912, 12:6, 59.

122 *Berkeley Daily Gazette*, November 4, 1912; *Oakland Tribune*, October 13, 1912, 12, "Anarchy and Confiscation in Taxation."

123 *San Francisco Chronicle*, September 26, 1912, 3; *Sausalito News*, October 5, 1912.

124 *Oakland Tribune*, October 30, 1912.

125 *Oakland Tribune*, October 10, 1912.

126 *Berkeley Daily Gazette*, November 9, 11, 1912.

127 *San Francisco News Letter*, November 16, 1912, 28.

128 *San Francisco Call*, November 20, 1912.

129 *World* (Oakland), August 16, 1912.

130 *Berkeley Daily Gazette*, November 25, 26, 1912.

131 *Berkeley Daily Gazette*, November 30, 1912.

132 *California Social Democrat*, December 21, 1912.

133 *Oakland Tribune*, November 22, December 2, 1912; *Berkeley Daily Gazette*, November 30, 1912, December 19, 1912; *World* (Oakland) December 7, 1912; *San Francisco Call*, December 7, 9, 1912.

134 J. Stitt Wilson, *Vocational Education*, Social Crusade Series No. 11 (Berkeley: published by the author, November 1, 1913); *California Social Democrat*, January 18, 1913, 6; *Berkeley Daily Gazette*, January 3, 1913.

135 *Berkeley Daily Gazette*, February 18, March 18, 1913.

136 "Realty Dealers Want License Ordinance Revoked" *Berkeley Daily Gazette*, January 21, 1913; "Are Laundrymen Worth More to Community Than Realty Men? Mayor Wilson's Social Question Brings Rise from Sellers of Land," *Berkeley Independent*, January 21, 1913: "Puts Realty Men Below Laundries," *Oakland Tribune*, January 21, 1913.

137 *Berkeley Daily Gazette*, January 30, February 20 (cites *Hollister Bee*), 22 (cites *Riverside Press*), 1913, 1; *San Jose Mercury News*, February 2, 1913, 6; *Chicago Tribune*, Jan 31, 1913 *Day Book* (Chicago), November 22, 1913.

138 *Berkeley Daily Gazette*, December 27, 1912.

139 *Berkeley Daily Gazette*, November 27, 1912.

140 *California Social Democrat*, February 8, 15, 22, 1913; *Berkeley Daily Gazette*, February 10, 1913, 1.

141 *San Francisco Call*, February 20, 24, 1913. J. Stitt Wilson, "Letter to Berkeley Socialists Declining the Nomination for the Mayoralty of Berkeley," February 19, 1913, reprinted in *Vocational Education*, 32–36.

142 *San Francisco Call*, February 20, 1913, "Mayor Wilson is not in contest for reelection." Wilson, "Letter to Berkeley Socialists Declining the Nomination."

143 *California Social Democrat*, February 8, 1913.

144 Ferrier, William Warren; *Berkeley, California: The Story of the Evolution of a Hamlet into a City of Culture and Commerce* (Berkeley, published by the author, 1933), 267–269; *Berkeley Daily Gazette*, December 27, 1912.

145 *Oakland Tribune*, February 10, 1913; *Berkeley Daily Gazette*, June 9, 1913.

146 *Berkeley Daily Gazette*, February 25, March 18, 1913.

147 *Berkeley Daily Gazette*, February 22, 1913.

148 *Berkeley Daily Gazette*, February 10, 27, 1913.

149 *Berkeley Daily Gazette*, October 6, 1941, 13; *World* (Oakland), October 19, November 2, 1912.

150 *Berkeley Daily Gazette*, April 30, 1913, 1.

151 *World* (Oakland) July 8, 1911.

152 *Sacramento Union*, November 9, 1910; January 17, 1914.

153 *Oakland Tribune*, March 4, 1913, 17; *Berkeley Daily Gazette*, March 3, 4, 1913.

154 *Berkeley Daily Gazette*, April 2, 4, 22, 1913.

155 *Berkeley Daily Gazette*, April 7, 1913.

156 *Berkeley Daily Gazette*, April 14, 1913.

157 *Berkeley Daily Gazette*, April 14, 1913; *House Journal: Proceedings of the House of Representatives of the State of Kansas, Eighteenth Biennial Session, Topeka, January 14 to March 17, 1913* (Topeka, 1913).

158 *San Francisco Call*, May 19, 1913; *California Social Democrat*, May 31, 1913.

159 *California Social Democrat*, November 30, 1912.

160 *California Social Democrat*, January 3, February 7, 1914, January 30. 1915; Oakland City Directory, 1913, 1914.

161 *Berkeley Daily Gazette*, January 20, 1921, 4.

162 *Berkeley Daily Gazette*, May 2, 7, 10, 29, 1913; *Rocky Mountain News* (Denver) May 6, 1913; *Commonwealth* (Everett) May 9, 1913; *Kansas City Times*, May 9, 1913.

163 John T. McRoy, "Fels Fund Dinner of the Manhattan Single Tax Club," *Single Tax Review*, January–February 1914, 53.

164 *Party Builder* (N.Y.) June 14, 1913; *Oakland Tribune*, June 8, 1913.

165 Robert Knight, *Industrial Relations in the San Francisco Bay Area*, 280–284.

166 *Berkeley Daily Gazette*, May 10, 29, June 20, 21, 23, 24, 25, 1913. *California Social Democrat*, June 28, 1913.

167 Robert Knight, *Industrial Relations in the San Francisco Bay Area*, 280–284.

168 *Berkeley Daily Gazette*, June 27, 1913.

Chapter 11. Campaigning Takes Its Toll

1   J. Stitt Wilson to Anne H. Martin, October 27, 1914, Anne Henrietta Martin Papers, Bancroft Library, University of California, Berkeley.

2   *California Social Democrat*, June 28, 1913.

3   *California Social Democrat*, November 22, 29, 1913, January 24, 1914.

4   *California Social Democrat*, March 7, 1914; *Daily Telegraph* (San Luis Obispo) July 7, 1913, 7.

5   *Chicago Tribune*, March 2, 1914, 7.

6   *California Social Democrat*, May 31, July 19, August 30, 1913; *Western Comrade*, August 1913, 158–9, October 1913, 237. Steven J. Ross, "Struggles for the Screen: Workers, Radicals and the Political Uses of Silent Film," *American Historical Review*, 96 no. 2 (April 1991) 333–367. It is hard to understand why, at a time when public speaking was so important, recordings were not made of any major Socialist speakers. Even the "recording" of a brief speech by Eugene Debs actually uses someone else's voice. http://historymatters.gmu.edu/d/5658/.

7   W. Stephen Bush, "The Sea Wolf" (review), *Moving Picture World*, November 1, 1913, 480.

8   Teresa Hurley and Jarrod Harrison, "Awed by the Women's Clubs: Women Voters and Moral Reform, 1913–1914," in *California Women and Politics*, Cherny, Irwin and Wilson, eds. 237–261. Mark Hopkins, "No Undue Familiarity: Gender, Vice and the Campaign to Regulate Dance Halls, 1911–1921" in *California Women and Politics*, Cherny, Irwin and Wilson, eds. 289–307.

9   J. Stitt Wilson, *The Harlots and the Pharisees: or, The Barbary Coast in a Barbarous Land* (Berkeley: published by the author, October 20, 1913), 1, 12.

10 *Berkeley Daily Gazette*, March 26, 1913.

11 Rev. C. F. Aked, "Mr. Stitt Wilson's Sneers a Discredit," *Chicago Examiner*, October 7, 1913, 16.

12 J. Stitt Wilson, "Revolutionary Christianity, or the Call of Christ to the Christian Church," *California Social Democrat*, November 8, 15, 22, 29, December 6, 1913.

13 *Berkeley Daily Gazette*, January 26, 1917.

14 *California Social Democrat*, March 14, 1914.

15 *California Social Democrat*, December 6, 20, 27, 1913, January 3, 1914; *San Francisco Call*, December 24, 29, 1913; *Berkeley Daily Gazette*, December 29, 1913, 3.

16 *California Social Democrat*, January 17, 1914.

17 *New York Call*, January 22, 1914.

18 Carl D. Thompson to Dear Comrade, January 31, 1914 with response from J. Stitt Wilson written below, dated received February 16, 1914, Socialist Party Papers, Duke University.

19 *Berkeley Daily Gazette*, February 7, 12, 15, April 7, 1913.

20 *California Social Democrat*, February 14, 21, 1914.

21 *California Social Democrat*, February 7, 21, 1914; *Riverside Daily Press*, March 4, 1914, 4; *Riverside Independent Enterprise*, March 4, 1914, 5.

22 *Marin Journal* (San Rafael, CA), August 6, 1914; *California Social Democrat*, July 25, 1914.

23 *Daily Independent* (Corona, CA), March 14, 1914; "Letter from J. Stitt Wilson to the Socialists of California," *California Social Democrat*, May 30, 1914.

24 J. Stitt Wilson, "Roosters Must Go," *Oakland Tribune*, July 20, 1922, 16; Rockwell D. Hunt, "Linden L.D. McCash, Doctor of Chiropractic," in *California and Californians*, Vol. V (San Francisco: Lewis Publishing Co., 1926) 298.

25 *Healdsburg Enterprise*, March 28, 1914; *Daily Telegraph* (San Luis Obispo), March 26, 1914.

26 *Lodi Sentinel*, April 9, 1914; *Sacramento Union*, April 12, 1914; *Red Bluff News*, April 17, 1914.

27 *California Social Democrat*, May 9, 1914.

28 *California Social Democrat*, July 11, 1914; *Sacramento Union*, April 14, 1914, 10; *Chicago Tribune*, May 13, 1914, 3.

29 *Berkeley Daily Gazette*, May 25, 1914.

30 *San Francisco Chronicle*, June 3, 1914, 4.

31 Noble, *Its Name Was M.U.D.*

32 *Washington Socialist*, June 4, 18, 1914, 2.

33 Frans Bostrom, "The History of the 1913 Secession in the Socialist Party of Washington," March 16, 1914. Accessed June 20, 2020 at https://archive.org/details/HistoryOfThe1913SecessionInTheSocialistPartyOfWashington.

34 *Seattle Daily Times*, June 23, 1914, 6.

35 *Christian Socialist*, July 15, 1914, 1–4.

36 *Christian Socialist*, August 1914.

37 *Christian Socialist*, July 15, 1914, 4.

38 "Wanted: A New God and a New Religion," *California Social Democrat*, October 3, 1914.

39 *Oakland Tribune*, August 6, 1914; *San Francisco Chronicle*, August 16, 1914.

40 *Rockford* (IL) *Republic*, September 23, 1914.

41 *California Social Democrat*, October 3, 1914.

42 *Sacramento Union*, September 30, 1914; *Press Democrat* (Santa Rosa), October 7, 1914; *Marin Journal* (San Rafael), October 8, 1914.

43 *California Social Democrat*, April 11, 1914.

44 *Santa Cruz Evening News*, October 23, 1914, 4.

45 Arthur Nichols Young, *The Single Tax Movement in the United States* (Princeton: Princeton University Press, 1916), 232.

46 Michael Paul Rogin and John L. Shover, *Political Change in California: Critical Elections and Social Movements, 1890–1966* (Westport: Greenwood, 1970), 62–89.

47 *California Social Democrat*, December 12, 26, 1914, January 2, 9, 23, 30, February 6, 13, 1915; *Berkeley Daily Gazette*, January 2, 11, 18, 25, February 1, 8, 15, 1915.

48 Homer Lea, 1909: *The Valor of Ignorance*. (New York: Harper and Brothers, 1909) and *The Day of the Saxon*. (New York: Harper and Bros., 1912). Charlotte Perkins Gilman, *The Man-Made World; or, Our Androcentric Culture* (New York: Charton Co., 1911).

49 *Berkeley Daily Gazette*, February 8, 1915; *California Social Democrat*, Jan 30, February 6, 13, 1915.

50 *Chicago Examiner*, February 22, 1915, 6.

51 *Berkeley Daily Gazette*, January 28, 1915.

52 *Oakland Tribune*, February 12, 15, 1915; *Berkeley Daily Gazette*, April 16, 1915, 4.

53 *California Social Democrat*, February 20, 1915.

54 *Berkeley Daily Gazette*, March 1, 1915, 7.

55 *Berkeley Daily Gazette*, March 22, 1915, 1.

56 *Berkeley Daily Gazette*, March 27, 1915, 1.

57 *Berkeley Daily Gazette*, April 2, 1915, 1.

58 *Berkeley Daily Gazette*, March 20, 1915, 1, 6.

59 *Berkeley Daily Gazette*, April 1, 1915, 4.

60 *Berkeley Daily Gazette*, April 10, 1915.

61 J. Stitt Wilson, "The Minimum Program of a Militant Christianity," in *Addresses: World's Social Progress Congress*, William Bell, ed. (Dayton: Otterbein Press, 1915) 22–34.

62 George E. Mowry, *The California Progressives* (Berkeley: University of California Press, 1951); H. Brett Melendy and Benjamin F. Gilbert, "Friend W. Richardson" in *The Governors of California* (Georgetown, CA: Talisman Press, 1965) 336–347.

63 J. Stitt Wilson to *American Socialist* (Chicago), April 6, 1915, Socialist Party of America Papers, Duke University.

64 *Berkeley Daily Gazette*, April 6, 1915, 1, 8.

65 *Berkeley Daily Gazette*, April 10, 1915, 1.

66 *Berkeley Daily Gazette*, April 13, 1915, 1, 7.

67 *Berkeley Daily Gazette*, April 15, 1915, 1, 4.

68 *Berkeley Daily Gazette*, April 16, 1915, 1, 4.

69 *Berkeley Daily Gazette*, April 16, 1915, 1, 4.

70 *Berkeley Daily Gazette*, April 17, 1915, 1.

71 *The City for the People*, April 21, 1915.

72 *Berkeley Daily Gazette*, April 26, 1915, 4; *Oakland Tribune*, April 26, 1915, 11.

73 *Riverside Daily Press*, June 5, 1915, 8.

74 *California Social Democrat*, July 10, 17, 1915; *Evening Tribune* (San Diego) July 9, 23, 1915.

75 Edwin Markham, *The Shoes of Happiness and Other Poems* (Garden City: Doubleday, Page, & Co., 1915). Inscribed copy in author's collection.

76 *Berkeley Daily Gazette*, August 16, 1915, 3; *Oakland Tribune*, August 26, 1915, 16.

77 *California Social Democrat*, October 23, 1915; *Western Comrade*, October 1915, 22.

78 *Sun* (N.Y.), September 5, 1915.

79 *Berkeley Daily Gazette*, September 28, 1915, 3.

80 *Watertown (N.Y.) Daily Times*, October 13, 1915, 10.

81 *New York Times*, October 31, 1915, 4.

82 *New York Call*, November 1, 1915.

83 *Day Book* (Chicago), November 17, 1915; *Berkeley Daily Gazette*, November 20, 1915.

84 *California Social Democrat*, January 8, 22, February 5, 1916; *Southern California Trojan* (Los Angeles) February 11, 16, 1916.

85 *Morning Echo* (Bakersfield), February 18, 20, 22, 23, 24.

86 *Bakersfield Californian*, February 22, 1916, 12.

87 *Morning Echo* (Bakersfield), February 26.

88 *Northwest Worker* (Everett) December 23, 1915, 1.

89 Ralph E. Shaffer, "Radicalism in California," 193.

90 J. Stitt Wilson, "A Letter to the Comrades," *California Social Democrat*, January 15, 1916, 2.

91 *Berkeley Daily Gazette*, February 12, 1917, 2.

92   Ed Herny, Shelley Rideout and Katie Wadell. *Berkeley Bohemia: Artists and Visionaries of the Early 20th Century* (Salt Lake City: Gibbs Smith, 2008).

93   *Berkeley Daily Gazette*, December 19, 1914, 1.

94   *Day Book* (Chicago) May 27, 1915.

95   *Oakland Tribune*, March 14, 1916.

96   *Day Book* (Chicago), April 5, 1916.

97   *Berkeley Daily Gazette*, March 15, 1916, 1.

98   *Berkeley Daily Gazette*, March 16, 1916, 3; *Washington Post*, April 2, 1916, 15; and many others.

99   *Los Angeles Herald*, March 25, 1916, 2.

100 *Riverside Daily Press*, April 7, 1916, 1.

101 *Berkeley Daily Gazette*, April 26, May 25, 26, 1916.

102 *Berkeley Daily Gazette*, May 26, 1916.

103 *San Francisco Chronicle*, June 4, 1916; *Oakland Tribune*, June 25, 1916.

104 *San Francisco Chronicle*, January 2, 1917, 9; *Riverside Independent Enterprise*, January 1, 1917, 6.

105 *California Social Democrat*, April 29, 1916; *Des Moines Daily News*, May 4, 14, 1916.

106 Inez R. Brown, Mary Roberts Coolidge et al, "The Undersigned are Supporting the Candidacy of Mayor Samuel C. Irving for Reelection," Bancroft Library, University of California, Berkeley (dated April 26, 1917).

107 *Berkeley Daily Gazette*, August 7, 1916, 5.

108 *Berkeley Daily Gazette*, September 18, October 11, 12, 1916.

109 *Seattle Daily Times*, November 24, 1916, 9; list of attendees on reverse of a press photo, web sites accessed June 20, 2020. https://kyozoufs.blob.core.windows.net/filestoragecs4/Pictures/_8/7341/7340217.jpg and https://www.pinterest.com/pin/390687336399791627/.

110 *Berkeley Daily Gazette*, November 23, 1916, 1; *Oakland Tribune*, November 26, 1916, 25.

111 *San Francisco Chronicle*, December 11, 1916, 5; January 25, 1917, 4.

112 Christopher William England, "Land and Liberty: Henry George, the Single Tax Movement and the Origins of 20th Century Liberalism," (PhD diss. Georgetown University, 2015), 293–295. England argues that the change in strategy was "solely attributable to the impatience of the Fels Fund," but the failure of Local Option to gather sufficient signatures suggests that volunteers, those most committed to the issue, preferred to work directly for the Single Tax.

113 *Single Tax Review*, May-June 1916, 161; July-August 1916, 229–30, 251; November-December 1916, 364–67.

114 *Single Tax Review*, January–February 1917, 35–6, 50–52; *The Public*, January 26, 1917, 87; February 2, 111; February 16, 158–9.

115 Luke North (James H. Griffes), "A Change in Management or a Vote of Confidence," *Everyman*, December 1918.

116 *The Public*, April 13, 1917, 362–3; April 27, 1917, 380–82; *Single Tax Review*, March–April 1917, 126; May–June 1917, 168–170; Jan–Feb 1918, 35–6, 50–52. *Riverside Daily Press*, January 23, 1917. *Morning Echo* (Bakersfield) April 4, 1917.

117 *Land and Freedom*, January–February 1934, 27–28; James Echols, "Jackson Ralston and the Last Single Tax Campaign," *California History*, 58 no.3 (Fall 1979) 256–263.

Chapter 12: Making America Safe for Democracy

1   A number of histories incorrectly list J. Stitt Wilson among the Socialists who left the Party to support the war. See for example, Daniel Bell, *Marxian Socialism in the United States*), 100–101; Jack Ross, *The Socialist Party of America*, 185.

2   *Berkeley Daily Gazette*, October 21, 1916, 1.

3   *Berkeley Daily Gazette*, February 8, 22, 1917. J. Stitt Wilson, "Open Letter to the Citizens of Berkeley," four-page campaign flier, Bancroft Library, Berkeley Politics folder, stamped March 27, 1917.

4   *Berkeley Daily Gazette*, April 29, 1909.

5   *Berkeley Daily Gazette*, February 10, 12, 22, 1917.

6   Marc A. Weiss, "Urban Land Developers and the Origins of Zoning Laws: The Case of Berkeley," *Berkeley Planning Journal*, 3 no. 1 (1986), 18.

7   *Los Angeles Herald*, January 23, 1917; *Sacramento Union*, Jan 28, 1917; State of California, *Senate Journal*, March 8, 1917, 586.

8   *Berkeley Daily Gazette*, October 21, 1916, 1; *Berkeley Daily Gazette*, April 2, 14, 1917.

9   *Berkeley Daily Gazette*, April 3, 5, 16, 1917.

10 *Berkeley Daily Gazette*, April 18, 1917.

11 J. Stitt Wilson, "J. Stitt Wilson: To the People of Berkeley," four-page flier, Bancroft Library, April 1917. *Berkeley Daily Gazette*, April 12, 1917, 2.

12 *Berkeley Daily Gazette*, April 13, 1917.

13 James Weinstein, *The Decline of Socialism in America, 1912–1925* (New York: Vintage Books, 1969).

14 *Berkeley Daily Gazette*, April 21, 1917, 1.

15 *Berkeley Daily Gazette*, April 14, 1917.

16 *Berkeley Daily Gazette*, April 16, 1917, 5.

17 David M. Kennedy, *Over Here: The First World War and American Society* (Oxford: Oxford University Press, 2004).

18 *Marin Journal*, April 12, 1917.

19 Bill Mills, *The League: The True Story of Average Americans on the Hunt for WWI Spies* (New York: Skyhorse Publishing, 2013); Kennedy, *Over Here*.

20 Diane M. T. North, *California at War: The State and the People during World War I* (Lawrence: University Press of Kansas, 2018), 226–228.

21 *Oakland Tribune*, April 15, 1917.

22 *Berkeley Daily Gazette*, March 27, 28, April 12, 13, 1917; *Oakland Tribune*, April 14, 1917.

23 *Berkeley Daily Gazette*, April 17, 1917, 1.

24 Arwen P. Mohun, *Risk: Negotiating Safety in American Society* (Baltimore, Johns Hopkins University Press, 2013) 141–162.

25 *Electric Railway Journal*, July 13, 1912, 61; *San Francisco Call*, September 21, 1911, 4; *Seattle Daily Times*, Jan 18, 1911, 8; *New Brunswick* (N.J.) *Times*, November 6, 1912, 7; *Berkeley Daily Gazette*, April 24, 1917, 2.

26   *Oakland Tribune*, August 2, 1898, 1; *Oakland Tribune*, November 19, 1911, 1; "Ural Sumner 'Fred' Hughes" posted on Ancestry.com on March 23, 2014, accessed June 20, 2020. https://www.ancestry.com/mediaui-viewer/tree/8102249/person/7027655028/media/7ea3c1c2-2a36-4d31-a1c1-f7753e582ffc?_phsrc=CzC93&_phstart=successSource.

27   Letterhead on Frederic S. Hughes to August Vollmer, April 6, 1917, in Berkeley Police Dept. Records, 1909–1932, Box 8, Hughes folder, Bancroft Library, University of California, Berkeley.

28   Alex Palmer, *The Santa Claus Man: The Rise and Fall of a Jazz Age Con Man and the Invention of Christmas in New York* (Guilford, Rowman & Littlefield, 2015) 213.

29   Palmer, *Santa Claus Man*, 155–162.

30   *Lowell Sun* (MA) May 9, 1916; *Moving Picture World*, June 3, 1916, 1668.

31   Palmer, *The Santa Claus Man*, 163.

32   *Anaconda Standard* (MT), June 4, 1916, 5; *Ogden Examiner* (UT), June 7, 1916.

33   Frederic Sumner Hughes, "Announcement to NHV Members," undated, in Berkeley Police Dept. Records, 1909–1932, Bancroft Library.

34   Letterhead on Hughes to Vollmer, April 6, 1917, in Berkeley Police Dept. Records, 1909–1932, Bancroft Library.

35   *Polk's Portland 1911 City Directory*, 732.

36   Rufus W. Putnam to Frederic S. Hughes, March 23, 1917, in Berkeley Police Dept. Records, 1909–1932, Bancroft Library.

37   Putnam to Hughes, March 23, 1917, in Berkeley Police Dept. Records, 1909–1932.

38   Hughes to Vollmer, April 6, 1917, in Berkeley Police Dept. Records, 1909–1932.

39   *Berkeley Daily Gazette*, April 7, 1917, 1.

40   *Berkeley Daily Gazette*, April 7, 1917, 1; April 25, 1917, 4.

41   *Oakland Tribune*, April 8, 1917, 37.

42   *Oregonian* (Portland), April 8, 1917, 3.

43   *Oakland Tribune*, April 7, 1917, 4.

44   *Denver Post*, April 7, 1917, 13; *Bakersfield Californian*, April 7, 1917; *Los Angeles Herald*, April 7, 1917.

45   F. S. Hughes, Field Secretary and Chief of Bureau, to Fellow Safeguard, May 14, 1917 in James Deitrick Papers, Stanford University Special Collections.

46   *Berkeley Daily Gazette*, April 7, 1917, 1; April 25, 1917, 4.

47   *Berkeley Daily Gazette*, April 21, 1917, 1.

48   *Berkeley Daily Gazette*, March 27, 28, April 12, 13, 1917; *Oakland Tribune*, April 14.

49   *Berkeley Daily Gazette*, April 17, 1917, 1.

50   *Berkeley Daily Gazette*, April 18, 1917, 2; *Berkeley Daily Gazette*, April 21, 1917, 1.

51   *Berkeley Daily Gazette*, April 18, 1917, 2; *Berkeley Daily Gazette*, April 21, 1917, 1.

52   *Berkeley Daily Gazette*, April 19, 1917, 1.

53   *Berkeley Daily Gazette*, April 20, 1917, 1.

54   *San Francisco Chronicle*, April 22, 1917, 41.

55   *Berkeley Daily Gazette*, April 21, 1917, 1.

56   *Berkeley Daily Gazette*, April 23, 1917, 4; April 27, 1917, 6.

57   *Oakland Tribune*, April 22, 1917, 39.

58 *Berkeley Daily Gazette*, April 24, 1917, 2.

59 *Berkeley Daily Gazette*, April 23, 1917, 1.

60 *Berkeley Daily Gazette*, April 26, 1917, 3, 6.

61 *Berkeley Daily Gazette*, April 25, 1917, 4.

62 *Berkeley Daily Gazette*, April 25, 27, 1917.

63 *Berkeley Daily Gazette*, April 30, 1917, 4.

64 *Berkeley Daily Gazette*, April 26, 1917, 3, 6.

65 *Berkeley Daily Gazette*, May 19, June 8, 1917; *Oakland Tribune*, August 5, 1917, 14. Diane M. T. North, *California at War*, 183–185.

66 *Oakland Tribune*, May 22, November 3, Dec 11, 1917; Jan 28, March 30, 1918; *Sacramento Union*, Jan 19, 1918.

67 *Sausalito News*, April 28, 1917; *Oregonian* (Portland), April 29, 1917, 8. A surviving membership card has the number 2676 (author's collection).

68 *Berkeley Daily Gazette*, May 15, 1917, 10.

69 Frederic Sumner Hughes, "Announcement to N.H.V. Members," undated, Berkeley Police Dept. Records, 1909–1932.

70 Hughes to Vollmer, May 30, June 7, 1917, in Berkeley Police Dept. Records, 1909–1932.

71 Pierson W. Banning to United States Army Intelligence Department, September 2, 1918 in National Archives and Record Administration, Record Group 165 Entry (A1) 65 *Records of the War Department General and Special Staffs. Military Intelligence Division. Security Classified Correspondence and Reports, 1917–1941*, Box 2141, File 9434-154.

72 *Evening Tribune* (San Diego), April 18, 1917; *San Francisco Chronicle*, April 18, 1917, 4; *Sausalito News* (CA) April 28, 1917; *Oregonian* (Portland), April 29, 1917, 8; Hughes to Vollmer, June 7, 1917, in Berkeley Police Dept. Records, 1909–1932.

73 Diane M. T. North, *California at War*, 143. H.F. Edson, "In Re: Carl Lembke–German Activities," September 6, 1917, National Archives, RG 165, File 10110-384, Box 2767.

74 National Archives and Records Administration, Investigative Reports of the Bureau of Investigation, 1908–1922, Old German files, 1909–1921, Case 8000-16847 (May 7, 1917), Case 8000-18264 (August 20, 1917), Case 174332 (April 5, 1918).

75 Hughes to Vollmer, May 30, June 7, 1917, in Berkeley Police Dept. Records, 1909–1932.

76 Frederic Sumner Hughes, "Announcement to N. H. V. Members," undated, in Berkeley Police Dept. Records, 1909–1932; Banning to Army Intelligence Department, September 2, 1918 in National Archives and Record Administration, Record Group 165.

77 Banning to Army Intelligence Department, September 2, 1918 in National Archives and Record Administration, Record Group 165.

78 *Oregonian* (Portland), April 29, 1917, 8.

79 "Announcement to NHV Members," undated, in Berkeley Police Dept. Records, 1909–1932, Box 8, Hughes folder, Bancroft Library.

80 *Berkeley Daily Gazette*, August 21, 1917, 8; *San Francisco Chronicle*, August 22, 1917, 4.

81   Joan M. Jensen, *The Price of Vigilance* (Chicago, Rand McNally, 1968); Mills, *The League*.

82   Jensen, *The Price of Vigilance*, 26.

83   H. Evans, Intelligence Officer, War Department, Headquarters Western Department, "Weekly Intelligence Summary," No. 10, October 13, 1917, National Archives RG 165 File 10016-12, Box 2239.

84   Banning to Army Intelligence Department, September 2, 1918 in National Archives and Record Administration, Record Group 165; Jensen, *The Price of Vigilance*, 122.

85   Banning to Army Intelligence Department, September 2, 1918 in National Archives and Record Administration, Record Group 165; National Archives and Records Administration, Investigative Reports of the Bureau of Investigation, 1908–1922, Old German files, 1909–1921, Case 8000-126936 (January 11, 1918).

86   Alameda County voter registration list for 1918; *Polk Husted Oakland-Berkeley-Alameda Directory*, 1918.

87   *Musical Courier*, August 28, 1919, 19.

88   Los Angeles County voter registration records, 1920, 1922, 1926; "Ural Sumner 'Fred' Hughes" posted on Ancestry.com on March 23, 2014, accessed June 20, 2020. https://www.ancestry.com/mediaui-viewer/tree/8102249/person/7027655028/media/7ea3c1c2-2a36-4d31-a1c1-f7753e582ffc?_phsrc=CzC93&_phstart=successSource.

89   North, *California at War*, 247, 266.

90   American Protective League, Berkeley Division to Samuel Pond, U.S. Food Administration, San Francisco, July 29, 1918, accessed June 5, 2018 at https://catalog.archives.gov/id/295922; Jensen, *The Price of Vigilance*.

91   North, *California at War*, 265.

92   Emerson Hough, *The Web: The Authorized History of the American Protective League* (Chicago, Reilly & Lee, 1919), 446.

93   *Riverside Daily Press*, November 7, 1917, 6.

94   *Riverside Daily Press*, November 8, 1917, 6; *San Bernardino Daily Sun*, March 23, 1918, 2.

95   *Santa Ana Register*, August 23, 1917.

96   James Weinstein, *The Corporate Ideal in the Liberal State: 1900–1918* (Boston, Beacon Press, 1968), 240–245.

97   *Berkeley Daily Gazette*, June 19, 1918, 4; *Kansas City Star*, April 28, 1918, 4; *Helena Independent Record*, May 27, 1918.

98   *Morning Echo* (Bakersfield), September 23, 1917, 9.

99   *Oakland Tribune*, September 8, 1918, 17.

100 *Oakland Tribune*, August 2, 1917, 4; September 12, 1917, 6.

101 Wilson, "My Crowded Years," 4.

102 *Evening Tribune* (San Diego), March 27, 29, 1918.

103 *Fresno Morning Republican*, September 2, 1918, 2.

104 *Riverside Daily Press*, May 20, 1918.

105 *Riverside Independent Enterprise*, May 19, 1918.

106 *Riverside Independent Enterprise*, March 24, 1918, 2.

107 *Morning Echo* (Bakersfield, CA) October 26, 1917, 10.

108 *Riverside Independent Enterprise*, May 21, 1918, 3.

109 *Riverside Daily Press*, May 16, 1918, 12.

110 *San Diego Union*, February 21, 27, March 7, 1918, 4.

111 Kennedy, *Over Here*, 49–51.

112 John Dewey, "The Social Possibilities of War," 1918, http://teachingamerican history.org/library/document/the-social-possibilities-of-war-2/, accessed October 4, 2020.

113 Joseph A. McCartin, *Labor's Great War: The Struggle for Industrial Democracy and the Origins of Modern American Labor Relations, 1912–1921* (Chapel Hill: University of North Carolina Press, 1997), 83.

114 *Evening Tribune* (San Diego) September 14, 1918, 8; *San Diego Union*, September 15, 16, 1918; *Riverside Daily Press*, September 16, 1918.

115 *San Francisco Examiner*, September 11, 1918.

116 *San Francisco Chronicle*, September 8, 1918, 1; *Oakland Tribune*, September 8, 1918.

117 *San Francisco Examiner*, September 11, 1918; *Berkeley Daily Gazette*, September 10, 1918.

118 Mr. & Mrs. J. Stitt Wilson, Gladys (Wilson) Conway, Violette (Wilson) Pichel, "Dear Friends," September 1918.

119 J. Stitt Wilson, "Postscript," November 11, 1918.

Chapter 13: From Socialism to the New Deal

1 David P. Setran, *The College "Y": Student Religion in the Era of Secularization* (London: Palgrave MacMillan, 2007); Christopher Evans, "The Social Gospel, the YMCA, and the Emergence of the Religious Left After World War I," in *The Religious Left in Modern America*, Leila Danielson, Marian Mollin and Doug Rossinow, eds. (London: Palgrave, 2018).

2 C. Howard Hopkins, *History of the YMCA in North America* (New York, Association Press, 1951), 364.

3 *Riverside Daily Press*, February 8, 1919, 10.

4 William McGuire King, "The Emergence of Social Gospel Radicalism: The Methodist Case," *Church History*, 50 no. 4 (December 1981): 436–449; Janine Giordano Drake, "War for the Soul of the Christian Nation: Christian Socialists versus the Federal Council of Churches, 1901–1912," *Labor History*, 14 no. 3 (Fall 2016): 55–80; Hopkins, *The Rise of the Social Gospel*, 291–292.

5 J. Stitt Wilson, *Constructive Christian Democracy: An Outline of Fundamentals in the Message and Movement of Applied Christianity*, Berkeley, April 1919. *Ottawa Campus* (Kansas), April 15, 1919; *Fayetteville Democrat*, April 7, 1919; *Denver Post*, June 17, 1919; *Philadelphia Inquirer*, June 21, 1919.

6 George Stewart, Jr. *Life of Henry B. Wright* (New York: Association Press, 1925), 90–91.

7 Charles W. Gilkey, "Religion Among American Students," *Journal of Religion*, 4 no. 1 (January 1924): 9.

8   David R. Porter to Rev. Canon Tissington Tatlow, D.D., October 10, 1928, Stitt Wilson folder, John Randolph Haynes Papers, University of California, Los Angeles.

9   Clarence P. Shedd, *Two Centuries of Student Christian Movements: Their Origin and Intercollegiate Life* (New York: Association Press, 1934), 393–394.

10   *Oregonian* (Portland), July 13, 1919.

11   San Jose Mercury News, July 12, 1919.

12   *Corona (California) Independent*, October 6, 1919, 8; *Seattle Daily Times*, October 7, 1919, 23; *Riverside Independent Enterprise*, October 25, 1919, 8; *Atlanta Constitution*, March 4, 1920, 9.

13   David A. Shannon, *The Socialist Party of America*, 128, 163.

14   *Berkeley Daily Gazette*, November 20, December 5, 9, 10, 1919, February 7, 1920, December 8, 1920, June 9, 1921; *Oakland Tribune*, May 29, 1917, December 4, 9, 1919, June 9, 1921. Seraphim F. Post, *The Story of the Postnikov Family*, no date (circa 1977) on file at the Berkeley Public Library.

15   J. Stitt Wilson to Dr. John R. Haynes, December 1, 1924; J.S. Edwards to J. Stitt Wilson, December 5, 1924; Stitt Wilson file, Haynes Collection.

16   Ed Herny, Shelley Rideout, Katie Wadell, *Berkeley Bohemia: Artists and Visionaries of the Early 20th Century* (Salt Lake City, Gibbs Smith, 2008) 90–94.

17   *Oakland Tribune*, January 6, 1922, November 22, 1925, January 14, 1926, March 6, 1926, May 11, 1926; *Berkeley Daily Gazette*, December 25, 1924, January 12, 1926.

18   *Hagerstown Daily Mail* (MD), February 12, 1926, 2 (among many, credit to NEA wire service).

19   *Oakland Tribune*, August 8, 1928; *Berkeley Daily Gazette*, September 4, 14, 1929, 5; *San Marino Tribune* (CA) May 18, 1934, 10.

20   *Oakland Tribune*, July 7, 1922, 12; J. Stitt Wilson, "Property Has No Rights," *World Tomorrow*, 5:4 (April 1922) 112–113; J. Stitt Wilson, "Jesus in the Labor Movement," *Intercollegian*, 40:2 (November 1922) 1–2; J. Stitt Wilson, address on "The Militant Church and Property," National Council of Cities of the Methodist Episcopal Church, Chicago, February 1922 in *The Militant Church and Property—The Militant Church and Public Opinion* (Berkeley: published by the author, no date (circa 1923)).

21   J. Stitt Wilson, *Constructive Christian Democracy: An Outline of Fundamentals* (Berkeley: published by the author, January 1922). *Capital Times* (Madison), October 16, 1920, 2; *Evening News* (San Jose), September 24, 1921, 8.

22   Wilson, *The Militant Church and Property*; *Waukesha Daily Freeman* (WI), October 17, 1921, 1.

23   J. Shiang Min Lee, "The Asilomar Conference," *Christian China*, 8:3 (March 1922) 214–215.

24   *Crisis*, December 1926, 108; *Greensboro Daily News*, March 23, 1928, 14.

25   Note: The student newspaper archives of some historically Black colleges may hold news stories that give more details of Wilson's talks to Black student audiences, but any such reports are not yet online in searchable form.

26   Reinhold Niebuhr, *Moral Man and Immoral Society* (New York: Scribners, 1932), 254.

27   *San Antonio Evening News*, July 31, 1919, 12.

28   *Daily Northwestern* (Evanston, IL) February 17, 1925; *Exponent* (Northern State

Teachers College, Aberdeen, SD) May 6, 1924; *Davidsonian* (Davidson College, Davidson, NC), February 11, 1926; J. Stitt Wilson, "A Constructive Criticism of Modern Education," in *Am I Getting an Education*, Doubleday (Garden City, Doran & Co., 1929).

29   J. Stitt Wilson, *The Christ-Spirit in the Animal World* (Berkeley: published by the author, June 1923).

30   *San Francisco Chronicle*, June 20, 1918, 5.

31   *Berkeley Daily Gazette*, January 14, 1920, February 17, August 3, 1921.

32   *Berkeley Daily Gazette*, January 14, 1920, February 17, August 3, 5, 1921, May 19, 1922; *Oakland Tribune*, August 31, 1921, December 7, 1921; *Dispatch—Democrat* (Ukiah), September 15, 1922.

33   *Oakland Tribune*, July 7, 1922, 12.

34   *San Francisco Call*, September 4, 1922.

35   *Sacramento Union*, August 19, 1922; *Sausalito News*, August 26, 1922; *Oakland Tribune*, October 11, 1922, 35.

36   William Issel and Robert W. Cherny, *San Francisco, 1865–1932: Power, Politics and Urban Development* (Berkeley: University of California Press, 1986) 94–97.

37   Berkeley Daily Gazette, September 15, 21, October 2, 1922; Riverside Daily Press, September 22, October 4, 1922; Bakersfield Californian, September 21, 1922, 2; Oakland Tribune, September 22, 28, 29, October 3, 1922.

38   Wilson to Haynes, July 8, 1928, 21–22, Stitt Wilson file, Haynes Collection.

39   *Berkeley Daily Gazette*, September 18, 1923, October 1, 1923.

40   *Oakland Tribune*, November 18, 1934, 60; *Echo* (Gloucestershire) May 8, 1923, 6.

41   *Oakland Tribune*, July 1, 1924.

42   *Riverside Daily Press*, October 25, 1924, 2; *Evening Tribune* (San Diego), October 27, 1924, 2.

43   La Follette campaign meeting flier, University of Iowa Library, accessed Oct. 4, 2020 at https://digital.lib.uiowa.edu/islandora/object/ui%3Atc_23261; Wilson to Haynes, November 17, 1924, Haynes Collection.

44   David Shannon, *The Socialist Party of America*, 163.

45   *The Crescent* (Pacific College of Oregon, Newberg, OR) April 29, 1925; *Berkeley Daily Gazette*, October 21, 1925, May 11, 1928; July 9, 1931; Debra N. Dietiker, "A History of the First Unitarian Church of San Jose, California," (M.A. thesis, San Jose State University, 1966), 45–47.

46   Tom Sitton, *John Randolph Haynes: California Progressive* (Stanford, Stanford University Press, 1992), 186.

47   Edwards to Wilson, Dec. 5, 1924; Haynes to Ellen Scripps, Dec. 12, 1924; Wilson to Haynes, October 23, 28, December 9, 1928, February 2, 1929, Haynes Collection, UCLA. Note: Prospective backers included J.R. Haynes; J.S. Edwards, a major orange grower who Wilson had helped convert to the social gospel; Martin Bekins, founder of a moving company; and Ellen Scripps, a co-founder of the Scripps newspaper chain.

48   *Berkeley Daily Gazette*, September 26, 1927; *The Grail*, Stephens College, Columbia Missouri, October 16, 1927.

49   Social Crusade Committee (Cardiff, Wales) to J. Stitt Wilson, September 1, 1928, John Randolph Haynes Collection, UCLA.

50   After the request for funds there is no direct indication of this payment, but the fact that Stitt Wilson sent Haynes extensive material on the two month Social Crusade suggests that he was showing Haynes that his money was well spent.

51   *Berkeley Daily Gazette*, September 25, 1928, 6.

52   *Shipley Times and Express*, July 28, 1928, 2; *Western Mail*, August 27, 1928, 10.

53   *The Social Crusader: A Messenger of Brotherhood and Social Justice (Souvenir Edition of the J. Stitt Wilson Crusade, Cardiff, Wales, July and August 1928*: Social Crusade Committee (Cardiff, Wales) to Wilson, September 1, 1928, John Randolph Haynes Collection, UCLA.

54   *Yorkshire Post*, September 3, 1928, 16; A.T. Sutton, Secretary, Bradford Independent Labour Party to J. Stitt Wilson, September 19, 1928, Haynes collection, UCLA.

55   *Berkeley Daily Gazette*, October 5, 1928, 9; October 26, 1928, 9.

56   Wilson to Haynes, October 28, 1928, Haynes Collection, UCLA.

57   U.K. outward bound passenger lists, ship Baltic, Liverpool to N.Y.C., departure June 15, 1929, accessed June 1, 2020 through Ancestry.com.

58   J. Stitt Wilson, "The Meaning of Prayer," *Social Crusader*, February & March 1929, 2, Haynes Collection.

59   J. Stitt Wilson, "Poverty—That is the Enemy," *Social Crusader*, February & March 1929, 2, in Haynes Collection.

60   Wilson to Haynes, December 9, 1928, February 2, 1929, May 1, 1929 Haynes Collection.

61   *Leeds Mercury*, May 21, 1929, 7; *Derby Daily Telegraph*, May 23, 1929, 7. *Berkeley Daily Gazette*, July 16, 1929, 3.

62   *Sheffield Daily Telegraph*, June 13, 1929, 6; *Leeds Mercury*, June 14, 1929, 8.

63   Wilson, "My Crowded Years" 4; Wilson to Haynes, March 30, 1930, Haynes Collection.

64   *Leeds Mercury*, December 2, 1929, 7; *Yorkshire Evening Post*, December 9, 1929, 8; *Sheffield Daily Telegraph*, December 14, 21, 1929; *Sheffield Independent*, December 14, 16, 1929; *Yorkshire Post*, January 14, 1930.

65   *Yorkshire Evening Post*, April 11, 1934; *Yorkshire Post*, June 20, 1938.

66   *Western Mail and South Wales News*, March 15, 22, 1930.

67   J. Stitt Wilson, *The Stitt Wilson Campaign*, Cardiff Wales, March 9th to April 6th, 1930, 2.

68   Wilson to Haynes, March 30, 1930, Haynes Collection.

69   *Berkeley Daily Gazette*, June 18, 1930, 3.

70   *San Francisco Chronicle*, September 21, 1930; *Oakland Tribune*, September 20, 1930.

71   *Berkeley Daily Gazette*, November 25, 1930, 6.

72   *Berkeley Daily Gazette*, June 30, 1931, 6; July 24, 1931, 5.

73   Council of Christian Associations, *Toward a New Economic Society: A Program for Students* (New York: Eddy & Page, 1931).

74   H. W. Brands, *Traitor to His Class: The Privileged Life and Radical Presidency of Franklin Delano Roosevelt* (New York: Random House, 2008), 240, 252.

75 *Berkeley Daily Gazette*, June 30, July 7, 11, 1931.

76 *Berkeley Daily Gazette*, July 7, 11, 24; *Oakland Tribune*, July 16, 24.

77 *New York Times*, September 19, 1931, 2; *Southwest Times* (Pulaski, VA) September 20, 1931, 2.

78 *Bakersfield Californian*, October 31, November 3, 1931.

79 *Intercollegian*, 50 (1932), 154.

80 *Oakland Tribune*, November 14, 1931, January 20, 1932; *Kansas City Star*, December 5, 1931; *Springfield Republican* (MA), December 8, 1931; *Berkeley Daily Gazette*, December 12, 1931, April 19, May 7, 1932; *Riverside Daily Press*, January 21, 1932; *Chicago Tribune*, February 11, 1932; *News-Post* (Frederick, MD) February 20, 1932; *San Diego Union*, April 2, 1932.

81 Paul A. Carter, *The Decline and Revival of the Social Gospel: Social and Political Liberalism in American Protestant Churches, 1920–1940* (Ithaca, Cornell University Press, 1956), 150, 151, 175.

82 *Berkeley Daily Gazette*, August 23, 1932, 5.

83 *Oakland Tribune*, September 15, 1932, 3; *Berkeley Daily Gazette*, September 24, 1932, 12.

84 *Oakland Tribune*, October 4, 6, 1932.

85 John Curl, *For All the People*, PM Press, Oakland, 2009, 164–184; Clark Kerr, "Productive Enterprises of the Unemployed, 1931–1938," (PhD diss. University of California, Berkeley, 1939), 389–390; *Berkeley Daily Gazette*, June 6, 1933.

86 Shannon, *The Socialist Party of America*, 227–228; Ross, *The Socialist Party of America*, 329–332.

87 *Berkeley Daily Gazette*, June 6, 1933, 3.

88 Donald I. Miller, *The New American Radicalism: Alfred M. Bingham and Non-Marxian Insurgency in the New Deal Era* (Port Washington, Kennikat Press, 1979), 75–76.

89 Paul Blanshard, J. Stitt Wilson, Harry W. Laidler, *Declaration of Independence of the Continental Congress of Economic Reconstruction*, Washington D.C., May 7, 1933.

90 *New Leader*, July 1, 1933.

91 *New Leader*, August 12, 1933.

92 *San Diego Union*, July 24, 1933, 2; *New Leader*, July 1, 1933.

93 J. Stitt Wilson to Peter Gulbrandsen, July 26, 1933, Peter Gulbrandsen Papers, Box 1, Stitt Wilson file, Bancroft Library, University of California, Berkeley.

94 *San Diego Union*, July 24, 1933, 2.

95 *Riverside Daily Press*, September 11, 1933, 1.

96 Paul Bullock, *Jerry Voorhis: The Idealist as Politician* (New York: Vantage Press, 1978), 24.

97 J. Stitt Wilson, State Chairman of California Congress of Workers and Famers to Alfred N. Bingham, Executive Secretary, Farmer-Labor Political Federation, September 21, 1933, Socialist Party of America Papers, Duke University.

98 Cletus E. Daniel, Bitter Harvest: *A History of California Farmworkers, 1870–1941* (Berkeley, University of California Press, 1981).

99 *Western Worker*, October 9, 1933, 2.

100 *Berkeley Daily Gazette*, April 8, 1933, 6; *San Diego Union*, July 23, 1933, 3.

101 *Mill Valley Record* (CA), November 3, 1933; *Oakland Tribune*, August 23, 1932, 6.

102 *San Diego Evening Tribune*, July 6, 1933.

103 *Oakland Tribune*, July 10, 1933; *Evening Tribune* (San Diego), July 10, 1933, 1.

104 *Oakland Tribune*, July 11, 1933.

105 *Healdsburg Tribune* (CA), July 14, 1933, 1; *Oakland Tribune*, July 18, 1933, 13; text on reverse of photo, Wide World News Photos, Jul 14, 1933 in author's collection.

106 *Healdsburg Tribune* (CA), December 7, 1933; *Sotoyome Scimitar* (Healdsburg, CA) February 1, 1934.

107 *Oakland Tribune*, November 29, 1933.

108 *Oakland Tribune*, March 26, 1934, 10; *Healdsburg Tribune*, June 25, 1934.

109 *Healdsburg Tribune* (CA), July 2, 1934.

110 *New Leader*, June 2, 1934.

111 Ross, *The Socialist Party of America*, 332–333.

112 Wilson to Bingham, September 21, 1933, Socialist Party of America Papers, Duke University. Underlining in the original.

113 Richard M. Valelly, *Radicalism in the States: The Minnesota Farmer-Labor Party and the American Political Economy* (Chicago, University of Chicago Press, 1989).

114 Curl, *For All the People*, 180–183.

115 Leonard Leader, "Upton Sinclair's EPIC Switch: A Dilemma for American Socialists," *Southern California Quarterly*, 62:4 (Winter 1980) 372; Ross, *The Socialist Party of America*, 364.

116 *Berkeley Daily Gazette*, May 22, 1934, 6.

117 *Oakland Tribune*, May 15, 1934; *Calexico Chronicle* (CA), February 26, 1934.

118 *Santa Ana Daily Evening Register*, January 24, 1934.

119 Shannon, *The Socialist Party of America*, 239–240.

120 J. Stitt Wilson, "Stitt Wilson Sees Danger to Party in Declaration," *New Leader*, June 30, 1934.

121 Upton Sinclair, *I, Candidate for Governor: And How I Got Licked*, University of California Press, Berkeley, 1994 (1935) 56; *Oakland Tribune*, June 22, 1934.

122 *Santa Ana Daily Evening Register*, July 18, 1934, 3.

123 Bullock, *Jerry Voorhis*, 16, 23, 25.

124 *Arcadia Tribune*, July 20, 1934; *San Diego Evening Tribune*, July 23, 1934; *Berkeley Daily Gazette*, August 16, 1934; *Oakland Tribune*, August 21, 23, 1934.

125 Sinclair, *I, Candidate for Governor: And How I Got Licked*.

126 *Santa Ana Daily Evening Register*, October 20, 1934, 4.

127 Web site: Hometown Pasadena, http://hometown-pasadena.com/history/pasaden a-became-part-of-upton-sinclair's-EPIC battleground-part-2-of-2/37653; *Berkeley Daily Gazette*, September 27, 1934, 6; *EPIC News*, October 24, November 2, 1934.

128 *Evening Tribune* (San Diego), January 15, 1935, 11; *San Diego Union*, January 17, 1935, 3.

129 Jerry Voorhis, "Stitt Wilson Heads Congress for Production for Use," *Upton Sinclair's EPIC News*, March 25, 1935.

130 *EPIC News*, May 13, 1935; Clarence F. McIntosh, "Upton Sinclair and the EPIC Movement, 1933–1936," PhD diss. Stanford University, 1955; Un-American

Activities in the U.S., Hearings before a Special Committee on Un-American Activities, House of Representatives, 76th Congress, United States Government Printing Office, Washington, D.C., 940.

131 Derek C. Jones and Donald J. Schneider, "Self-Help Production Cooperatives: Government-Administered Cooperatives During the Depression," in *Worker Cooperatives in America*, Robert Jackall and Henry M. Levin eds. (Berkeley, University of California Press, 1984), 62.

132 *Oakland Tribune*, August 23, 1935, 11.

133 Adolf Sturmthal, *The Tragedy of European Labour, 1918–1939* (London: Victor Gollancz, 1944).

134 Adolf Sturmthal, *The Tragedy of European Labour.*

135 *Socialist Call* (N.Y.) February 1, 1936, 5.

136 *New York Times*, February 22, 1936, 2; *Berkeley Daily Gazette*, February 22, 1936, 2.

137 *Berkeley Daily Gazette*, March 2, 1936, 5.

138 *Berkeley Daily Gazette*, March 13, 1936, 11.

139 *Oakland Tribune*, June 9, 14, August 2, 24, 1936.

140 *Oakland Tribune*, August 26, 1936.

141 *Oakland Tribune*, September 9, 1936, 1; *Berkeley Daily Gazette*, September 9, 1936, 16.

142 *Oakland Tribune*, September 17, October 12, 21, 1936. *Covina Citizen*, October 28, 1936, 1; *San Diego Union*, October 29, 1936.

143 Appendix to the Congressional Record, April 15, 1937, 879–882, Extension of Remarks of Hon. Compton I. White, "Address of J. Stitt Wilson of Berkeley, Calif."

144 *San Francisco Chronicle*, October 17, 1937; *Nevada State Journal* (Reno) October 17, 1937; *Socialist Call* (N.Y.), May 21, 1938; Robert E. Burke, *Olson's New Deal for California* (Berkeley, University of California Press, 1953) 14–15, 20.

145 *Rural Observer* (San Francisco), June 1938; *Berkeley Daily Gazette*, May 23, 1939.

146 *Oakland Tribune*, May 22, 1939; *Berkeley Daily Gazette*, July 26, August 12, September 25, 26, October 22, 1939.

147 *Berkeley Daily Gazette*, Nov. 25, 1938, 6.

148 Robert E. Burke, *Olson's New Deal for California*, 140–143. *Oakland Tribune*, March 14, April 5, 10, 26, May 3, 1940; *Corona Independent* (CA), April 30, 1940.

149 *Berkeley Daily Gazette*, March 20, 1936, August 27, 1940.

150 *Berkeley Daily Gazette*, April 17, 1941.

151 *Berkeley Daily Gazette*, April 25, 1938, 11; *Oakland Tribune*, June 12, 1940; *Berkeley Daily Gazette*, March 4, 5, 8, April 26, 1941.

152 *Oakland Tribune*, December 1, 1941, 10.

153 *Oakland Tribune*, December 1, 1941, 10.

154 *Berkeley Daily Gazette*, December 26, 1941, 6.

155 Wilson, "Autobiography," 11.

156 Wilson, "Autobiography," 93.

157 Wilson, "Autobiography," 119.

158 *Berkeley Daily Gazette*, May 30, 1942, 5.

159 Wilson, "My Crowded Years," 5.

160 *Berkeley Daily Gazette*, August 29, 1942, 6.

INDEX